Living Fishes of the World

With photographs by

FRITZ GORO

GENE WOLFSHEIMER

JOHN TASHJIAN

HANS AND KLAUS PAYSAN

STAN WAYMAN

and

MARINE STUDIOS

Atlantic Spadefish
(*Chaetodipterus faber*)
FRITZ GORO

Living Fishes of the World

by *EARL S. HERALD*

Curator of the Steinhart Aquarium,
California Academy of Sciences

A CHANTICLEER PRESS EDITION

DOUBLEDAY & COMPANY Inc.

Garden City, New York

PUBLISHED BY DOUBLEDAY & COMPANY, INC. 1961

Garden City, New York
Ninth Printing 1972

PLANNED AND PRODUCED BY CHANTICLEER PRESS, INC., NEW YORK

THE WORLD OF NATURE SERIES

Living Mammals of the World by Ivan T. Sanderson

Living Reptiles of the World by Karl P. Schmidt
and Robert F. Inger

Living Birds of the World by E. Thomas Gilliard

Living Insects of the World by Alexander B. Klots
and Elsie B. Klots

*The Lower Animals: Living Invertebrates of the
World* by Ralph Buchsbaum and Lorus J. Milne,
in collaboration with Mildred Buchsbaum
and Margery Milne

Living Fishes of the World by Earl S. Herald

Living Amphibians of the World by Doris M. Cochran

1485
ISBN: 0–385–00988–7

Library of Congress Catalog Card No. 61–6384

PRINTED IN THE UNITED STATES OF AMERICA

Preface

THE rapid growth of skin diving, together with the development of inexpensive underwater camera housing, has resulted in a great increase of interest in aquatic life and in the observation and photography of fishes. Thirty years ago there was not a single photograph showing the cleaning activities of the remarkable parasite-removing wrasses and of other fishes as well as invertebrates that perform this same function. Yet in this volume we are able to present three photos showing this strange activity. Assembling outstanding photographs requires a tremendous amount of work and perseverance, and to Chanticleer Press is due the credit for bringing together the remarkable group of pictures presented in these pages.

In the text an effort was made to avoid going over material ably covered in many books on tropical fish, and more emphasis is placed on groups less often covered in popular works. The text is organized along systematic classification lines, following the scheme long used by the British Museum but with some modification based on recent revisions.

Every writer of such a survey as this must depend heavily on other earlier books; a number of essential works have been listed in the selected bibliography at the end of this volume. Preparation of such a book also calls for aid from many colleagues in special areas: invaluable assistance of this kind in various sections of the manuscript was provided by Mr. Donald Simpson, Dr. Robert Rofen, and Dr. Stanley Weitzman. Many others have helped in innumerable ways, and the author is particularly indebted to the following: James Atz, Herbert R. Axelrod, Reeve Bailey, Rolf Bolin, William Braker, Vernon Brock, Christopher Coates, Robert Dempster, Douglas Faulkner, W. I. Follett, William Gosline, Carl Hubbs, Frank Mather III, George Myers, Robert T. Orr, John Randall, C. Richard Robins, Leonard Schultz, Stewart Springer, John Tee Van, F. G. Wood, Jr., Capt. William Gray, and Mrs. Lillian Dempster. Editing of the manuscript by Milton Rugoff and J. R. de la Torre Bueno and photographic procurement and coordination by Miss Jean Tennant have been much appreciated. The final typing has been efficiently handled by Mrs. Phyllis Corbin.

Most important of all has been the long and painstaking work of my wife, Olivia, in making ichthyological jargon give way to standard English.

EARL S. HERALD

Steinhart Aquarium
California Academy of Sciences
San Francisco 18, California
January, 1961

Contents

BONY FISHES (continued)

Living Fishes of the World

Introduction

IN the golden age of fishes, about 320 million years ago, aquatic forms were the most important and the most advanced animals on earth. Yet everything we know about the fishes of that period has been learned from the occasional specimen that died and floated to the bottom where its body was imprisoned in the sedimentary oozes that later became Devonian rocks. Even before this time, some of the jawless vertebrates known as ostracoderms, the forerunners of the present-day hagfishes and lampreys, had appeared. Next came fishes with jaws, including the primitive cartilaginous fishes, which were the ancestors of the sharks and rays. Much later, but still in the Devonian period, the primitive bony fishes made their appearance. Down through the centuries, the earliest types—the jawless fishes and the sharks and rays—flourished, then became much less abundant, until a great many species had become extinct. At the same time, the fishes with bony skeletons increased greatly both in numbers and in species, until today they are the dominant group of aquatic vertebrates. Some of those early fishes, known as crossopterygians, had flipper-like fins. They made attempts to get out on land, and a few succeeded, leading eventually to the development of amphibians.

At this point someone is likely to ask: "Just what special features make an animal a fish rather than an amphibian or some other kind of animal?" We think of a typical fish as having scales, and yet there are many that lack them. We know that fishes are found in water, but there are a number that spend a great deal of time out of water. Most fishes have gills and respire by absorbing oxygen from the water as it passes over the gill filaments, but there are exceptions that have only vestigial gills often inadequate for respiration; in these fishes, breathing may be carried out by a lung, or by vascular areas above the gills and in the mouth, that absorb oxygen directly from the air. Fishes usually have fins on the top of the back, on the tail, and under the body behind the vent, as well as paired pectoral (arm) fins and paired pelvic (leg) fins, but there are fishes that lack some or all of these. (See Appendix for anatomical diagrams and glossary.) So we must look at the internal anatomy to find out why a fish is so classified. The fishlike vertebrates all have a supporting structure down the back. In the primitive forms it is a cartilaginous rod; in the more complex species it becomes partially or wholly ossified to form a backbone. The heart of most fishes has two chambers, whereas the amphibian heart is slightly more complex, having three chambers.

The success of the fishes in adapting themselves to various habitats is well shown by their distribution in the waters of the world: they are found everywhere except in waters that are toxic. It is difficult to be sure how many species of fishes there actually are, but conservative estimates place the number at around twenty-five thousand; these are divided into approximately thirty-six orders and more than four hundred families. The difference between salt and fresh water has proved a physiological barrier to most kinds of fishes, yet others have managed to adapt, and move back and forth between the two kinds of water without difficulty. The most rigid living requirements among fishes are undoubtedly those concerned with spawning. Fresh-water fishes living in the ocean, such as the salmon, always return to fresh water to spawn, and salt-water fishes living in fresh water, such as some of the gobies of the Pacific islands, always return to the ocean to spawn. Only a very few, like certain species of the African mouthbreeder genus *Tilapia,* are able to spawn in either salt, brackish, or fresh water.

Temperature is often a factor in both north-south or latitudinal distribution and vertical distribution. Although the temperature-tolerance range of an individual species may be less than 15 or 20 degrees Fahrenheit, the total range of all species is from freezing waters to those of more than 100 degrees. The temperature of the fish's body fluctuates with the temperature of the surrounding water. This fluctuation of body temperature with environment is also found among the amphibians and reptiles, and for this reason all three are known as cold-blooded vertebrates. In contrast, the body temperature of the warm-blooded vertebrates, the birds and mammals, is fairly uniform.

gelfish (*Pterophyllum scalare*); fresh water; Rio Negro and Amazon basins (Hans and us Paysan).

Sensory organs among the fishes show a tremendous amount of variation. For example, fish vision varies from amazingly acute perception to complete blindness. Some species are able to see the slightest underwater movement from as far off as fifty feet. Loss of sight in the blind species is sometimes compensated by sensitive barbels and other tactile organs on the head and body. In the muddy waters of Africa and South America there are fishes, such as the mormyrids and knifefishes, with small electric organs that discharge impulses which tell the fish about its surroundings. This apparently is also true of the Japanese marine skates, which have electrical tissue in the tail.

In certain fishes, especially the sharks, smell is very important in locating food. Copper compounds used in large oceanaria to control parasites have been said to clog the nostrils of some large sharks, causing them to lose their appetites and eventually starve to death. Experiments with blocking the nostrils of migrant salmon returning to fresh water to spawn revealed that the salmons' ability to select their parent stream was dependent upon their sense of smell.

The sense of taste is important to some fishes in locating food. Certain catfishes of the genus *Ictalurus* have taste buds covering most of the outside of the body; food coming in contact with these taste buds is quickly devoured. Along the sides of the body many fishes have a lateral line or a system of lines, usually in the form of a tube with a series of pores that open to the outside. These pores lead to sensory cells that "sense" vibrations in the water. The equilibrium system of fishes is found in the semicircular canals of the inner ear, hidden in the brain case. The ear bones or otoliths of these canals are sometimes useful in age determination, and in croakers and some other fishes are also important in species identification.

The air bladder is usually an essential feature to the fishes in which it is present. It is located in the upper part of the abdominal cavity and is used as a hydrostatic organ, enabling the fish to float at any given level without sinking or rising. It also may function as a resonance chamber in sound production, and in some fishes it has a respiratory function.

Most reproduction in the fish world is by means of external fertilization, in which the eggs spewed out by the female are fertilized at the same time by milt extruded in the immediate area by the male. There are, however, a number of live-bearers as well as some egg-layers that practice internal fertilization. This is true of the sharks and rays, which have large eggs covered with a chitinous material; in some sharks the eggs hatch within the mother so that the young are born alive. Among the most highly specialized reproductive habits are those of the pipefishes and seahorses: the male, in this case, becomes an incubator for the eggs, which the female either attaches to his body or places in his special brood pouch.

The extreme diversity of the fishes is illustrated in many other ways. There are species well adapted to almost every kind of watery habitat, from the teeming reefs of the tropics to the almost barren waters of high mountain ranges. The color patterns of fishes run the gamut from brightly colored, exotic combinations to drab monotones and others capable of changing to match the background. Some species are edible, some toxic, and some venomous to touch. All of these and many more make up the subject of the following pages, the living fishes of the world.

Jawless Fishes

(*Class Agnatha*)

THIS very primitive and surprisingly well-adapted group includes only two kinds of living fishes, the hags and the lampreys. They are often referred to as the cyclostomes, a term derived from the circular appearance of the suctorial mouth with its rasping teeth. Although the number of species is small, perhaps no more than forty-five, they have been able to survive with anatomical peculiarities, chiefly of omission, that would prove fatal in the more advanced forms. For example, the hags and lampreys lack bones, jaws, paired limbs and girdles, a sympathetic nervous system, a spleen, and scales. Support of the body is provided by cartilage or fibrous material, with an unsegmented notochord serving the same purpose as the backbone in higher fishes. Respiration takes place in a series of six to fourteen gill pouches, which may open individually or by a common tube both to the throat and to the outside of the body. There is only a single nostril. Fertilization is external. Some species of hags and lampreys are restricted to a marine habitat, whereas others occur only in fresh water or in both fresh and salt water.

HAGFISHES—Family Myxinidae

Occasionally when a haddock fisherman, having dumped his catch on the deck, begins to examine the fishes, he discovers that some of them are hollow, veritable "bags of bones." When he shakes one of these vigorously, out tumbles the culprit, a hagfish, usually called a hag. This unwelcome intruder, having drilled into the fish with its rasplike teeth, has worked like a termite, leaving the exterior intact but consuming most of the edible interior portions. Such an experience is not unusual, for hags are serious pests in some areas, wreaking great damage upon the catches of many kinds of fishes, including haddock, hake, cod, mackerel, rock cod, and flatfish, to mention a few. Hags are scavengers, and are not successful in feeding upon fast, free-moving fishes. In some regions polychaete worms are a normal part of their diet.

The hag shows all the primitive features of the jawless fishes, such as a cartilage skeleton, a single nostril, the absence of paired limbs and girdles, and the absence of a sympathetic nervous system, a spleen, and scales. This voracious scavenger is a blind, elongate, wormlike fish usually less than 30 inches in length, with a slightly rounded tail, and several thick, finger-like whiskers extending from around the mouth. In the mouth are two rows of sharp, broadly triangular teeth, the number of which is useful in species identification. Internally, these are followed by a digestive tract that is a simple straight tube.

For many years hags were thought to be hermaphroditic, but then it was discovered that although both sex organs may be present in any given individual, only one organ, either testis or ovary, is functional, the other remaining in a rudimentary state. The egg measures about 1 inch in length and is covered with a horny material, at each end of which there is a small tassel. A maximum of thirty eggs has been recorded from internal examination of a single female. There appears to be no definite spawning period, for eggs may be laid during any month of the year. Despite the fact that the other group of cyclostomes, the lampreys, has a distinct larval stage known as an ammocoete, this stage has not been discovered among the hags and perhaps does not exist.

The amazing physiological nature of the hag can sometimes be seen if it is handled roughly and then dropped into a bucket of water. In a short time the water will be entirely converted to a slimy mucus. The activity of many mucous pores along the sides of the body has resulted in the name "slime eel" being often applied to the hag.

The three genera of hags may be identified by differences in the gill pouches. The six species of *Myxine* all have these pouches connected through a tube to a single exterior opening on each side. This tube is absent in the Japanese *Paramyxine,* which has sixteen individual gill openings on each side, and in *Eptatretus,* which has five to fourteen. About twenty species of hags are recognized. They are found in temperate or cold salt water no warmer than 55° Fahrenheit. Usually they do not survive in brackish or fresh water. The depth range is from 100 to 3100 feet.

The maximum length of the hags is approximately 31 inches, which is recorded for the common Atlantic *Myxine glutinosa;* surprisingly enough, members of the European population of this species are only slightly more than half this size, with a maximum length of less than 17 inches.

The Pacific hag, *Eptatretus stouti,* has proved an excellent test animal in heart-function studies, because the absence of heart nerves as well as other sympathetic nerves has made it possible to obtain information from the hag heart that could not be learned from other animal groups.

In some areas hags are extremely abundant; they are usually found in soft mud or clay bottoms, where they spend a good part of the time embedded, with only the snout and some of the whiskers protruding. The food is located entirely by smell. When progressing toward a food source, the hag comes out of the mud and swims horizontally with an undulating motion. Biologists have learned that it will swim toward a trap constructed from a wide-mouthed five-gallon can baited with a few putrid fish heads. Many holes driven into the can with a large spike permit the odor of the bait to be disseminated in all directions; these openings also permit the slender-bodied hag to squeeze into the can, but not to escape.

LAMPREYS—Family Petromyzontidae

The recent history of commercial fishing in the American Great Lakes region is one of disastrous decline from a yearly catch of eleven million pounds of lake trout and other fishes to practically nothing. All of this has taken place in less than three decades and is entirely the work of a parasitic landlocked lamprey, *Petromyzon marinus.* This eel-like lamprey is normally a marine species that occurs on both sides of the Atlantic and migrates into fresh water to spawn. Gradually through the years, it has moved into the Great Lakes, probably through the New York State Barge Canal and the Welland Canal, and has become firmly established there. Because of the serious economic loss resulting from the depreda-

Mouth and oral disk of the Sea Lamprey (*Petromyzon marinus*); fresh and salt water on both sides of the North Atlantic (E. P. Haddon: U.S. Fish and Wildlife Service).

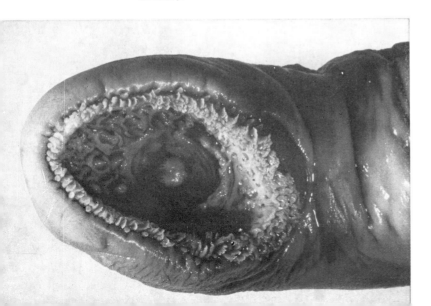

tions of lampreys, a widespread research and control program has been initiated in the Great Lakes region. The maximum length of the adult *Petromyzon marinus* is about 3 feet. Although it is capable of rapid, undulating swimming, it does much of its traveling attached to host fishes while sucking out their life juices. It attaches itself to the victim with its rasping teeth and keeps the victim's blood in a fluid state by means of an anticoagulating substance in its saliva. When the victim is drained, the vampire-like lamprey attaches itself to another host. Sea lampreys ingest only blood, whereas some of the fresh-water species also ingest a small amount of flesh.

During the spring months of March through May *Petromyzon marinus* usually moves into shallow-water streams to spawn. It can even ascend falls, if they are not too high, by attaching itself to rocks with its oral disk and working itself upward. Having located a rocky bottom suitable for spawning, a male and female usually work together to prepare the nest. They pick up rocks with the mouth and use them to form a depression, about two or three feet in diameter and perhaps six inches deep, in which the eggs are to be laid. As the female lays as many as 200,000 eggs, the male, wound around her, spews milt over the nest. Shortly thereafter the parents die.

In about two weeks the eggs hatch. Several days later the blind, toothless, wormlike larvae, known as ammocoetes, moves out of the nest and into adjacent mud and silt areas where burrowing is easy and microplanktonic food is readily available. Four to six years later this same ammocoete, now having grown to a length of as much as 6 inches, begins its transformation to the true lamprey. During this radical metamorphosis many anatomical changes take place, only a few of which need be mentioned here. The rudimentary eyes become functional, and soon the changing ammocoete acquires a new kind of mouth with a full compliment of 112 to 125 horny rasping teeth. The digestive tract is altered, and the bile duct and gall bladder disappear. Following these changes, the youngster starts its move downstream and into the parasitic phase of its life history. Sexual maturity is attained in twelve to twenty months. The lamprey does not necessarily return to the stream of its birth, and is very selective, spawning only in certain types of streams. In some cases the selection is limited; for example, all Cayuga Lake (New York) lampreys spawn in Cayuga Inlet, the only feeder of that lake that is not too precipitous for them to ascend.

Petromyzon marinus, the only member of its genus, occurs, as previously mentioned, along both coasts of the Atlantic. In a few places, as in the Great Lakes, there are land-locked permanent fresh-water populations. In addition to *Petromyzon,* six other genera of lampreys are recognized in a family total of about twenty-five species. Some, such as the Pacific American *Lampetra ayresii,* are confined entirely to fresh water, but all of them have a life history similar to that of *Petromyzon marinus.* In North America there are actually thirteen species of lampreys, six of which are parasitic and the remaining seven nonparasitic. The major difference in the life history is that the nonparasitic forms do not feed as adults; as a result they never grow larger than the larvae from which they are transformed.

An adult lamprey looks so much like an eel that one of the names often applied is "lamprey eel." However, it is not related to the eels, and like its cousin, the hagfish, it lacks the jaws and many other characteristics of the more advanced fishes. The adult lamprey has seven pairs of gill pouches which open separately to the exterior; internally they are connected to a tube which empties into the mouth. This is advantageous to the parasitic lamprey since it allows it to respire by pumping water in and out of each gill pouch while sucking the lifeblood from a host fish. The gill pouches themselves are supported by a complex cartilaginous structure known as the branchial basket. The digestive tract has on one side a small ridge which is probably the forerunner of the spiral valve or typhlosole of the sharks and rays. The ear has only two semicircular canals. Depending upon the genus, there may be one or two dorsal fins, and these are separate from the tail fin. Identification

Spawning Sea Lamprey (*Petromyzon marinus*); fresh and salt water on both sides of the North Atlantic; landlocked in fresh water in many places, including the Great Lakes (U.S. Fish and Wildlife Service).

of species is often based on teeth arrangement.

The use of lampreys as food has had an erratic history. In the Middle Ages they were considered a delicacy. Although lampreys are no longer fished as food, they were sold in markets in New England as late as the 1850's. The larvae can be used as bait.

Cartilage Fishes

(*Class Chondrichthyes*)

IN this zoological class, which includes the sharks, skates, rays (subclass Elasmobranchi), and chimaeroids (subclass Holocephali), the cartilage skeleton of the hags and lampreys is retained and further developed. In some cases there is an indication of calcification, particularly around the vertebrae. The most important difference, however, is that among these more advanced fishes there is a well-developed lower jaw and that both jaws have bony teeth. The sharks, skates, and rays have an upper jaw that is separate from the cranium although it may be locally attached, whereas the chimaeroids have the upper jaw permanently fused to the cranium. The circulatory system is more complex than in the jawless fishes, with a series of heart valves preceded by a

chamber, the *bulbus conus arteriosus.* The nervous system is reasonably complete, and the spleen is present. The fins are paired. The scales, of the type known as placoid, are developed in the same manner as a tooth, and in this respect are entirely different from the scales of bony fishes. The gills, four to seven in number, have individual openings, or clefts, to the outside. Many species have a pair of spiracles on the top of the head, a vestige of a former pair of gill clefts. In the digestive tract there is a unique spiral valve which effectively increases the absorptive area of the tract. All of the Chondrichthyes carry out internal fertilization by means of a pair of elongate claspers located on the inner edge of the ventral fins of the male. None of these fishes has an air or swim bladder. Almost six hundred species of sharks, skates, rays, and chimaeroids belong to this class.

Sharks (*Order Selachii*)

Many sharks can be identified without difficulty, but there are some kinds that look as much like rays as like sharks, so it is necessary to discuss the anatomical peculiarities that differentiate these two groups. First in importance is the position of the gill openings. Sharks have five to seven gill clefts on each side of the head, usually forward of and slightly above the pectoral fins, whereas the rays have their five clefts on the under side of the pectorals, which are greatly enlarged and expanded. Sharks breathe like normal bony fishes, taking water in through the mouth and passing it out over the gills. Most of the rays modify this procedure by bringing water in through the spiracles and out through the gills. The free eyelid which can be seen on the upper portion of the eye of a shark is absent on the skates and rays. There are a number of internal anatomical features that are equally distinctive.

About 250 kinds of sharks are known; these are divided into some nineteen families allocated to seven suborders. The divisions within the subordinal groups are based on the presence or absence of (1) the anal fin, (2) the nictitating membrane on the eye, (3) one or two dorsal fins with or without spines, and (4) whether there are five, six, or seven gill openings. Some of these subordinal groups will be discussed in connection with the individual families.

FRILLED SHARK—Family Chlamydoselachidae

The frilled shark is distinguished by the presence of six gill slits, with only the first gill opening extending under the neck from one side to the other. The presence or absence of this continuous gill opening is quite important, since it serves to segregate the frilled shark from the sixgill cow shark.

In appearance the very slender frilled shark is suggestive of a marine snake or monster. This resemblance is further increased by the very large mouth filled with many sharp and fearsome teeth. The dorsal and anal fins are small and located far back on the body, just in front of the tail. The tail itself has lost all resemblance to the typical lopsided shark tail, the ventral lobe being invisible and the elongate upper lobe extending backward like a broadened whip.

Most sharks have a vibration-sensitive lateral-line system with special cells located inside a hollow tube along the side of the body. The primitive frilled shark, however, has only an open groove with the sensitive cells exposed to the water at all times. Another interesting feature of the frilled shark is found in the reproductive system. This species is ovoviviparous—that is, it lays eggs, but the eggs are hatched within the mother so that the young are born alive. A gravid female may carry ten to fifteen embryos, each of which develops from a gigantic egg measuring 4¾ inches in its long axis. The gestation period is very long, actually approaching two years. The adult shark may reach a length of 6½ feet, but the rate of growth is not known. Throughout life the color is a light brown without distinguishing marks.

Since the frilled shark is a deep-water species, it may have a wider distribution than is known at present. A number of specimens have been caught off Japan, two have been taken off California, and the remainder off European coasts from Norway to Portugal. Most of the captures have been in deep water, although a few have occurred at the surface. The frilled shark feeds chiefly on deep-water octopuses and squids.

SIXGILL and SEVENGILL COWSHARKS —Family Hexanchidae

By counting the number of gill openings along the side of a shark's head one can determine very quickly whether he is dealing with a primitive shark belonging to the sixgill and sevengill group or with one of the main groups of sharks, which always have five gill openings.

Only one shark, *Hexanchus griseus,* has six separate gill openings on each side of the head. The frilled shark also has six openings, but the first is continuous from one side of the neck to the other. Although *Hexanchus griseus* has been tagged with a number of scientific names in various parts of the world, most ichthyologists are now in agreement that there is probably only one species. The adult sixgill has a broad head, a heavy, thick body, and a very long tail. The color ranges from shades of nondescript gray to brown with no distinctive markings. These giant deep-water sharks sometimes weigh as much as seventeen hundred pounds, with an estimated length of 17 feet. There is also a report of a giant sixgill measuring slightly more than 26 feet caught off Cornwall, England, more than one hundred years ago. No other sixgills of this size have been found.

On the Pacific coast of North America this fish is known from British Columbia to southern California, and it apparently has a similar distribution governed by temperature along the Chilean coast of South America. It has not been taken in the central Pacific, although it is known from Japan to Australia, from the Indian Ocean, and from South Africa. It is found on both coasts of the Atlantic and in the Mediterranean. Most of the recent American Atlantic records have been from northern Cuba, where a deep-water long-line fishery has been operating. Despite the fact that it has been caught in depths greater than one mile, it also occurs in shallow water. It is strange that on the American Pacific coast it rarely enters San Francisco Bay, only two specimens having been caught there; yet it commonly occurs in Tomales Bay, which is only a few miles to the north and is much shallower.

The sixgill feeds mostly on fishes and crustaceans. One theory is that the shark remains quietly at the bottom in deep water during the day and comes to the surface only at night for feeding.

The young, which are born alive, are surprisingly small when compared with the adults, some measuring no more than 16 inches. The females appear to be fairly prolific: There is a report of a 14-foot female from which 108 embryos were removed.

The Pacific sevengill gives a deceptively docile appearance in the water, cruising along languidly and apparently with little effort. It swims constantly, and has never been seen to rest on the bottom. It has a large head, a slender body, and a very long tail. The teeth are recessed, so that their sharp points and tremendous potentialities are not fully evident until the brute is pulled up on deck. Then one should stand back and beware, for the snapping mouth and thrashing body of even a sevengill measuring no more than 6 feet are very dangerous.

Identification of a sevengill shark is very simple, for, as the name implies, there are seven gill slits along each side of the head rather than the usual five or, in some species, six. Two distinct kinds of sevengills are recognized. The first is a small, point-headed type, genus *Heptranchias,* that matures at a length of about 3 feet. The largest recent record of a point-headed sevengill was one measuring 7 feet. The other is a larger, broad-headed type, genus *Notorhynchus,* that probably matures at a length of about 10 feet. In each case there is disagreement among the authorities as to whether one or several species are involved.

In the Atlantic the sharp-headed *Heptranchias perlo* is widely distributed, although not abundant except in the Mediterranean. In Japan there is a sevengill with a pointed head that appears to be identical with the one in the Atlantic. This may also be true of the Australian population, although the latter is sometimes dealt with separately under the name *Heptranchias dakini.*

The Australian sevengill is caught in trawl nets operating at depths of twelve hundred feet. The Atlantic sevengill occurs at depths of fourteen hundred feet in Cuba and Portugal, but is also found in shallow water in West African lagoons.

Very little is known about the reproductive rate of the sevengills. We do know that the young are born alive and may be as small as 10 inches at birth. Some indication of the number of young in one litter is found in the report of a female that contained nine embryos when caught.

The broad-headed Pacific sevengill, *Notorhynchus maculatum,* normally lives offshore and is seldom caught in very shallow water. One exception is the southern end of San Francisco Bay, where a nursery ground is located. The females, which range in size up to 10 and perhaps 15 feet, are thought to come into the bay to drop their young, although no fisherman has as yet caught a really large female in this area. On September 14, 1952, we examined 1871 sharks and bat stingrays caught in the southern end of the bay. Of this total, 301, or about 16 per cent, were sevengills. The smallest was 25 inches in length and weighed one and a half pounds; the largest measured 83 inches and weighed eighty-four pounds. By the time the sevengill has reached a weight of a hundred pounds and a length of 89 inches it usually leaves the bay. Sevengills of less than a hundred pounds are sexually immature. The broad-headed sevengill has a distinctive color pattern—a dark gray background with a number of black spots scattered irregularly over the body.

Although few people today consider the sevengill an edible shark, it is interesting to note that Ayres wrote in 1855 when he first described the species from San Francisco Bay: "It is taken during the summer by the Chinese fishermen in no small quantities. But as sharks rank high with them in the scale of edible fishes, we have not been able to obtain from them a complete specimen." From another source Ayres later obtained a 23-inch juvenile which became the type of the species.

Albino elasmobranchs are extremely rare, and hence it is of interest to note that the only albino sevengill ever taken was caught in San Francisco Bay. It was 34 inches long.

On the Pacific coast the broad-headed sevengill ranges from British Columbia to southern California. It has also been recorded from the Mediterranean, South Africa, Argentina, Japan, China, Australia, New Zealand, and the Indian Ocean. Here again there is a question as to whether more than one species is involved.

SAND SHARKS—Family Carchariidae

Numerous sharp, wicked-looking teeth protruding from the mouth of the sand tiger shark, *Carcharias taurus,* make this species fit almost perfectly the popular conception of a dangerous shark. Despite its grim appearance, there are no records on the Ameri-

Sand Tiger Shark (*Carcharias taurus*) with two remoras attached; marine; both sides of the temperate and tropical Atlantic (New York Zoological Society).

can side of the Atlantic of its having attacked humans. However, in South Africa it is considered very dangerous and capable of unprovoked attack. Although the sand tiger is primarily a shallow-water shark, it usually swims constantly and seldom rests on the bottom. This constant swimming is generally characteristic of deep-water sharks. Although sharks do not have air bladders, the sand tiger has developed the peculiar ability to swallow air and retain it in the stomach, thus allowing the stomach to act as a hydrostatic organ. It is fairly common on both sides of the Atlantic, but not necessarily during the entire year, as the populations seem to fluctuate with the water temperature. Along the American coast the normal range is from the Gulf of Maine to Florida, with an isolated population in Brazil. The largest sand tiger ever caught measured 10 feet 5 inches and probably weighed more than three hundred pounds.

Females begin to bear young after reaching a length of about 7 feet. Only two embryos develop at a time, one in each horn of the uterus. After they consume the yolk within their own egg capsule, they become cannibalistic, eating the other eggs as they come down the oviduct. Even before being born, these sharks should be treated with respect: one biologist, performing a shark Caesarean, was bitten by one of these embryonic monsters.

December 30, 1958, was memorable at Florida's Marine Studios because it was the day that the first sand tiger was born in captivity. At the end of the first week it measured about 40 inches in length and showed signs of thriving—it had already attempted to supplement its diet with a bite out of a diver's boot.

The sand tiger has few relatives. There are only about five other species in the genus, and these few make up the entire family Carchariidae. The other species range through the eastern Atlantic and Mediterranean, and along the coasts of Argentina, Australia, Japan, China, and India.

GOBLIN SHARKS—Family Scapanorhynchidae

The strangest-looking shark of them all is the deep-sea goblin shark, of which there is probably only a single species, *Scapanorhynchus owstoni*. The conspicuous, long, sharp teeth of the overlapping upper jaw curl down over those of the lower jaw. From about the level of the eyes a long, pointed, paddle-shaped nose measuring about twice the length of the upper jaw extends forward. This bizarre shark has the usual complement of pectoral, pelvic, dorsal, and anal fins, and an extremely long tail fin. Its maximum length is about 14 feet. It is known from very deep water off Japan, India, and Portugal. Its discovery in the Indian Ocean was due to malfunctioning of a cable at a depth of 4500 feet. When the tender brought the cable to the surface for inspection, a broken tooth of the goblin shark was found wedged between the strands of wire. Apparently the shark had been feeding on animal life growing on the cable.

MACKEREL SHARKS—Family Isuridae

"Monsters of the sea" might be a more appropriate name for the mackerel sharks, since this family includes some of the world's most dangerous fishes. The most widely known is the great white shark, *Carcharodon carcharias*, commonly called the man-eater. Sharks of this group are heavy-bodied and usually have a nearly symmetrical tail, resembling that of the tuna rather than the lopsided tail of the typical shark. It is probable that all of these fast-moving sharks swim constantly and do not rest on the bottom at any time. Speed in the water requires careful stabilization, and for this purpose the mackerel sharks have large keels along the sides of the tail just in front of the fin. Further hydrodynamic control is gained by means of the characteristically large pectoral fins, whose length is about equal to that of the head. The dorsal fin is of moderate size and is followed by a small second dorsal. The pelvic fins are also small, about half the height of the dorsal. The position of the anal fin in relation to the second dorsal, usually directly above it, can often prove useful in identification.

Preliminary identification among the mackerel sharks can be made by means of the profile of the teeth. For example, the upper center teeth of the great white shark or maneater are broadly triangular with saw-toothed edges, whereas those of the other mackerel sharks, such as the Atlantic porbeagle and the mako, are very slender and quite smooth. One mark that can sometimes be used to distinguish the maneater is a conspicuous black spot in the axil or base of the pectoral fin. Apart from this, the color of the maneater is not outstanding. It is a dark grayish black on the back, shading to an off-white on the undersurface.

The largest maneater ever caught measured 36½ feet in length, and was taken at Port Fairey, Australia. Although it dates back more than ninety years, the jaws have been preserved intact in the collection of the British Museum. In contrast with this giant, most of the large maneaters caught today are in the 20- to 25-foot range. Because of the great thickness of the body, these sharks are massive fish. For example, a small shark 17 feet long can weigh as much as 2800 pounds. There is a record of a 21-foot Cuban specimen weighing 7100 pounds, with a liver that weighed slightly more than 1000 pounds.

Evidence indicates that the female maneater must reach a length of at least 13 feet before attaining sexual maturity. Although this species is thought to bear living young, very little is known about its early developmental stages.

The maneater is a fish of the open seas and is found less frequently inshore. Despite the fact that it is usually captured near the surface, there is one Cuban record from a depth of 4200 feet. When the maneater is found in very shallow water, it is usually in areas adjacent to deep water. Although it is most abundant in tropical areas around the world, it does range into temperate waters. On the American coasts it has been taken as far north as the state of

Washington in the Pacific, and the St. Pierre bank just south of Newfoundland in the Atlantic.

The temperament of the maneater is reputed to be invariably bad. Although it is reported to attack readily anything and everything, skin divers who have encountered this monster have usually survived to tell the tale. There seem to be indications that the maneater may sometimes be just as wary and frightened of the skin diver as the latter is of the maneater.

Apparently the maneater samples anything that looks like food, including humans, and there are even records of rowboats having been attacked. Whole animals of considerable size are sometimes taken, the stomach contents of maneaters revealing the intact bodies of a hundred-pound sea lion, a fifty-pound seal, and a Newfoundland dog, as well as sharks 6 and 7 feet in length.

Although the maneater is a good-sized brute and puts up a respectable struggle when hooked, there are records of fish as large as 1329 pounds having been landed with angling tackle in as short a time as fifty-three minutes. By contrast, another member of the mackerel shark family, the mako, sometimes called the sharp-nosed mackerel shark, is noted for its spectacular activity when hooked. Not only is it considered a faster swimmer than the great white shark, but when caught it acts like a marlin, leaping clear of the water and providing the angler with a tough test of his abilities. Perhaps correlated with the increased speed of the mako is the fact that this fish is more streamlined than other members of the mackerel shark family and has longer stabilizing keels along the sides of the caudal peduncle.

Two species of makos are recognized. The Atlantic *Isurus oxyrhinchus* and the Indo-Pacific and Australian *Isurus glauca* are both believed to reach a maximum length of about 12 feet, which would probably correspond to a maximum weight of about 1200 pounds. The largest authenticated record is of an Atlantic mako 10 feet 6 inches long weighing 1005 pounds. Although these sharks have a world-wide distribution in tropical seas, none has been taken in the southern latitudes of South America. However, it is known from the South African area.

In the old days, the Maoris of New Zealand prized the center teeth of the mako, using them for ear ornaments. For fear of marring the teeth, the Maoris did not employ hooks to catch the fish; instead, prebaiting was used to bring the mako close enough to a canoe so that a noose could be slipped over the forward part of the fish's body. The early chronicler failed to tell how the Maoris handled the powerful mako at this point, but certainly it would be a ticklish proposition at best.

Whenever possible, the mako takes its food at one gulp. This is well illustrated by a 120-pound swordfish found intact in the stomach of a 730-pound Bahaman mako. With much larger swordfish, attack is usually made from the rear; thus the mako removes the entire tail of the prey with one bite.

The color of the mako is quite distinctive—a dark blue above and a pure white underneath. It can be distinguished from the maneater by its narrow, smooth teeth, and from the common mackerel shark or porbeagle by the fact that the two center teeth in each jaw are much more slender than the others. In addition, there are no lateral cusps on each tooth, whereas these are present on both the maneater and the porbeagle.

The mako with its tremendous speed is unquestionably a dangerous shark. It has been known to attack small boats, and undoubtedly will attack a swimmer although it does not have the reputation of being a maneater.

Like the mako, the common Atlantic mackerel shark or porbeagle, *Lamna nasus,* has a related species on the American Pacific coast—*Lamna ditropis*. In addition to the differences in the teeth, mentioned above, these two species can be further distinguished from the other members of the mackerel family by the presence of two stabilizing keels instead of one along the sides of the tail. The main

Mako Shark (*Isurus oxyrynchus*); marine, pelagic; both sides of the Atlantic (Michael Lerner Expedition of The American Museum of Natural History).

keel is in the same lateral position as on the mako and the maneater. In addition, there is a small keel just below this but limited to the tail fin. The porbeagle and its Pacific counterpart are thick-bodied like the maneater, but although potentially dangerous, they have not been implicated in attacks on man. However, they are a plague to many fishermen because of their persistence in feeding on netted fish and leaving nets in shreads. Unlike the mako, they offer little resistance to capture despite their tremendous speed in the water. In color they are similar to the mako, being bluish black above and white on the lower sides and belly. In addition, the Pacific mackerel shark has black blotches over the belly.

The maneater and the mako are found throughout both temperate and tropical waters, whereas the porbeagle and the Pacific mackerel shark are primarily temperate-water species. The Pacific species ranges from Japan and Alaska down to southern California. The Atlantic mackerel shark lives in the area between the Gulf of St. Lawrence and South Carolina, and on the European coasts from the North Sea to the Mediterranean. It also occurs along the northwestern coasts of Africa. Mackerel sharks with a double tail keel also occur off South America and Australia. Although they have been described as distinct species, further study may show them to be identical with the Pacific *Lamna ditropis*.

Ten feet is usually accepted as the maximum length of the common Atlantic and Pacific mackerel sharks, with the females attaining sexual maturity at about 5 feet. Very little is known about the development of these sharks. There is, however, a report of a 6½-foot female *Lamna ditropis* caught in southern California that contained four young, each weighing eighteen pounds and measuring 30 inches.

THRESHER SHARKS—Family Alopiidae

An extremely long whiplike tail approximately equal to the length of the body provides the thresher shark with tremendous driving power, enabling it to round up schools of small fishes by rapidly encircling them. Slapping the surface of the water with its tail also helps it to frighten the fishes into tighter formation so that it can feed on them more readily. In the central Pacific, threshers are often foul-hooked on deep-set tuna lines, probably as a result of attempting to herd the dead bait with the tail. Despite its ferocious nature toward schooling fishes, the thresher is entirely harmless to man.

Although the threshers as a group are primarily offshore and tropical in distribution, they do come into temperate waters in considerable numbers. At times during the summer months they are very common off the New England coast. In the Santa Barbara Island area of California they are fished commercially during the summer.

As might be expected, the threasher family is a small one, having only a single genus and perhaps four species. The best-known species is the common thresher, *Alopias vulpinus,* which has an extended distribution on both sides of the Atlantic as well as in the eastern Pacific. In the western Pacific it is replaced by *Alopias pelagicus.* Other species, the big-eyed threshers, named for their extremely large eyes, are suspected of being a deep-water species. Records of their capture are rare, though they are probably more common than is indicated. They are undoubtedly often mistakenly identified as the common thresher. There are two species of the big-eye, *Alopias superciliosus,* known from Cuba, Florida, and Madeira, and *Alopias profundus,* from Formosa.

The largest threshers measure more than 20 feet in length and weigh more than one thousand pounds. The female thresher probably matures at about 14 feet and usually carries only two or four young. The newborn are 4½ to 5 feet long. When examining one of these youngsters for the first time, one is astounded at the length of the tail as compared with the small body. The tail of the young is even longer proportionally than that of the adult, and, in fact, seems to dwarf the rest of the fish.

BASKING SHARK—Family Cetorhinidae

"Basking shark" is an appropriate name for this leviathan of the sea, because of its habit of spending much of its time just floating at the surface or cruising slowly with the dorsal fin awash.

The giant basking shark, *Cetorhinus maximus,* is the world's second-largest fish, sometimes reaching a length of 45 feet. It can best be described as a mackerel shark that has dropped its carnivorous food habit and substituted a plankton diet. Like the mackerel sharks, it has a nearly symmetrical tuna-like tail with heavy lateral supports or stabilizing keels. A plankton diet naturally requires it to strain tremendous volumes of water. To meet this demand the basking shark has greatly enlarged gill openings extending from the top of the head and neck to almost the center section underneath. As the water flows into the mouth and out over the gills, the straining of the plankton is accomplished by many long, slender rakers attached to the inside of each gill arch and extending into the throat. The first and fifth gill arches have a single row of rakers, whereas the second, third, and fourth have a double row. A single row may have as many as twelve hundred rakers measuring between 2 and 4 inches in length. This fine meshwork provides the straining mechanism

needed to sieve sufficient food for an animal which at an average size of 30 feet will weight more than four and one-quarter tons. An apparent exception to this generalization is that some basking sharks have been described as being without gill rakers. This was the case with a small male of 19 feet that accidentally swam into a submerged drydock in San Francisco Bay. One recent theory is that the gill rakers are absorbed in some basking sharks during the winter months and are regenerated during the summer months.

The basking shark has two dorsal fins. The first, located in the center of the body, is rather large and is equal in height to about one-half the length of the head. The second dorsal is about one-quarter of the height of the first dorsal and is about equal in height to the anal fin. The pectorals are slightly longer than the height of the dorsal, and the pelvics are about half the height of the dorsal. The color of the basking shark varies from a nondescript over-all gray to a brown or black. The teeth are very small, and apparently have little function since the basking shark feeds on plankton.

The record length for the basking shark is usually given as 50 feet, but perhaps this should more conservatively be listed as 45. The average maximum range is 30 to 35 feet. The young are thought to be born alive and to be approximately 5 or 6 feet in length at this time. Males do not mature until they reach a length of 15 or 20 feet.

The basking shark has been described from many regions of the world, but most of the records are from temperate waters. They may occur singly or in schools numbering as many as one hundred. Sizable populations exist off the European coasts and off the southern California coast. Some authorities recognize a single world-wide species, but others think that several species may be involved. Little is known about the movements of these giant fishes. Tagging them to gain this information would probably not be too difficult, since the basking shark is not considered dangerous. Skin divers swim around them without fear and have even taken rides sitting on the caudal peduncle, the slender part of the tail just ahead of the tail fin.

It is somewhat surprising that the two largest fishes are both sharks and that both of them feed on plankton, usually near the surface. In distribution they are somewhat segregated, since the whale shark usually prefers tropical waters while the basking shark is found in more temperate seas. The two are easy to distinguish by the conspicuous white spots present on the back of the whale shark, which are lacking on the basking shark.

Fishing for basking sharks is usually conducted

from small boats by means of harpoons. This is necessary because of the shark's habit of swimming close to the surface. Most of the fisheries are sporadic in their operation, since overfishing would reduce the stock to the point where it would no longer be profitable. In past years fisheries were conducted along the European coasts, in the New England area, off central California, and off the coasts of Peru and Ecuador. Because of its oil the liver is the most valuable part of the basking shark, although sometimes the carcass is rendered for fish meal. The liver in a shark usually makes up about 10 per cent of its total weight. For example, a 30-foot basker weighing 8600 pounds would have a liver weighing 860 pounds, from which a high percentage yield in oil would be obtained. Six hundred gallons is the greatest volume of oil ever obtained from a single basking shark liver. The liver oil contains no vitamins and is used chiefly in certain leather-tanning processes.

A unique method for capture of these giant sharks has been developed in the central California coastal area. The fishermen employ a small spotting plane, which locates the school, then radios back to the mobile "killer boat," in this case a six-wheeled combat amphibian vehicle. The amphibian crew, upon learning of the location of the school, drives up the beach to a point opposite the plane, which continues circling over the sharks. It then goes out through the surf, and the harpooning begins. Each harpooned shark is tied to a buoy, where it remains briefly until the carcass is sold by long-distance phone. The sharks are then towed ashore, pulled onto a truck, and hauled to the processing plant. During 1947 about a hundred of these giant sharks were taken by this technique in the Pismo Beach area of California.

Some years ago an exceptional film record, *Men of Aran,* was made of the basking shark fishery along the west coast of Ireland. For anyone interested in knowing more about these gigantic sharks the film is still available through documentary film services.

WHALE SHARK—Family Rhincodontidae

Of all the fishes known to mankind, none has had more written about it, based on fewer specimens, than that docile giant of the sea, the whale shark, *Rhincodon typus.* Despite this deluge of literature, we still know surprisingly little about the species. Because of its distinct characteristics, it is easy to identify. It is the only spotted shark that has the mouth at the tip of the head; it also has ridges along the sides of the body; and it grows to a length of at least 45 feet. It is of interest to note that many articles have been written describing collisions of sailing ships and power vessels with this lethargic shark; in some cases the shark has remained impaled on the

bow of the ship for many hours. Skin divers report these fishes to be so docile that one can swim around them with impunity.

Like the massive basking shark, the whale shark feeds on very small food items, ranging from schools of little fishes and squid to crustaceans. Any small food must of course be sieved from the water as it passes into the mouth and out over the gills. This is accomplished by an intricate network of strainers or gill rakers extending into the throat from the individual base of each gill arch. Because of this type of diet one might expect the whale shark to be lacking in teeth. However, there are numerous small teeth arranged in some 310 rows in each jaw, but only about 10 or 15 rows can function at any one time.

Feeding activities sometimes cause the whale shark to assume a vertical position with the head uppermost. In Cuban waters it is often observed in this position among schools of tuna where both are feeding on sardines and other small surface fishes. In the past this observation has given rise to stories of whale sharks feeding upon tuna.

Whale sharks are egg-layers. Sixteen eggs were found in a Ceylon specimen and a living 14-inch shark in an egg case measuring 12 x 3½ x 3½ inches was found in the Gulf of Mexico.

Whale sharks are recorded from all tropical waters of the world. On the American Atlantic coasts the center of abundance seems to lie in the Caribbean region. Occasional individuals have been found as far north as New York and as far south as Brazil. Another population center is in the Gulf of California, particularly around Cape San Lucas. These sharks are fairly common in some areas in the Philippines and in the Red Sea. At one time there was a fishery for them off the northwest coast of India.

CARPET and NURSE SHARKS
—Family Orectolobidae

The sharks in this family are similar in appearance to the scyliorhinid catsharks but can readily be distinguished from them and all others by the presence of a conspicuous pair of external grooves, one on each side, running from the mouth to the nostril. Each of these oronasal grooves, as they are called, has at its anterior end a thick, fleshy barbel, which further aids in identification. The carpet shark has in addition to this a fringe of fleshy palps around the sides of the head. The orectolobids have two dorsal fins and spiracles, but lack the nictitating eye membrane; the tail is not turned upward but is in line with the rest of the body. Most of them are small, inshore forms, but there are a few of the perhaps two dozen species in the family that reach a large size—such as the Atlantic nurse shark, *Ginglymos-*

Harpooned Whale Shark (*Rhincodon typus*) being followed by ichthyologist William Beebe; marine; all tropical seas (John TeeVan: courtesy Harcourt, Brace & Co.).

toma cirratum, which has a maximum length of 14 feet, or the Pacific zebra shark, *Stegostoma fasciatum,* with a maximum length of 11 feet. The Atlantic nurse shark when full grown is quite heavy as well as large; an 8-foot specimen may well weigh 350 pounds. With the single exception of this species, the carpet and nurse sharks are found exclusively in the tropical Indo-Pacific area. The Atlantic nurse shark is common in shallow water from the Florida keys southward into the West Indies and down to Brazil. It occasionally comes as far north as Cape Lookout, North Carolina, and also occurs along the tropical West African coasts.

The Atlantic nurse shark is of particular interest since it is the first Atlantic shark to have made its way to the Hawaiian Islands. As a matter of fact, the sharks did not reach this new environment by natural means but by being transported in a sealed plastic bag filled with sea water and oxygen. This story goes back several years to the time when a litter of young nurse sharks, each about 1 foot in length, had just been born in one of the large tanks of the Seaquarium in Miami (Plate 2). These young sharks were subsequently shipped to the Steinhart Aquarium in San Francisco, and shortly thereafter one of them was sent to Honolulu's Waikiki Aquarium. Despite these relocations all of the litter survived, growing rapidly on a diet of cut fish, although their normal food in the wild is composed largely of invertebrates. Nurse sharks, like the other orectolobids, usually do well in captivity.

The fact that nurse sharks are born alive brings up an interesting point about the orectolobid family: in three of the seven genera the young are born alive; in the remaining four the females lay eggs. The

nurse sharks and others of the family that are born alive are hatched from eggs within the uterus of the mother. The special term for this type of reproduction is ovoviviparity.

The Atlantic nurse shark is not considered dangerous under normal circumstances; however, if molested it can become so. There is a record of a Miami skin diver's catching a 5-foot nurse shark by the tail and then letting it go, only to have the shark turn and sink its teeth into his thigh. Although he was in thirty feet of water, the diver's companions were able to release his leg from the shark's jaws, and, much the wiser, he subsequently recovered.

Unfortunately, accidents involving other members of the orectolobid family, particularly the Australian carpet sharks known as wobbegongs, are often much more serious. Several species of wobbegongs are recognized. Because of their brilliant markings, often white on a rich brown background, their hides are sometimes used in the shark-leather industry. The largest wobbegong is *Orectolobus maculatus,* which reaches a length of 10½ feet and ranges from Queensland to South and West Australia and Tasmania. Like all wobbegongs, it rests on the bottom in the daytime and forages at night. In some cases accidents have occurred when a swimmer or wader has stepped near or upon a wobbegong, but in others the shark has attacked the intruder.

CATSHARKS—Family Scyliorhinidae

Some of the most beautiful elasmobranchs in the world are found among the catsharks, for a number of the species in this large family have picturesque patterns with exotic stripes, bars, and mottling. Only one other group, the carpet sharks, rivals the cat-

[23

Egg cases of the Spotted Dogfish (*Scyliorhinus stellaris*); marine; European coasts (Otto Croy).

sharks in this regard. Some of the scyliorhinids have strange habits. Among these are the swell sharks that swallow air and as a result blow up like a balloon, and the South African "skaamoogs" or "shy eye" sharks such as *Haploblepharus edwardsi* and *Holohalaelurus regani* that attempt to hide from their captors by curling their tails over their heads, thus hiding their eyes.

Most of the scyliorhinids are small, inshore forms less than 3 feet in length; however, there are some deep-water species, such as the thirteen members of the genus *Apristurus*, a group that is found on both sides of the Atlantic as well as in the Pacific.

The scyliorhinids usually have two dorsal fins, and the tail is in a straight line with the rest of the body, not bent upward. Spiracles are present, but the nictitating membrane is absent from the eyes. In some respects the catsharks are similar to the orectolobid nurse sharks, but may be distinguished from them by the fact that as a rule the cats lack the groove between the nostril and the mouth; and if this groove is present, as it is in a few species, the fleshy whisker of the nurse shark is lacking. All catsharks lay rectangular eggs that usually have a single tendril attached to each corner.

The two common European spotted dogfishes, *Scyliorhinus caniculus* and *Scyliorhinus stellaris* belong to the catshark family, as does another small species caught in 240 to 750 feet of water off New Jersey, the chain dogfish, *Scyliorhinus retifer*. Although there are other less common middle-water and deep-water species on both Atlantic coasts and on the American Pacific coast, the center of distribution with the greatest number of species of catsharks is in the Indo-Pacific region. The most spectacular color pattern among the catsharks is found in the adult South African "skaamoog" previously mentioned (*Holohalaelurus regani*); the body is covered with cryptic markings suggesting Egyptian hieroglyphics. The young, however, show only a mottled pattern.

In the water the swell shark seems ordinary, but when pulled out of that element it blows up like a balloon. Swell sharks are small and live in shallow water in both temperate and tropical zones. The maximum length for all six species in the single genus, *Cephaloscyllium,* is around 4 feet. They range throughout the eastern Pacific from California to Chile, Japan, Australia, New Zealand, and Africa, but are absent from the Atlantic.

Probably the best-known swell shark is the California species, *Cephaloscyllium uter*. It has a limited distribution from Monterey Bay southward into Lower California waters. In some sections it is common in kelp beds and is often caught in lobster traps. Despite its small size it has a very large mouth with a wicked set of teeth, which are surprisingly effective in catching fishes. When pulled up on deck, the swell shark swallows air, filling the stomach until the center of the body is at least twice its normal diameter. If thrown back into the water, it floats until it is able to discharge this burden. The ability to get rid of the swallowed air varies greatly from one shark to another. Some accomplish this with great facility and are quickly able to swim back to the bottom; others require as much as four or five days. During all of this time the swell shark floats helplessly at the surface. When this inability to release the air occurs in the aquarium, much massage is required from sympathetic aquarists. It is difficult to understand the value of this peculiar mechanism to the swell shark. Most certainly a floating shark would become a quick victim of any large predator in the area. On the other hand, it should be noted that sharks do not have air bladders, which normally act as hydrostatic organs for other fishes. A very few species such as the Atlantic sand tiger, *Carcharius taurus*, swallow air, retaining it in the stomach, which then functions as an air bladder. Perhaps at one time in the past this was also true of the swell sharks.

The rectangular egg case of the swell shark is light tan in color and is somewhat transparent, so that when it is held up to the light, the developing egg or embryo can easily be examined. Although many have tried, no one as yet has succeeded in hatching the eggs in an aquarium.

FALSE CATSHARKS—Family Pseudotriakidae

There are only two known species of these large and rare deep-sea sharks, one from the Atlantic, *Pseudotriakis microdon,* and one from Japan, *Pseudotriakis acrages.* Instant identification of these sharks can be made by observing the long base of the dorsal fin, for it is even longer than the tail fin, a condition found in no other shark. Fewer than a dozen specimens of the Atlantic form have been taken, the largest measuring slightly less than 10 feet. Most of those captured on both sides of the Atlantic have been caught at depths of approximately one thousand to five thousand feet, although they may also occur in shallower water, since there is a record of a dead one having washed ashore at Amagansett, Long Island, New York.

SMOOTH DOGFISHES—Family Triakidae

The smooth dogfishes form a group intermediate between the nurse sharks and catsharks (families Orectolobidae and Scyliorhinidae) and the requiem sharks (family Carcharinidae). The smooth dogs have the body profile and many of the anatomical characteristics of the latter, but their dentition is more like that of the former. The family includes fewer than thirty species in perhaps seven or eight genera. These sharks are small in size, usually measuring less than 5 feet; they are inshore species and often fairly abundant. One of the best known and the second most abundant shark on the American Atlantic coast is the smooth dogfish, *Mustelus canis.* It ranges all the way from Cape Cod on the north to Brazil and Uruguay on the south. Between Cape Cod and North Carolina there is a seasonal north-south migration pattern which is correlated with water temperature. Many details of the biology and life history of the smooth dog are known: females mature by the time they reach a length of 3½ feet; mating takes

place during the summer; and the average litter of about sixteen is born the following spring or summer, the gestation period being about ten months. In food habits, they seem to eat anything that is available, ranging from a great variety of small fishes to all kinds of invertebrates, even worms. One of the interesting characteristics of this shark is its ability to change its pigment over a period of two days from its usual grayish color to a "pale, translucent pearly tint." The smooth dog is not considered an edible species, and the sports fisherman finds it uninteresting. Its one contribution to mankind is its abundance, providing an adequate supply for classroom dissection and study.

The most abundant shark on the American Pacific coast, the drab brown smoothhound, *Rhinotriacis henlei,* is also a member of this family. To illustrate its abundance, my colleagues and I have data on 7211 sharks and bat rays caught in San Francisco Bay between 1948 and 1954. Of this group, 3076, or 42.5 per cent, were brown smoothhounds. The average length of the males in this group was about 20 inches; that of the females 31 inches.

The American Pacific leopard shark, *Triakis semifasciata,* is brilliantly marked with black saddles across the back. It normally ranges from Oregon to Lower California, and holds the record for long-distance air travel to places not in its range. By way of explanation, I should point out that many public aquaria in the United States and Europe maintain with other institutions a program for continuous exchange of living fishes. Since San Francisco Bay is a nursery ground for young leopard sharks, this species has become the "stock in trade" of Steinhart Aquarium, and consequently has been shipped in sealed bags filled with water and oxygen to many different aquaria. These sharks, in being tested for air shipment, were found to have a surprising tolerance for carbon dioxide. Because of this high tolerance, they have been able to survive greater distances of air travel than the majority of fishes. Most fishes will die if the concentration of free carbon dioxide in the water goes above twenty parts per million, even though the water is saturated with oxygen. Sharks, and some eels, can survive easily even if the carbon dioxide goes as high as seventy parts per million.

The spotted shark of the Mediterranean and South Africa, *Mustelus punctulatus,* has the body covered with many small black dots; it is slightly larger than the other members of the triakid family, reaching a length of 6 feet. The whitetip shark, *Triaenodon obesus,* is conspicuously present from the Red Sea to Polynesia and Panama. As the name implies, the ends of the two dorsals and the caudal fin are tipped in white.

Smoothhound Shark (*Mustelus mustelus*); marine; European coasts (Hans and Klaus Paysan).

REQUIEM SHARKS—Family Carcharhinidae

The requiem or carcharhinid sharks form the largest family among the elasmobranch fishes, with a total of more than sixty species distributed among some fifteen genera. Two species of the carcharinids, the tiger shark and the Lake Nicaragua fresh-water shark, are noted for their attacks on man. Several other species could be designated as dangerous to humans under certain circumstances. Another species, the soupfin, has been extremely valuable as a source of liver oil and vitamin A. Many of the species in this family do not have common names, and for a number of them, precise identification without detailed study is very difficult.

All members of the requiem shark family have the appearance of "typical sharks." There are two dorsal fins, paired pectoral and pelvic fins, an anal fin, and a long, lopsided tail with the upper lobe much elongated. There are no gill rakers attached to the gill arches, nor are there barbels around the mouth. Spiracles are present in some genera but absent in others. The young are born alive. For the most part the members of this family are tropical in distribution.

The notorious tiger shark, *Galeocerdo cuvieri*, is widely known for its omnivorous food habits. It eats anything available, including mammals, birds, fishes, lobsters, horseshoe crabs, garbage, coal, tin cans, and, finally, people. If sea turtles are available, they are taken with great relish.

The tiger shark is easily identified because of its distinctive markings. The ground color is grayish brown and is lighter on the undersurfaces. The principal markings are in the form of vertical bars along the sides. In addition, there may be a spottiness or mottling, or perhaps a reticulated pattern, along the upper surface of the body. The teeth are saw-toothed in formation and have a deep notch on one side, and the base of each tooth is quite broad.

The young may be born at any time of the year.

The number in a litter ranges from as few as ten to as many as eighty-two, with the average somewhere between thirty and fifty. Data is not available on the rate of growth, but we do know that as adults these are large and powerful sharks, with a maximum length in American waters of 18 feet. Information on several Australian tiger sharks indicates weights of approximately fourteen hundred pounds for individuals 14 feet in length.

The tiger shark occurs in tropical waters around the world, and in some regions it moves northward into temperate waters. Although it should probably be considered primarily an offshore surface shark, there are many records of the tiger's pursuing fish into water so shallow that fishermen standing on the shore have been able to catch the brutes. This species is not known from north European coasts, although a stray was once captured in Iceland. However, it is found off the African coasts but theoretically is absent from the Mediterranean. In the Caribbean as well as in Florida it is a common shark. In the summer it sometimes comes as far north as Long Island; however, these occurrences are sporadic. On the American Pacific coast the tiger shark rarely comes as far north as southern California, there being only two captures in that region.

Because of the large amount of oil available from the liver, and to a lesser extent because of the value of the hide, the tiger shark has often been fished commercially. The oil is used in tanning.

In the aquarium the tiger shark feeds in a casual fashion, much as though it could hardly be bothered to eat. And yet at times it has been known to take food with great ferocity.

A large tiger shark was the principal culprit in a series of events in Sydney, Australia, that began on April 17, 1935, and subsequently became known as the Shark Arm Murder Case. It started with a fisherman who captured a 14-foot tiger shark and brought it to the Coogee Aquarium for public display. This aquarium specializes in sharks, and—as I noticed at the time I visited it—any recently acquired large shark proves a tremendous attraction. Such was the case with this 14-foot specimen. The shark adapted very well to its new surroundings and began feeding immediately. However, eight days later it stopped feeding, and then was actually seen to regurgitate a human arm. The arm was tattooed and had a piece of rope attached to the wrist. From the tattoo mark the police were able to verify that the arm had belonged to one James Smith, who had disappeared shortly before. As the investigation proceeded, it became evident that James Smith had had a serious falling out with his cronies over a bit of skulduggery, and had apparently been murdered. It was thought that the body had been dismembered, crammed into a weighted container, and dumped at sea. In some manner the tiger shark had picked up the arm, and it had remained undigested in the creature's stomach for more than eight days.

Since shark digestion is normally rather rapid, it may seem surprising that human flesh should remain undigested for such a long time within the stomach of a large specimen. However, there are a number of cases which indicate that such delayed digestion is normal for the reaction rate of shark digestive juices upon human flesh.

Fourteen dollars for a pound of liver—the most expensive liver in the world; that is the price that the vitamin-rich livers of the American Pacific soupfin shark were bringing at the height of the expanded fishery during World War II. During this bonanza a ton of unprocessed soupfin shark was worth about $2500. In one instance, a two-man fishing boat operating out of Crescent City, California, made a $30,000 catch in two days of fishing.

Before World War II, Norway had been the chief source of vitamin-rich cod-liver oil. With Norway then blockaded and the supply of cod-liver oil cut off, shark liver assumed new importance as a source of vitamins, and the result was a boom that lasted until the end of the war. This boom was augmented by the discovery that massive doses of vitamin A given to aircraft pilots would prevent nosebleeds during combat acrobatics and would also increase acuity of night vision. Following the termination of hostilities, fish-liver oils from many countries began to flood the market. At the same time new methods of manufacturing inexpensive synthetic vitamins were developed, and the value of shark livers rapidly declined. In 1950 the last shark boat on the Pacific coast went out of business.

Sharks were fished for livers in many parts of the world, including Florida and the Caribbean. The two best liver sharks were both found on the American Pacific coast: the soupfin, *Galeorhinus zyopterus,*

and the dogfish, *Squalus acanthias.* The latter also occurs in the Atlantic. Previously both of these had been considered pest sharks, the bane of the fisherman's existence, because of their depredations on nets and the catch therein.

One useful side aspect of the shark fisheries was the biological investigations carried out at the same time. More was learned about the biology of the liver sharks than had been previously known about any other elasmobranchs. The first surprising discovery was that in the northern part of the soupfin range (northern California to British Columbia) most of the individuals were males. In the central California area a 50:50 ratio prevailed between the sexes, but in southern California and in Lower California females predominated. In 1942 and 1943 about five thousand soupfins were caught near Santa Catalina Island west of Los Angeles. Only thirty-one of this vast number were males. In areas where both sexes are present the females are generally found in depths of less than 180 feet, whereas the males are found in deeper waters, up to 1350 feet. With this geographic distribution of the sexes it would seem logical that the soupfin should prove to be a migratory species. Although little tagging has been carried out, there have been six recaptures of marked fish, indicating considerable movement. However, no pattern is evident from this small sample. The longest migration, eleven hundred miles northward, was carried out in three and one-third months by a fifty-five-inch female. This fish was tagged at Venice, California, and recaptured at Hecate Strait in British Columbia. One male, tagged in Oregon, moved seventy-five miles in two days.

Both males and females mature at about 5 feet. The maximum length of females is usually 6½ feet and that of males about 6 feet. The respective maximum weights are one hundred pounds and sixty pounds. The soupfin is ovoviviparous, the young being born alive. Litters range in number from six to fifty-two, with an average of thirty-five. Gestation requires about a year.

The soupfin is sometimes confused with both the brown and the gray smoothhound sharks. They can usually be differentiated because the soupfin has large, sharp, wicked teeth and a second dorsal fin, which with the anal fin directly opposite and beneath it forms a diamond in profile. As might be expected, the smoothhounds have smooth teeth, and the second dorsal is not opposite the anal fin.

Soupfins are fast-swimming sharks and cannot survive in small tanks since they keep bumping their noses. However, in large tanks they can usually live for a number of months, although getting them to feed may be difficult.

Along the southern coasts of the Australian continent, from Brisbane on the east to Geraldton on the west, there is an abundant Australian species, the school shark, *Galeorhinus australis.* In many respects it is similar to the American Pacific soupfin, and perhaps some day the two species may prove to be identical. Although the soupfin is of negligible significance as a food fish, the Australian species is an important market item; during World War II it also provided one of the main sources of vitamin A for that region. Returns from 6 per cent of more than six thousand marked sharks showed that they formed a homogenous population, with movements into shallow water during the summer and into deeper offshore water during the winter. There was no indication of a sex segregation pattern such as that of the American soupfin. One tagging record was quite exceptional: a male aged thirteen and one-half years and measuring 45 inches was tagged in Tasmania on April 6, 1949, and was recaptured nine and one-half years later (now 70 inches in length) just a few miles away. Studies by A. M. Olsen showed that the male school shark must be eight years old (47 inches long) before it matures and the female at least ten years (53 inches). Since the females reproduce only every second year, with an average litter of twenty-eight, the reproductive potential of the entire population is low, and the effect of over-fishing is soon evident.

From the standpoint of color the great blue shark, *Prionarce glauca,* is well named. Its upper surface is a dark blue, approaching indigo, and grading by almost imperceptible degrees to a gleaming white on the undersurface. As is the case with many other fishes, the beautiful blue color disappears soon after death. Identification of the blue shark is based upon a combination of characteristics beginning with the distinctive color. It has a sharp nose and very long pectoral fins, a slender body, and an elongate upper tail lobe with a notch near the top of it.

The great blue shark has been reported from both tropical and temperate waters around the world. Although several species have been described, most authorities at the present time recognize only a single one. The largest specimen ever captured measured 12 feet 7 inches, and like all blue sharks was very slender. Blue sharks measuring as much as 9 feet weigh no more than 164 pounds. Females mature at a length of about 7½ feet. The maximum number of young in a litter is fifty-four, which was reported from the Mediterranean. In the Pacific litters usually range from four to forty.

The great blue shark has never been fished commercially, and despite its abundance in some regions, it is not particularly popular with the sports fisher-

men. Although it is truly an oceanic species, being most abundant offshore, it does occur inshore at various places along the European, African, and American shores. On the American Pacific coast it invades some of the deep-water bays such as those at Monterey and La Jolla, but is absent in shallow-water bays such as at San Francisco. On the American Atlantic coast it is a common summer visitor in the Long Island and Gulf of Maine areas, but strangely enough is entirely absent at all times from the inshore coast line between Florida and Chesapeake Bay. This mysterious absence will undoubtedly prove to be due to temperature barriers if the information gained from the Pacific investigations can also be applied to the Atlantic.

These Pacific shark investigations were incidental to long-range tuna studies carried out by the Honolulu laboratories of the United States Fish and Wildlife Service. Their data included full oceanographic information on the conditions existing at the time of capture of more than six thousand sharks representing twelve species. These were taken over a wide expanse of several thousand square miles of the central and eastern Pacific. Twenty-five hundred of the total number caught were great blue sharks.

In studying the blue shark several important field observations were made. Blue sharks were never observed swimming at the surface in the equatorial latitudes, but they were often present at the surface in more northern latitudes. Also the young were apparently born in the north, for they were often caught there and were not caught in the equatorial areas. It was found that 99 per cent of the great blue sharks lived within a temperature range of 45 to 69 degrees F.

Thus temperature provided the obvious answer to the field observations; in the north the optimum temperature was located near the surface, but in the southern latitudes this same isotherm was below as much as five hundred feet of warmer water. In the latter area one had to fish much deeper to catch the same blue sharks.

The American Atlantic lemon shark, *Negaprion brevirostris,* is one of the commonest inshore shallow-water species, ranging from North Carolina to Brazil. It is occasionally found in brackish and even in fresh water. The body of the lemon shark usually has a yellowish tinge, hence the name. The upper surface may range from yellowish brown to bluish gray, and the undersurfaces may be white, yellow, or grayish olive. Besides the color, two characteristics help to identify this shark: a second dorsal fin which is almost as large as the first dorsal; and some very small teeth, usually one to three, in the center of both the upper and lower jaws. These teeth are

Sandbar Shark (*Carcharhinus milberti*); marine; both sides of the tropical and temperate Atlantic (Fritz Goro: *Life* Magazine, at Marine Studios).

about half the size of those on each side, and thus provide a conspicuous means of identification. Newborn lemon sharks are found from May to September and measure about 2 feet in length. Maturity is reached at about 7½ feet, maximum length being about 11 feet. Very little weight data is available, but there is a report of one specimen of 9 feet 6 inches that weighed 265 pounds. Lemon sharks have sometimes been fished commerically, although they are not a mainstay of the shark fishery. The lemon shark is the only member of the genus *Negaprion* known from the Atlantic, but it has four cousins in the Pacific. All share the identifying anatomical peculiarities as well as the habit of inshore shallow-water living.

The lemon shark proved to be an interesting and valuable test animal in a series of psychological studies conducted by Dr. Eugenie Clark, Director of Florida's Cape Haze Marine Laboratory and also a well-known skin diver and author of books on underwater activity. The sharks were trained to press their noses against a submerged target and then swim to the side for a distance of seven feet to receive a food reward. For ten weeks during the winter, the temperature dropped so low that the sharks lost their interest in food; however, they retained the learned feeding pattern developed during the test period, as was shown when the water warmed up again.

The silky shark, *Carcharhinus floridanus*, is very common offshore in both the Atlantic and the Pacific. Yet strangely enough it was not described in a

scientific journal until 1943, and it was not until 1953 that it was tentatively identified from the Pacific. As the leading authorities, Henry B. Bigelow and William C. Schroeder, put it in their treatise on Atlantic sharks: "That a shark so common, so large and easily recognized should have continued unknown for so long casts an unflattering light on scientific knowledge of the group to which it belongs."

The silky shark is a member of the ridged-back group of carcharinid sharks, having an obvious ridge down the center of the back between the first and second dorsal fins. The pectoral fins are extremely long, the eyes are small, and the second dorsal and anal fins have long, separate projections extending from their bases. The name of the species comes from the silky feel of the outside of the body, which is due to the many small and finely set denticles, the shark equivalent of scales. The denticles of the silky shark usually have three ridges across them. In the Atlantic the silky shark is sometimes confused with *Carcharhinus falciformis,* which is similar in appearance but has shorter pectorals, seven instead of three ridges on the denticles, and a broader snout.

In the central and eastern Pacific the silky sharks have a limited distribution, the range extending only about ten degrees of latitude on each side of the equator. In some areas within this 1200-mile band the silkies are very common. Catch records for 4133 sharks caught in this region by the U.S. Fish and Wildlife Service show that 2174, or 52½ per cent, were silkies. The silkies—along with the whitetips, which occur in the same area—are the bane of the

[29

Springer's Blacktip Shark (*Carcharhinus springeri*); marine; Bahamas and Gulf of Mexico (Fritz Goro: *Life* Magazine).

tuna fishermen's existence, since they delight in removing chunks from fish caught on the tuna set lines.

The most common shark in the Atlantic and Pacific offshore waters is a gray shark that usually has whitish tips on the pectoral fins, on the first dorsal fin, and sometimes on the upper lobe of the tail fin. This whitetip shark, *Carcharhinus longimanus,* is not to be confused with the whitetip of the Indian and Pacific oceans, *Triaenodon obesus,* mentioned earlier. Several features besides the color pattern are useful in identification. These are (1) long pectorals, (2) a short snout, and (3) a first dorsal fin that is broadly rounded at the top (most shark dorsals come to somewhat of a point at the top). In addition, the rear tip of the anal fin is very long, extending to the small notch just in front of the tail fin. This species reaches a maximum length of about 13 feet.

Since it is primarily a tropical species, the whitetip does not normally occur along either coast of the United States. It is common in the Mediterranean, and in the Atlantic it ranges from Uruguay to the West Indies. On at least one occasion it is thought to have appeared in the Gulf Stream off New England.

Detailed studies in the central and eastern Pacific show that whitetips are found only in a north-south band about 2400 miles wide extending from 20 degrees north latitude to 20 degrees south latitude. In this region the whitetips, along with the silky sharks, are responsible for most of the damage to the catches of tuna long-line boats. Occasionally very young whitetip sharks are found in the shallow water of coral-reef areas of the Pacific offshore islands. Some years ago, while studying the fishes at Palmyra Island, one of the northern Line Islands, I was struck by the fact that the sizes of whitetip sharks roughly correlated with the distance from the shore, the young being close to the beach and the adults only in the offshore areas.

In very shallow water throughout most of the Indo-Pacific region, and perhaps even off Africa, there is found a small grayish shark not over 6 feet long that can be identified from as far as it can be seen by the black tips on the fins. Although it is not dangerous to man, the blacktip, *Carcharhinus melanopterus,* is a very inquisitive shark. It is not uncommon for a skin diver to jump into an intertidal pool and instantly be surrounded by several curious blacktips. This is a bit unnerving to the swimmer, even though he may have read all of the books which state emphatically that this species never nibbles at the unwary spear fisherman.

Low tide on a tropical reef forces all of the fishes into deeper water. The first shark to return to the exposed reefs with the incoming tide is the Pacific blacktip. Sometimes it forages in water as shallow as six to twelve inches. This species is not found in deep water, and in this respect is entirely different from the two common species of Atlantic blacktips.

The small Atlantic blacktip, *Carcharhinus limbatus,* and the large Atlantic blacktip, *Carcharhinus maculipinnis,* are invariably confused. There are several individual features on which identification may be based, but careful examination is required to distinguish the two. On the small blacktip the dorsal base begins at a point farther forward on the body than it does on the large blacktip. This, however, is a variable feature. The lower teeth of the large blacktip are entirely smooth, whereas those of the small blacktip have very fine sawlike edges. The small blacktip reaches a normal maximum length of about 6½ feet, but the large blacktip is thought to grow somewhat larger. The large blacktip is known from

Florida, Cuba, and Puerto Rico. The small blacktip is common off Florida, Mississippi, Louisiana, and Texas, as well as in the Bahamas. During the warm summer months it has sometimes been caught as far north as Long Island. It is a fast-swimming shark and has the amazing habit of jumping into the air like a porpoise. On one occasion it was observed to spin three times before dropping back into the water.

Many sharks and rays are able to live in brackish water, and in some cases they can migrate into fresh water for unknown periods of time. However, only one shark has been able to make the permanent conversion from salt to fresh water and to establish a large population therein. This is the maneating Lake Nicaragua shark, *Carcharhinus nicaraguensis,* which is usually recognized as a distinct species limited entirely to fresh water. Actually, it is closely related to the common Atlantic bull, cub, or ground shark, *Carcharhinus leucas.* Since this latter species has been known to make migrations for great distances into fresh-water streams and rivers—for example 160 miles into the Atchafalaya River, Louisiana—it is probable that this is what happened many ages ago through the San Juan River into Lake Nicaragua. At a later geological period the sharks became land-locked through diastrophic activity which produced rapids and falls in the river and stopped further migration into or out of the lake. At the present time the Lake Nicaragua shark is separable by minor anatomical differences from the salt-water cub shark. The most surprising difference between these two, however, is in the records of human attack charged against them. The cub or bull shark, which is found in shallow water from North Carolina to Brazil, is considered by many to be dangerous to man, and yet documented records of such attacks are few in number. By contrast, there are many authenticated records of the Lake Nicaragua shark's attacking bathers, often with fatal results. The vital question, then, is whether the fresh-water habitat has changed the physiology of the shark, or whether the records for attack by the bull or cub shark are not as accurate as might be desired.

The Lake Nicaragua maneater is a gray, heavy-bodied shark that reaches a maximum length of 8 or perhaps even 10 feet. Recorded weights show that specimens no longer than 4 feet may weigh as much as fifty pounds. This is a bottom-dwelling shark and readily takes almost any kind of bait that is offered. Although it does come into shallow water, it usually does not show at the surface. Characteristically, it has a very broad, rounded snout with a short nose, long pectorals, and a moderately long first dorsal fin.

Lake Nicaragua, the home of the man-killer, has some interesting features. It is 96 miles long and 39 miles wide, covering some 3060 square miles. The surface of the lake is 106 feet above sea level; however, the maximum depth is 200 feet, or 94 feet below sea level. Although the lake is only twelve miles from the Pacific, its drainage flows in the opposite direction for some seventy miles, emptying by means of the San Juan River into the Atlantic. Lake Nicaragua is connected by the Tipitapa River with Lake Managua, but *Carcharhinus nicaraguensis* is not known from the latter lake.

Many times in the years since 1826 plans for a canal from the Atlantic to the Pacific through Lake Nicaragua have been initiated. The plan is still very much alive, and if this construction were carried out, it would be interesting to study the effect of the canal on the fresh-water shark population.

HAMMERHEAD SHARKS—Family Sphyrnidae

The year 1959 saw several fatal and near-fatal shark attacks along the American Pacific coast line. One of these involved a big hammerhead at La Jolla, California; the intended victim, a skin diver, was equipped with a power spear which he was able to fire down the throat of the monster, thus ending the attack. Unfortunately, hammerhead victims are usually not as lucky as the man just described. The first American fatality on record was caused by a big hammerhead captured off Long Island, New York, about 1815. The stomach contained portions of a human body. Records of unprovoked hammerhead

Left, Common or Smooth Hammerhead (*Sphyrna zygaena*); marine; world-wide in tropical and temperate seas. Right, Scalloped Hammerhead (*Sphyrna lewini*); marine; both sides of temperate and tropical Atlantic (Stewart Springer).

attacks upon humans are also known from other parts of the world. These incidents emphasize the fact that large hammerheads are very aggressive and dangerous, especially to the swimmer.

The hammerhead is one of the most readily identified of all sharks. The head is extended laterally in the form of flattened, somewhat thickened lobes, at the tips of which are located the eyes and nostrils. The distance between the eyes of a 15-foot hammerhead weighing fifteen hundred pounds may be as much as 36 inches. In some species the individual hammer lobes may almost equal in length the width of the rest of the head, whereas in others, such as the bonnet sharks, the lateral extensions of the hammer are much shorter, being equal to about one-third of the width of the head.

"Shovelhead" is a much better name for the bonnet shark, since the head looks exactly like a spade with a rounded outer margin. These are small sharks, with a maximum length of 5 or 6 feet. Unlike the big hammerheads, they are not dangerous. *Sphyrna tiburo,* the Atlantic bonnet or shovelhead, is a very common shallow-water shark throughout most of its lengthy range from Brazil to Massachusetts. The same species is also thought to occur in the Pacific. The large hammerheads with the extended "hammers" are usually found in deeper water than the bonnet sharks.

Among the characteristics upon which classification of the individual species is based is the shape of the forward edge of the head, which may be straight or rounded and with or without scallops or indentations. Another distinguishing feature is the position of the eyes and the nostrils. Since some of these head characteristics are modified by growth, a detailed reference such as *The Fishes of the Western North Atlantic* (Part 1: "Lancelets, Cyclostomes and Sharks"), by Henry B. Bigelow and William C. Schroeder, is needed in order to be certain of specific identification.

The hammerheads occur in all tropical seas and during summer periods may move northward or southward into temperate waters. The common hammerhead, *Sphyrna zygaena,* occurs on the African and European coasts of the Atlantic as well as on both Atlantic and Pacific American coasts. The great hammerhead, *Sphyrna tudes,* is probably the largest species in the family, with many records of lengths up to 15 feet. It occurs in most of the same areas as the common hammerhead.

The common hammerhead is about 20 inches long when born, and the litter may include as many as thirty-seven individuals. Growth is rapid. At a length of 12 feet this species may weigh as much as nine hundred pounds.

There has been much speculation about reasons for the development of the hammer as well as about the function it may serve the fish. One theory is that the extended hammers serve as balancers and make up to a certain extent for the lack of stabilizing keels along the sides of the tail as well as for the shortened pectoral fins. Problems of this kind might well be solved by observation and experiment in large oceanaria. However, there is something in either the psychology or the physiology of the adult hammerhead that prevents it from surviving in captivity, although numerous painstaking attempts have been made to keep it alive. Within a few minutes or at most a few hours after capture, the large hammerhead is invariably moribund. Fortunately for the study of the biology of these interesting sharks, newborn and young hammerheads have recently been kept alive at the University of Hawaii's Marine Station at Coconut Island.

One fine day a few years ago I happened to drive out on the Santa Monica pier in southern California. Hanging from the end of the pier was the first hammerhead that had been caught in local waters in twenty years. Never having examined a hammerhead, I obtained permission to cut down the hundred-pounder, and then proceeded with my study. Part of the data garnered was that the stomach contents included some fish detritus, a 15-inch mackerel, and, of all things, a beer can—which, aside from the testimonial to the particular brand of beer, demonstrates the omnivorous feeding habits of hammerheads. These sharks are primarily fish-eaters, but like many other sharks and scavengers, anything that flashes in the water may be considered food.

HORNSHARKS—*Family Heterodontidae*

The hornshark family is a small but very interesting group with only a single genus and not more than ten species. These sharks do not occur in the Atlantic or the Mediterranean, although they are found throughout most of the other temperate and tropical waters of the world. The California hornshark, *Heterodontus francisci,* ranges from Morro Bay, California, to Cape San Lucas and into the Gulf of California. The Australian *Heterodontus philippi* ranges through eastern and southern Australian waters. Few of the hornsharks exceed a length of 4½ or 5 feet.

The mark of the hornshark is a large, heavy spine at the forward margin of each of the two dorsal fins. The mouth is unlike that of any other shark. The dental plates curve upward from the upper and downward from the lower jaws and are covered with many minute, sharp teeth. This peculiar mouth, together with the lateral nostrils, produces a piglike

[continued on page 49]

1. Texas Skate (*Raja texana*); marine; Gulf of Mexico (photographed at Seaquarium by Stan Wayman: Rapho Guillumette)

2. Young Nurse Shark (*Ginglymostoma cirratum*); marine; shore on both sides of tropical and temperate Atlantic (photographed at Seaquarium by Stan Wayman: Rapho Guillumet)

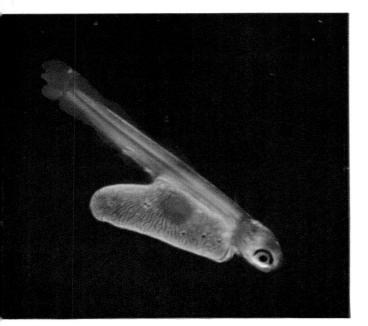

3. Larval Trout (*Salmo carpio*) with yolk sac still attached (30 days old); fresh water; Lake Garda, Italy (Mario Pasotti)

4. Eastern Brook Trout (*Salvelinus fontinalis*) jumping for a fly; fresh water; northeastern North America; widely introduced elsewhere (Treat Davidson: National Audubon)

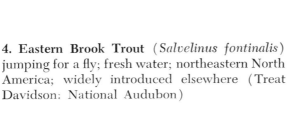

5. **Reticulate Bichir** (*Polypterus weeksi*); fresh water, upper Congo (John Tashjian at Steinhart Aquarium)

6. **Ornate Bichir** (*Polypterus ornatipinnis*); fresh water; upper Congo (John Tashjian at Steinhart Aquarium)

7. **Pike** (*Esox lucius*); fresh water; Eurasia and North America (Ernst Zollinger)

11. **Jewel Tetras** (*Hyphessobrycon callis* fresh water; Guiana to Rio Paraguay (Wolfsheimer)

8. **Silver Hatchetfish** (*Carnegiella marthae*); fresh water; Amazon basin (Herbert R. Axelrod)

9. Banded Distichodus (*Distichodus sexfasciatus*); fresh water; African Congo (Gene Wolfsheimer)

10. Pike Characid (*Boulengerella lucius*); fresh water; Amazon basin (Harald Schultz)

12. **Common Piranha** (*Serrasalmus nattereri*); fresh water; Amazon basin (John Tashjian at Steinhart Aquarium)

13. and 14. **Brazilian Black Piranha** (*Serrasalmus* sp.); fresh water; Amazon Basin (Harald Schultz)

15. Clown Loaches (*Botia macracanthus*); fresh water; Sumatra and Borneo
(Gene Wolfsheimer)

16. Tiger Barbs (*Puntius hexazona*); fresh water; Sumatra and Malay Peninsula
(Gene Wolfsheimer)

17. American Minnows; showing a Coastal Shiner (*Notropis petersoni*), North Carolina to Florida, and a Sailfin Shiner (*Notropis hypselopterus*), southeast United States (Herbert R. Axelrod)

18. Sumatran Barbs (*Puntius tetrazona*); fresh water; Sumatra and Borneo (Gene Wolfsheimer)

19. **Tench** (*Tinca tinca*); fresh water; Europe (Ernst Zollinger)

20. **Schwanenfeld's Barb** (*Puntius schwanenfeldi*); fresh water; Borneo to Thailand (Gene Wolfsheimer)

21. Veiltail Goldfish (*Carassius auratus*); fresh water; Asia, but now widely introduced in all temperate waters (Willard Luce: Shostal)

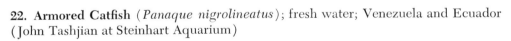

22. Armored Catfish (*Panaque nigrolineatus*); fresh water; Venezuela and Ecuador (John Tashjian at Steinhart Aquarium)

23. Electric Catfish (*Malapterurus electricus*); fresh water; western and central Africa
(John Tashjian at Steinhart Aquarium)

24. Spotted Upside Down Catfish (*Syno-dontis angelicus*); fresh water; western Africa (John Tashjian at Steinhart Aquarium)

25. Dragon Moray Eel (*Muraena pardalis*); marine; tropical Pacific (Douglas Faulkner at Waikiki Aquarium)

26. **Blackedge Morays** (*Gymnothorax nigromarginatus*); marine; Florida and Gulf of Mexico (Ernest Libby at Marine Studios)

27. **Rainbow Wrasse** (*Labroides phthirophagus*) removing parasites from a moray eel (*Gymnothorax eurostus*); marine; tropical Pacific (Douglas Faulkner at Waikiki Aquarium)

29. Green Moray (*Gymnothorax funebris*); marine; New Jersey and Bermuda to Rio de Janeiro and including Gulf of Mexico (Edmond L. Fisher)

30. European Fresh-water Eel (*Anguilla anguilla*); temperate and tropical Atlantic and European fresh water (Mario Pasotti)

California Moray Eel (*Gymnothorax mordax*) visiting parasite-removing imp (*Hippolysmata californica*); marine; southern California (photographed clay cave off La Jolla at a depth of 90 feet by Ron Church)

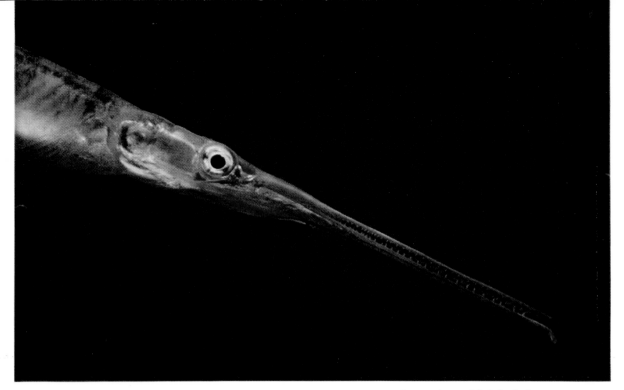

31. Needlefish (*Potomorrhaphis guianensis*); fresh water; Amazon basin (Harald Schultz)

32. Black and Sailfin Mollies, males (*Mollienesia latipinna*); fresh and brackish water; South Carolina to Mexico (Herbert R. Axelrod)

[continued from page 32]

appearance when the shark is seen from the front. As might be expected, this similarity has resulted in the common name "pig shark."

Courting activity is initiated by the male hornshark's biting at the female on almost any available part of the body. In copulation the male uses only one of the claspers, which puts into the clasper a 45-degree warp that remains for several days. The hornshark's egg is a fluted, cylindrical object with a spiral shelflike rim around the outside. It is very dark in color and covered with hard chitinous material, and it usually measures 4 inches in length and 2 inches in width. In the aquarium, *Heterodontus californicus* usually deposits single eggs during the months of February and March. Some of the newly laid eggs are occasionally attacked by female hornsharks and crushed between the teeth. Whether or not this is done by the same female that laid the eggs is not known. Incubation time within the egg is usually about seven months for the California species. The newly hatched hornshark is about 8 inches in length. The few records of hornsharks in captivity indicate that they do well under these conditions and live for a number of years.

SAW SHARKS—Family Pristiophoridae

In the region in which they occur, saw sharks are considered a delicacy. Off South Africa and Australia they are trawled at depths ranging from sixty to twelve hundred feet. Actually, there are two distinct kinds of elasmobranch fishes with saws attached to the front end of the head, the sawfishes and the saw sharks, and the two are constantly confused. They can, however, easily be distinguished by the position of the gills in relation to the pectoral fins. The four known species of saw sharks have small pectoral fins with the gill openings just ahead of these fins. By contrast, the sawfishes (family Pristidae) have the gill openings located on the underside of the greatly enlarged pectorals. These latter fishes, then, must be classified as rays. They will be discussed later.

The pristiophorid saw sharks are all small, with a maximum length of less than 4 feet. About halfway out on the underside of the saw are two long whiskers, which probably have some tactile function. The teeth of the saw are alternately large and small, and in this respect are entirely different from the even teeth of the raylike sawfishes. *Pliotrema warreni* from South Africa has six gill openings, whereas the other three species, all belonging to *Pristiophorus*, have only five gill openings. One of the most widely distributed species is *Pristiophorus cirratus*, which is found from South Africa through the Indo-Australian region.

SPINY DOGFISHES—Family Squalidae

The presence of a spine in front of each of the two dorsal fins and the absence of the anal fin serve to identify the spiny dogfishes of the family Squalidae. It may be noted that the hornsharks, family Heterodontidae, also have spines in front of the twin dorsals, but they retain the anal fin. When removed alive from a fishing net, the spiny dogfishes have the habit of wildly thrashing the tail about, which may result in the fisherman's being stabbed with one of the dorsal spines. In the case of the common spiny dogfish, *Squalus acanthias,* injury with one of these spines can be very painful, and according to some even mortal, because of the injection of a toxin released by the rupture of a small venom gland hidden in a groove on the back of each dorsal spine. Other members of the family apparently do not have this venom gland.

The common spiny dogfish, its gray body covered with small indistinct white spots, is undoubtedly the best known of the approximately fifty species in the family. It is primarily a temperate-water species, but also ranges less commonly into arctic and tropical waters. It is abundant along the European coasts and on both the American Atlantic and Pacific coasts; for example, an estimated 27,000,000 were caught off Massachusetts in 1913. In addition, there are sharks that look very much like this European-American form in other parts of the world; and although most of these have been given individual specific names, it is quite probable that there is only the one species. In 1952 a dogfish tagged on the American Pacific coast was caught on the Japanese coast after an elapsed time of seven years and a minimum distance of four thousand miles.

Females of the common spiny dogfish, sometimes called piked dogfish, reach a maximum length of 4 feet and a weight of fifteen or even twenty pounds; the males are always smaller than the females. This species has one of the longest gestation periods of any of the sharks, the range being from eighteen to twenty-two months. The newborn are usually around 7 to 10 inches in length and are born from eggs that hatch within the uterus of the mother (ovoviviparity). They grow rapidly, and from tagging data it is known that they live for many years.

In Europe the dogfish is fished commercially for sale in the fresh-fish market; however; in the United States it is not a profitable market item. During the war years it was fished for the value of its liver, but with the development of synthetic vitamin A the fishery collapsed.

Along the Atlantic coast dogfish have a seasonal migration pattern which is correlated with temperature. They congregate in fast-moving schools, which are here today and gone tomorrow; but wherever they are, they make tremendous inroads on the local fish population and destroy a great deal of fishing gear. For this reason there have been before the United States Congress on more than one occasion proposals to pay a bounty for the capture of these fishes. It is surprising, in view of this voracious background, that when the dogfish is brought into the aquarium, it is often difficult to get it to feed. If placed in a small tank (2000 gallons or less), it bangs its head against the tank walls until its sharp nose is so worn down that death results; however, in a large circular tank (100,000 gallons or more) it seems to adapt more readily. If someone should figure out a way to make the dogfish a really valuable commodity, thus effectively reducing the population of these fishes, he would be blessed by all fishermen.

Whereas the common dogfish is an inshore and relatively shallow-water species, some of the other members of the family are strictly deep-water in habitat. This is true of the ten species of the genus *Etmopterus*, whose members have light organs. This genus is of particular interest because it contains the smallest known shark, the Atlantic American *Etmopterus hillianus;* females of this species mature at a length of 12 inches and males at 10 inches. The largest specimen known measured less than 14 inches. The Mediterranean and eastern Atlantic *Etmopterus spinax* is somewhat larger, reaching a length of 24 inches.

SPINELESS DOGFISHES—Family Dalatiidae

For all practical purposes, these sharks are spiny dogfishes similar to those of the previous family except that they have lost the spine in front of the second dorsal fin, and in most cases have also lost the one in front of the first dorsal; like the spiny dogs, they lack the anal fin. Eight species placed in six genera are recognized, but only two will be mentioned. The first is *Isistius brasiliensis,* a small pelagic species maturing at a length of 18 inches and known from the tropical waters of the Atlantic, Pacific, and Indian oceans. It has been taken at the surface far from shore under night lights, and is suspected of being a deep-water species. It is of interest because it is the most brilliantly luminescent of all the sharks; observers have described the living fish as giving off a vivid greenish light from the undersurface of the trunk. Few specimens have been taken, and little is known of its food habits or biology.

The second species is the Greenland or Gurry shark, *Somniosus microcephalus,* which is a veritable **giant** compared with the other dogfishes, for it reaches a length of 21 feet (2250 pounds) and perhaps even 24 feet. Actually, there are four kinds of these cold-water sharks: besides the Greenland species, there is one in the North Pacific, *Somniosus pacificus,* one in the Antarctic, *S. antarcticus;* and a smaller temperate-water form in the Mediterranean, *S. rostratus.* Of these the Greenland shark is the best known, since it has been fished commercially for many years. For example, around 1905 as many as thirty thousand sharks a year were caught off Greenland in depths ranging from six hundred to eighteen hundred feet. Thirty gallons of liver oil can be obtained from a large specimen. The flesh is sometimes eaten, but first it must be dried since it contains a violent toxin that is removed by the drying. One of the mysteries of the Greenland shark is that a species so savage where its food is concerned, as shown by stomach contents containing an entire reindeer, seals, etc., can be so lethargic when caught; it is as unresisting as a log when pulled out of the water.

ALLIGATOR DOGFISH—Family Echinorhinidae

The alligator dogfish, *Echinorhinus brucus,* sometimes called bramble shark, is similar in appearance to the spiny dogfishes and at one time was placed in the same family. It has two dorsals without spines, and it lacks the anal fin. The principal identifying mark that will instantly serve to segregate it from all other sharks is the presence over the outside of the body of many small platelike denticles, each of which has one or more small hooks in the center. As an adult, *Echinorhinus* is a heavy-bodied shark, reaching a length of 10 feet and a weight of five hundred pounds. Although it is a rarity in some areas, it is found in all tropical seas, occasionally extending its range into temperate waters. Off Portugal it is normally caught at depths of thirteen hundred to three thousand feet, but in the North Sea it has been taken in much shallower water. The species is not common along the American coastline, only one specimen having been taken off Cape Cod in 1878 and another north of Los Angeles in 1939. It is known to feed on spiny dogfishes, *Squalus acanthias,* as well as other fishes. Certain South African tribal groups consider the liver oil a very potent medicine, so that in this area the oil commands a high price.

ANGEL SHARKS—Family Squatinidae

In many respects the angel shark is a true missing link, having some features that are sharklike and others that are raylike. The broad flattened head and trunk make the angel shark look as though it were a distant cousin of the guitarfish. Like the latter species, it has conspicuous spiracles, two small dorsal fins, and no anal fin; however, the mouth is moved to the anterior edge of the head. The nostrils are just above the mouth, and each nostril is equipped with two very conspicuous whiskers which extend into the entrance of the mouth. The profile of these whiskers is important in determining the various species of angel sharks. The anterior edges of the large pectoral wings are not attached to the head as they are in the guitarfish. There are six to seven rows of heart valves—again, a skate or ray characteristic—but the gill openings are on the sides of the head rather than under the pectoral wings. The angel shark also has sharklike free eyelids and a typical sharklike motion when swimming.

The largest angel shark is the European species, *Squatina squatina,* which has a maximum length of perhaps 8 feet and a weight of 160 pounds. The other ten species of the single genus in the family rarely grow longer than 4 or 5 feet. The majority are inshore species, seldom straying into very deep water. However, there is a record of a specimen of the Atlantic American *Squatina dumeril* from a depth of 4200 feet. Some species move into shallow water to drop their young. Others show evidence of a yearly migration, the details of which are unknown. As indicated by the distribution of the Pacific American *Squatina californica* (Alaska to Lower California), these sharks are principally temperate-water species.

Angel sharks are not dangerous to the swimmer; however, out of the water they are of a very nasty disposition, as many an unwary fisherman can testify. The shark often swings its body from side to side if picked up by the tail, and also clicks its jaws shut with resounding snaps that emphasize the dangerous nature of its spikelike teeth. In captivity it usually refuses to feed and thus may survive for only a few weeks or months.

SHARK ATTACK

Any experienced skin diver can go into great detail on the activity pattern of a curious shark, telling how it continues to circle about, each time coming a bit closer to the uneasy diver. The point at which the curious shark becomes an attacking shark is influenced by a number of factors, a few of which are under the control of the diver. Fortunately, many sharks never go beyond the curious stage, provided there are no recently speared fish in the immediate vicinity of the diver. Therefore one of the cardinal rules for the skin diver working in shark-infested waters is not to attach speared fishes to his body. Obviously the best procedure would be to get the fish out of the water and into a diving launch if one is available.

Sharks are often interested only in the fish and not in the diver. On one occasion, while studying fishes on the outer Bikini reef during the 1946 atomic-bomb investigations, I picked up a thirty-pound grouper that had been killed by the fish poison we were using and threw it to another man working in the turbulent water some twelve feet away. The fish slipped out of my hand and went only half the distance. Just as the other man started for it, a big fin cut through the water between us, and suddenly there was only half a grouper floating there in front of us. Incidentally, the other man never went back into the water during the remainder of the field work.

Even a normally docile species can have its temperament radically affected merely by the presence of blood or fish juices in the water. For example, the California leopard shark is a friendly species, yet on one occasion at Eureka, California, a leopard shark did attack a diver, tearing the swimming flipper from his foot.

One action that is likely to change a docile shark into a dangerous one is to impede its progress. Two instances in which Atlantic nurse sharks have bitten divers have resulted from the divers catching the sharks by the tail. On a number of occasions, spearing has resulted in large sharks turning upon both divers and boats.

Any skin diver would be incredulous if it were suggested that a guitarfish could be dangerous, and yet one did circle a diver in Southern California and then attempt to bite his leg.

All of this points to the fact that there are renegade or perhaps psychotic sharks and elasmobranchs, as there are among most other living creatures, that do not conform to the normal pattern for the species. In a small species of shark this might not be too significant; however, any shark that is larger than 10 feet in length must be considered potentially dangerous.

The feeding excitement of a single shark is usually increased if it happens to be part of a feeding school. For example, the Atlantic nurse sharks in Steinhart Aquarium share a tank with Hawaiian moray eels, and the only time that they do not get along well together is during feeding. Under the effects of a feeding frenzy a nurse shark will sometimes mistake a moray eel for one of the dead fish thrown into the tank. It is usually several minutes and many injuries later before the nurse shark discovers its mistake and the moray eel is able to withdraw into hiding. A parallel can be found in the advice given visitors to the national parks, "Never feed a bear"; for although the bear appreciates your kindness, it does not understand where the food ends and where your hand begins. Undoubtedly this also applies to many of our so-called harmless sharks.

One of the strangest aspects of shark attack is the bumping technique employed by some of the large species. This consists of the shark's ramming into the object that has attracted it; and if the object happens to be a paddleboard, the swimmer is often thrown off into the water. Usually the shark does not bite the victim, but bumps into him with sufficient force to cause serious injuries from contact with its rough skin. In one instance the bumping was so serious that it required subsequent amputation of the man's leg.

Dr. V. M. Coppleson, the authority on shark attack, estimates that as many people are injured by shark bumps as by shark bites.* Several theories have been offered to explain these bumping tactics. One suggestion is that the shark is testing for juices to determine the object's edibility. Others have thought that this was the shark's idea of fun, perhaps akin to the playful techniques of the porpoises which have been demonstrated at large oceanaria in the United States.

Aquarists have long known that the volume of food intake among elasmobranchs as well as other fishes is correlated with the temperature of the water. It is not surprising, then, to find that the number of shark attacks around the world show a correlation with water temperature. Records show that most shark attacks have taken place in water of 70 degrees or more, and correspondingly that there have been fewer attacks in water ranging down to 60 degrees. This goes back to the fact that the sharks most dangerous to man are primarily tropical in distribution. In the tropics, shark attacks take place during any time of the year, but in temperate zones they are usually limited to the warmer months. For example, Florida sharks lose interest in food when the temperature drops to 66 degrees, and when it goes down to 61 degrees they stop feeding entirely. A record of nineteen shark attacks in Florida showed none during the winter months of November through January. The most dangerous months were June and July, when ten attacks occurred. All of the attacks on the American Pacific coast have taken place during the summer months.

Dr. Coppleson's records of sixty-one Australian attacks show that slightly more than half of them (thirty-three) took place between two and six o'clock in the afternoon. The most surprising part of his data is that man-eating sharks prefer men to

women, twenty to one. As yet no one has come up with a suitable explanation for this astounding ratio.

SHARK REPELLENTS

During World War II a great deal of study was devoted to the problem of how to prevent shark attacks. If a flyer were forced to abandon his aircraft over shark-infested seas, what course of action should he take in the water to avoid becoming a shark fatality? The most logical solution to this problem seemed to be a shark repellent that a combat flyer or a swimmer could carry with him.

It was agreed among shark specialists that a suitable repellent should have two effects. First, it should reduce the shark's ability to locate food in the water through its sense of smell, so that blood or other chemical attractors would then be ineffective; and second, it should obscure the intended food from the shark. More than seventy substances were tested to determine their value as shark repellents. It was found that the most effective materials were those that contained copper—in this case, copper acetate. It might be mentioned that large sharks in oceanaria often refuse to feed in captivity. This is now attributed to the effect of the copper compounds introduced into the water to control parasites. The copper is thought to cause a mucous formation within the shark's nostrils, thus detracting from a normal interest in food. For use as a repellent the copper acetate was combined with a nigrosene dye in the proportion of 20 per cent to 80 per cent.

When this repellent was poured into the water along with trash fish from the stern of a Gulf shrimp boat, the effect of the substance upon hundreds of feeding sharks was immediate and astounding. Investigators felt that this was the answer to the problem. On the basis of tests of this kind, shark repellent was packaged and made an item of issue for the armed forces. Each package could be attached to the life vest or parachute. A pull cord enabled the wearer to remove the repellent from the packet quickly, so that, theoretically, he would be protected from hungry sharks. From the standpoint of the man, this was a very important psychological factor. The only trouble was that although the repellent was effective on certain Atlantic sharks, it was quite ineffective on many Pacific species. About the time that this fatal difference in the natures of Atlantic and Pacific sharks was discovered, the war ended, and there was no immediate need for further studies. However, in 1958 the armed forces and various governmental agencies again joined in sponsoring a program to learn as much as possible about shark behavior. Through these studies it is hoped that a repellent that will work on all sharks will be found.

---

* For the most detailed records of shark attacks on a world basis, the reader is referred to Dr. Coppleson's study, *Shark Attack* (Sydney, Angus and Roberston, 1959.)

Skates and Rays (*Order Batoidei*)

Several external features set the skates and rays apart from the other elasmobranchs. The greatly enlarged pectoral fins are attached to the sides of the head, and the gills are on the undersides of these fins. If the bottom-dwelling skates or rays were to bring water into the mouth and out over the gills during normal respiration, all of the bottom mud and detritus would be included. In order to avoid this, these forms have been forced to change their method of respiration, bringing the water in through spiracles on top of the head and then out through the gill chambers. Those rays that do not live on the bottom, such as the mantas, breathe like normal fishes. The free upper eyelid of the shark is absent in the skates and rays. About 340 species of this order are known at the present time.

ELECTRIC RAYS—Family Torpedinidae

On San Francisco Bay the old Chinese fishermen tell you, "Pick up electric ray by tail—no trouble." If both your hands and the tail of the ray are dry, this is correct, since the large paired electric organs are located in the wings, next to the head. Theoretically, it would be possible for a person to pick up a large electric ray and, holding one wing in each hand, receive a lethal jolt through the chest and heart, thus electrocuting himself. More than two hundred volts have been recorded from some of these fishes, although the majority produce no more than seventy-five or eighty volts, and some even less than twenty-five volts. As would be expected, the voltage drops radically with successive discharges. Several days are then required for the ray to recharge its "battery" and bring it up to normal strength.

Historically, the electric ray has been known from the time of the early Greeks. Not only do we find it depicted in their pottery motifs, but it was also mentioned in the writings of Hippocrates, Plato, and Socrates. In early Roman times the standard cure for gout was a shock from the torpedo or electric ray. Today these fishes have no commercial value, but zoologically they are important because of their strange electric organs.

The ability to discharge an electric current voluntarily can be useful to a fish in several ways. If the voltage and amperage are sufficient, the discharge can be used as a protective mechanism, or it can be used to stun overly active food. If microvoltages are produced, they may serve as a means of orientation, helping the fish to avoid obstacles. The discharge would then function in much the same manner as underwater sonar or as the high-frequency squeaks produced by bats. For a fish that has poor eyesight or habitually lives in muddy water, this sonar ability is essential. In some cases these electrical impulses actually serve as a method of communication with others of the same species.

In the electric rays the discharge is a means of protection as well as of food immobilization. Sometimes the slightest provocation will produce an entire chain of electrical outbursts. Dropping a newly arrived California electric ray into a tank with leopard sharks usually results in one or more of the leopards receiving a jolt that initiates frenzied swimming. On occasion shocked leopards have been known to jump straight up in the air and fall into the work corridor behind a tank.

Anatomically, the paired electric organs are composed of modified muscle tissue. The smallest unit of the individual organ is the electric disk, sometimes called the electric plate or prism. It contains a clear gelatinous material in which there are usually many nuclei. Each disk is separated from the next by fibrous connective tissue. As many as four hundred disks may be arranged vertically to form a single column that extends from the top to the bottom surface of the wing. The number of columns may vary from one hundred and fifty to one thousand, depending upon the species. When discharging, the electric ray is positive on the upper surface and negative on the undersurface. By contrast, the electric eel is positive on the head and negative on the tail, whereas the electric catfish is negative on the head and positive on the tail. These differences in polarity are of course due to differences in the arrangement of the electric plates or disks.

Some electric rays, such as *Torpedo californica,* often starve to death in captivity. Fortunately, they can be force fed if one is careful. This usually involves bringing the ray to the surface of the water in a net and then deftly flipping it by the tail so that it is upside down. Moving the net slightly out of the water forces the ray to gasp for life-saving water. Having selected a fish about the exact size of the electric ray's mouth, the aquarist forces the food into the mouth between gasps. This is where technique is important, for pressure must be kept on the fish until it is in the mouth and past the gullet, and at the same time the aquarist's hand must avoid the ray's violently moving wing tips whose internal electrical generators may be discharging at maximum.

At the Plymouth Aquarium in England, Dr. D. P. Wilson worked out an experimental feeding technique to determine the time of discharge of the batteries. A dead 9-inch horse mackerel with embedded electrodes and attached wires was trailed

Lesser Electric Ray (*Narcine brasiliensis*); marine; North Carolina to Brazil (Marine Studios).

past a resting *Torpedo nobiliana*. Suddenly the ray pounced on the fish; at the very instant when it folded its wings and head over the mackerel, a strong shock was registered on the meter (amplitude not recorded). At no other time during the feeding did the ray give off discharges.

About eleven genera, including three dozen species, of electric rays are recognized. They are found in all of the oceans of the world from tropical to temperate climates. In their normal habitat electric rays form a sparse population and usually do not occur in the tremendous numbers characteristic of some of the other sharks and rays. Their food is composed of small crustaceans, which some species siphon into the mouth with extreme rapidity. Like many of the other rays, the electric rays are ovoviviparous; that is, they lay eggs which are hatched within the parent. Thus the young are born alive.

The genus *Torpedo,* with its fourteen species, is the largest in the family. A typical *Torpedo* has a well-rounded disk with a reasonably well-developed tail and tail fin. Like other members of the family it lacks the venom spine. Two small dorsal fins are present on the tail. Some of the other genera of electric rays have a single dorsal fin or are entirely lacking in this feature. The eyes are small, and in some species vestigial; others are totally blind. In vertical distribution, the electric rays are found from the intertidal zone into water as deep as three thousand feet. The largest species is probably the American Atlantic *Torpedo nobiliana,* which is known to reach a length of more than 5 feet and a weight of 160 or perhaps even 200 pounds. The smallest species is the Australian numbfish, *Narcine tasmaniensis,* with a maximum adult size of no more than 17 inches.

Another Australian crampfish or numbfish, *Hypnarce monopterygium,* is the strangest of all the electric rays. The body is a nondescript semi-oval blob, and the tail is reduced to practically nothing. The original description of this oddity was first presented to the scientific world in 1795, and at that time it was described as a new angler fish.

In addition to the electric rays, only one other group of elasmobranch fishes has electric organs. These are certain skates that have small areas of electric tissue in the tail muscle. They will be dealt with later.

Diplobatus pictus from British Guinea could well be considered a "missing link" or transitional species between the electric rays and the next family of elasmobranch fishes, the guitarfishes. It looks exactly like a guitarfish, and yet it has electric organs.

GUITARFISHES—Family Rhinobatidae

Looking at a guitarfish for the first time, one gets the impression that the animal is suffering from chromosomal indecision, being unable to make up its mind whether to become a shark or a ray. The elongate body is flattened along the sides of the head and trunk, with the pectorals extended as small raylike wings. But the gills are on the underside of the pectoral fins, so it must be called a ray.

These fishes are found in tropical and temperate waters around the world. Many species travel in schools, sometimes in tremendous numbers. A length of 5 or 6 feet is a respectable size for the majority of adult guitarfishes. The one exception is the giant Indo-Pacific *Rhynchobatos djiddensis*, which reaches a weight of five hundred pounds and a length of 10 feet. This genus, along with *Rhina*, is sometimes placed in a separate family, the Rhynchobatidae. Anatomically, these differ from the rest of the guitarfishes in that the position of the pectoral is considerably forward of the origin of the pelvic fins. Also the caudal fin is notched in the center, whereas the other guitarfishes have a more symmetrical tail.

The guitarfishes are shallow-water bottom feeders, often being found in bays and estuaries. Small crustaceans are the preferred food items. The teeth are well adapted to this type of food supply, for they are very small, numerous, and arranged in as as many as sixty-five or seventy rows.

Sports fishermen abhor the guitarfish, since it is so docile that it never puts up a good fight. On the other hand, it is a source of enjoyment to the skin diver, who can generally outswim it and then capture it by the tail. As might be expected, none of the guitarfishes is normally dangerous to man, yet there is a record of an attack on a skin diver at La Jolla, California. He was collecting sand dollars at a depth of eighteen feet and was working without breathing apparatus. While he was at the bottom in an upside down position, a pair of California guitarfish approached him. The female passed by, but the male proceeded to bite him on the calf. Fortunately, the blunt pavement-like teeth of the guitarfish can produce no more than an abrasion. This was observed by the victim's diving partner, Conrad Limbaugh, noted diver and ichthyological consultant, who was astounded by this unheard-of behavior.

Guitarfishes are ovoviviparous, the young hatching from the eggs before they leave the body of the mother. Several species of guitarfishes have been kept in captivity; they usually do well and survive for many years.

In all, nine genera of guitarfishes are recognized. Eight of these genera account for fifteen species, and the remaining genus, *Rhinobatos,* includes at least thirty additional species.

All of the species of guitarfishes look much the same; however, a few do have striking specific differences. The Atlantic spotted guitarfish, *Rhinobatos lentiginosus,* can easily be recognized by the numerous small whitish dots covering the upper surface of the body and tail. It is found from North Carolina to Yucatan. *Rhinobatos rhinobatos,* the common Mediterranean guitarfish, ranges from Portugal to Angola, Africa. The Brazilian guitarfish, *Rhinobatos horkelii,* is a nondescript brownish species common in many areas along the South American coast. Only a specialist could distinguish it from the American Pacific *Rhinobatos productus,* which ranges from Monterey Bay south into the Gulf of California.

Studies I have made on this form indicate that the sexes are probably segregated during certain periods of the year. For example, records on 564 specimens caught in Monterey Bay during a seven-year period show that there were about two females for every male. Average weight for males is a fraction less than nine pounds with a maximum of nineteen, and for females, slightly less than seventeen pounds with a maximum of twenty-nine. Stomach contents revealed a preponderance of small crabs and an occasional small fish.

SAWFISHES—Family Pristidae

By attaching an ancient double-edged, saw-toothed sword to the nose of a guitarfish, one is able to produce the basic anatomical peculiarities of the sawfish. Unfortunately, the sawfishes and the saw sharks are invariably confused. The sawfish is a ray, as is shown by the position of the gills on the underside of the pectoral fins. By contrast, the saw sharks, family Pristiophoridae, have the gill openings on the sides of the body slightly above the pectoral fins. This latter family has been described earlier.

Very little information is available on the growth of sawfishes. However, at Marine Studios, Florida, five sawfishes have been in captivity for nearly nine years, during which time the largest has grown from a length of 8 feet 2 inches to 11 feet. Only about six species of these giant rays are known. There are recorded lengths of more than 35 feet and weights of more than five thousand pounds.

The sawfishes are ovoviviparous, the young being born alive. Although fecundity studies have not been made, there is a record of a 15½-foot female caught off Ceylon that contained twenty-three young. Like the spines of unborn stingrays, the sawteeth are flexible until after birth. Thus birth can take place without injury to the mother.

Sawfishes commonly occur in tropical salt and brackish waters around the world. They migrate readily into fresh water; for example, Lake Nicaragua has a well-established population that is now suspected of being landlocked. In some areas they are very abundant. In the Indian River in Florida one fisherman captured more than three hundred during a single season.

Classification of the sawfishes is dependent upon the presence or absence of a notch in the tail, the number of teeth along the sides of the saw or rostrum, and the position of the dorsal fins. The common sawfish of the western Atlantic, *Pristis pecti-*

Common or Smalltooth Sawfish (*Pristis pectinatus*); marine, brackish, and fresh water; both sides of tropical and temperate Atlantic (Fritz Goro: *Life* Magazine, at Marine Studios).

natus, can easily be identified by the lack of the tail notch and by the presence of twenty-five to thirty-two pairs of rostral teeth. By comparison, the eastern Atlantic *Pristis pristis* has only sixteen to twenty pairs of rostral teeth.

The saw is a handy tool. The sawfish uses it not only in digging up the sandy bottom, but also in clubbing its prey. The sawfish swims rapidly through a school of fishes, flailing the saw from side to side, thus wounding or impaling many victims. It then cruises about, eating its prey at its leisure.

Despite the sawfish's fearful reputation among some native peoples, it is fairly docile in captivity. From Marine Studios, Florida, F. G. Wood, Jr. has written some interesting notes on their specimens:

> All of our sawfish are fed by hand by the divers during the regular feeding programs. The only precaution taken is to ward off any wild swings of the saw with the metal feeding basket. Evidently swinging the saw is so closely associated with taking food that the sawfish still tend to move the saw from side to side when a fish is being shoved into the mouth. On a few occasions when a hungry sawfish has gone unnoticed by the diver it has swung its saw against his shanks with sufficient force to puncture his diving suit. Nevertheless, the divers are not afraid of the sawfish, nor do they dislike them the way they do the sea turtles which bite quite indiscriminately.

SKATES—Family Rajidae

The typical skate is a flat-bodied elasmobranch with a widely expanded pair of pectoral wings extending forward around the head as a thin, shelflike plate. In some species a nose or rostral cartilage provides support for a forward extension, giving the skate an extremely elongate nose. The eyes are usually conspicuous on the top of the head and immediately adjacent are the spiracles. The tail is slender and often short, and has two small dorsal fins. The mouth and adjacent nostrils as well as the five paired gill openings are on the undersurface (Plate 1). The teeth are small, numerous, usually rounded, and arranged in several series. The skate's food is usually composed of bottom-dwelling invertebrates, although some of the European species seem to be quite adept at catching small fishes such as herring. Mature females are much larger than mature males; the latter may be distinguished by the presence of claspers attached to the inner surface of the ventral fins. Sometime after copulation the females lay flattened, rectangular eggs encased in a leather-like protective sheath made of keratin. Each corner of the egg has a slender finger or tendril by which it often becomes anchored to objects on the bottom. Egg incubation time for six European species of skates on which studies were made ranged from four and one-half to fourteen months.

Skates are found in most temperate and tropical ocean waters and occasionally in brackish water, but are strangely absent from the Hawaiian Islands, Micronesia, and Polynesia, as well as from the northeastern coastal area of South America. Although they have a wide variety of habitats, they are most frequently found upon sand, gravel, or mud bottoms in shallow water at depths of less than 600 feet. There are, however, a few species such as the American Pacific *Raja abyssicola* that have been taken at depths as great as 7200 feet.

More than one hundred species of skates have been described in the scientific journals, the majority of them assigned to the large genus *Raja*. Of the more than forty species along the American Atlantic coast, one of the commonest is the little skate or hedgehog skate, *Raja erinacea,* which ranges from South Carolina to Nova Scotia. When fully grown it is only about 20 inches in length and weighs slightly more than a pound. By contrast, there are several species such as the New Zealand *Zearaja nasuta* that reach a length of more than 6 feet and a weight probably greater than seventy pounds. The American Pacific big skate, *Raja binoculata,* has a maximum length of 8 feet.

The eight other genera in the family include about twenty species, although some specialists assign four of these to separate families. For example, one of these families is the Acanthobatidae, whose three members lack the paired dorsal fins and have a nose that is greatly extended like the nose of a supersonic jet. Of these three, both the African *Acanthobatis marmoratus* and *Springeria dubia* have the elongate nose as a simple slim extension, but *Springeria folirostris* from the Gulf of Mexico has lateral extensions on the nose about the size of half a fifty-cent piece, giving it a leaflike appearance. The New Zealand *Arhynchobatis* has a single dorsal fin and is also placed in a separate family by some ichthyologists.

Some skates have electric organs formed from modified musculature along the sides of the tail. Anatomically, these organs are highly variable. The nerve supply to the electric organs of skates comes from the spinal nerves, whereas that of the electric rays (whose electric organs are located in the wings) is from the cranial nerves. Although the voltage of the skates' electric organs is known to be small, little detailed information is available on the electrical output. Recent investigations have shown that all twenty-two species of skates in Japanese waters have this electrical tail tissue. Strangely enough, the skates in southern Japanese waters are typically shallow-water species and have larger electric organs than the northern species, which usually occur in deeper water. The skate authority, Dr. Reizo Ishiyama, has suggested that all skates may eventually prove to have electrogenic ability.

Along some of the European coasts skates are trawled commercially and sold in the fresh-fish markets; the American species are not so desirable as food items, and there is little demand for them.

STINGRAYS, WHIPRAYS, BUTTERFLY RAYS, and ROUND RAYS—Family Dasyatidae

Fortunately for us, only two families of rays have venom spines. Usually a single flattened and tapered spine is attached to the dorsal surface of the tail. Many sharp, small teeth along the sides of the spine give the stingray its fearful reputation. About 118 species are involved, but only a small percentage of that number are really abundant. The first of the two families, the dasyatid stingrays, may easily be distinguished from the second, the holorhinid eagle rays, by the fact that the wing fins of the former extend around in front of the head as a thin, flattened shelf, whereas in the latter this wing fin extension forms a thick, fleshy lip.

In the dasyatid stingrays the tail is usually very slender and tapering, and in most species is much longer than the body disk. In some forms the single poison spine on the top of the tail can be replaced if it is lost; in others there is thought to be a routine replacement. This perhaps explains why some stingrays have two spines at the same time, and on rare

Thornback Ray (*Raja clavata*), female; marine; European coasts, Black Sea to Baltic (Hans and Klaus Paysan).

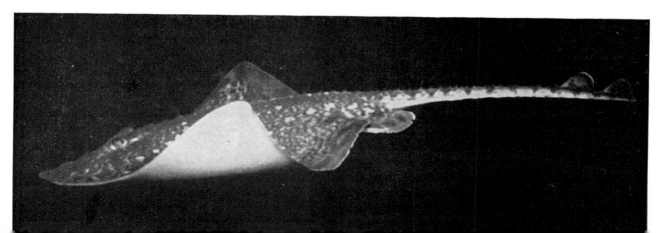

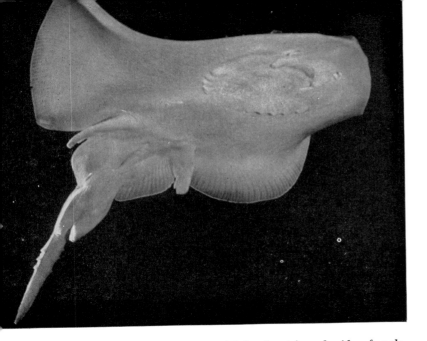

Thornback Ray (*Raja clavata*) underside of male, showing mouth and five pairs of gill openings; marine; European coasts, Black Sea to Baltic (Hans and Klaus Paysan).

occasions even three or four. Since the tail is very flexible, it can usually swing the hardened spine against objects in almost any direction. Some rays always switch the tail sideways, whereas others invariably throw it vertically forward toward the head. Large stingrays are capable of driving the venom spine through the planking of a wooden boat or completely through an arm or leg. If a spine with its venom gland intact is accidentally driven into the abdomen of a swimmer, death invariably results.

The cleaned spines have long been used as weapons by native peoples in the Indo-Pacific region. A single large spine as a spear tip is very effective, but occasionally a bundle of spines is used. In tropical areas stingrays are utilized as food. In the Congo, the tails have been used as whips and the skins as drumheads.

Ichthyologists classify the eighty-nine species of dasyatid rays into ten genera. *Dasyatis,* with some thirty species, is the largest genus, and also contains the largest rays. The other nine genera account for the remaining fifty-nine species. All possess the venom spine with the exception of the two species of the African genus *Urogymnus* and one Atlantic butterfly ray, *Gymnura micrura*. Most of the species are restricted to salt water, but a few occasionally migrate into brackish and fresh water. In South America there are several species of *Potamotrygon* which never leave fresh water. All dasyatid stingrays are shallow-water forms, seldom going deeper than 360 feet.

The dasyatid stingrays run the gamut of size from mature round rays weighing only 1½ pounds and measuring 12 inches across the wings to the giant Australian stingray weighing 750 pounds and measuring 6 to 7 feet across the wings.

Like the eagle rays, the dasyatids have powerful grinding teeth which enable them to crack the toughest clam shells. However, in contrast to the banded teeth of the eagle rays, the teeth of the dasyatids are small, numerous, and arranged in many rows. The digging action of the pectoral wings on the sandy bottom enables the stingray to excavate downward toward choice bivalves hidden under the sand. The stingray's normal food consists of any crustaceans, clams, or fish that are readily available in the area. These are quickly sucked into the mouth and ground to pieces.

The young are born alive, as the entire family falls into the category which the biologists call ovoviviparous, that is, one in which the female produces eggs that are hatched within the parent.

Needless to say, one should never walk barefoot in a sandy or muddy area where stingrays might possibly occur. Neither should he dive headfirst into water in such areas or skin dive in prone position close to the bottom. Such actions may well result in serious and sometimes fatal injury by stingrays.

The venom glands of the stingray are usually located in paired grooves that run the length of the poison spine. When the integument covering the spine is torn as a result of contact with a fishing net or some unsuspecting person's foot, the combined skin and venom glands are carried with the integument, and often remain in the wound. A study of more than four thousand California round stingrays, *Urolophus halleri,* revealed that 45 per cent had lost the integumentary sheath as well as the venom glands. The larger and older the stingray is, the greater is the possibility of its having lost the venom glands and protective sheath. This explains why some people who have been stabbed by stingray spines have received only mechanical injury without venom.

Although few stingray venoms have been studied, it is suspected that most of them share the same characteristics. For example, the venom of the round stingray affects the circulatory system. Its most serious effect is upon the heart muscle, producing an irregular beat or actual stoppage of the heart. Together with this are other changes that affect the respiratory and urinary systems as well as the central nervous system. As far as is known, stingray wounds of the extremities alone are never fatal, but this cannot be said of abdominal wounds. In one case a twelve-year-old Mexican boy, loading a shrimp net aboard a trawler, received an abdominal wound from a large *Dasyatis longus*. He died in less than two hours.

The treatment for stingray wounds as recommended by Dr. Findlay Russell and his associates consists of: (1) immediate irrigation together with a careful search to find and remove the integumentary sheath and venom glands; (2) immersion of the wounded extremity in water as hot as the patient can stand for a period of thirty minutes to one hour; (3) a second cleansing of the wound and a further search for any remaining bits of venom gland or integument; (4) dermal sutures to be applied if necessary; and (5) the use of antitetanus agent.

EAGLE RAYS, BAT RAYS, and COW-NOSED RAYS—Family Myliobatidae

A large fleshy pad extending around the front end of the head, giving the appearance of a flabby upper lip, is the mark of the eagle rays and their relatives, the bat rays and the cow-nosed rays. Actually the cow-nosed rays, *Rhinoptera*, carry this development one step further by having the fleshy lobe divided into a right and a left portion. The three members of the genus of duck-billed rays, *Aetomylaeus*, lack the venom spine, but the remaining four genera, totaling twenty-six species, have this poison apparatus well developed. Since some of these rays are reported to reach a weight of eight hundred pounds and a length of 15 feet, the stinger becomes a formidable weapon. It is located just behind the dorsal fin and fairly well forward on the whiplike tail.

Like the dasyatid rays, the eagle rays are noted for their pavement-like teeth. No one has tested the grinding power of these massive molars, but it must be tremendous, for they can easily crush the heaviest clamshells. One genus, *Aetobatus*, has a single broad band of molars in each jaw. The other genera usually have seven rows of teeth above and below, although several species of cow-nosed rays are known to have nine rows.

The food of the eagle rays is to a certain extent dependent upon the supply, but actually any food item that gets in the way will usually find itself sucked into the powerful jaws. Studies of stomach contents have revealed clams of many species, including commercial oysters; also crabs, lobsters, shrimp, peanut worms, nereid worms, sea pens, marine snails, and small fishes.

Although the young are born alive, the eagle rays are actually ovoviviparous, that is, the eggs are hatched within the uterus. Each of the two horns of the uterus is richly supplied with numerous villi which provide nourishment for the growing embryos during their uterine life. As a rule, equal numbers of young are found within each horn of the uterus, the exact number being determined by the size of the mother and the species involved. The young are born tail first, with the wings rolled up over the body like a double-rolled Mexican tortilla. Even as the newborn starts its aquatic life, it shows the spectacular swimming movements for which the adult eagle rays are noted. As gracefully as the flight of a soaring bird, they swim through the water with perfect ease and control.

The eagle rays and their cousins range widely through the tropical seas of the world, with a few species occurring in temperate and even cold waters. As a group they are not overly abundant, although some species have occasional dense populations. In San Francisco Bay the bat stingray, *Myliobatis californicus*, forms only about 5 per cent of the total elasmobranch population. On the other hand, the same species in Lower California has been observed from a helicopter in schools of many thousands.

Detailed studies on more than one thousand specimens showed that although the record female weighed 209 pounds, only a few females actually reached a weight of more than 140 pounds. The males were somewhat puny, rarely weighing more than 25 pounds. A female weighed at least 52 pounds before she could reproduce, but a male was mature at 10 pounds. The size of the female determined the number of young. A 60-pound female would bear perhaps six young, three in each horn of the uterus, whereas a 140-pound female would carry at least ten or twelve young. At birth the youngsters weighed about 1 pound.

In the past there has been much controversy over the orientation of the youngster within the uterus, the argument being that if the young were born tail first, which is the case, the poison spine might impale the

Bluntnose Stingray (*Dasyatis sayi*) digging into sand; marine, inshore; Massauchusetts to Brazil (Fritz Goro: *Life* Magazine, at Lerner Marine Laboratory).

At right: Sheepshead (*Archosargus probatocephalus*); marine and brackish water; Novia Scotia to Gulf of Mexico. At left: Bluntnose Stingray (*Dasyatis sayi*); marine, inshore; Massachusetts to Brazil (Fritz Goro: *Life* Magazine, at Lerner Marine Laboratory, Bimini).

mother during the birth process. Nature has taken care of this by making the venom spine rubbery and covering it with a heavy dermal sheath. The spine hardens quickly after birth, and within a few days the young are quite adept in its use, even more so than the adults. Holding a recently born youngster by the head, one finds that its tail flicks forward like a rapier trying to find the location of the hand. Not only can it be aimed straight forward, but it can be aimed equally well to the side. By contrast, the adult can whip the tail straight forward only.

As yet we have no exact knowledge of the migration of bat rays, but we do know that they move into shallow bays and estuaries to drop their young. In central California this occurs in June and July, and there is but a single brood each year.

Working at shark-fishing contests for many years, we have attempted to keep alive the newborn rays that have been removed by Caesarean section from the moribund mothers. In the aquarium these youngsters are susceptible to a multitude of recognizable but undescribed diseases, so that great care is required to bring them through. To date our longevity record for these aquarium-grown rays is eighteen months. One difficulty in keeping bat rays in good

health in captivity is that they are slow feeders. If they are to receive enough food, it must be made available to them for several hours each day. The competition usually present in an aquarium makes it difficult to achieve this essential condition.

In the past, San Francisco Bay was noted for its commercial clam and oyster beds, all protected from bat rays by redwood stake fences. To be fully effective, the individual stakes had to be about six inches apart. Many a fisherman was ruined because the stakes were broken during neap tides and stormy weather, allowing hordes of stingrays to enter the flats. A bat ray, or any of the other eagle rays for that matter, moves through a clam bed wreaking the same kind of havoc that a gold dredge does in virgin timber country. In either case, it takes a long time for restoration of the area.

A peculiar lobed, fleshy fold just below the eyes, looking for all the world like a split upper lip, gives the cow-nosed ray its name and also provides a quick method of identification. This feature and the presence in some of the species of eight or nine rows of grinding molar teeth are the principal characteristics that segregate the cow-nose from the rest of the eagle rays. As might be expected, the usual poison spine is

60]

present. Only one genus, *Rhinoptera,* is recognized. Some authors classify this genus in a separate family, the Rhinopteridae.

The American cow-nose, *Rhinoptera bonasus,* occurs sporadically from New England to Brazil but is strangely absent from the Caribbean. *Rhinoptera braziliensis* is found through much of the South American tropical marine water, whereas *R. marginata* occurs through the Mediterranean and down the northwestern African coast. Like some of the other rays, the cow-noses are jumpers, on occasion leaping high in the air. Maximum size across the wing tips is about 7 feet.

The spotted duckbilled ray, sometimes called spotted eagle ray, *Aetobatus narinari,* is one of the most beautiful of the large rays. The spots serve as a simple means of identification, and this can be further confirmed by the single band of teeth in each jaw. Although the duckbill is primarily an inshore species, it does have a wide distribution, being found on both sides of the tropical Atlantic. It is a tremendous jumper, probably having more ability along this line than any other member of the family. The small value derived from its sale as food in some tropical fish markets is greatly outweighed by the damage it causes to commercial clam beds.

DEVIL RAYS—*Family Mobulidae*

More has been written about the dangerous giant devil rays than about any of the other batoids. Their fearful reputation, however, seems to be little deserved, for many competent scientists including skin divers report them to be rather docile. Because they are extremely large and powerful they must be treated with respect, but they are not belligerent under normal circumstances.

Cow-nose Rays (*Rhinoptera bonasus*); marine, inshore; Cape Cod to Rio de Janeiro (Gulfarium, Florida).

The devil ray is best described as an overgrown eagle ray that forsook bottom feeding for the more time-consuming surface feeding. Nature has provided the devil ray with a pair of slender feeding fins that are useful in driving small crustaceans and other planktonic food into its cavernous scooplike mouth. These fins are attached on each side at the front of the head and are directed forward. Working as agile palps, they fan the food toward the mouth as the giant ray cruises through swarms of the most suitable prey in the area. An excess of small food in the gills can be a serious problem and has been known to result in suffocation in some species of fishes. Fortunately, the devil rays are provided with a special gill-protective mechanism located in the throat at the entrance to the gills. It is composed of a fine lattice work of many-spined small protuberances which effectively hold the food in the mouth until it can be swallowed. At the same time, these strainers allow water to pass into the gills. It should be noted that although the majority of rays respire by bringing water to the gills through the spiracles, it is suspected that the devil rays abandon this procedure and follow that used by the bony fishes—that is, bringing water into the mouth and then into the gill cavity.

Although the devil rays have long been noted for their giant size, the smallest member of the family, the Australian *Mobula diabolis,* is a veritable pigmy. When full grown it measures only 2 feet across the wing tips. By contrast, the largest known *Manta* measured 22 feet across the wing tips and probably weighed more than 3500 pounds.

Most of the devil rays are jumpers. Witnessing a ton or more of devilfish coming out of the water at one time is an experience not easily forgotten. Even when not jumping, the devilfish often reveals its presence by lazily flipping the tips of its pectoral fins out of the water.

Devil rays, like the eagle rays, are ovoviviparous, the young being born alive but hatched within the parent. Unfortunately there is very little data on the number of young in a brood. Some species are believed to carry only a single embryo at a time, probably because of the extremely large size of the embryo. For example, there is a record of an embryo of *Manta birostris* that weighed twenty pounds and had a wing spread of 45 inches.

Because of their large size devil rays are not easy to study. One would normally expect to examine a series of specimens of any species of small fish. Ob-

Biologists walking a newly captured Atlantic Manta (*Manta birostris*); marine, pelagic; tropical and temperate Atlantic (Seaquarium, Miami).

viously such a series of these titans of the sea is out of the question. Because of the paucity of material there is general disagreement among specialists as to the number of species in the family. For example, there have been ten species of *Manta* described from the Indo-Pacific region. Perhaps there actually are ten species; however, one authority recently lumped them all into a single species, with the added possibility that this single species might be identical with the Atlantic *Manta birostris*. Nevertheless ichthyologists are generally in agreement on the division of the family into perhaps four genera, based on whether the mouth is at the anterior end of the head or under the head as well as on the presence or absence of teeth.

The genus *Ceratobatis* with its single species, *robertsi,* is known from one specimen from Jamaica. It is a unique genus in that the teeth are found only in the upper jaw; otherwise it is a typical *Mobula.* Members of the genus *Manta* have teeth in the lower jaw only. A number of species of this genus are known from the tropical regions of the world. The remaining genera, *Mobula* and *Indomanta,* have teeth in both jaws. The six species of *Mobula* are distinguished by having the mouth on the lower surface of the head. The one species of *Indomanta,* known only from Karachi, has the mouth in the center of the head.

Among the devilfishes the tail poison spine may be present in one species of a genus and absent in another. For example, the common western Atlantic *Mobula hypostoma* lacks the spine, whereas the very similar but larger eastern Atlantic and Mediterranean *Mobula mobular* invariably has one or more spines.

Devil rays occur singly or in pairs, and some species are occasionally found in small schools. One afternoon in the Palmyra Island Channel (about five hundred miles southwest of Honolulu) our research group from the George Vanderbilt Foundation came upon a group of ten young mantas feeding near the surface. One of the mantas, a 280-pound male, was quickly speared and pushed back to the ship over the bow of the ten-man rubber life raft. On deck I proceeded to study the internal anatomy of my first manta. Dissections of this type are messy at best, and just at that moment the shipowner's wife came on deck for the first time after a week of seasickness. One look at the manta's anatomy strewn out all over the deck returned her to the stateroom for another week.

Before moving on to the more advanced fishes, it is worth noting that the largest of the fishes with cartilage skeletons are plankton feeders. Among the sharks this includes the whale and basking sharks, and among the rays, the giant manta. By comparison, the largest plankton feeders among the fishes with bony skeletons are relatively small.

The Chimaeroids

(*Subclass Holocephali*)

THE chimaeroids, sometimes called ratfishes, ghost sharks, or elephant fishes, have characteristics that in some respects appear to be intermediate between those of the sharks and the bony fishes. However, most authorities today agree that they have evolved from a sharklike ancestor and are actually highly aberrant sharks. Among the primitive sharklike characteristics that the chimaeroids retain is a cartilage skeleton; also, they lay eggs encased in horny capsules, and the males have paired claspers used for internal fertilization. On the other hand, they do show some of the characteristics of bony fishes, such as a dermal opercle covering the four pairs of gill openings and an anal opening that does not empty into a cloaca but opens separately to the exterior just forward of the urogenital aperture. Whereas the sharks and rays have an upper jaw that is free from the skull, or in some cases attached only by a ligament, the chimaeroids have the upper jaw immovably fused to the cranium—hence the subclass designation Holocephali, meaning "wholehead." The most startling feature of this group of fishes is the presence of a special clasper just in front of the eyes on the head of the male. Although it is thought to have some function in courtship, the actual method of using this clasper still remains somewhat of a mystery. This is also true of another pair of male claspers located in small pockets just forward of the pelvic fins. Empty pockets without claspers are sometimes present on females.

The entire chimaeroid group is a small one, with only a single order, Chimaerae, containing three families and a maximum of about twenty-eight species. The families are easily segregated by the shape of the nose—rounded, pointed, or plow-shaped. For the most part the chimaeroids are marine species living in deep water.

SHORT-NOSED CHIMAERAS or RATFISHES
—Family Chimaeridae

The majority of the chimaeras belong to this family, and all have the same general appearance as *Hydrolagus colliei,* illustrated in the adjacent photograph. The nose is rounded without an extension; this single feature instantly segregates the seventeen species (two genera) in this family from the other two families. The first genus, *Chimaera,* has a separate anal fin which is entirely distinct from the caudal fin, whereas the second genus, *Hydrolagus,* has the anal and caudal fins as one, with continuous fin rays.

The short-nosed chimaerids have many distinctive characteristics. The circuitous mucus canals on the head are very prominent, and so is the long poison spine at the front of the first dorsal fin. This venom spine is saw-toothed along its back edge, where there is also a groove that contains the poison gland. The unfortunate few who have accidentally come in contact with this spine have described the pain as long-lasting and excruciating. The venom has not been studied. The long, rodent-like tail is responsible for the name "ratfish." This resemblance is even more remarkable when one watches the ratfish swimming in an aquarium tank. The large pectoral fins sweep the water gracefully and slowly, making the fish look very fragile, and for some reason mouselike. Most ratfishes do not respond well to handling. Of a dozen *Hydrolagus colliei* brought into the aquarium, perhaps one or two will survive for several months. The longevity record in captivity for this species is held by University of Washington aquarists, who were able to keep one alive for more than two years.

Ratfishes contain a liver oil that is highly prized for its qualities in the lubrication of precision equipment; they also have a limited use as a food item.

Chimaera montrosa is the most commonly encountered European species, being found from Norway to the Mediterranean. It is absent from equatorial waters but is again present in the South African region. It is one of the largest species, often reaching a length of 5 feet. The American Pacific *Hydrolagus colliei* is smaller, having a maximum measurement of not more than 3 feet. It occurs offshore from Lower California to Alaska, and in some limited areas is occasionally so abundant that fishermen find their trawl nets entirely filled with this species.

Ratfish (*Hydrolagus colliei*) in the act of laying two eggs; marine; Alaska to Lower California (Steinhart Aquarium, California Academy of Sciences).

LONG-NOSED CHIMAERAS
—Family Rhinochimaeridae

The elongate stiletto-like nose of the rhinochimaerids reminds one of the nose contour of supersonic jet aircraft. This long nose immediately distinguishes them from the other chimaerids; further segregation is based on the fact that the paired claspers of the male are each in the form of a single rod, not double or triple rods as in some species. Because these fishes are found only in the depths, their recorded range lying between 2250 and 8500 feet, they are rare in collections; for example, only a small number of specimens of *Harriotta raleighana* have ever been taken—about nine from the western North Atlantic and even fewer from the Atlantic European region. The four recognized species of long-nosed chimaeras are divided into three genera according to the condition of the anal fin and the teeth. If the anal fin is not continuous with the tail, the specimen falls into the genus *Neoharriotta,* which has but a single species, *pinnata,* from South Africa. If the anal fin is continuous with the tail and the dental plates are rough, the genus is *Harriotta,* with the single North Atlantic species, *raleighana;* but if the anal fin is continuous with the tail fin and the dental plates are smooth, the genus is *Rhinochimaera,* which has two species: *pacifica* in Japan and *atlantica,* in the Atlantic.

PLOW-NOSED or ELEPHANT CHIMAERAS
—Family Callorhinchidae

The honor of having the most peculiar appearance of any of the strange chimaeroids goes to the plow-nosed, sometimes called elephant, chimaeras. The flexible nose extension actually turns down and backward toward the mouth, looking for all the world like a plow or hoe. Because of this spectacular proboscis, no other fish could possibly be confused with *Callorhinchus.* It occurs only in the oceans of the southern hemisphere in temperate and even colder water down to depths of at least six hundred feet. Four species have been described, but some scientists have suggested that they should perhaps be considered as a single wide-ranging form with populations in South Africa, South America, New Zealand, Tasmania, and Australia. In Tasmania *Callorhinchus* is reported to enter shallow-water harbors and even rivers. Because the flesh is edible and this species reaches a fairly respectable size (twenty pounds at a length of 3½ feet), it has sometimes been fished commercially in this area.

At the Porto Bello Marine Hatchery in New Zealand, biologists were able to remove the embryos from the egg cases of *Callorhinchus*, and eventually the young elephant fishes hatched. Unfortunately they refused to feed, and, like some of the fast-swimming sharks, banged their noses repeatedly against the tank walls and destroyed the plowlike nose.

Bony Fishes

(*Class Pisces*)

ALTHOUGH the name "bony fishes" implies a skeleton of bone, the primitive members of this group still make use of the cartilage skeleton of the sharks and rays, only the cranium being covered with dermal bones. The individual gill clefts of the elasmobranchs are now covered by a new structure, a single gill flap or opercle on each side, which effectively covers all of the gill filaments beneath it. The paired claspers of the elasmobranchs are lacking, and fertilization of the eggs is usually external. In the few groups where fertilization is internal, there is a single copulatory organ modified from the anal fin. An air bladder or a primitive lung is usually present. In some of the more primitive bony fishes the elasmobranch spiral valve in the intestine is retained.

Zoologists usually divide the living bony fishes into two principal groups or subclasses: the archaic Paleopterygi, containing only two orders and three families, the bichirs, sturgeons, and paddlefishes; and the Neopterygi, an enormous group of more than thirty orders and several hundred families, containing the great majority of bony fishes.

Bichirs (*Order Cladistia*)

—Family Polypteridae

Polypterus, the generic name for the bichirs, means "many fins"; yet when the fish is observed swimming in the water, this characteristic is usually not apparent. However, if the bichir is alerted or agitated, the five to eighteen finlets along the top of the back rise in unison, and it then presents the classic appearance usually shown in textbook illustrations. Each of these strange finlets is composed of a single spine to which is attached one or several fin rays, giving the finlet a flaglike appearance. In other fishes, the fin rays of a fin or finlet are attached to the

body adjacent to the spine rather than to the spine itself.

The polypterids are a small African family with only eleven species allocated to two genera. The genus of the bichirs, *Polypterus,* includes ten of the eleven species. The remaining species is the reed fish, *Erpetoichthys* (sometimes called *Calamoichthys*) *calabaricus.* It has a greatly elongated snakelike body, but it retains the typical bichir head. Also, it lacks the pelvic or ventral fins and has only a single fin ray attached to the finlet spines. The reed fish is found throughout most of the rivers of tropical West Africa. The bichirs are found in the same area but also range northward into the Nile.

The various species of bichirs are easily segregated by a combination of structural differences, including jaw position, number of dorsal finlets, scale count,

Bichir or Lobefin (*Polypterus weeksi*), showing flaglike dorsal spines on back; fresh water; Congo (New York Zoological Society).

and color pattern. Maximum size of the polypterids is between 2 and 3 feet; but because they are very slender, their weight is of little significance. Unfortunately this interesting primitive family is without known fossil ancestors. Since they are very similar in appearance to the ancient and extinct paleoniscids, formerly one of the predominant fish groups, it is probable that one of these days the missing link between the polypterids and the paleoniscids will be discovered.

Structurally, the bichirs and the reed fish have many features that clearly show why they are set aside in a separate order, the Cladistia. The scales are covered with ganoin and are rhombic in shape. Under the throat is a pair of large gular plates. The spiracles are conspicuously present. The newly hatched bichir has feathery external gills functioning in the same manner as the external gills of lungfishes. These strange gills are attached above the normal gills, actually to the hyoid arch, and are present for only a few weeks, usually a much shorter time than those of the lungfish. In some respects these are comparable to the embryonic gills of larval sharks which are lost before birth. The digestive tract of the bichir retains the spiral valve found also in the sharks, rays, sturgeons, bowfin, lungfishes and coelacanth. The lungs of the polypterids are somewhat similar to those of the lungfishes, but not so efficient, for although they receive arterial blood, they are lacking in alveolar structure. The right lung is the larger; both develop from a single offshoot of the pharynx. The bichir can live out of water for many hours but not many days. Like other primitive fishes, the bichirs have lopsided or heterocercal tails, in which the vertebral column swings upward into the dorsal fin lobe. Although they appear to have symmetrical tails, the symmetry is only on the surface, the lower lobe of the tail having filled in exteriorly, giving it this appearance.

Polypterus is fascinating to watch in a deep aquarium tank. When the bichir is in need of air, it struggles laboriously to the surface; then, taking a quick gulp of air, it moves toward the bottom with twice the surfacing speed. A new fish added to the tank is investigated with a stalking technique suggestive of a cat approaching a large rodent. The bichir moves slowly forward with the pectoral fins fluttering and the dorsal spines erected, ready to back off or go forward depending upon the outcome of the reconnaissance. When the bichir is in a hurry, the dorsal spines and the pectoral fins are held close to the body, and the fish travels with a slithering eel-like motion. Care must be taken in handling the bichir out of the water, since the spines are quite sharp and can lacerate the hand badly.

In some regions natives use bichirs for food, usually cooking them in hot ashes much as potatoes are cooked in other countries. Although the fine bones make them difficult to eat, the tasty flesh is considered well worth the effort. Small polypterids are sometimes impaled on a stick and toasted over an open fire.

Because of their peculiar external structure, the larvae of the bichirs have been carefully studied. However, little is known about the breeding habits or general life history. Spawning apparently takes place at the time of the floods. During these periods *Polypterus* moves out of the rivers and into the swamps, where gravid females and fry are found during the months of August and September.

Sturgeons (Order Chondrostei)
—Family Acipenseridae

The sturgeons are fishes of temperate waters and are found only in the northern hemisphere. What they lack in number of species, only about twenty-four, is made up in size of the individuals. Many sturgeons have been caught whose weights exceeded two thousand pounds. Some species are found only in fresh water. Others spend a portion of their lives in the ocean but return to fresh water to spawn. The zoogeographical center of their distribution is the region of central and eastern Europe extending into Asia. In this area there are about fifteen species of sturgeons, compared with only about nine species in North America.

In appearance, the sturgeon is an impressive sharklike fish with a body that is scaleless except for five series of sharp-pointed, heavy, platelike scales along the sides. The turned-up tail and the spiracles which are found in some species add to the sharklike appearance. In front of the underslung mouth, hanging down from the snout, are four long whiskers that work like a mine detector as the sturgeon moves over the bottom. The separate dorsal spines of the bichirs are missing in the sturgeons. But, like that of the bichirs, the ancestry of the sturgeons undoubtedly goes back to the same ancient paleoniscids.

As the sturgeon cruises slowly over the bottom, the sensitivity of the fleshy whiskers trailing in the sand makes up to some extent for the fish's poor eyesight. As soon as the whiskers pass over food, the protrusable mouth drops down with an elevator-like action and the food is rapidly siphoned into the hungry maw. The sturgeon is one of the few fishes that are known to have taste buds outside of the mouth. It is probable that these taste buds are also effective in locating food. In comparison with other fishes, the sturgeon is a very slow feeder. Moreover, the food it eats is small compared to its own size, so that in its normal habitat it must devote a great deal of time to foraging. For feeding, both the American lake sturgeon, *Acipenser fulvescens,* and the shovelnose sturgeon, *Scaphirhynchus platorynchus,* prefer a bottom that is clear sand or gravel where there is adequate invertebrate life. Food items include snails, crawfish, insect larvae, and such small fish as can be caught. In the aquarium many sturgeons do well on a diet of chopped fish. However, it takes them so long to find their food that if hungry, fast-swimming fishes are also in the tank, the sturgeons may starve to death. Some sturgeons refuse to eat in captivity, but they can survive for many weeks without food.

found more often in brackish and salt water than the white sturgeon. Its recorded maximum weight is 350 pounds, with a maximum length of 7 feet.

The eastern American lake or rock sturgeon has been known to reach a weight of 300 pounds and a length of 8 feet, whereas the shovelnose or hackleback rarely reaches a weight of 6 pounds and a length of 3 feet. Of the marine sturgeons, the Atlantic *Acipenser sturio,* which is probably the same species on both sides of the Atlantic, reaches a maximum of 500 pounds and 10 feet. The largest sturgeon of all is the giant beluga, *Huso huso,* from the Caspian and Black seas as well as the Volga River. Berg lists a world record for this species at a magnificent weight of 2860 pounds and a length of 28 feet. The

Left, Atlantic Sturgeon (*Acipenser oxyrhynchus* or *sturio*); marine, entering fresh water; both sides of the North Atlantic south to Florida and the Black Sea. Right, Shovelnose Sturgeon (*Scaphirhynchus platorynchus*); fresh water; central U.S.A. (New York Zoological Society).

The food supply of the ocean-going sturgeon is chiefly confined to small invertebrates, many of which live on mud bottom rather than on the clear bottom favored for feeding by the American land-locked species. Examinations of stomach contents of marine sturgeons have revealed shrimp, clams, worms, crustaceans, and a much higher percentage of fish than is caught by their fresh-water cousins.

The largest American species, and incidentally the largest American fresh-water fish, is the Pacific coast white sturgeon, *Acipenser transmontanus.* There is an unverified 1897 record of a British Columbia female weighing about 1800 pounds. The next-largest female recorded weighed 1285 pounds and was caught at Vancouver, Washington, in June 1912. In recent years, however, the largest individuals have usually weighed less than 300 pounds. The other American Pacific sturgeon, *Acipenser medirostris,* is

age of this fish was unknown, but one individual of seventy-five years weighed 2200 pounds and measured 13 feet. Several other Eurasian species attain weights in excess of 1000 pounds. The large size of these fishes and the tremendous egg production of the females (as many as five million eggs) have been responsible for the age-old success of the sturgeon and caviar fisheries in this part of the world.

Caviar can be processed from the roe or eggs of many different kinds of fishes. Originally this epicurean delicacy came from several species of sturgeons in the Caspian and Black seas and the Volga River areas of eastern Europe. Later caviar production spread to western Europe, and within the past hundred years to the United States.

Although the technique of preparation varies with the geographical area and the species, it involves the same fundamental processes. The unripe or green eggs are usually removed from the newly killed female by opening the abdominal cavity. In some cases, stripping the eggs from the living fish has been practiced in a manner similar to that used in trout hatcheries. This conservation measure allows the female to be returned to the water for subsequent production of more caviar. Once the roe has been taken from the sturgeon, the next step is to free it from the egg membranes. This is sometimes done by beating, but in other instances it is done more gently by rubbing the masses of eggs over a screen. If the egg masses are beaten to remove the membranes, they are then put through a sieve to separate the eggs from the extraneous material. If the separation is done by rubbing the egg masses over a screen, the screen itself allows the eggs to pass through, retaining the undesirable membranes. Then the freed eggs are carefully mixed with salt, which rapidly becomes brine as the salt extracts the liquid from the eggs. The brine is drained from the eggs, which are then ready to be packed commercially. The degree of salting and the resultant consistency of the caviar determine the quality of the product. The best Russian caviar is almost liquid and is difficult to preserve because of the low percentage of salt in it.

Isinglass is another by-product of the sturgeon fisheries. It is made from air bladders and at times has been more valuable than caviar.

The four genera of sturgeons are differentiated by the presence of spiracles and pseudobranchiae in *Huso* and *Acipenser* and the absence of these structures in *Scaphirhynchus* and *Kessleria*. Further differentiation is based on whether the gill membranes are united, the type of gill rakers, the size of the air bladder, and other detailed characteristics.

Huso is limited to two species, one of which is the giant beluga *Huso huso,* previously mentioned, while the other is *Huso dauricus* from the Okhotsk Sea and the Amur River basin. The largest genus in the family is *Acipenser,* with some sixteen species. *Scaphirhynchus,* with three species, is found in the United States and Mexico, while *Kessleria,* also with three species, is found in Syr-Daria and Amu-Daria, U.S.S.R.

Significant reduction in a sturgeon population may well result from only moderate fishing pressure. Although large females sometimes produce as many as two and a half million to five million eggs, there are indications that sexual maturity is not achieved in some species of sturgeons until the female reaches an age of about twenty years and a length of some 4 feet. It is obvious that the loss through fishing of the slow-growing large adults in a sturgeon population would result in a quick decrease in reproductive potential.

Unfortunately, the history of sturgeon fisheries has often been one of overexploitation and subsequent decline in both size and number of fishes caught. In some cases drastic action in the form of a permanently closed season has been required. For example, in 1872 as many as five thousand sturgeon per month were caught in California's Sacramento River. By 1917 the catch had dwindled to practically nothing; consequently fishing was no longer permitted and the sturgeon was placed on the protected list. As a result of this restriction, thirty-seven years later the population had built up to the point where a limited sport-fishing season could be opened in 1954.

Tagging studies of the migration of white sturgeon in the Columbia River have been undertaken by the Oregon State Fish Commission. During the fall and winter immature and medium-sized sturgeon move upstream, where they remain until early spring and then move downstream again. This is suspected of being a feeding migration. Average migration speed is one-half mile a day with a maximum of five miles a day. In the winter months the sturgeon move to deeper water but during the spring tend to congregate in the shallows. Only an occasional sturgeon goes out into the ocean and into other streams and rivers at any time.

Apparently most species of sturgeons are spring spawners. American landlocked sturgeons prefer shallow water for spawning, and if possible they generally ascend small streams for this purpose. Marine sturgeons migrate into rivers and streams to spawn. The Russian beluga moves from the Caspian Sea up the Volga River and spawns in deep holes, some of which may be 120 feet deep. In the American rock or lake sturgeon, ripening of eggs in the ovary is a continuous process, and small numbers of eggs are deposited here and there as the female moves about foraging. The incubation period of the fertilized egg is influenced not only by the species of sturgeon but also by the temperature of the water. Hatching may take place in less than two weeks, but on occasion may not occur for almost three months.

The newly hatched larva is about ½ inch in length. Just in front of the mouth is a shallow pigmented groove, a vestige of the sucking disk found in certain other primitive fishes such as the bowfin, gars, and lungfishes. Growth of the larva is rapid for a number of months and then slows down. Although the beluga reaches a length of 15 inches in one year, the lake sturgeon requires twenty years to attain a length of 4 feet, when it also reaches sexual maturity.

One of the most startling cases of parasitism of a vertebrate animal is to be found in the Volga River sturgeons. A small coelenterate, a primitive animal related to the sea anemones, is parasitic upon sturgeon eggs while they are still contained within the body of the mother. After the egg has been laid, the eggshell breaks and the coelenterate swims away, having consumed the contents of the egg. The original infection mechanism is unknown.

THE PADDLEFISHES—Family Polyodontidae

There are only two kinds of paddlefishes, one in the Yangtse River valley, *Psephurus gladius,* and the other in the Mississippi valley, *Polyodon spathula.* Together they make up a strange family of cartilage-bone fishes, the Polyodontidae.

When examining a paddlefish it is easy to see why on several occasions it has been described as a new species of shark. However, the monstrous paddle attached to its nose immediately challenges this identification. Although there is one shark, the deep-sea goblin, that has a paddle-like extension on its nose, this is quite small compared with that of the paddlefish, which is equal to about one-third the length of the fish. Under the paddle there are four very small barbels suggestive of the sturgeon family. The body of the paddlefish is smooth and scaleless. A cartilage skeleton supporting the body and a shark-like spiral valve in the intestine are among the primitive features of this archaic fish.

For many years larval paddlefish were unknown. It was not until 1933 that fry less than 1 inch long were discovered. These pale, translucent fry are entirely lacking the paddle, although they do have a large bump on the nose. In quick field identification they are easily mistaken for sturgeon larvae. The explanation for the delayed knowledge of the young stages lies in the fact that spawning usually takes place in the most turbulent portions of the Mississippi or other waters, and, of course, collecting under such conditions is extremely difficult.

The actual size of the smallest known American paddlefish is $1\frac{1}{16}$ of an inch. Changes in body proportions are rapid at this size. By the time the fish has grown to a length of $1\frac{3}{8}$ inches the nose has changed from an insignificant bump to a respectable beak or rostrum equal to one-sixth of the total length. With further growth this relationship continues to change until the body proportions of the young adult are achieved—that is, until the paddle is equal to one-third of the total length of the fish. For example, an adult paddlefish measuring 6 feet would have a paddle 4 inches wide and about 24 inches long, measured from the upper edge of the mouth. It is surprising that although the very young paddlefish have teeth, the adults have none; yet both young and old feed on the same kind of food.

Although little growth data is available, some indication of the rate of growth is shown by a few isolated reports. A series of twenty-six paddlefish from an Iowa pond increased in size from an average of 18 inches to 30 inches in a period of twenty-seven months. One exceptional group in Fort Gibson Reservoir, Oklahoma, grew 28.4 inches in the first year, yet previous groups of paddlefish in this same reservoir had grown only 32 inches in three years.

Looking at the paddle, one would guess that it was used as a sensitive probe for mud-dwelling organisms. Nothing could be further from the truth, for although the paddle is very sensitive and easily damaged in captivity, it seems to serve no useful function. Instead of probing with its paddle, the paddlefish catches its food by swimming about with its mouth wide open. Small crustaceans and planktonic organisms are strained from the water by the long gill rakers on the inner sides of the gills.

In the aquarium the paddlefish can be changed from a planktonic to a cut-fish diet, but this usually requires much patience on the part of the aquarist.

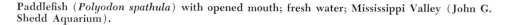

Paddlefish (*Polyodon spathula*) with opened mouth; fresh water; Mississippi Valley (John G. Shedd Aquarium).

Watching the feeding through the glass, the visitor is astounded when the paddlefish opens its mouth. The entire back part of the head drops down, and one gets the feeling that he is watching something that is anatomically impossible.

The average adult American paddlefish found today weighs from thirty to fifty pounds. Sexual maturity is reached at a weight of twenty to thirty pounds, which is usually not before the seventh or eighth year. There is some indication that the paddlefish may show reproductive periodicity and not spawn every year.

The largest recorded American paddlefish weighed 168 pounds and measured slightly more than 6 feet. The Chinese paddlefish, however, grows much larger. There are records, although unauthenticated, of individual fish reaching 20 feet. The largest reported by recent ichthyologists has been around 12 feet.

The original distribution of the American paddlefish was over most of the Mississippi valley from North Dakota to New York and down to South Carolina. Because of dams, pollution, and many other factors, it is now greatly restricted in its range and is abundant only in certain limited areas.

The early Americans did not consider the paddlefish edible. Later it became commercially acceptable but not a first-class fish. Although they are sometimes mixed with sturgeon roe, the greenish black paddlefish eggs can by themselves be made into a good caviar.

Bowfin (*Order Protospondyli*)

—Family Amiidae

Dogfish, grindle, spotfin, and mudfish are just a few of the names that have been applied to the archaic bowfin, *Amia calva,* a fish that in ancient times was widely distributed through the fresh waters of North America but is now restricted to the waters of the eastern United States. This is an easy fish to identify because of the long, spineless dorsal fin (about fifty-eight rays) that runs from the forward part of the back down to the base of the tail. On the upper part of the caudal peduncle just in front of the tail there is usually a large dark spot. On the male this spot is edged with orange or yellow, but on the female the edging is absent and sometimes the spot is also missing. On the underside of the head between the two lower jawbones is a large and distinctive gular plate, which is a further aid in identification. The head is covered with bony plates and the rest of the body with heavy cycloid scales. The ventral fins are abdominal in position, located almost in the center of the body. The tail is basically

lopsided or heterocercal, although externally it appears symmetrical.

Internally the bowfin has some interesting features. The skeleton is composed principally of bone with double concave vertebrae; there is a vestige of the primitive spiral valve of the sharks and rays; and the well-developed air bladder has a cellular internal surface so that it can act as a lung, enabling the bowfin to live in water almost devoid of oxygen or to survive out of water for as long as twenty-four hours. Large bowfins may reach a length of 3 feet and a weight of more than eight pounds, although the usual maximum length is around 2 feet. Since bowfins eat all kinds of fishes and invertebrates, they are considered such a destructive factor that in some areas where they are extremely abundant eradication measures have been instituted. In some parts of the South they are used for food, but in the North they are trash fish.

The preferred spawning sites are weedy areas along the margins of lakes and streams. The male bowfin not only builds the nest but also guards it after the female lays her eggs, and chaperones the youngsters for a short time after they are hatched. Like lungfishes and sturgeons, the newly hatched bowfin has an adhesive organ on the snout that enables it to attach itself to aquatic vegetation. Growth is rapid; a year-old bowfin may be 5 to 9 inches long.

Gars (*Order Ginglymodi*)

—Family Lepisosteidae

Many a skin diver working in fresh water has aimed his spear at a gar only to see the weapon ricochet from the gar's heavy external armor. Close examination of this formidable protective covering reveals that it is composed of ganoin scales arranged in diamond- or rhombic-shaped flat plates which do not overlap like normal fish scales.

Gars are usually found in shallow, weedy areas. Much of the time they show little movement, appearing to be suspended in mid-water. However, when necessary, they can move extremely fast, especially when food is available. Like crocodilians, gars slash sideways at food, which is effectively pierced and held captive by the long, needle-sharp teeth. Most fishermen consider gars the scourge of the fish world, not only because of their predaceous nature but also because of their ability to steal bait from the hook. Gars are generally not used as food, although the Seminole Indians in the Florida Everglades include them in their diet. Small gars are fantastically abundant in many sections of the glades; the Indians remove the head and tail, then shuck them out by making a slit from one end to the other along the undersurface of the body. The giant tropical gar, *Lepisosteus tristoechus,* with lengths of 10 and perhaps 12 feet, is reported to be a food fish in the markets of Tampico, Mexico. Gar scales have a limited use in making ornaments and jewelry.

The vertebrae of gars are decidedly reptilian in nature. Most fishes have vertebrae that are concave at both ends, but gars have ball-and-socket joints, with the interior end of each vertebra being convex and the posterior end concave. Both the anal and dorsal fins are without spines and have fewer than

gars for one of their commonest parasites, the abominable fish louse, *Argulus.* These small, flat crustaceans, measuring about ¼ inch in diameter, are almost impossible to kill with most chemicals without also killing the fish. However, *Argulus* cannot survive in salt water, so that a salt-water bath for one or two weeks will usually rid the gars of this affliction. Although gars live for years in fresh water aquaria, some will not feed readily in salt water. This fact probably explains why the large commercial oceanaria have often not been successful in displaying these fishes.

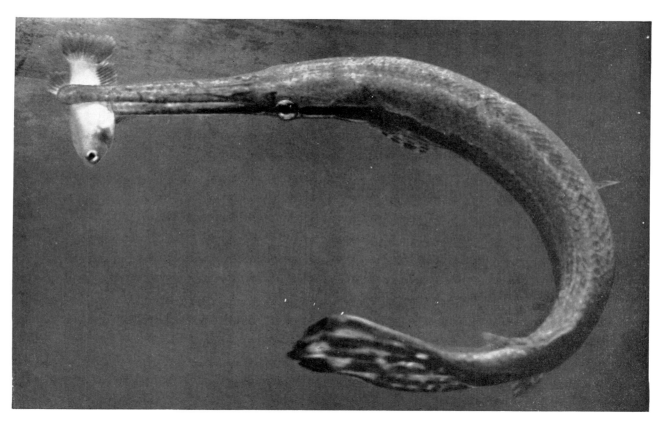

Young Longnose Gar (*Lepisosteus osseus*) catching food; fresh water; Mississippi basin eastward through seaboard states (Gene Wolfsheimer).

a dozen rays each; these two fins are located far back on the body, just in front of the heterocercal tail. Although the tail fin looks symmetrical, the vertebrae inside actually swing upward in the typical lopsided fashion of the shark and sturgeon tail.

About eight species of gars are recognized; limited in distribution to North America from southeastern Canada to Costa Rica, they do not occur west of the Rocky Mountains. Although primarily a fresh-water family, some, such as the two or three species of alligator gars, do move into salt water. Aquarists make use of this fact in treating alligator

The most widely distributed member of the family is the longnose gar, *Lepisosteus osseus;* it ranges from the Mississippi basin eastward through all of the seaboard states. Its long jaws provide a ready means of identification: the length of the jaws in front of the eyes is about three times the length of the head behind the eyes. Other species of gars have much shorter jaws, usually no longer than twice the distance from the eye to the opercle or end of the head. Unlike the other gars, the longnose does not seem to mind a current of water, and it is often found in clear water.

The shortnose gar, *Lepisosteus platostomus,* lacks the mottled color pattern of its cousin, the otherwise very similar spotted gar, *L. productus.* The largest lepisosteid ever caught in the United States was an alligator gar, *Lepisosteus spatula,* that weighed 302 pounds and measured almost 10 feet. This species has the most limited distribution of all the gars, being mostly restricted to the southern states.

Isospondylous Fishes

(*Order Isospondyli*)

There are many familiar names among the soft-rayed fishes of this primitive group—herring, smelt, salmon, and trout, to mention a few. Also among them are certain deep-sea forms noted for the photophores, or light organs, along the sides of the body.

The name Isospondyli, meaning "equal vertebra," is given to this order because the vertebrae at the head end of these fishes are essentially the same as those at the tail end, a condition not found in more advanced fishes. The Isospondyli have soft-rayed fins, lacking the fin spines of the more advanced groups. The ventral fins are located on the abdomen and are supported by the pelvic girdle, which is not attached to the pectoral girdle as in the more complex fishes. The air bladder is connected to the throat by means of an open duct and in some cases functions as a primitive lung. Many of the fishes in this group have a small, fleshy adipose fin located on the back about halfway between the dorsal fin and the tail fin. About thirty-four families assigned to nine suborders are included in the Isospondyli.

TENPOUNDER and TARPON—Family Elopidae

The fishes of the elopid family resemble externally many of the other more primitive isospondylous species, especially the milkfish and bonefishes: all of them have a long, deeply forked tail and a single dorsal fin of soft rays, placed about the center of the body and more or less opposite the ventral fins. However, the tenpounder and the tarpon do have one distinguishing mark which the others lack—a fairly large, bony gular plate located under the mouth, between the two mandibles. There are also many sharp, small teeth in the mouth. Although primarily marine, these fishes are also known from brackish and even fresh waters. The larval forms of the elopids are similar to those of the albulids or bonefishes—that is, bandlike and transparent—and they shrink radically in length at the time of metamorphosis to the juvenile stage.

There is probably only a single species of tenpounder, *Elops saurus,* although as many as seven have been recognized. It occurs around the world in tropical and subtropical seas, reaching a length of 3 feet and a weight of thirty pounds. It has large pseudobranchiae in the gill area, and grooves into which the dorsal and anal fins can be depressed. In addition, the dorsal fin is normal in structure, whereas in the other genus in the elopid family—that of the tarpons, *Megalops*—the last ray of the dorsal is extended as a long filament. Also, the tarpons lack the pseudobranchiae and the grooves for the dorsal and ventral fins, and they are much heavier bodied than the tenpounders.

Because of its explosive reaction to being hooked, the Atlantic tarpon, *Megalops atlanticus,* has long been known as one of the most spectacular game fishes. It rushes to the surface, leaping high out of the water in an effort to shake out the hook; an exciting battle ensues, lasting until the fish is totally exhausted. A number of 200-pound tarpon have been taken by sportsmen, but the record is a giant 8-foot individual that weighed an estimated 340 pounds. In the summertime the Atlantic tarpon ranges as far north as Cape Cod, but it is most abundant in tropical areas. One of the favored sports fishing areas is the Panuco River near Tampico, Mexico, where fishes as heavy as 240 pounds can be caught.

The Pacific tarpon, *Megalops cyprinoides,* is a much smaller species than its Atlantic cousin, seldom growing as long as 40 inches. It ranges from Africa through the Indo-Pacific to Guam.

Unfortunately, neither of the two tarpons nor the tenpounder is a good food fish, although all three are sometimes eaten.

The Elopidae constitute probably the most primitive family of the suborder Clupeoidea of the Isospondyli. Ten more families are included in this suborder, but only the most important will be discussed.

BONEFISH or LADYFISH—Family Albulidae

The salt-water angler considers the silvery bonefish one of the best sport fishes to be caught on light tackle. On the other hand, ichthyologists find the bonefish interesting because of its strange eel-like larval stage. This leptocephalus larva, as it is called, is in many respects similar to that of the eels. Two species of bonefish are recognized: *Albula vulpes,* which is cosmopolitan in shallow, warm, marine waters, and *Dixonina nemoptera,* which is found only in the West Indies. The latter differs from *Albula* in that the last ray of both the dorsal and anal fins is modified as a long, extended filament. Identification is easy because of the thick, transparent cartilage that covers the pointed head and because of the characteristic profile of the head with its receding mouth. The teeth are numerous, small, blunt, and rounded. The dorsal fin with its ten to fourteen soft rays is in the center of the body opposite the ventrals, and the caudal fin is deeply forked. Adult bonefish range in size up to about 3½ feet, with a maximum weight of eighteen pounds. Although they are sometimes sold in markets, they have many small fine bones, which limit the way in which they can be prepared for the table.

SLICKHEAD FISHES—Family Alepocephalidae

This is a large group of small, dark-colored, slender-bodied deep-sea fishes, most of which are seldom seen except in research collections. Although there is a considerable amount of anatomical variability within the family, most of the slickheads have a lateral line and lack both air bladder and adipose fin. The anal fin and the single dorsal are usually opposite each other, and both are set far back on the body. A few of the species have photophores. Probably the strangest member of the family is *Dolichopteryx,* which has telescopic eyes elongated vertically and long extensions of the pectoral rays reaching nearly the entire length of the body.

HERRINGS—Family Clupeidae

Watching a small school of sardines or herring move through the water together in perfect unison, one is impressed by their beauty of motion and ability to act as a single unit. In the northern hemisphere they mostly school in a counterclockwise direction, whereas their cousins in the southern hemisphere theoretically school clockwise. Most of the clupeids are small fishes, less than 18 inches in length; but there are a few larger ones, such as the American shad, which may reach 30 inches. Economically, the herrings, sardines, and their relatives form one of the world's most important groups of food fishes, not only in their value to humans but also as a seemingly endless food reservoir for a great many carnivorous aquatic vertebrates. Family identification of these fish is no great problem, since most of the approximately 175 species and 46 genera are similar in appearance. Identification of individual species, however, is another matter, since even the specialists are not in agreement about all of them.

All of the clupeids are noted for their oily flesh. The body itself is deeply compressed laterally and covered with deciduous scales, which form a knifelike ridge along the center line of the undersurface of the body. The presence of this sharp ridge determines whether the fish belongs to the clupeids or, if the ridge is absent, to the round herring family (Dussumieriidae). The dorsal fin is placed near the center of the body, the adipose fin is missing, and the tail fin is deeply forked. The large, usually toothless

mouth works like a siphon to suck in small planktonic organisms, which are caught on the gill rakers in the throat. Some clupeids have as many as two hundred slender rakers on each gill arch. Tuna fishermen have found that many clupeids cannot survive in live-bait tanks if too much air is bubbled through the tanks, since the bubbles are caught on the gill rakers, forming a mat that prevents the fish from respiring normally and causing asphyxiation. Some species with comparatively few gill rakers feed on food larger than the microplankton preferred by the sardines and others with many gill rakers. Although the majority of clupeids are primarily marine, many move easily into brackish and fresh water. There are several genera with some members that live in fresh or brackish water, for example, *Microthrissa* and *Pellonula* in West Africa and South Africa, *Stolothrissa* in Lake Tanganyika, and *Pseudochirocentrodon* in the Amazon. Their optimum temperature range is considerable—all the way from the warmest water in the tropics to very cold water in the far north, dependent of course upon the species.

Spawning activity shows a great deal of variation among the clupeids. The Pacific American sardine, *Sardinops caerulea,* spawns offshore during the spring and summer months and has surface-floating eggs; whereas others like the American shad, *Alosa sapidissima,* migrate into rivers, spawning in fresh water. It is of interest to note that the American shad, normally an Atlantic species, has on at least three different occasions been introduced into California's Sacramento River, the last time in 1880. This has resulted in a well-established population which has a spawning pattern very similar to that of the Atlantic members of the species. The Pacific herring, *Clupea pallasi,* moves into shallow-water bays at spawning time, the eggs being deposited on seaweeds and other suitable surfaces. The latter activity is always indicated above the water by the descent of hordes of predators, from sea gulls feeding on the eggs to man catching the fish. The Atlantic

Atlantic Tarpon (*Megalops atlanticus*); marine, brackish, and fresh water; both sides of the Atlantic in tropical and temperate waters (Fritz Goro: *Life*).

Atlantic Herring (*Clupea harengus*); marine, moving occasionally into fresh water; both sides of the North Atlantic (D. P. Sharman).

herring, *Clupea harengus*, is also a demersal spawner, leaving its eggs on the bottom attached to shells and weeds of various types; however, it does not necessarily move into shallow water to spawn, for the eggs have been brought up from as deep as eighty feet. This single species, which reaches a length of about a foot and may live for twenty years, is one of the most important food fishes on both sides of the North Atlantic. Wars and battles have been waged over herring fishing rights over the years. Tremendous fisheries have been developed in a number of places —in the North Sea, around the British Isles, and on the American coasts.

Other important members of the clupeid family include the American menhaden, *Brevoortia tyrannus*, which, although not a food fish, is used extensively to manufacture fish meal. The alewife, *Pomolobus pseudoharengus*, with a maximum length of 11 inches, not only is found in marine waters from Nova Scotia to Florida but also has moved inland into the fresh waters of all the seaboard states. The skipjack herring, *Pomolobus chrysochloris*, with a length of about 21 inches, is a Gulf of Mexico species that is also widely distributed in fresh water from the Mississippi River eastward but does not reach the Atlantic coastal states; it is considered an excellent food fish. The thread herring, *Opisthonema oglinum*, is a Caribbean species that sometimes comes northward along the American Atlantic coast line. It has a characteristically long, threadlike extension of the last fin rays of the dorsal. A comparable species, *Opisthonema libertate*, exists on the American Pacific coast. In the Australian region one of the most important commercial species is the pilchard, *Sardinops neopilchardus*; in South Africa another member of this genus, *S. sagax*, is also commercially valuable.

Experimental studies with the clupeids are sometimes difficult because of the deciduous scales previously mentioned. When one of these fishes is touched with a net, it seems as if a thousand scales fall off;

and if the fish happens to be in an aquarium, it probably will not live much longer. It is not an uncommon experience to bring in as many as a thousand Pacific sardines and after one month have only ten alive in spite of the most careful handling. Yet those that do survive sometimes live for many months.

GIZZARD SHAD—Family Dorosomidae

These fishes derive their name from the peculiar muscular stomach which all of the approximately half-dozen species in the family possess. Externally, they look like clupeid threadfin herring, being very deep-bodied, with a sharp ridge along the abdomen and with the last rays of the dorsal fin extended as a long filament. The Atlantic gizzard shad, *Dorosoma cepedianum*, which reaches a length of 20 inches, has been widely introduced as a forage fish into many areas of the central and eastern United States and now covers most of that area. Throughout the Indo-Pacific there is found a smaller gizzard shad, *Dorosoma nasus*; it is primarily a marine species and does not acclimate so readily to fresh water as does its American relative. Several additional species are found in Australian waters; they range in size from 5 to 15 inches.

ROUND HERRING—Family Dussumieriidae

The round herrings differ from the clupeid herrings in that the abdomen is rounded and the center rows of sharp scales forming a knifelike edge along the abdomen are missing. Fewer than fifteen species divided into four genera are recognized. The majority of species are tropical marine in habitat, but there are some that range northward into temperate waters. Although these fishes sometimes appear locally in large groups, they do not occur in vast schools as do some of the clupeid herrings. Probably the most abundant round herrings are two species of small, slender, silvery fishes belonging to the genus *Spratelloides*. Throughout the tropical Indo-Pacific whenever one hangs a night light over the side of a ship, these fishes move into the lighted area in tremendous swarms. Although they measure no more than 4 inches in maximum length, they are harvested commercially in some areas and made into a tasty fish paste.

Dussumieria hasseltii, widely distributed through the tropical Pacific, is a 6-inch fish that is of minor importance as a food item. The largest round herrings, which reach a length of about 15 inches, belong to the genus *Eutrumeus*; included in this group are the common round herring of the Atlantic coast, *E. teres*; *E. acuminatus* of the American Pacific coast; and *E. micropus* of South Africa and the tropical Indo-Pacific.

WOLF HERRING or DORAB
—Family Chirocentridae

The fact that the wolf herring is one of the most voracious carnivores in the sea is surprising, since most of the other herring-like fishes feed on small food, many of them on microplankton. Anatomically, the wolf herring, *Chirocentrus dorab,* has one major feature as an adult that sets it apart from all other herrings. This is the presence of a spiral valve in the intestine, a development found elsewhere only in the sharks and rays and a few of the primitive bony fishes. The wolf herring also has other non-herring characteristics such as large canine teeth, few gill rakers, and a total absence of the numerous appendages or caeca normally attached to the pyloric part of the digestive tract of herrings. Externally, *Chirocentrus* looks much like an overgrown herring, with the characteristic knifelike edge along the undersurface of the abdomen. However, its maximum recorded length of 12 feet is about five times that of the largest of the other herring-like fishes. The dorab ranges widely from the central Pacific to Africa.

ANCHOVIES—*Family Engraulidae*

The mouth of the anchovy is set far back on the underside of the head, and the lower jaw is small and inconspicuous, so that the fish appears to be chinless. This characteristic of the head and chin instantly enables one to recognize any of the almost one hundred species in the family. Except for the chin, the anchovy looks much like a small round herring. The single dorsal fin is almost at the center of the body; the ventral fins are abdominal in position, often opposite the dorsal; and the tail fin is deeply notched. The adipose fin and lateral line are absent. The anchovies are small fishes that are always found in schools, never singly. The majority of them are less than 5 inches in length, very few growing as large as 9 inches. Spawning usually takes place during the spring or summer. The eggs float and are easy to identify since they are oval in shape, whereas most other fish eggs are spherical. After a few days, hatching occurs, and the young anchovy begins its life, which at a maximum is probably no more than seven years. Anchovies are economically valuable as food for human consumption as well as for live and frozen bait for fishermen. Their greatest abundance is in tropical marine waters; brackish water does not bother them, and a few live even in fresh water.

The strangest member of the family is the whiskered anchovy, *Thrissocles setifer,* of the Indo-Australian region. The maxillary bone of this fish is extended for almost three times the length of the head, reaching nearly as far back as the anal fin. Two other members of this genus have extended, but shorter, maxillaries. What possible value this peculiar development can have for the fish is as yet undetermined.

Other aberrant members of the anchovy family are found in the strange genus *Coilia* of the Indo-Australian region; these fishes retain the chinless appearance of the anchovy, but add to it a long, tapering, ratlike tail with a minute caudal fin at the tip. The anal fin extends along much of the underside, often having more than one hundred rays.

The northern anchovy, *Engraulis mordax,* a large species (9 inches) ranging from British Columbia to the tip of Lower California, is one of the most important American Pacific engraulids. The anchoveta, *Cetengraulis mysticetus,* a wide-ranging species found from southern California to Peru, is a smaller species and is in much demand as live bait by the tuna fishermen. Most of the fishing by the tuna clippers for this live bait is carried on in Mexican and Central American waters.

The European anchovy, *Engraulis encrasicholus,* is the basis for valuable fisheries from the Mediterranean Sea to Norway. Much of the catch is processed into anchovy sauce and paste.

Anchoviella commersonii, found abundantly in many areas from the Philippines to South Africa, is a food fish of moderate value.

MILKFISH—*Family Chanidae*

Despite its many fine bones, the milkfish, *Chanos chanos,* is usually a valuable food fish throughout its range from the tropical American coast to Africa. It is a large, silvery fish reaching a length of 5 feet. Identification can usually be made through the following combination of factors: (1) the dorsal fin opposite the ventrals; (2) the toothless mouth; and (3) the large, deeply forked tail. In profile the milkfish bears a marked resemblance to the tenpounder (family Elopidae), but the latter has teeth.

The milkfish spawns in shallow, brackish water, usually during the months of March through May, a single fish producing as many as 9,000,000 eggs. In many areas, such as the Philippines, the fry, measuring about ½ inch, are collected and transported in special earthenware pots to brackish or fresh-water ponds. Milkfish fry are not cannibalistic, but other larval fishes that are normally found in the same areas, such as the tenpounder, goby, sea bass, and tarpon, are noted for this trait; therefore these others must be separated from the milkfish before stocking the ponds. The fry grow rapidly, feeding on the blue-green and green algae which are cultivated as fish food in the same ponds. Harvesting of the pond-raised milkfish is usually done during the rainy season, when other marine fishes are scarce in the mar-

Atlantic Salmon (*Salmo salar*) migrating upstream for spawning; marine and fresh water; North Atlantic south to Maine and Spain (Ronald Thompson: Annan Photo Features).

kets, and thus they are sold at a maximum price. During the dry season the milkfish ponds are often used to evaporate salt water for the production of solar salt.

Except during the spawning season, the milkfish is typically an open-water species, but it is not uncommon for them to venture into shallow lagoons and brackish and fresh-water areas where the depth of water is not even sufficient to cover the upper portions of the body. Under such conditions they can easily be spotted by the elongate dorsal fin projecting above the water. In these shallow-water areas they are able to survive in water so hot (about 90 degrees F.) that a human being cannot comfortably stand in it.

TROUT and SALMON—Family Salmonidae

Among fresh-water sportsmen, trout and salmon are probably the best known and most popular of all the fishes. The family Salmonidae, to which these fishes belong, is a small one made up of five genera and perhaps less than two dozen species. Salmonids all have an identifying small, fleshy adipose fin on the dorsal surface of the body opposite the anal fin. Although originally limited to the northern hemisphere, they have been introduced successfully into many parts of the southern hemisphere.

Trout are usually restricted to fresh water, but there are a few types, such as the steelhead, that regularly migrate to the ocean between spawnings, and many of the species do so under favorable conditions. Many popular articles and books on the salmon have made its life history well known; typically, it spends most of its adult life in the ocean, returning only to fresh water to spawn and die. However, there are exceptions to this rule. The landlocked fresh-water salmon, such as the kokanee, *Oncorhynchus nerka kennerlyi*, a type of Pacific sockeye, never make the trip to the ocean. The Atlantic salmon, *Salmo salar*, which is actually an ocean-run trout, also has landlocked populations such as the sebago in some of the eastern North American lakes, as well as other populations in some of the European lakes. Salmon and trout are normally found in cold and temperate waters, thriving at temperatures below the 50-to-65-degree range. Some of the Mexican trout such as *Salmo nelsoni,* however, live easily in waters as warm as 80 degrees, although temperatures of this level are usually lethal to most salmonids.

Details of spawning vary with the species, but usually the spawners move upstream in the spring or occasionally in the autumn. Sometimes they have to fight their way against tremendous obstacles, even jumping falls (Plate 4), until they find suitable gravel bottoms that can be excavated by the female. During this upsteam migration, some males, particularly those of the Pacific salmon and to a lesser extent the trout, develop temendous hooked jaws. This gives them a grotesque appearance that is further accentuated in some species by the fact that they do not feed during this migration and develop an emaciated look. Coming to the exceptions again, we find that although most trout and salmon are stream spawners, there are at least two species, the brook trout, *Salvelinus fontinalis,* and the lake trout, *Salvelinus* (formerly *Cristivomer*) *namaycush,* that use the gravel beds of their home lakes for spawning; but this statement of course is not true of those brook trout that live in streams. Having dug a depression in the gravel, the female spews out eggs into the depression, and at almost the same moment the male covers the eggs with spermatozoa, known as milt. Finally the female pushes gravel over the eggs so that they are protected from egg-eating predators as well as from being washed downstream. Several of these spawning pockets may be filled with eggs before a pair have completed their reproductive functions. If the spawning pair happen to be Pacific salmon, they soon die; but if they are trout, they may spawn for a number of years. The temperature of the water determines how soon the eggs hatch, the time required ranging from as many as eighty days in 40-degree water to as few as nineteen days in water of 60 degrees. Upon hatching, the larval trout or salmon has a large bulbous abdomen containing the egg sac, which provides the fry with its necessary food for the next few weeks of life (Plate 3). The larval salmonid usually stays in the gravel until the egg sac is absorbed, then works its way upward to become free-swimming. Its growth rate depends upon the food available and the temperature of the water. In one year it may grow only 3 inches or as much as 12 inches. Ocean-run trout often move downstream to salt water at the end of the first year; this is also true of some salmon, but other salmon fry may remain in the stream for as long as four years before migrating.

Trout and salmon eggs in the "eyed" stage can be shipped without difficulty. Hence these fishes have been widely distributed all over the world, and therefore the present distribution of any given species may bear little relationship to its original range. For example, the European brown trout, *Salmo trutta,* was brought into North America many years ago by fish culturists, and since then has been widely planted over the continent in almost every area having suitable waters. The adult brown trout can be identified quite easily by the reddish spots on the sides of the body, each surrounded by a light-colored area. *Salmo carpio* (Plate 3) is a species related to the brown trout. It is found only in Lake Garda, Italy.

Because of the large pair of horizontal streaks or cut marks under the throat, the cutthroat trout, *Salmo clarki,* is one of the most spectacular of the salmonids. Several subspecies of this spotted trout, including a sea-run form, have been described. Its normal range is western North America.

The charr or brook trout, *Salvelinus fontinalis* of eastern North America and, through introduction, Europe has a mottled pattern, usually with red spots on the sides. Identification can usually be made by the distinct white border along the anterior margins of the ventral and anal fins. Sea-run forms of the brook trout are present in some of the northern areas, for example along the Canadian coasts. In western North America the brook trout is replaced by another species of the same genus, the Dolly Varden trout, *Salvelinus malma,* which ranges from Alaska to the McCloud River in California.

The lake or mackinaw trout, *Salvelinus namaycush,* lives in deeper water than any of the other fresh-water salmonids, often as deep as four hundred feet. Valuable commercial fisheries for this species have in the past operated in the Great Lakes of North America, but the depredations of the parasitic sea lamprey have cut the populations of this fish almost to nothing. (For other aspects of this important biological control problem, see the earlier section on lampreys.) Introduction of the lake trout into California's Lake Tahoe in 1895 has resulted in a well-established permanent population with adults ranging up to twenty-eight pounds, but since the lake trout eats anything that gets in its way, it has been

Young Lake Trout (*Salvelinus* [*Cristivomer*] *namaycush*); fresh water; North America southward as far as the Great Lakes region; introduced elsewhere in many deep-water lakes (Treat Davidson).

responsible for the disappearance of the Lahontan subspecies of the cutthroat trout, *Salmo clarki henshawi,* from these same waters.

The rainbow trout, *Salmo gairdneri,* and its several subspecies are highly popular with western American sportsmen. The brilliant reddish band along the side of the body is the principal identification mark. The rainbow has an important ocean-run form popularly known as the steelhead and recognized technically under the name *Salmo gairdneri gairdneri.* It is usually less conspicuously banded than the fresh-water rainbow, and its black spots are more evident. The term "steelhead" has been loosely bandied about: at one time it was applied to any type of ocean-run trout, so that one might speak of steelhead rainbow, steelhead cutthroat, steelhead brook trout, and so forth. Recent usage, however, has limited its application to the ocean-run form of the rainbow only.

The golden trout, *Salmo aguabonita,* is the high-mountain trout of western North America; it is seldom found at elevations of less than eight thousand feet. As an adult it retains the parr marks, the vertical bars found on the sides of all juvenile trout. In habitat the European counterpart of the golden trout is the Alpine trout, *Salvelinus alpinus,* of the high mountains of central Europe.

Weights of trout and salmon as well as other sports fishes are often the subjects of much discussion, and in some cases it is evident that the records need additional authentication. Both the lake trout and the Atlantic salmon (Scotland) have been reported from commercial catches at weights of around 100 pounds; however, the normal maximum as indicated by rod and reel records is 63 pounds for the former and 79 pounds for the latter. Other maximum weights include the Lahontan cutthroat at 41 pounds; brown trout, 39½ pounds; rainbow, 37 pounds; Dolly Varden, 32 pounds; brook, 14½ pounds; and golden, 11 pounds.

The six species of Pacific salmon are grouped together in the genus *Oncorhynchus;* these are larger fishes than the trout, with some, such as the king or quinnat salmon, *Oncorhynchus tshawytscha,* reaching a weight of as much as 100 pounds. The presence of more rays in the anal fins of the Pacific salmon also serves to distinguish them from the trout. *Oncorhynchus* ranges from northern California to Alaska, Siberia, and Japan. One species, the king salmon, has been successfully introduced into New Zealand waters, where important fisheries have now developed. All of the Pacific salmon are anadromous; that is, they live in the ocean as adults but return to the stream in which they were hatched to spawn, after which they die. The great mystery has been how these fishes that travel many hundreds of miles in the ocean can unerringly return to their parent stream. Actually, there is a variable amount of error. For example, 14.9 per cent of the silver salmon, *Oncorhynchus kisutch,* fingerlings hatched and tagged in Waddell Creek on the northern California coast strayed upon their return as adults to an adjacent creek four and one-half miles away. Only 1.9 per cent of the returning steelhead trout strayed to the adjacent creek.

In 1951 two American ichthyologists, A. D. Hasler and W. Wisby, advanced the olfaction theory of homing perception, explaining how adult salmonids were able to locate their parent stream. Laboratory tests indicated that the salmon undoubtedly reacted by smell to organic matter and other substances in the water. In a field test, the investigators captured sexually mature coho or silver salmon from two branches of the Issquah River in Washington. Before returning these fish downstream, they plugged the nasal sacs of one-half of the group with cotton, leaving the other fishes untouched. Then they released all of the salmon, allowing them again to migrate upstream. Those fish without the nasal plugs were able to discriminate between the two streams so that they returned to the branch from which they had been taken. However, the ones with the nasal plugs were not able to make this discrimination, and their return upstream followed a random pattern.

No discussion of the salmonid fishes would be complete without some mention of the fabulous ayu of Japan. This interesting fish, known technically as *Plecoglossus altivelis,* reaches a length of about a foot. It is a marine species but migrates into fresh water to spawn. Because of the fact that it has a number of anatomical peculiarities, including plate-like teeth, it has been variously classified, first as a salmon, then as an osmerid smelt, and finally in a family by itself, the Plecoglossidae. The remarkable thing about this fish is the special method of catching it by using captive sea birds—cormorants, to be exact. A ring is slipped over the cormorant's head and down to the base of the neck. The bird is then turned loose to catch the ayu as they migrate upstream. This it does with great rapidity, but the ring prevents the fish from being swallowed. Upon their return to the owner, the cormorants are upended and the ayu drop out of the throat. The bird is then rewarded with some less valuable fish.

WHITEFISHES—Family Coregonidae

The whitefishes share many of the characteristics of the salmon and trout; in fact, at one time they were all placed in the same family. Like the salmonids, the whitefishes are a family of the northern hemisphere, ranging from arctic waters southward. From the standpoint of food value to man, they are undoubtedly one of the most important fresh-water groups. Again like the trout and salmon, these fishes have a small adipose fin on the top of the back between the dorsal and the tail fin, but the whitefishes and the grayling have much larger scales and smaller mouths than either the trout or the salmon. The whitefishes are all notoriously uniform in color: a silvery white that is slightly darker on the back. Coregonids usually spawn in the fall, always in fresh water, where the majority live. Only a few species such as the European *Coregonus oxyrhynchus* live in salt water, and these return to fresh water to spawn. In the American Great Lakes there are extensive populations of several species of whitefishes for which large commercial fisheries have been developed. In recent years, however, the effects of the parasitic sea lamprey, and perhaps of overfishing, have reduced the numbers of these fishes to the point where many of the fisheries are no longer profitable.

The largest species in the family is the lake whitefish, *Coregonus clupeaformis,* which usually reaches a weight of about four pounds, although there is a record of one that weighed twenty-six pounds. Another well-known species is the shallow-water cisco, *Coregonus artedii,* sometimes called "lake herring." The kiyi, *Coregonus kiyi,* found at depths ranging between 180 and 600 feet, is a representative of the deep-water whitefishes or chubs.

GRAYLING—Family Thymallidae

The long and beautiful flaglike dorsal fin of the grayling is always a welcome sight to the angler, who prizes this cold-water northern species both as a food and as a sport fish. Like the trout and salmon, the grayling has a small adipose fin located on the back halfway between the dorsal and the tail fin. In contrast to the salmonids, the grayling has a very small mouth, and fewer and larger scales along the sides of the body. It is entirely restricted to fresh water. Grayling spawn in the spring of the year, selecting shallow-water areas where the bottom is either sand or gravel. The grayling egg is about half the size of those of trout, and under artificial hatching methods requires much agitation, usually by a stream of water.

Grayling occur in the northernmost parts of both North America and Eurasia. Several species have been described, *Thymallus thymallus* being the common European species, and *T. arcticus* the American form. The latter is found as far south as the southern limits of Canada and in a few places in the United States, chiefly in Montana. It previously occurred in Michigan, but that population is now extinct. The largest grayling ever caught weighed around four pounds, but the largest sizes usually encountered in the wild are in the one-to-two-pound range, with lengths of 12 to 16 inches.

TRUE SMELTS—Family Osmeridae

The osmerid smelts are small inshore fishes of temperate or cold water in the northern hemisphere;

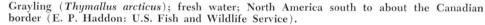

Grayling (*Thymallus arcticus*); fresh water; North America south to about the Canadian border (E. P. Haddon: U.S. Fish and Wildlife Service).

none of them exceeds 14 inches in length. An important feature in the identification of the true or osmerid smelts is the presence of a small adipose fin on the dorsal surface of the body, usually opposite the anal fin. This is lacking on the members of the atherinid smelt or silverside family, which is often confused with the osmerid group. About thirteen species of osmerid smelts are known, most of them being found in the Pacific. They do not occur in the southern hemisphere or in the Indian Ocean. In some regions they are noted for their tremendous abundance; for example, it is not unusual in San Francisco Bay for Chinese shrimp nets to catch more than sixty thousand 3-inch Sacramento smelt, *Spirinchus thaleichthys,* during a single three-hour fishing period. Because of their phenomenal abundance, osmerids often serve as the basis or smallest member of many predator food chains in which each fish is eaten by a larger one. Prosperous fisheries for adult osmerids exist in many places in the northern hemisphere. Often the fishing season is correlated with the time of the spawning run into fresh water; on the giant Columbia River many tons of osmerids are caught during the spring months.

One of the largest members of the family is the eulachon, *Thaleichthys pacificus,* a 12-inch species of the American Pacific Northwest. It is sometimes called "candlefish" because of its oily flesh. The early Indians actually used the dried fish attached to a stick as a torch.

In California the fresh-water smelt, *Hypomesus olidus,* spends nearly all of its life in the fresh waters of the Sacramento River delta, but this same species in Japan is a marine form, migrating into fresh water only to spawn.

Other species also have fresh-water populations. The common American Atlantic smelt, *Osmerus mordax,* normally ranges from the Gulf of St. Lawrence to Virginia. In 1912 fishes of this species were introduced into the Great Lakes region, where they have multiplied so greatly that today there is a commercial fishery maintained for them.

The surf smelt, *Hypomesus pretiosus,* found from Alaska to southern California, lives most of its life in the surf and is an important bait species for both commercial and sport fishermen.

The European smelt, *Osmerus eperlanus,* is a valuable commercial species throughout its range from the Seine to the Baltic; freshly caught fish have been described as having the odor of cucumbers.

GALAXIIDS—Family Galaxiidae

From the standpoint of distribution, the fresh-water galaxiids are a strange group. They are found only in the southern hemisphere: in New Zealand,

Australia, South Africa, and the tip of South America. One theory explaining this strange distribution is that all the countries in which the galaxiids occur were once joined to form a large southern continent. Although many hypotheses have been offered, as yet no entirely suitable explanation for their distribution has been found. Of interest is the fact that these fishes inhabit many places in the southern hemisphere that are comparable to the habitats of the trout in the northern hemisphere.

All of the galaxiids are elongate, scaleless fishes, with the single dorsal and single anal fin set far back on the body just in front of the tail fin. The adipose fin is lacking, and one genus, *Neochanna,* lacks the ventral fins. The majority of the three dozen or so species in the family are quite small, with maximum lengths ranging between 4 and 6 inches.

The largest galaxiid known, a New Zealand species, *Galaxias alepidotus,* was discovered in 1775. Like the other members of the family, its appearance is in some respects similar to that of the northern pikes, genus *Esox*—in fact, its discoverer described it as a pike. This giant galaxiid has an average length of about 12 inches, the record being 23 inches; but since it is a very slender species, its weight at this length is still less than three pounds. Its normal habitat is spring-fed creeks near the sea. Identification can be made by the small yellow hieroglyphic-like markings on the body.

The New Zealand brown mudfish, *Neochanna apoda,* is fully grown at about 6 inches. Its chief claim to fame other than its lack of ventral fins is its ability to exist for several weeks in dried mud, much as the South American and African lungfishes do (the Australian lungfish has lost this ability). The Tasmanian eel mudtrout, *Saxilaga anguilliformis,* has the same habitat, but whether it can survive in dried mud is not known.

The whitebait, *Galaxias attenuatus,* found in both Australia and New Zealand, is a small species that is mature at about 4 inches; it is the only member of the family found in more than one region. This is no doubt explained by the fact that it spawns in fresh and brackish water but spends a good part of its juvenile and adult life in salt water.

Some of the Australian species of the galaxiids are brightly banded, the 1½-inch black striped minnow, *Brachygalaxias pusillus,* from west Australia being a good example of this. The common South African species is the mountain galaxiid, *Galaxias zebratus,* which measures about 3½ inches.

[continued on page

33. Three color phases of the Common Atla[...] American Seahorse (*Hippocampus hudsoni[...]* marine; Nova Scotia to Argentina (photograp[...] at Seaquarium by Stan Wayman: Rapho Gu[...] mette)

34. Yellow Seahorse (*Hippocampus kuda*); marine; tropical Indo-Pacific (Hans-Joachim Schramm)

35. Trumpetfish (*Aulostomus maculatus*); marine; both sides of the tropical Atlantic (Edmond L. Fisher)

36. Bay Pipefish (*Syngnathus griseolineatus*); marine, in eel grass; California to Alaska (John Tashjian at Steinhart Aquarium)

37. Striped Squirrelfish (*Holocentrus xantherythrus*); marine Hawaiian Islands (John Tashjian at Steinhart Aquarium)

38. Longspine Squirrelfish (*Holocentrus rufus*); **marine**; Bermuda and North Carolina to Colombia (Edmond L. Fisher)

9. Wistful Squirrelfish (*Holotrachys lima*); marine; tropical Indo-Pacific (John Tashjian at Steinhart Aquarium)

40. Deepwater Squirrelfish (*Ostichthys japonicus*); marine; tropical Pacific (Douglas Faulkner at Waikiki Aquarium)

41. Golden-striped Groupers (*Grammistes sexlineatus*); marine; tropical Indo-Pacific (Gene Wolfsheimer)

42. Blue-spotted Argus (*Cephalopholis argus*); marine; tropical Indo-Pacific (John Tashjian at Steinhart Aquarium)

43. Spotted Grouper (*Epinephalus elongatus*); marine; tropical Pacific excluding Hawaiian Islands (John Tashjian at Steinhart Aquarium)

44. Pigmy Sunfish (*Enneacanthus gloriosus*); fresh water; lowland areas of eastern and southern United States (Gene Wolfsheimer)

45. Mottled Grouper (*Epinephelus fuscoguttatus*); marine; central tropical Indo-Pacific (Mike Wilson: Pix)

46. Catalufa (*Priacanthus arenatus*); marine; both sides of temperate and tropical Atlantic; from Massachusetts to Argentina (Edmond L. Fisher)

47. Barred Cardinal Fish (*Apogon binotatus*); marine; Bermuda and Florida Keys to Venezuela (Fritz Goro: *Life* Magazine)

48. Spotfin Butterfly Fish (*Chaetodon ocellatus*); marine; Massachusetts to Brazil including Gulf of Mexico (Ernest Libby at Marine Studios)

49. Young Striped Butterfly Fish (*Chaetodon melanotus* var.); marine; tropical Indo-Pacific (Gene Wolfsheimer)

50. and **51. Longnose Butterfly Fish** (*Chelmon rostratus*); marine; tropical Indo-Pacific from northern Australia to Mauritius (Hans and Klaus Paysan)

52. Queen Angelfish
(*Holacanthus ciliaris*); marine; northeastern and southwestern Gulf of Mexico to Bahia, Brazil (Wilhelm Hoppe)

53. Potter's Angelfish (*Centropyge potteri*); marine; Hawaiian Islands (Douglas Faulkner at Waikiki Aquarium)

54. Queen Angelfish, full view (photographed at Seaquarium by Stan Wayman: Rapho Guillumette)

55. Blue Angelfish (*Pomacanthus semicirculatus*); marine; tropical Indo-Pacific (Gene Wolfsheimer)

56. Young Imperial Angelfish (*Pomacanthus imperator*); marine; tropical Indo-Pacific (Gene Wolfsheimer)

57. French Angelfish (*Pomacanthus arcuatus*); marine; both sides of tropical Atlantic, Florida Keys to Rio de Janeiro (Conrad Limbaugh)

58. Regal Angelfish (*Pygoplites diacanthus*); marine; central tropical Indo-Pacific (Hans and Klaus Paysan)

59. Clown Butterfly Fish (*Chaetodon ornatissimus*); marine; tropical Pacific (Douglas Faulkner at Waikiki Aquarium)

60. Saddleback Butterfly Fish (*Chaetodon ephippium*); marine; tropical Pacific (Douglas Faulkner at Waikiki Aquarium)

[continued from page 80]

BRISTLEMOUTHS—Family Gonostomatidae

The bristlemouths are the first of nine families of deep-sea isospondylous fishes, all of which are grouped in the suborder Stomiatoidea.

The most abundant fishes in the entire world belong to this family; and yet as a rule one never sees these very small fishes unless he studies the stomach contents of larger carnivorous forms that feed in the depths or examines the catch from deep-haul plankton nets. These fishes look like miniature herring with a series of photophores or light organs along the sides of the body. Of interest is the fact that one genus and species, *Photichthys argenteus,* known from the Atlantic and New Zealand, has many anatomical features similar to those of the tenpounder, *Elops,* described earlier. Some species have a small adipose fin just forward of the tail fin. A 3-inch fish is considered a giant in this family. There are probably about thirty-two species in all.

Despite the abundance of these fishes and their importance in food cycles, very few studies of them, other than classification, have been conducted. However, recent investigation (1958) by United States Fish and Wildlife Service biologists Ahlstrom and Counts on the development and distribution of *Vinciguerria lucetia* of the eastern Pacific has brought to light some interesting data. The floating spherical egg, measuring about $\frac{1}{34}$ of an inch in diameter, hatches into a larva which is confusingly like that of the sardine. Only at metamorphosis does the first evidence of photophores appear as a paired series of white spots that later become dark with pigment. The adult $2\frac{1}{2}$-inch fish has from seventy-eight to eighty-three photophores on each side, the number varying with latitude.

One other genus of bristlemouths, *Cyclothone,* is of importance from the standpoint of abundance; its half-dozen or so species are world-wide in distribution and often are the most abundant fishes that come up in the deep-plankton net. It is not difficult to identify them since they are so fragile that when they are brought up in a net, they always look as though they had been beaten and tossed about.

HATCHET FISHES—Family Sternoptychidae

The hatchet fishes are startling in appearance and well named, for they look as though they could be picked up by the slender tail and used to chop a miniature block of wood. All of the approximately fifteen species are small—less than $3\frac{1}{2}$ inches in length—and silvery. They have the usual photophores along the lateral margins of the underside of the body, and one genus, *Argyropelecus,* has telescopic eyes aimed upward. These fishes are world-wide in distribution in tropical and temperate waters and are found only in the depths. Although not nearly so abundant as the bristlemouths, in some areas they provide important food for deep-swimming tuna.

DEEP-SEA CHIN-WHISKER FISHES

Members of several families of world-wide deep-sea fishes have a single whisker-like barbel attached to the underside of the chin. In some species the barbel may have treelike branches and even may contain a luminescent photophore similar to the light organs always present along the lower sides of the body. This barbel varies considerably in length from some that are very short, hardly longer than the head, to others that are as much as nine times the length of the fish (*Ultimostomias mirabilis*). All of these fishes have dagger-like teeth, some with small hooks on the ends. Three families in this chin-whisker group are noted for their elongated snake-like bodies: the scaleless dragonfishes, the scaly dragonfishes, and the black dragonfishes. The family of the scaleless dragonfishes, Melanostomiatidae, includes about 115 species, some of which, such as those of the genus *Bathophilus,* have the ventral fins moved upward on the sides of the body to about the midline, giving them a most peculiar appearance. The family of the scaly dragonfishes, Stomiatidae, is a smaller one, containing about eight species most of which are widely distributed; however, one species, *Stomioides nicholsi,* is known only from the Gulf of Maine. As the name indicates, their chief identifying feature is their scales. The third family of chin-barbel snakelike fishes, the Idiacanthidae, contains only five species, known as the black dragonfishes. In some respects they resemble the scaleless dragonfishes, but are set apart from them because of the remarkable larval stage through which all black dragonfishes pass. The larval *Idiacanthus* has the eyes set entirely off the head by slender stalks of unbelievable length. A larva measuring only $\frac{5}{8}$ inch in length would have eye stalks extending from the

Hatchetfish (*Argyropelecus* sp.); marine, deep water; Bay of Biscay (J. B. Gilpin Brown).

head for a distance equivalent to one-third of its total length. By the time the fish is full grown at 1½ inches, the eye stalks are absorbed and the eyes are pulled in against the head in normal position.

Two families of deep-sea fishes with bodies of moderate length are included in the chin-barbel group. The snaggle-toothed fishes, family Astronesthidae, include about thirty-five species, most of which have a small adipose fin between the dorsal and the tail fins. Like many other deep-sea species, these are fishes with large mouths and large stomachs. Not only do they have powerful dentition but they are also armed in the throat with sharp teeth attached to the gill arches. The second family with chin barbels and bodies of moderate length is the Malacosteidae, called the loose-jawed fishes. These remarkable fishes all possess a hyoid gill slit. Of the fourteen species in the family, five in the two genera *Malacosteus* and *Photostomias* lack the chin barbel; but *Ultimostomias mirabilis,* the fish with the longest chin barbel of them all—nine times the length of the body—is also a member of this small family.

VIPER FISHES—Family Chauliodontidae

The tremendous fanglike teeth of the viper fishes give them a weird appearance. Because of the striking picture they present, they are often used in illustrations to represent the tremendous fauna of deep-sea fishes. Actually, there are only three species of vipers, but they occur in many of the deep-ocean areas of the world, from tropical to very cold water. In size they are not very large—only about 10 inches long at the most—but they do have some distinctive characteristics besides the needle-sharp teeth. These include both a dorsal and a ventral adipose fin, an extremely long first ray of the dorsal fin, and photophores or light organs along the sides, sometimes extending almost to the tail. The first neck vertebra is exceptionally long—it is equivalent to the

combined length of the succeeding five vertebrae. This extra-long vertebra undoubtedly acts as a shock absorber; when the fish throws its mouth wide open, the upper fangs are directed straight forward, and the impact as they spear the victim is taken by this elongated first cervical vertebra. When the mouth is closed, the overlapping upper and lower fangs prevent the victim's escape.

An interesting study made by Rudolph Haffner of Wesleyan University shows some surprising facts about the three species and six subspecies of *Chauliodus.* They apparently make extensive vertical migrations but never come to the surface, living by day between 1500 and 7500 feet and by night moving upward above 1500 feet. Each population is limited in its distribution by the salinity and temperature characteristics of the water mass in which it resides.

BONY TONGUES—Family Osteoglossidae

The four genera and five species in this family are restricted to the fresh waters of Africa, South America, and the Malay-Australian region. All of these fishes are similar in appearance, with prominent scales, large eyes, and bony plates covering the head. The dorsal and anal fins are placed so far back on the body that they appear continuous with the tail fin. Not only do the bony tongues have interesting habits, but they also have a very peculiar distribution. The giant arapaima of the Amazon resembles and is most closely related to the shorter-bodied African *Clupisudis* (formerly *Heterotis*), whereas the other South American species, the arawana, *Osteoglossum,* resembles and is most closely related to the two species of Malay-Australian *Scleropages;* both of these latter two genera have conspicuous chin barbels. The arapaima and *Clupisudis* are nest builders, but breeding of the arawana and *Scleropages* is unknown. Except for the presence

Pacific Viperfish (*Chauliodus macouni*); marine, deep water; Alaska to southern California (Toshio Asaeda, Crocker-Stanford Expedition, 1938).

Arapaima (*Arapaima gigas*); fresh water; Amazon basin (New York Zoological Society).

of *Scleropages* in Borneo, Sumatra, and Malaya, the distribution of these fishes parallels that of the lung-fishes.

The largest species in the family is the fabulous *Arapaima gigas,* called paiche in Peru, pirarucú in Brazil, and arapaima in British Guiana. It has long been considered the largest strictly fresh-water fish in the world; however, the South American catfish *Brachyplatystoma filamentosum* may be as large or even larger. Arapaima are reported to reach a length of 15 feet, but conservative writers place the average at 7 to 8 feet, with a weight of about two hundred pounds. In spite of its being a large, heavy-bodied fish, it moves with smooth and sinuous grace, which explains why aquarists prize it so highly. It has large, olive-green scales, and the posterior part of the body upon which the three unpaired fins are grouped is of a tint that is increasingly reddish toward the tail until at the caudal peduncle it becomes crimson. The air bladder occupies a large area above the abdominal cavity and, as in all isospondylous fishes, is connected by an open duct to the throat. Since the lining of the air bladder is richly supplied with blood vessels, it effectively serves the fish as a lung.

With the approach of breeding season, usually during April or May, arapaima move into clear shallow areas with sandy bottoms. Here the nests are constructed by hollowing them out with the fins. Each nest measures about twenty inches in diameter and about six inches in depth. The same nest may be used in successive seasons.

As indicated by records from the Shedd Aquarium in Chicago, growth of captive arapaima is very rapid. In the young stages the rate of growth varies from one to almost three inches a month. One specimen grew from 8 to 64 inches in five years.

Importations of the arapaima have been made to nearly all the major public aquaria in the United States, where, with one exception, it has been reported to be a very difficult fish to raise. Its chief difficulty seems to be a lamentable tendency to try to swim through the walls of the tank. This has been solved in several cases by introducing another fish, which the arapaima will follow around. In each case, the introduced fish was its only South American relative, and also its favorite bait, the arawana.

With the exception of British Guiana, where for some reason it is not esteemed as food, the arapaima is fished extensively throughout its South American range; it is generally cut into long strips and dried in the sun. In one year, 1917, some three million pounds of dried pirarucú were shipped from Manaos to Belem.

The African counterpart of the arapaima, *Clupisudis niloticus,* is a much smaller fish, seldom growing longer than 3 feet, yet as a nest digger it seems to have greater ability than its cousin. The nests are about four feet in diameter and have walls several inches thick made of the vegetation removed from the center.

The two fleshy barbels at the tip of the lower jaw instantly identify the South American arawana, *Osteoglossum bicirrhosum.* It occurs over the same range as the arapaima and has a maximum length of about 2 feet. The mouth, particularly large and prominent, with the jaws angling upward at about 45 degrees, somewhat resembles the ramp on a landing barge. The arawana spends most of its time leisurely cruising just below the surface of the water.

[99

Arawana (*Osteoglossum bicirrhosum*); fresh water; Amazon basin (Georg Mandahl-Barth, Danmarks Akvarium).

It is seldom still, and in captivity generally swims in a slow, deliberate, circular pattern. When alarmed, however, it can take off with an amazing burst of speed. On one occasion, while an aquarium tank was being cleaned, an arawana went straight up into the air for at least ten feet and, fortunately, came down vertically. One fish that was confined for a time in a large but narrow tank would, when making its turn, promptly bite its own tail. When removed to a larger tank this behavior ceased.

The breeding habits of the arawana are unknown, but it is suspected of being a mouth breeder of some type, incubating the eggs in the mouth or throat. Supporting evidence for this belief is the presence of a large pouchlike space between the bones of the lower jaw. Its Asiatic relatives, the *Scleropages,* are also thought to be mouth breeders. Two species of this latter genus are recognized: *Scleropages formosus* from Borneo, Sumatra, and the Malay region, and *S. leichhardtii* from New Guinea and Australia.

BUTTERFLY FISH—Family Pantodontidae

In the fresh waters of western Africa there is found one of the strangest of the so-called flying fishes, *Pantodon buchholzi.* "Butterfly fish" is the name most often applied to this fascinating species, which spends most of its time swimming just under the surface and is capable of leaping out of the water for a distance of six or more feet. The large pectoral fins probably enable *Pantodon* to do a small amount of gliding during this jump, but it is not true flight such as that shown by the South American hatchet fishes, which actually vibrate their pectoral fins while in the air. The most amazing characteristic of *Pantodon* is found in the ventral fins, the rays of which extend downward as long, slender fingers without interconnecting membranes. Although the butterfly

fish is classified in the same suborder as the giant arapaima of South America, it is a veritable pygmy by comparison, for it never grows much longer than 5 inches. Like the adult, the eggs and fry float at the surface of the water. Few spawnings have been observed in captivity, so that much still remains to be learned of this exotic fresh-water butterfly fish. The entire family Pantodontidae is made up of the single species described above.

MOONEYE—Family Hiodontidae

The mooneye family is a small one, containing only three species of fresh-water herring-like fishes limited in distribution to the northern central and eastern parts of North America. The mooneye or toothed herring, *Hiodon tergisus,* is characterized by a very large eye and a silvery color; it reaches a length of 17 inches and a weight of two and one-half pounds, although the majority are shorter than 12 inches. It is usually found in clear water and is a good game fish but not a desirable food item.

The goldeneye, *Hiodon alosoides,* is similar to the mooneye in general appearance but in color is dark blue above and silvery on the sides, with a slight touch of golden color on the eye. It may be distinguished from the mooneye by the sharp ridge along the underside of the belly in front of the ventral fins. Its maximum size is around 20 inches, with a weight of slightly more than two pounds. Unlike the mooneye, the goldeneye will tolerate muddy and turbid water. The Hiodontidae and the next family, the Notopteridae, together make up the Notopteroidea, one of the seven suborders of the isospondylous fishes.

FEATHERBACKS—Family Notopteridae

Featherbacks are easily identified by the very long anal fin, which begins just behind the head and extends along the undersurface of the body to the tip of the tail. The tail fin, as such, is not evident. In the center of the back is a small, slender dorsal fin, from which the fish derives the name "featherback." In swimming, the dorsal fin acts as a rudder and the rippling anal fin—a beautiful sight—provides the main propulsion. The four species of featherbacks live in fresh water; and although they have small bones, they are usually considered choice food fishes. The largest species is the banded *Notopterus chitala,* which in India reaches a length of 3 feet but in most of the rest of the Indo-Australian region seldom grows as long as 2½ feet. The biology of this species has been studied in detail in Thailand; the male was found to guard the eggs with great care during the incubation period of five or six days. Because of the market value of the featherback, the Thailand Fisheries Department has encouraged the spawning of these fishes by placing posts in the ponds where they are abundant in order to provide artificial spawning sites. On such posts each female will deposit eggs ranging in number from five thousand to ten thousand during a single season.

Notopterus notopterus occurs in the same areas as *N. chitala;* and although it is a smaller species, it is equally valued as food. The West African *Notopterus afer* has a spectacular banded and reticulated pattern. Also in West Africa is found the false featherfin, *Xenomystis nigri,* which has a nondescript brownish coloring; its sole claim to generic recognition is the fact that it lacks the dorsal fin. It is a small fish, not exceeding 6 inches in length. Unlike the species of *Notopterus,* which are generally noted for their belligerent dispositions, *Xenomystis* is a docile species and will live peaceably with other fishes in an aquarium.

MORMYRIDS—Family Mormyridae

The astonished aquarium visitor, seeing an elephant-nosed mormyrid for the first time, is apt to exclaim: "What a silly-looking animal—it doesn't even look like a fish!" Apparently the ancient Egyptians were equally impressed by its unique appearance, for carved and painted mormyrids have often been found as decorations in the friezes of the tombs. Recently I was privileged to examine a 4-inch bronze mormyrid, a perfect replica of *Mormyrus caballus,* a species from the upper Nile that has a moderately long snout. A small cobra and the "Horns of Hathor" on the forward part of this amulet indicate that it was worn by a sixteenth-dynasty Pharaoh as a neck ornament some three thousand years ago.

There is a considerable range of variability in the snouts of the mormyrids. *Gnathonemus curvirostris*

African Butterfly Fish (*Pantodon buchholtzi*); fresh water; western central Africa (Gene Wolfsheimer).

and several related species all have enormously elongated snouts, with a small mouth at the end of this curved and inflexible rostral extension. *Gnathonemus petersi* presents another extreme, for in this species only the lower lip is elongated; a fish measuring 5 inches might have a lower lip ½ inch in length. The fact that this Ubangi-type lip is flexible increases its value as a device for locating food material on the bottom. To complete the range of variation, *Marcusenius* and some related genera have rounded noses that are not extended, with the mouth shoved back on the underside of the head.

Having once carefully examined a mormyrid (see photographs), it is usually possible to identify other members of the family by recognition of the typical "mormyrid look." Besides the characteristic extension of the snout in some species, most mormyrids have an abnormally narrow caudal peduncle, that slender part of the tail between the main body and the caudal fin; the latter is always deeply forked, a feature that serves as another identifying characteristic. Typically, the single dorsal and single anal

Left, False Featherback (*Xenomystis nigri*); fresh water; western central Africa. Right, Featherback (*Notopterus chitala*); fresh water; Thailand to Indonesia (John Tashjian at Steinhart Aquarium).

fin are placed back on the body, usually opposite each other.

The mormyrids form a fairly large family of more than 110 species and about 11 genera. The majority of them are bottom feeders, grubbing in the mud for worms, insect larvae, and other invertebrates. Although many are less than 6 inches long as adults, though the water is so muddy that the visibility range is zero. This electrical activity may be correlated with the fact that the mormyrids have the largest cerebellum of any of the fishes; since this part of the brain controls motor activity, it would obviously control the electrical organs, which are modified muscle tissue.

Ubangi Mormyrid (*Gnathonemus petersi*); fresh water; Congo (Hans and Klaus Paysan).

there are several that reach lengths of 5 feet. Most of the larger species are used as food, sometimes eaten fresh but mostly dried.

The elongated snout of the elephant-nosed fish is only one of the strange attributes possessed by members of this African family. Scientists have discovered in recent years that many, and probably all, of the mormyrids are capable of electrogenic activity; that is, they have modified muscle tissue in the form of electric organs capable of putting out microvoltages. These minute and usually fairly constant discharges set up around the fish an electrical field that works as a screening device. Any object coming within this field, such as other fishes, food, or enemies, can be instantly pinpointed as to location even

One of the most aberrant of the mormyrids is a species long known for its electrogenic ability, *Gymnarchus niloticus,* which is sometimes placed in a separate family, the Gymnarchidae. It is best described as a mormyrid that has lost the ventral, anal, and tail fins, but perhaps by way of compensation has gained a long dorsal fin which, starting just behind the head, runs almost the entire length of the eel-like body. *Gymnarchus* reaches a length of 5 feet and in some areas in considered an excellent food fish. It constructs a peculiar floating nest with a hole-like entrance on one side. The newly hatched gymnarchids have long gill filaments much like those of the embryo sharks.

The continuous electrical discharges sent out from

the tail of *Gymnarchus* have long been studied by biologists. Recent investigations by Professors H. W. Lissmann, K. E. Machin of Cambridge University, and others have shown that *Gymnarchus* can differentiate between objects which are geometrically and optically identical but have different electrical conductivity. On the other hand, it cannot distinguish between externally identical objects of similar electrical conductivity although they may be of different chemical composition.

Ichthyologists are intrigued with the similarities between the African mormyrids and the South American gymnotids, a group that includes the electric eel, the knifefishes, and their relatives. Although these two groups are not even slightly related and are separated by the Atlantic Ocean, many of them are very similar in appearance and behavior. In swimming, both groups move forward and backward with equal ease, and both mormyrids and gymnotids have electric organs. The mormyrids, however, are able to produce a steadier and more uniform electrical discharge than the gymnotids, which have a somewhat erratic electrical pattern.

Because of their peculiar anatomical characteristics, the mormyrids are recognized as a separate group, one of the seven suborders of the isospondylous fishes.

SANDFISH or BEAKED SALMON —Family Gonorhynchidae

Although as many as four species of this strange family have been recognized in recent years, there is a strong probability that there is only a single one, *Gonorhynchus gonorhynchus*. It occurs in marine waters around Japan, Australia, New Zealand, the Hawaiian Islands, and South Africa. The sandfish is a very slender species with a usual maximum length of 15 inches, although lengths of 2 feet have been recorded. It is not difficult to identify because of its unique features. The mouth is set back on the underside of the pointed head, and in front of it there is a single conspicuous barbel or whisker. The tail fin is black at its base and changes abruptly to white or red at the tip. The inside of the mouth and gill area is black or purple. The belly is reddish white, the lateral scales purplish blue edged with brown. The head and body are covered with very small, beady ctenoid scales. *Gonorhynchus* occurs in sandy areas, from the shallows down to depths of almost five hundred feet. Although it is often brought in by trawlers in South Africa, it has no value there as a food fish; however, it is eaten in New Zealand, where it is considered a gourmet item. Using isopod crustaceans as bait, New Zealand sportsmen catch sandfish, or "sand eels" as they call them, in shallow

Elephant-nose Mormyrid (*Gnathonemus numenius*); fresh water; Congo (New York Zoological Society).

water where the bottom is sandy. In this region the sandfish has been observed to burrow into the sand with great speed, using its angular snout as an effective plow. Because of its many distinctive features, *Gonorhynchus* is given subordinal rank among the isospondylous fishes.

Pike and Their Relatives
(Order Haplomi)

This is a small order, with many features similar to those of the isospondylous fishes, which include the salmon, trout, and herrings, but differing from them in the absence of a part of the shoulder girdle known as the mesocoracoid. In this respect the haplomous fishes are intermediate between the large isospondylous group and the equally large and important Ostariophysi, which includes the minnows, carp, and catfishes. In the haplomous fishes the air bladder has an opening that is continuous with the gut; all of the fins have soft rays without spines; and the ventral fins are abdominal in position. This group of fishes is restricted to the northern hemisphere; it includes three families and about a dozen species.

PIKE, PICKEREL, and MUSKELLUNGE —Family Esocidae

Characteristically, all members of this family have ducklike shovel bills and an efficient set of sharp and wicked teeth that show when the mouth is opened. These fishes are effective carnivores, and are logically at the pinnacle of any aquatic food chain. Examination of their stomach contents reveals that they are primarily fish eaters, but also readily accept frogs, small birds, and mammals. The northern pike, *Esox lucius* (Plate 7), is the most wide-ranging member of the family, being found over most of North America from about the latitude of the state

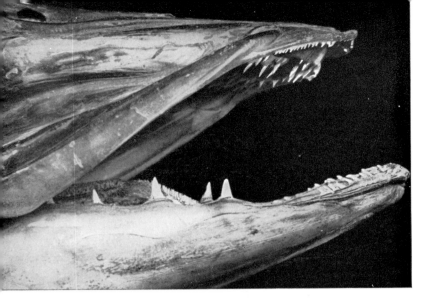

Jaws of Northern Pike (*Esox lucius*); fresh water; Eurasia and North America (W. Harstrick; Bavaria Verlag).

of Ohio northward, with the exception of the westernmost portion of the continent. It also occurs through many parts of Europe and Asia. As an adult the northern pike is a large fish with a maximum recorded weight of forty-six pounds and a length of 54 inches. The pike follows the family pattern of spawning during the spring months, usually in shallow, weedy areas, where the eggs are scattered indiscriminately.

As a group the esocids are very susceptible to slight changes in environment, such changes having often been held responsible for the disappearance of these fishes in areas where they were formerly abundant. Hybridization is known to occur among some of the species: for example, between the northern pike and the muskellunge, and between the two species of pickerel. As is well known, the esocids are very important sport and commercial species.

Identification of pike and other members of the family is sometimes difficult because of the similarity in appearance of the various species; however, examination of the scalation along the sides of the head provides the means of differentiation. The northern pike has a complete series of scales from

Muskellunge (*Esox masquinongy*); fresh water; Great Lakes and vicinity (New York Zoological Society).

top to bottom on the area of the cheek just behind the eye; and on the opercle, which is just posterior to the cheek, only the upper half is scaled. The muskellunge, *Esox masquinongy*, has identical scalation on the opercle, but can be differentiated from the pike by the fact that only the upper half of the cheek is scaled. However, if both the cheek and opercle are fully scaled from top to bottom, the fish is one of two pickerels, either the grass pickerel, *Esox americanus* (with dark bands on the sides) or the chain pickerel, *Esox niger* (with chainlike reticulations on the sides).

The muskellunge surpasses even the northern pike in size, its maximum weight being recorded at 102 pounds with the angler's record at 70 pounds. In distribution it is also markedly different, being restricted to a much smaller area, which does not now extend beyond the Great Lakes and adjacent areas. It is apparently becoming less common even in this limited range.

The chain pickerel reaches a length of 24 inches and occurs from Nova Scotia to Texas in a band several hundred miles inland from the coast. The grass pickerel is much smaller, with a maximum length of only 12 to 14 inches, and is found in the eastern United States with the exception of a band a few hundred miles wide along the eastern seaboard.

The last member of the family, the black-spotted *Esox reicherti*, is important in eastern Siberia.

MUD MINNOWS—Family Umbridae

The mud minnow looks like a junior edition of the pikes and pickerels but has a rounded snout instead of the elongated shovel-bill profile. The largest of the three species is the central mud minnow, *Umbra limi*, which may reach a length of 6 inches, although 2 inches or less is the commonest size. It is found in silt-bottomed lakes and ponds through the upper Mississippi basin and into the Great Lakes area. The eastern mud minnow, *Umbra pygmaea*, is a smaller species, usually with a 3-inch maximum length; it is found along the Atlantic seaboard from New York to Florida. The third species, the western mud minnow, *Novumbra hubbsi*, measuring about 4 inches, is known from the Chehalis River in Washington.

The name mud minnow is an appropriate one, for these fishes often dig themselves into the mud tail first, either to hide or to estivate. Because of its lung, the African lungfish has been known to survive in a mud cocoon for years. The mud minnows do not have lungs, but they do have a remarkable ability to survive in oxygen-deficient water; in fact, they can survive for several days and perhaps weeks in highly viscous mud. Their abundance makes them a readily available food supply for larger carnivorous species. Mud minnows are often used by fishermen as bait.

A recent study of the ecology of the central mud minnow, *Umbra limi,* conducted near the campus of the University of Notre Dame in Indiana, showed that the fish were usually found along the sides of the stream under dense vegetation, and that at any one time approximately as many were swimming in the space between the mud bottom and the floating vegetation as were buried in the mud. With the approach of the early spring breeding season, the males developed a bluish green iridescence on the anal fin, this fin being slightly larger than that of the female. Females carried as few as 220 eggs or as many as 1489. Stomach contents indicated that the mud minnow was strictly carnivorous, with any type of small animal being fair prey.

ALASKA BLACKFISH—*Family Dalliidae*

The Alaska blackfish, *Dallia pectoralis,* is an arctic version of the mud minnow and is as abundant in many of the far northern sections of Arctic America and Siberia as the mud minnows are in the more temperate areas. The blackfish, with its maximum length of 8 inches, is somewhat larger than the mud minnow; it also has a great many more pectoral fin rays—thirty-three to thirty-six, as compared with the eighteen to twenty-three of the mud minnow.

There are many famous "sourdough" stories of the ability of the blackfish to withstand cold—how it can actually become frozen in the wintertime and return to its normal activity when the ice thaws. One day in the Steinhart Aquarium laboratory we decided to test the veracity of these tales by freezing three blackfish, each about 4 inches long, into solid ice blocks. This was accomplished without difficulty, and twelve hours later the slow thawing process was started. In several hours the pectoral fins were released and started to move gently. In a few more hours the fishes were entirely free and seemed able to swim without too much difficulty. But the next day they were all dead. This small test does not prove that the blackfish cannot be frozen and subsequently survive. However, it is suspected that in order for the fish to survive, its tissues must not become frozen, for once ice crystals form within the cells of the body, no tissue can regain its normal activity.

Iniomous Fishes (*Order Iniomi*)

The iniomous fishes form a group that in some respects is transitional between the more primitive isospondylous forms previously discussed and the more advanced groups to be described later. The majority are small fishes, many living in the depths of the oceans; a number of these deep-sea forms have light-producing organs or photophores along the sides of the body. The fins have soft rays without spines, and the ventrals are abdominal in position. Most of the species have a small adipose fin on the upper surface of the caudal peduncle just in front of the tail. The air bladder is usually lacking. More than three hundred living species have been recognized. They are divided into two suborders—the Myctophoidea, with seven families, and the Alepisauroidea, with six families.

LIZARD FISHES—*Family Synodidae*

Lizard fishes not only look like reptiles, but they also act like reptiles. Most of their time is spent sitting on the bottom with the body at a slight angle, propped up on the front end by the ventral fins, like a jet fighter ready to take off. This inactivity ends as soon as small food fishes swim into the area; the lizard fish then darts upward with great rapidity, usually swallowing the prey in one gulp. The numerous stiletto-like teeth in both jaws, together with the teeth on the tongue, prevent even the most agile fishes from escaping. In captivity lizard fishes are very particular about their food; it is almost impossible to accustom them to feeding on dead material. Thus if the aquarium does not have live fishes available as food, the lizard fishes do not survive for long.

Most species of lizard fishes are less than 12 inches in length, although there are some, such as the Indo-Pacific *Saurida undosquamis,* that reach a length of 20 inches. Incidentally, this species is one of the few in the family that is considered a good food fish. In some areas its preferred habitat is on the bottom at depths between 90 and 130 feet. Most lizard fishes are inshore shallow-water forms, usually living on sandy bottom adjacent to rocky or reef areas. With the pectoral fins they sometimes burrow down into the sand until only the tips of the eyes show. Although the synodids are a tropical group, there are a few species that move northward during the summer into temperate waters. Included in this category are the American Atlantic *Synodus foetens,* which is found from Cape Cod to Brazil, and the American Pacific *Synodus lucioceps,* which comes as far north as Point Conception on the California coast. Some of the lizard fishes are widely distributed; for example, *Synodus synodus* has been able to establish itself on both sides of the tropical Atlantic, and *Trachinocephalus myops* is widely distributed not only in the Atlantic but also in the Pacific.

About three dozen species of lizard fishes are recognized; all exhibit the characteristic cylindrical shape and reptile-like head. Most of the species have a small adipose fin on the back between the dorsal and tail fins. The blotched color pattern shown in the photo of *Synodus intermedius* is typical of the family.

The young stages of the lizard fishes are most interesting, for in some species the very slender whitish larval form does not even vaguely resemble the adult until it reaches a length of 2 inches or more.

THREAD-SAIL FISHES—*Family Aulopidae*

The thread-sail fishes are often considered the most generalized of all the iniomous forms. The family is a small one, containing about five species, which live at moderate depths in the Indo-Pacific region and the Atlantic. They look much like the lizard fishes, having a small adipose fin on the upper side of the caudal peduncle, but the head is shorter and the dorsal fin is larger than those of the lizard fishes. *Aulopus japonica* is a small light-red species reaching a length of 8 inches; it is found at depths of about three hundred feet along the southern Japanese coasts, and is considered a delicacy. The Australian Sergeant Baker, *Aulopus purpurissatus,* is a larger species, attaining a length of 2 feet; its normal food is composed of mollusks and crustaceans. *Aulopus filamentosus* is known from the Mediterranean, Madeira, and the Canary Islands.

GREENEYES—*Family Chlorophthalmidae*

The greeneyes are much like the thread-sail fishes in appearance, but their fins are more normal in size and they are usually found in much deeper water. About eleven species are known; *Chlorophthalmus chalybeius* occurs off the United States Atlantic coast.

GRID-EYE FISHES—*Family Ipnopidae*

The deep-sea ipnopids are remarkable in that in some species the structure of the eye is greatly modified, with a flattened cornea and an enlarged retina, to form a very sensitive structure that is undoubtedly efficient in receiving the faint luminescence coming from the light organs of other fishes. Other members of the fourteen species in the family have luminous patches in the place of the eyes, and still others have scales covering the area.

SPIDER FISHES—*Family Bathypteroidae*

Strange indeed are these extremely deep-sea spider fishes. The first fin rays of the pelvic fins are greatly elongated and stiffened so that the spider fish uses them as landing gear—sitting on the bottom with the tips of the pelvic and tail fins forming a resting tripod. The upper fin rays of the pectorals may also be greatly elongated, reaching almost to the tail; however, there appears to be a certain amount of sexual dimorphism in regard to the lengths of some of these fin rays. About thirteen species are known, most of them in the genus *Bathypterois*.

LANTERN FISHES—*Family Myctophidae*

The lantern fishes, with their neatly arranged photophores or light organs along the sides, form a moderately large family of perhaps 150 species. Because of the daily vertical migrations of some of the lantern fishes, they are among the few truly deep-sea fishes often seen by the curious seafaring person. All it takes is a light hung over the side of the ship on a moonless night while the vessel drifts over fairly deep water. If there are lantern fishes about, they will soon be darting around the light. With the approach of day they disappear, starting their return trip into the depths. A deep-haul plankton net pulled through the same waters in the daytime will usually show that the identical species that was around the night light is as much as one-half mile down in the depths at midday. It is probable that some of these small fishes spend all of their time swimming up and then turning around and swimming down again. Lantern

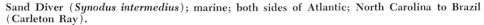

Sand Diver (*Synodus intermedius*); marine; both sides of Atlantic; North Carolina to Brazil (Carleton Ray).

fishes are small, the majority in the 3-to-6-inch range, with a few being adult at 1 inch.

Classification of the lantern fishes is dependent upon the exact position and number of photophores; a precise nomenclature has developed around the designation of these light organs. For example, two of the main genera are separated by differences in the praecaudal photophores (the light organs on the caudal peduncle just in front of the tail fin). If there are two of these praecaudal photophores, the species belongs to the genus *Myctophum,* but if there are three to six, the genus is *Lampanyctus.*

One of the common lantern fishes of the Atlantic and Mediterranean, *Myctophum punctatum,* has been studied in detail. The adults are about 4 inches in length, with many light organs along the sides. Females have three to five luminescent plates on the underside of the tail just in front of the tail fin, and males have one to three plates on the upper surface of the tail. In the Mediterranean, spawning takes place during the winter and early spring months. Until the time of metamorphosis at about three-quarters of an inch, the transparent larvae are more abundant in the surface waters, but following the change to the adult form, they begin to move downward into deeper water.

BOMBAY DUCK—Family Harpodontidae

The Bombay duck, *Harpodon nehereus,* is an interesting fish; it looks like a blunt-nosed lizard fish with extremely long pectoral and ventral fins. Although it grows as long as 16 inches, most of those caught commercially are much smaller. The flesh of this fish, dried and used as hors d'oeuvre or as an accompaniment to curries, is called Bombay duck; by usage the name has become attached to the fish itself. It is caught in tremendous numbers in the Ganges area and other parts of India, and is eaten fresh as well as in the dried state.

In Indian waters the distribution of the Bombay duck is to a certain extent correlated with salinity, for it occurs commonly in river mouths and estuaries. There are marked fluctuations in its abundance, which seems to be affected by fresh-water runoff. It occurs along the northern coasts of both eastern and western India, but is absent from the southern tip as well as from Ceylon. Besides the Bombay duck there are four other species in the genus *Harpodon,* which ranges from Zanzibar to Australia.

The family Harpodontidae also has a deep-water genus, *Bathysaurus,* which probably includes only a single species, *ferox,* although several species have been described. It looks like a very "toothy" lizard fish, but it lacks the adipose fin, and the snout is considerably elongated. Maximum adult size is around

2 feet. Its normal depth range is 3,000 to 9,000 feet, and it probably occurs in all oceans.

BARRACUDINAS—Family Paralepididae

The deep-sea barracudinas are pale, usually small, slender-bodied fishes with a frightening array of teeth, although a microscope may be required to appreciate this dentition. They are fairly abundant in mid-water depths of all oceans, except the South Atlantic and the Arctic, down to about two miles. Stomach contents of large carnivorous fishes living at these same depths indicate that the barracudinas are one of the main sources of protein for these larger fishes. It is suspected that as adults the barracudinas are very fast swimmers; such speed would explain why no sexually mature adults of any of the forty-eight known species have ever been caught. The largest barracudina recorded (*Paralepis barysoma*) was caught in the Antarctic and measured about 2 feet. Unlike the lantern fishes and others living in the depths, most of the barracudinas are entirely lacking in luminescent light organs. The one known exception is *Lestidium,* which has one or two light-producing organs on the belly, in the form of internal ducts that have been observed to glow when the fish is taken out of the water.

Of the ten genera in the family, the members of only one (*Lestidium*) are known to make vertical migrations. During the day they are found at depths usually greater than one-half mile, but at night they move upward so that they are near the surface.

In the two deep-water bays of Balayan and Batangas, south of Manila, the fishermen make use of powerful lights to attract fishes at night. Barracudinas, usually *Lestidium,* are often taken in these catches and are sold the next morning in the local markets for a few centavos a dozen, which is what I paid when I collected my first specimens.

Although no one has as yet been able to keep these barracudinas alive in an aquarium, observers in the bathyscaphe report that they usually orient themselves vertically, with the head downward.

PEARLEYES—Family Scopelarchidae

The deep-sea fishes of the family Scopelarchidae are small, having a maximum known length of about 8 inches. The adults are thought to be fast swimmers, since they are apparently able to avoid not only plankton nets but also larger predators. In fact, there is only a single record of scopelarchids having been found in the stomachs of deep-sea predaceous species that normally feed on many other types of small fishes. This suspected ability to swim fast may explain why knowledge of most of the eighteen species in this family of five genera rests almost entirely on larval and juvenile specimens collected by deep-hauling plankton nets. Six hundred feet is as shallow as any of these strange fishes has been collected, and they seldom occur over the continental shelf. Their usual habitat is over the deepest water in the Atlantic, Pacific, and Indian oceans, ranging from six hundred feet down to at least a mile and three-quarters.

Not only do the scopelarchids have internal anatomical features that are quite distinct, but they also have two external distinguishing marks that clearly set

always of interest to the newspapers. The reason for this is quite obvious upon examination of the fish, for it reaches a length of 6 feet and is equipped with a ferocious set of long, fanglike teeth that would do justice to the most bloodthirsty shark or barracuda. On top of the body is a long, high, sail-like dorsal fin that starts just behind the head and extends down the back almost to the small adipose fin just ahead of the tail. Two species are recognized: the Atlantic *Alepisaurus ferox* and the Pacific *A. borealis.*

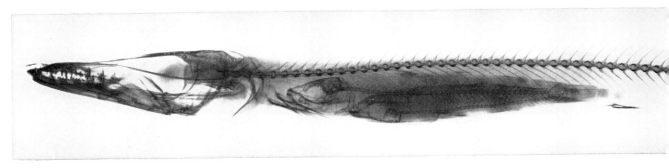

Radiograph of Barracudina (*Lestidium pofi*); marine; Pacific: Celebes to Line Islands; first record of the barracudina as a fish-eater (Robert R. Rofen).

them apart from all other members of the alepisauroid or lancet-fish group. These are the presence of (1) large, compressed, hooked teeth on the tongue, and (2) telescopic eyes. The eyes do not always aim in the same direction. In some species they may be directed forward; in others, upward; and in some, slightly backward. With the exception of these features, the scopelarchids are similar in appearance to the barracudinas, family Paralepididae.

SABER-TOOTH FISHES—Family Evermannellidae

There are only six known species of the small saber-tooth fishes. These are found in the depths of the Indian and Atlantic oceans as well as the Mediterranean Sea, and there is a single record from the Pacific—from the Banda Sea. Besides having exceptional, paired, saber-type teeth, the evermannellids have one major claim to fame; they can swallow fishes much larger than themselves. Along with *Chiasmodon,* the black swallower, and the hammerjaw, *Omosudis,* they undoubtedly hold the record in the fish world for this type of deglutition.

The saber-tooth fishes are apparently fast swimmers, for only two large adults have ever been taken. The larger of these measured 6½ inches. On the head of the saber-tooth fishes are pits that are suspected of being luminous.

LANCET FISHES—Family Alepisauridae

Whenever a lancet fish is washed ashore in an area where they are seldom seen at the surface, it is

The lancet fishes are the wolves of the midwater depths of the ocean; examination of their stomachs has revealed that they eat everything that gets in the way. Actually this has been a great boon to the ichthyologist, who must depend upon feeding habits of carnivorous fishes of this type for knowledge of many of the very rare deep-sea fishes. There seem to be three methods by which lancet fishes appear at the surface: (1) as a part of the catch of long-line fisheries, for example, off Japan and Portugal; (2) as a result of sickness or parasite infestation (worm infestations are common) which drives them out of their normal depth; and (3) as a hydrostatic result of ingested food acting like a balloon and forcing the lancet fish upward.

HAMMERJAW—Family Omosudidae

The hammerjaw, family Omosudidae, is represented by a single deep-water species, *Omosudis lowii.* It is best described as similar to a lancet fish, *Alepisaurus,* but distinguished from it by a dorsal fin having a few short rays as compared to the long, many-rayed fin of the lancet. Hammerjaws are found at depths between 2400 and 6000 feet, the juveniles usually occurring in the upper margin and the adults in the deeper part of the range. They occur in tropical and temperate waters of all oceans, but always in deep water and never over the continental shelf. Apparently the young are affected by light, for catch records indicate that they move downward during the daytime and upward at night.

The hammerjaw is another fish that as an adult can outswim a plankton net or mid-water trawl, for although the juveniles can be captured this way, few adults are taken by this method. Stomach examinations of larger predators of other species are the chief source of specimens.

The largest specimen ever collected measured 9 inches. The hammerjaw is essentially a carnivore, as evidenced by stomach examinations, which reveal a preference for squid and small fishes.

The name "hammerjaw" is derived from the large hammer-like lower jaw; this structure undoubtedly aids the fish in holding its food, which is often larger than the *Omosudis* itself. The best example of this is a larval *Omosudis* ¼ inch long that had devoured another fish measuring three times that length.

The hammerjaw has a very peculiar pectoral girdle: the supra cleithral elements are external, thus allowing the girdle to slide and expand when the hammerjaw is swallowing oversized food.

JAVELIN FISH—Family Anotopteridae

Anotopterus pharao, the sole member of the family Anotopteridae, is best described as an aberrant paralepidid externally marked by the absence of the dorsal fin and internally by development of the intermuscular bones. The largest known specimen of this elongate, carnivorous fish measured 34 inches. Fewer than fifty specimens have been collected. These were taken from the Atlantic, Pacific, and the Antarctic seas. Although not known from the Indian Ocean, it is suspected of being world-wide in distribution, ranging from temperate to polar waters and vertically from the surface at nighttime to mid-water levels in the daytime. Most of the known specimens have come from the stomachs of larger predators such as the lancet fish, *Alepisaurus,* halibut, antarctic whales, and California albacore tuna.

Deep-sea Giganturid Fishes (Order Giganturoidea)

—Family Giganturidae

The classification of these small, voracious fishes of the depths, represented by four known species from the Atlantic and Indian oceans, has long puzzled ichthyologists. One hypothesis is that they are intermediate between the shallow-water synodid lizard fishes previously discussed (order Iniomi) and the deep-sea gulper eels (order Lyomeri).

The giganturids are characterized by their lack of anatomical parts that are usually essential to other fishes. They lack ventral fins, maxillary and palatine bones, as well as the post temporal and supra cleithrum. The telescopic eyes, directed forward, seem to give them exceptional eyesight. They have needle-sharp depressible teeth, and the lower lobe of the tail is greatly extended. The dorsal and anal fins are placed far back on the body, and the pectoral fins are quite large for the size of the fish. This is thought to be a necessary development in order to allow the fishes to swallow food larger than themselves. For example, a 3-inch *Gigantura vorax* was found to contain a 5½-inch *Chauliodus,* which it had attacked from the center and had eaten with the body bent into a V. During the time this food was being ingested it would obviously be difficult for the giganturid to respire normally through the mouth. Consequently, it is thought that under such circumstances the large pectorals come to the rescue by driving water into the cavernous gill openings, thus reversing the normal breathing procedure.

The few specimens of *Gigantura* that have been collected ranged from 2¼ to 4⅜ inches in length; they were taken at depths of approximately fifteen hundred to six thousand feet.

Deep-sea Gulper Eels

(Order Lyomeri)

The name "gulper eel" has long been used for these fantastic fishes, but the term "gulper fish" is much more appropriate; for although the Lyomeri look like eels, they are not even distantly related. In fact, the exact relationship of the Lyomeri is still somewhat of a mystery. It has been suggested that they are most closely related to the deep-sea whale fishes (family Cetomimidae) of the order Berycomorphi, to be discussed later. Nine species are known, assigned to three genera in three families. Included in this group are some large fishes that reach a length of 6 feet. Some of the species have light-producing organs; and as a rule, they are all black in color. They are found at depths ranging between six hundred and nine thousand feet.

The two species of *Eurypharynx* (family Eurypharyngidae) have the largest mouths of any of the gulpers and surprisingly small stomachs that are not distensible. They are thought to use the tremendous mouth as a seining device for catching small planktonic organisms as they swim through the water with the mouth always open. Supporting this view is the fact that the skin of the mouth and body is so fragile that *Eurypharynx* would probably find it impossible to hold onto any active food. By contrast, stomach contents from members of the other two families show that they are voracious carnivores.

The five species of *Saccopharynx* (family Saccopharyngidae) have mouths nearly as large as those of *Eurypharynx,* but they also have many sharp teeth and very large distensible stomachs, which, of course, are essential for predators that eat other fishes larger than themselves.

The remaining two gulpers, both members of the genus *Monognathus* (family Monognathidae) are an ichthyological enigma. Their mouths are average in size, as contrasted with the tremendous mouths of the other gulpers; they lack the pectoral fins; and most amazing of all, they have no upper jaws, the maxillary and premaxillary bones being entirely absent. They also lack the opercular bones and the pharyngeal skeleton, as well as the parasphenoid and pterygoid bones. Very few specimens of *Monognathus* have been taken, and more material is needed before the relationship of this strange family can be worked out. It is of interest to note that an authority on this group, Dr. James Böhlke of the Academy of Natural Sciences of Philadelphia, has postulated that these monognathids may eventually prove to be post-larval forms of the saccopharyngid gulper eels.

Characins, Minnows, Catfishes, and Their Relatives (*Order Ostariophysi*)

At least six thousand kinds of fishes, by a conservative estimate, belong to this important group, which is almost entirely confined to fresh water. These various fishes are placed in a single order because all of them possess an interesting anatomical structure known as the Weberian apparatus, which is actually a series of small bones connecting the air or swim bladder with the internal ear. These bones are formed by modification of the anterior vertebrae. Although the function of the Weberian apparatus is not fully understood, there is evidence indicating that it may be a factor in the increased acuteness in hearing of certain ostariophysan fishes. These bones are also thought to add to the fish's ability to detect minute changes in the volume of gas within the swim bladder; by regulating these volumetric fluctuations, the fish gains better hydrostatic control and can more easily maintain its position in the water with less swimming effort. One group of these fishes, the loaches, are quite remarkable in that they are able to detect changes in barometric pressure; this ability is thought (but has not been proved) to be a function of the Weberian apparatus.

Unfortunately, there is no single external anatomical characteristic with classification value equivalent to that of the internal Weberian bones by which ostariophysan fishes can be easily identified. There is a wide range of variation, but in general these fishes have their pelvic or ventral fins attached near the center of the abdomen, and there is a single dorsal fin with soft rays. In certain carps and catfishes the dorsal fin is preceded by a single, usually large, spine. In the characins and catfishes there is normally an adipose fin, usually without rays, between the dorsal and tail fins. Whisker-like barbels are found on the catfishes and sometimes on the minnows and carps. Most of these ostariophysan fishes have scales, but in some catfishes these are replaced by bony plates.

Ostariophysan fishes are found on all continents of the world with the exception of Australia and Antarctica. Two suborders are usually recognized: (1) the Cyprinoidea, with two main divisions, (a) the characins and gymnotid knifefishes, and (b) the minnows, suckers, loaches, and hillstream fishes—a total of about ten families; and (2) the Siluroidea, containing approximately twenty-eight families of catfishes.

CHARACINS or CHARACIDS
—Family Characidae

This family was originally known as Characinidae and the fishes as characins. Later the family name was changed to Characidae, with characid becoming the preferred common name. However, the old name characin is still retained in common usage, so that today these fishes may be correctly called either characids or characins. Actually, there is great diversification in body form among this large group of fishes, as is well indicated by the fact that the family is sometimes split into six individual families and as many as thirty subfamilies.

The distribution of the characins is limited to Central and South America and tropical Africa. They look somewhat like the minnows and carps (family Cyprinidae), but can usually be distinguished from them by the presence of teeth in the jaws and of a small, fleshy adipose fin on the back between the dorsal and tail fins, and the absence of the specialized pharyngeal teeth and throat musculature of the minnows. Characins come in many shapes and sizes, the smallest being less than 1 inch in length, and the largest more than 5 feet long. Some are vegetarians, some are omnivorous, and a few are dangerous carnivores.

Whenever the name piranha is used, the word killer invariably accompanies it and has indeed become almost a synonym for it. For perhaps four of almost a score of species of South American characins, this is a well-deserved epithet. A most vivid description of these ferocious fishes was written by Professor George Myers of Stanford University, in his monograph on the piranha (*Aquarium Journal,* San Francisco, February and March, 1949). He says:

A fish only a foot long with teeth so sharp and jaws so strong that it can chop out a piece of flesh from a man or an alligator as neatly as a razor, or clip off a finger or a toe, bone and all, with the dispatch of a meat-cleaver! A fish afraid of nothing, which attacks any animal, whatever its size, like lightning! A fish which never attacks singly but always in schools of a hundred or a thousand! A fish which is actually attracted by splashing and commotion in the water! And a fish which, when it smells blood, turns into a raging demon! This is the piranha, feared as no other animal is feared throughout the whole length of South America. The piranha is the most dangerous fish in the Amazon and perhaps in the world.

Of the four most dangerous piranhas, the common and widely distributed *Serrasalmus nattereri* (Plate 12) is the species most often seen in tropical fish stores and public aquaria. One of the largest of these four deadly species is *Serrasalmus piraya,* which reaches a length of 2 feet, and is found in the River São Francisco in eastern Brazil. Most of the other species are much smaller. At least two of the four species are known as black piranhas (Plates 13 and 14) because of their very dark color. At various times in the past the United States government and some state fish and game agencies have considered legislation limiting the importation of piranhas because of their dangerous nature. Such proposals have never been adopted because, as was always pointed out, piranhas had never spawned in captivity and hence there seemed little possibility that their importation could result in permanent populations in natural waters. The situation, however, has now changed; in 1960 William Braker at Chicago's John G. Shedd Aquarium reported spawnings of one of the less dangerous of the piranhas, *Serrasalmus spilopleura.* These fishes bred when they were 7 inches long, having lived in a 1200-gallon tank for the previous three years. The female carefully deposited the eggs on aquatic plants, which is contrary to the helter-skelter spawning behavior of most of the other characins. The male then assumed his duty of guarding the eggs as well as the newly hatched fry, which became mobile in about five days.

The piranhas' diet is composed of smaller fishes, usually other characins, and it is only by accident that they feed on some unfortunate large animal. The efficiency of these fishes' teeth is phenomenal; the record in this field is undoubtedly that of a hundred-pound capybara that was reduced to a skeleton

in less than one minute. Since piranhas are excellent food items, they are sometimes caught on hook and line; but unless very strong leader wire is used, they simply cut the line with their teeth and swim away. Out of the water, and even when apparently dead, they are still dangerous, for they may snap their jaws when touched, slicing an unguarded finger or toe.

Despite its fearful reputation, the piranha when kept in an aquarium seems to become a different fish physiologically. Perhaps alone or with only one or two others, it loses the boldness it has when surrounded by a school of its kind. Although it sometimes shows how sharp its teeth are by biting a piece off another fish or slicing through a net or an aquarist's finger, it is usually a nervous and jittery fish, easily frightened by any sudden movement or by a net being placed in the tank. It is common aquarium practice to place less valuable decoy fishes with the piranhas, so that if they feel inclined to slaughter another fish, they may attack the decoy rather than one of their own kind.

There are several close relatives of the piranhas that feed chiefly on plants. These are the silver dollar fishes of the genus *Metynnis* and the genus *Myleus,* great favorites among the tropical fish hobbyists. In appearance they are confusingly like piranhas, but they can usually be distinguished by their lack of the jutting lower jaw and razor-sharp teeth as well as by their more docile dispositions. The silver dollars, like the piranhas, are good food fishes. Some of them reach a length of 2 feet, although 4 to 6 inches is the usual maximum size in aquaria.

One very interesting carnivorous characid is the long-jawed, pikelike *Boulengerella lucius* (Plate 10), a species that often hides among plants near the surface, then suddenly darts at a small fish, pinions it between its jaws, and quickly swallows it. This pike characid grows to a length of about 2 feet and it is not dangerous to humans. However, another carnivorous characid, the tiger fish of the African Congo, *Hydrocyon goliath,* is definitely feared by man. Its body is shaped like that of a trout, and it attains a weight of 125 pounds. Because of its large, conical, tearing teeth it has been suspected of attacking natives in the water, although not positively implicated. When alive and out of the water, it is extremely dangerous to handle because of its dagger-sharp teeth.

There are hordes of small characids with slender to fairly deep bodies, some with beautiful coloring, in South America, and a smaller number in Africa. They are largely omnivorous, eating almost anything that they can get their mouths around. A representative of this group is the South American jewel tetra,

Hyphessobrycon callistus (Plate 11). Many of these small fishes are imported from Africa and especially from South America for aquarists. Such names as "glo-lite tetra," "neon tetra," "cardinal tetra," and "head-and-tail-light" speak for themselves. They are truly beautiful fishes with brilliant colors.

Another South American group, the flying characins, often called flying hatchet fishes, are the only fishes that have true flight in the sense that they actually propel themselves through the air with the aid of their pectoral fins. (The well-known marine flying fishes merely glide; their "wings" do not move during flight.) The flying characins are all rather small; the largest do not grow longer than 4 inches. *Carnegiella marthae* (Plate 8) is one of the pygmies, reaching only a little over 1 inch in length. These fishes spend their time near the surface of the water, where they feed largely on insects. They apparently escape their enemies by flight. What appear to be greatly extended abdomens in the photograph are actually expanded shoulder girdles supporting the

Headstander (*Abramites microcephalus*); fresh water; lower Amazon (Gene Wolfsheimer).

muscles of the pectoral fins. This apparatus makes up about one-fourth of the total weight of the fish, and it is used to move the pectoral fins during flight as well as during swimming. Once a flying characin leaves the water, it does not change its course; it has no self-directional flight such as occurs in insects and birds. Instead, its flight seems to be simply a means of extending the distance and perhaps increasing the speed of the initial jump. The buzzing sound of the pectoral fins can be heard while the fish is in the air. Aquarists have often learned of the flying and jumping abilities of these fishes by finding them on the floor several feet away from an uncovered aquarium. There are about nine species in this group of characids; they occur from Panama south through tropical South America to the mouth of the Rio La Plata.

Several of the characids have odd swimming habits. Some, such as the tailstander, *Poecilobrycon eques,* swim with their heads up; some, such as the headstander, *Abramites,* normally swim with their heads down; and others, such as *Anostomus,* may occasionally even feed while upside down. At San Francisco's Steinhart Aquarium, *Anostomus anostomus* has been seen to scrape mucus from the backs of Australian lungfish, often standing on its back to do so. Characids that swim with their heads downward usually have terminal mouths and are bottom grubbers: for example, those of the genus *Chilodus.* However, some of the headstanders, such as *Abramites* and *Anostomus,* that have their mouths at the top or almost at the top of their snouts apparently scrape algae or other organisms from rocks and plants. With the mouth in this position it seems to be quite convenient, and perhaps occasionally even necessary, for these fishes to feed while turned over on their backs.

Poecilobrycon eques belongs to a group of some nine small, slender South American characids known as pencil fishes. This species and one other member of the genus stand on their tails. The reason for this behavior is unknown—all the other species in this group manage very nicely swimming in a horizontal manner. The pencil fishes are beautiful, peaceful little creatures and make extremely good aquarium fishes.

The genus *Leporinus* is a large one of some forty species, most of which are confined to the Amazon basin. As adults, some reach a length of 18 inches. Although they do well in captivity and live for a number of years, they are somewhat belligerent and are constantly picking at something. The presence of a leafy vegetable, such as lettuce, provides both food and decoy material, preventing *Leporinus* from nipping at its companions in the tank. The banded

Leporinus fasciatus is one of the most spectacular species. Its courting pattern, as observed at San Francisco's Steinhart Aquarium, begins when the fishes are about 8 inches in length, with a pair circling widely around the tank. An entire loss of the red color on the undersurface of the body easily distinguishes these courting fishes from the others.

The African genus *Distichodus* includes more than two dozen fairly belligerent, deep-bodied characids, many of which are brightly colored and herbivorous. The banded distichodus, *Distichodus sexfasciatus* (Plate 9), has been imported in recent years and has found some popularity with tropical fish fanciers. It is of interest to note that Hawaii has been studying these fishes with an eye to the possibility of introducing them into fresh-water canals to keep down the growth of aquatic weeds.

Perhaps one of the most interesting things about the fishes of the family Characidae is the fact that anatomically many of them resemble fishes of other groups and families. For example, there are characids that look and act like trout, some that look like North American darters, and one tiny species that looks like a salt-water herring. There is one, *Ichthyoelephas*—meaning elephant fish—that looks something like a sucker (family Catostomidae). There is a blind characid, *Anoptichthys jordani,* living in caves in Mexico, that looks much like the blind African barb, which is in another family. Some of the strangest species have no counterparts in the fish world. For example, one large-scaled African characid named *Phago* has a flattened head and beaklike jaws with which it feeds on the scales and fins of other larger fishes. Some cichlids also feed this way, but they do not look at all like *Phago*. The South American characids of the genus *Paradon* have comblike teeth and a mouth where one would expect the chin to be; they apparently scrape their food from the bottom. Characids of the genus *Curimata* have toothless mouths and look very much like marine and brackish-water mullets; they also probably feed in the same way as mullets.

The breeding habits of most characids are not unusual. The majority of them scatter eggs, which vary in their adhesive qualities, among aquatic plants and tree roots, then leave the eggs and young to fend for themselves. In many small characids, such as *Hyphessobrycon callistus* (Plate 11), the male drives the female into a thicket of plants, where she drops from five to ten eggs at a time at intervals of several minutes until all her ripe eggs have been extruded; this process usually requires one to three hours. Many of the larger characids, such as species of *Leporinus,* are reported to undergo seasonal migrations, spawning near the headwaters of streams. During these migrations small streams often become almost choked with fishes.

Banded Leporinus (*Leporinus fasciatus*); fresh water; Guianas through the Amazon basin to the La Plata River (Gene Wolfsheimer).

A few of the characids, however, have very strange spawning behavior. One species, the 1½-inch *Copeina arnoldi,* for example, is reported to lay its eggs out of the water. The breeding pair jump out of the water together, landing perhaps on a rock or a leaf along the shore of a small forest brook or stream. The female, with her fins locked to those of the male, extrudes from six to twelve eggs in a small gelatinous mass on the leaf or rock; then the parents fall back into the water. This process is repeated several times at the same site until all the eggs have been laid, forming a clump about two inches in diameter, all joined together. The male then assumes the duty of keeping the eggs wet by splashing water over them with his tail about every ten to fifteen minutes. After three days the eggs hatch and the young fall into the water. Apparently the male does not guard the young.

By way of summation, it may be noted that the beautiful and exotic characids are in a large measure responsible for the popularity of the multimillion-dollar tropical fish hobby all over the world. To some extent, this is also true of the next family, which contains the gymnotid eels or knifefishes.

GYMNOTID EELS, KNIFEFISHES, and THE ELECTRIC EEL—Family Gymnotidae

This bizarre group of streamlined fishes is anatomically similar to the characids in certain fundamental respects, but much more elongated and without dorsal and ventral fins. Although the gymnotids are obviously related to the characids, there are no known intermediate forms. In spite of the name "eel" which is applied to a number of these fishes, they are not, of course, true eels. An increasingly large number of fishes in this family have been found to have electric organs which enable them to establish electrical fields around their bodies as an aid in the location of enemies, obstacles, and food. The number of discharge impulses per second of these organs may be as high as a thousand, as in the case of *Apteronotus albifrons*.

The gymnotids are usually easy to recognize by such features as: (1) the cylindrical to ribbon-like body, (2) small, beady eyes; (3) a slender, usually pointed, tail with or without a fin; (4) the absence of a true dorsal fin with fin rays; and (5)—the most important factor—the long, undulating, anal fin, which extends along the underside of the body for three-fourths to four-fifths of the length of the fish. This long fin is responsible for the great mobility of

Electric Eel (*Electrophorus electricus*); fresh water; central and northwestern South America; hands indicate length of abdominal cavity (Fritz Goro: *Life* Magazine, at New York Aquarium).

the gymnotids; it enables them to move forward or backward and up or down with equal ease. Some of these fishes have a long, slender, and highly mobile tail that extends beyond the anal fin and is used as a tactile organ, enabling the fish to "feel" its way backward, where it obviously cannot see. For example, in an aquarium, a knifefish often establishes a daytime hide-out between rocks or among dense plants. The presence of live food causes it to emerge head-first from this abode to attack the food; after having eaten, it moves back into its lair tail first, propelled by the rippling anal fin.

Having the vital organs in the anterior end of its body serves the knifefish as a natural protective measure against its many enemies. A predator can bite a large portion out of the tail of the knifefish without causing its death; because of the extremely rapid regeneration of this part of the body, the wound is quickly healed. A survey in British Guiana showed that as many as 40 per cent of adult knifefish had wounds or scars where pieces had been bitten out of their bodies by hungry enemies.

One of the most amazing aspects of the South American gymnotid eels is that an almost identical type of development has taken place in a totally unrelated family of African fishes, the elephantnose mormyrids. Some of the mormyrids and gymnotids are superficially so similar that, without studying them, one might suspect that they belonged to the same family. However, there is some dissimilarity with respect to their electrogenic powers; the African species put out a continuous electrical discharge and the South American species release a more intermittent type.

The gymnotid family as a whole ranges from Guatemala in Central America southward to the River La Plata in Argentina and Paraguay. The total number of species is probably fewer than fifty. A great deal remains to be learned of the natural history of these fishes; unfortunately none of them has ever bred in captivity.

The gymnotid eels and knifefishes may be divided into four groups, and some authorities place each of these groups in a separate family. The first group is represented by *Rhamphichthys rostratus*, a long-snouted, valuable food fish that reaches a length of 4½ feet. It is distinguished from the other gymnotids by the fact that the anal opening is on the undersurface of the head, directly below the eye, and the anal fin starts in front of the pectoral fins.

The next group, the stenarchids, includes most of the species of knifefishes. Some of these, such as *Hypopomus brevirostris*, have modified gills for aerial respiration. Knifefishes of this genus are often imported for sale to tropical fish fanciers, although

Glass Knifefish (*Eigenmannia virescens*); fresh water; northern South America south to the La Plata River (New York Zoological Society).

the collectors in South America are sometimes met by an unusual obstacle: certain groups of native Indians refuse to collect them because they believe that these fishes are the ghosts of their own ancestors. The members of the genus *Apteronotus* are of special interest, since several of them possess a long, slender, streamer-like appendage in the place of the dorsal fin. The Amazonian *Apteronotus anas* has a very broad, long snout, and looks much like the African mormyrid *Gymnarchus niloticus*. One essential difference is that *Apteronotus* has a long anal fin and no true dorsal fin, whereas *Gymnarchus* has a long dorsal fin and no anal fin.

The third group of knifefishes contains the well-known banded knifefish, *Gymnotus carapo*, one of the first species to be known to the scientific world, having been described by Linnaeus. As a full-grown adult it is about 24 inches in length and has about twenty wavy, whitish bands around the dark body. The banded knifefish is an air breather.

The fourth and final group includes only one species, the spectacular electric eel, *Electrophorus electricus*. Anatomically, the body of the electric eel, like that of the gymnotid knifefishes, seems somewhat disproportionate, for the digestive tract and all of the essential organs occupy only a small part at the front end of the body, with the distance from the tip of the snout to the vent being only about one-fifth of the total length. The remainder of the body contains the electric organs, which are so potent that the electric eel is one of the few South American fishes that has no enemies (other than man). There are two small pectoral fins which act as stabilizers. The only other fin is an extended anal, with about 350 rays, running from the vent to the tip of the tail. By means of its undulations the eel moves up or down and backward or forward with equal ease. Since it is an air breather, it must come to the sur-

face at least once every fifteen minutes, usually oftener, to get a new air supply. If not permitted to do this, the eel will drown. *Electrophorus* lacks lungs, and the gills are not used to any marked extent in respiration; instead, there are special patches of vascular tissue in the mouth that enable the fish to obtain oxygen directly from the air. This feature makes the electric eel an ideal experimental animal for neurologists and physiologists, since it can safely remain out of water for several hours if the body and inside of the mouth are kept moist.

Six hundred volts of direct current is a lot of electricity, especially when one considers that this is what a traveler might encounter while wading a shallow Brazilian stream containing 6-foot electric eels. Fortunately, the amperage of this discharge is low—only about one-half to three-fourths of an ampere, so that even six hundred volts may not necessarily be a lethal shock. Actually, the electric eel has three different kinds of batteries, and it is the main battery, filling most of the body, that puts out the high voltage. A shock from this battery consists of a train of waves, each lasting about .002 second. The first is of small magnitude, followed .005 second later by three to six more, also .005 second apart, but this time of high voltage. This main battery is used for defense and for immobilizing food before it is eaten. In addition, there is a detection type of battery, known as the bundles of Sachs, and a third distinct battery, the Hunters organ, which apparently works in conjunction with the main battery.

If a pair of electrodes attached to a voltmeter is placed on the tail of an electric eel, the fish will demonstrate a definite linear polarity, being positive toward the head and negative toward the tail, which incidentally is the reverse of the polarity found in the African electric catfish. The amount of voltage registered on the meter is proportional to the distance between the electrodes: the greater the distance, the higher the reading.

C. W. Coates, Director of the New York Aquarium and an authority on the electric eel, has recorded electrical output as high as 650 volts; however, he finds that the average maximum is around 350 volts, which is attained by the electric eel when it reaches a length of 3 feet. Further growth increases the amperage but not the voltage. This leads one to wonder about the electrogenic ability of a 9½-foot giant, the largest electric eel known.

When the electric eel is young, it has small and beady but functional eyes. As it grows older the eyes become clouded, perhaps as a result of electricity discharged by other eels. From that time on the eel must locate its food by means of its detection battery. This special battery, one of the three electric organs, sends out small but fairly constant discharges, which bounce back from any object in the area and are received by a number of pits on the eel's head. If the electric eel is in a docile mood, the discharge rate of this detection battery is twenty to thirty impulses per second. However, if the eel is excited by the presence of an unrecognized obstruction or food, the discharge rate may go up to fifty impulses per second. Experimentally, the receiving pits can be temporarily covered, with the resulting effect that the eel is unable to find its food even though it may repeatedly bump into it.

The secret of keeping electric eels alive in captivity lies partly in keeping them in water that is not changed too often. The eels apparently exude, in their own body slime, a protective antibiotic which also permeates the water. If the water is changed too often, this protection is washed away, and as a result the eels develop their own specific ulcer disease, which is usually fatal. Electric eels have not been bred in captivity, and little is known of their life history. They disappear from their usual Amazonian haunts during breeding season; later, when they return, one of the parents takes care of the young until they are 4 to 6 inches in length.

Minnows, Suckers, Loaches, and Hillstream Fishes (Group Cypriniformes)

The second major division within the ostariophysan suborder Cyprinoidea consists of the minnow-like fishes and their relatives. This very large group probably originated in southern Asia, then spread to northern Asia, Europe, and North America.

MINNOWS and CARPS—Family Cyprinidae

Any small silvery fish is usually called a "minnow" by the layman. Ichthyologically, the term should be restricted to members of the large family Cyprinidae, a predominantly fresh-water group composed mostly of small fishes. Although the majority of the cyprinids are under 18 inches in length, the size range is fairly wide, some species being adult at less than 1½ inches and others, such as the giant Indian mahseers, reaching lengths of 9 feet. The total number of species included in the family probably exceeds twelve hundred; the last major American checklist (1930) listed three hundred species for North and Central America alone. Minnows occur in all kinds of habitats throughout the temperate and tropical regions of the world with the exception of South America, Madagascar, and Australia. The species themselves range from lethargic, grubbing herbivores to hard-hitting, predaceous carnivores, the majority being omnivorous. With the approach of breeding season many cyprinid males, and in a few species females also, develop conspicuous tubercles on the head or over the entire upper surface of the body.

Minnows have soft rays without true spines; however, in some of the carps and barbs the first ray of the dorsal fin is hardened into a stiff spinelike structure, and sometimes the first ray of the anal fin is also hardened. They have toothless jaws but compensate for this by having strong throat teeth, which are very important in classification; there are a number of species so closely related that the best method of differentiation is by dissection of the throat teeth and their subsequent careful examination under a microscope. Some species have barbels around the mouth. All minnows lack the adipose fin; the scales are of the cycloid type.

Although a few native cyprinids and the carp, which has been introduced, are fished commercially in North America, as a human food resource the minnows of this continent are not nearly so important as their relatives in other parts of the world. However, they are vitally important in the aquatic economy, chiefly in that they serve as small-sized food for larger, less bony, and more edible game fishes. Also, they are used as live bait by sports fishermen to a great extent; indeed in some areas the scarcity of minnows has become so critical that fish and game authorities have had to close streams and other waters to minnow fishing. Many commercial minnow farms, some of which can produce as many as 350,000 "head" per acre, have been established to satisfy this need. In the southeastern United States the minnows usually selected for commercial production are the fathead, *Pimephales promelas;* the goldfish, *Carassius auratus;* and the golden shiner,

Notemigonus crysoleucas. In other areas different minnows are used.

Typical examples of the smaller and more attractive American minnows are members of the large genus *Notropis,* for instance the 2-inch coastal shiner, *Notropis petersoni,* and the 2½-inch sailfin shiner, *Notropis hypselopterus* (Plate 17).

Other American minnows include some interesting forms such as the 8-inch stoneroller, *Campostoma anomalum,* which is widely distributed over the eastern United States; it is noted for the fact that its very long intestine is looped many times around its air bladder. During breeding season the males develop a reddish color and conspicuous tubercles over the upper part of the body. The stoneroller is readily identified by the presence of a narrow black bar on the anal fin and one on the dorsal fin.

Of the several genera of dace, those of the genus *Chrosomus* are among the most brightly colored. The 3-inch southern red-belly dace, *Chrosomus erythrogaster,* has along the sides of the body a red stripe bordered by a darker stripe above and below. Its range is from Pennsylvania and Minnesota to Alabama.

The chubs of the genus *Hybopsis* include perhaps two dozen small fishes, the majority less than 4 inches in length. But at least one species—the plains flathead chub, *Hybopsis gracilis,* occurring through-out most of the central United States—reaches a length of 12 inches.

A number of species of minnows are found only in western North America. Typical examples of these fishes are the 12-inch split-tail, *Pogonichthys macrolepidotus,* which has a deeply forked tail with the upper lobe slightly longer than the lower and is found in the Sacramento River system of California; and the 3-foot hardhead, *Mylopharodon conocephalus,* which occurs in the same area.

Among the widely ranging European and Asiatic minnows, the golden tench, *Tinca tinca* (Plate 19), is one of the most common species. It has two barbels on the mouth and a larger number of small scales—usually between ninety-five and one hundred—along the lateral line; the number of these scales is often useful in identification. The tench usually occurs in quiet ponds where the bottom is muddy. Although an eight-pounder is a large fish, there are specimens reported to have weighed seventeen pounds at a length of some 28 inches. Because of the fact that it is sometimes considered a tasty fish by Europeans, it has been introduced at various places in the United States where these people have settled; if competition with other fishes is not too great, it readily becomes established in a new area.

Other common European cyprinids include the barbel-less, 4-inch bait minnow, *Phoxinus phoxinus,*

Blind Cave Barb (*Caecobarbus geertsi*); fresh water; caves near Thysville, lower Congo (New York Zoological Society).

Female Bitterling (*Rhodeus sericeus*) depositing eggs in living clam; fresh water; central and eastern Europe (J. J. Duyvene de Wit).

which has a series of vertical, blackish bars on the sides; and the eight- to ten-pound chub, *Leuciscus cephalus,* which is a surface-dwelling river species, often a favorite of anglers but disdained by chefs. Also common are the two- to four-pound roach, *Rutilus rutilus,* which is a slow, muddy-water fish and one of the few cyprinids occasionally found in brackish water; and the 6-inch gudgeon, *Gobio gobio,* which is a two-barreled species usually found on the bottom; *Gobio* takes the baited hook readily, and at one time was the object of small established fisheries.

The old-world barbs are a very large group that has become widely known through the importation of many of the smaller, more attractive species for sale to the tropical-fish hobbyists. Among these are the tiger barb, *Puntius hexazona* (Plate 16), from Sumatra and the Malay Peninsula; the Sumatran barb, *Puntius tetrazona* (Plate 18), from Sumatra and Borneo; and Schwanenfeld's barb, *Puntius schwanenfeldi* (Plate 20), from the Borneo-to-Thailand area. Many species of barbs have been successfully bred in the aquarium; they seem to follow a fairly typical pattern of scattering their adhesive eggs around through a planted area; since the parents often eat the eggs, the adults are usually removed to other tanks after spawning.

The largest members of the minnow family are the Indian mahseers, of which there are a number of species; they are noted for their game-fish qualities as well as for their edibility. *Puntius* (*Tor*) *putitoria* is the largest species, reaching a length of 9 feet; since it has only about twenty-five scales along the lateral line, a fish of this size has individual scales almost large enough to cover the entire palm of the hand. Some of the mahseers have a fantastic development of very fleshy lips, which may be present in some individuals and absent in others of the same species collected in the same area.

The rasboras are another well-known group of Asiatic minnows. The 2-inch Malayan *Rasbora heteromorpha* is one of the most popular species; it is easily recognized by a characteristic black triangle on the posterior part of the body, the apex of the triangle being pointed toward the tail.

Aquarists are familiar with the genus *Labeo* through the importation of such species as the 4-inch "red-tailed black shark," *Labeo bicolor,* which has a brilliant red tail contrasted with a midnight-black color on the rest of the body. Equally attractive is the 12- to 24-inch Indonesian "black shark," *Labeo* (*Morulius*) *chrysophekadion,* which has a very high dorsal fin and a velvety black body. Aquarists consider these to be very beautiful fishes but sometimes not worth the bother of keeping, since they mutilate everything around them, including plants and other fishes. The genus *Labeo* is a large one with many species, ranging from Africa through Asia to Indonesia.

The strangest reproductive habits among the cyprinids are undoubtedly those of the Central European bitterling, *Rhodeus sericeus,* a rather deep-bodied species that reaches a length of about 3½ inches. The female develops a long ovipositor which at breeding season allows the eggs to be passed into the mantle cavity of one of the fresh-water clams or mussels. The eggs incubate and hatch within the living clam. The species of clam used is apparently unimportant—experimental studies have shown that at least two species of American clams will also serve as the host incubator. In Japan there is a related species, *Acheilognathus lanceolata,* that has similar reproductive habits.

Is the carp a curse or a blessing? In any discussion involving this ubiquitous fish, this is a question that is never entirely settled. To the sports fisherman it is certainly a curse, for in many areas it has entirely taken over the habitat to the exclusion of other more edible and sporting species that were previously present. And yet in those areas of the world where low-cost protein is scarce, if pond water is available, the carp is indeed a blessing because of its ease of cultivation. An idea of the productiveness of these fishes can be gained from data concerning pond-fish cultivation: a one-acre pond planted with carp and fertilized by farm manures can produce more than one thousand pounds of fish in a given time, whereas the same pond planted with American large-mouth black bass and a forage fish will produce less than two hundred pounds of the game fish in the same period of time.

The common carp, *Cyprinus carpio,* was originally native to the region from the Black and Caspian seas to Turkestan; from there it has spread by introduction through most of the temperate waters of the world. The carp has four barbels, two at each side of the mouth; these barbels are lacking on the somewhat similar goldfish. Hybrids between carp and goldfish are common; they usually have very small barbels. Carp usually have thirty-two to thirty-eight scales along the lateral line, whereas goldfishes usually have twenty-five to thirty-one. Both carp and goldfish have a large spine at the front of the anal fin and one in front of the dorsal fin; each of

these spines is serrated along its posterior edge. Although carp are mature at 12 inches, they have been known to grow as large as 40 inches and to weigh up to sixty pounds.

The Japanese have developed a golden carp that is a spectacular show fish. Several kinds of aberrant carps are recognized: the most common of these are the mirror carp, in which the abnormally large scales are limited to one or two rows along the sides of the body, and the leather carp, which is a scaleless form.

The nondescript wild goldfish, *Carassius auratus,* sometimes called johnny carp, Missouri minnow, and incorrectly cruscian carp, or in Japan, funa, is a rather plain, brownish, carplike species from which down through the ages all of the present-day goldfish varieties have been developed, either by natural selection or by artificial breeding. Many different types of domestic goldfish are recognized, a number

Carp (*Cyprinus carpio*); fresh water; world-wide through introduction (Otto Croy).

of the varieties having been pioneered by the Japanese. The comet, with its normal V tail, is one of the simpler types; in the United States young fish of this kind are widely distributed to pet and variety stores and usually sold for about twenty-five cents. The veiltail (Plate 21), which has a characteristic three-lobed tail, is another inexpensive, common variety. The blackmoor is a velvety black species with a veil tail and bulbous "pop eyes" that extend out from the head. The celestial telescopes usually have the typical goldfish coloration; they do not have a dorsal fin and the lenses of the bulbous eyes are

Celestial Telescope Goldfish (*Carassius auratus*); fresh water; one of many special varieties developed by aquarists (Wilhelm Hoppe).

rotated so that they look upward although the fish is swimming forward. The lionheads also lack the dorsal fin and have thick, tumorous-appearing material over the forepart of the head. Some of these highly aberrant varieties are difficult to raise, and perfect specimens are sometimes worth several hundred dollars.

SUCKERS—Family Catostomidae

The suckers are chiefly an American family and are usually bottom-grubbing fishes. Their fins are arranged in a manner so similar to that of the minnows that identification may at times be difficult, especially since some of the one hundred or more described species look like minnows and some of the minnows also look like suckers. Both suckers and minnows have toothless jaws; but, generally speaking, the minnow's mouth is at the end of the head whereas that of the sucker—a highly protrusible,

sucking mouth surrounded by large, fleshy lips—is usually located on the underside of the head. One of the principal differences in the two families is in the arrangement of the pharyngeal teeth, which must be removed by dissection in order to be studied. The suckers usually have one row of ten or more fairly fine teeth along the last gill arch, whereas the minnows have fewer teeth in a single row, but sometimes may have two or occasionally three rows, depending upon the species. Hubbs and Lagler, in their book *Fishes of the Great Lakes Region* (Cranbrook Institute of Science, 1958), have worked out a good scheme for differentiating the American suckers from the American minnows. Their rule is that if the distance from the front of the anal fin to the snout is more than two and one-half times the distance from the front of the anal fin to the tail fin, the fish is a sucker; if the first distance is less than two and one-half times the second, the fish is a minnow. One exception to this rule is the carp, which belongs to the minnow family; however, it can be distinguished from the suckers by the spine in front of the dorsal fin.

The three species of buffalo fishes look more like carp or goldfish than they do like suckers; this is especially true of the 3-foot largemouth buffalo fish, *Ictiobus cyprinellus*, which has a terminal mouth. This species is fairly common through the central part of the United States.

The quillback carpsucker, *Carpiodes cyprinus*, one of four species in the genus, can be identified by its long, flagpole-like second dorsal ray, which is about twice as long as the other rays. It ranges through the central and eastern part of the United States and is harvested commercially in Lake Erie and other sections. It is a fairly large species, reaching a length of about 26 inches and a weight of about twelve pounds.

The redhorse suckers of the genus *Moxostoma* include more than two dozen American species. In all of them the upper lip is very protractile and the lower lip is continuous, with no division in the center. The blacktail redhorse, *Moxostoma poecilurum*, from the coastal streams of the Gulf of Mexico, is one of the most interesting forms; the lower lobe of its tail fin is black and is longer than the upper lobe.

The flannelmouth sucker, *Catostomus latipinnis*, from the Colorado River drainage, is a typical member of the genus *Catostomus*, which is the largest group of suckers in the western part of the United States. Some members of this genus grow as large as 2 feet.

One of the most easily identified suckers is the 18-inch spotted sucker, *Minytrema melanops*, which has a black spot on each individual scale; it ranges through the larger streams of the eastern United States.

The 2-foot humpback sucker, *Xyrauchen texanus,* which lives throughout the Colorado River Basin, has been confronted with the same problem as the Indian hillstream fishes—that of trying to hold its position in a fast current—but instead of developing sucking devices, it has solved the problem in a different manner. The profile behind the head rises abruptly to form an inverted, boatlike keel above the body. As the swift waters of the river pass over *Xyrauchen's* body, they hydrodynamically tend to push it against the substrate; thus, the result is the same as that accomplished by the complicated sucking devices of other fishes. There are very few suckers in Asia, but one of these, the Chinese *Myxocyprinus asiaticus,* has a high-keeled back similar to that of *Xyrauchen.*

LOACHES—Family Cobitidae

The loaches are small, usually elongated, Old World fishes with six to twelve barbels around the mouth; some of them resemble catfishes, but instead of the typical catfish spines, they have soft-rayed fins, usually with few rays. Some have a movable spine either in front of each eye or below it; the function of this spine is as yet unknown. Although they lack jaw teeth, they usually have pharyngeal teeth. The scales are small and sometimes difficult to see. Because of their method of intestinal respiration, some loaches are able to survive in oxygen-deficient water that would be lethal to other species; they swallow air, and as it passes through their digestive tracts, they absorb oxygen from it.

A number of these loaches, including several species in the genus *Botia,* are popular with aquarists. The clown loach, *Botia macracanthus* (Plate 15), from Borneo and Sumatra, is a brilliantly colored orange species with three black bands around the vertically compressed body. Like other members of the genus, it has beneath each eye a sharp, movable, knifelike spine, the point of which is directed toward the tail of the fish. The clown loach is a very hardy species noted for its habit of uprooting the vegetation in a tank. In captivity it survives for as long as twenty-five years; although reported to reach a length of 12 inches, in the average aquarium it seldom grows much larger than 3 or 4 inches. The banded loach, *Botia hymenophysa,* is gray with a series of more than twenty narrow, dark bands around the body; it ranges from Thailand through Indonesia and reaches a maximum length of about 1 foot.

The coolie loach, *Acanthophthalmus kuhli,* is a common 3½-inch multibanded, snakelike species found throughout the Thailand-to-Java region; it has six barbels around the mouth and a short spine in front of each eye. At times it has been imported in tremendous numbers for the tropical-fish trade. Several other species of the same genus are occasionally imported from the same areas; among these is the half-banded coolie loach, *A. semicinctus,* a species in which the bands are in the form of saddles that do not extend below the midline.

The 4-inch spotted weatherfish or spined loach, *Cobitis taenia,* has six barbels, and belongs to another genus in which there is also a hinged spine beneath each eye. It has a wide temperature tolerance, surviving easily in water ranging from 40 to 80 degrees F. This species has been divided into a number of subspecies throughout its range—from Britain and western Europe to China. Careful genetic studies have shown the existence of several distinct physiological strains, some of which produce partially sterile male offspring. For spawning purposes the spined loach sometimes selects an area where the bottom is muddy; the eggs are scattered over the bottom and later covered with mud by the swimming activity of the parents. In Japan there is a similar spotted species, *Cobitis biwae,* that is sometimes used as food; in the past it was imported in great numbers into the United States, where it became a popular aquarium fish.

The European weatherfish, *Misgurnus fossilis,* is apparently more sensitive to changes in barometric pressure than are the other loaches; this sensitivity is shown by its increased activity, which has often been cited as a harbinger of stormy weather. Although the weatherfish may reach a length of almost 20 inches, the average size of those encountered is 8 to 10 inches; in captivity it may survive for as long as twenty-two years.

GYRINOCHEILIDS—Family Gyrinocheilidae

Gyrinocheilus aymonieri is a remarkable 10-inch hillstream-type herbivore that was originally classified as a loach, then as a minnow, then in both families at the same time, and finally in a separate family, as is done here. This strange fish occurs in Thailand and adjacent areas, and there is one other slightly larger species, *G. pustulosus,* in Borneo. *Gyrinocheilus* has a peculiar method of respiration, in that it does not bring water in through the mouth as most fishes do. The external gill openings are divided into an upper section and a lower section; water enters the upper section through a special inhalant channel by which it passes to the pharynx and then comes back over the gills and out the lower section. Only one other type of fish is known to have a similar breathing arrangement: this is a high-mountain catfish of the genus *Arges,* found in the South American Andes. The respiratory rate of *Gyrinocheilus* is extremely rapid, having been recorded as high as 230 to 240 times per minute in a 5-inch fish. This method of breathing is of great advantage to the fish: since the mouth is not needed for respiration, it can be used to browse continually or to hold onto rocks in the swift mountain streams in which *Gyrinocheilus* often lives. This family is easily recognized by the large, fleshy lip surrounding the forward part of the jaw; this lip reminds one of the mammalian lip structure of the dugong and the manatee.

HILLSTREAM FISHES—Family Homalopteridae

The homalopterids are small fresh-water fishes from southern and eastern Asia and the Indo-Australian archipelago. They generally have rounded heads and streamlined bodies adapted to life on the bottom in very swift mountain streams. To avoid being swept downstream, they have had to develop a special method of holding onto rocks and other protuberances. This has been accomplished by the development of a large sucking disk on the underside of the fish; the margins of the disk are formed by the pectoral and ventral fins, which extend laterally from the body, thus aiding in providing a cuplike undersurface. These fishes build up a semivacuum between the substrate and the underside of their bodies by means of a pumping action of the pectoral fins, which removes the water under the body. The sucking disk is carried to its greatest development in the genus *Gastromyzon,* found in Borneo and China; the ventral fins of these fishes are continuous along their inner margins and have a large number of rays. Most other genera have separate ventrals with fewer rays. The hillstream fishes are similar to the loaches in many respects; although they lack the movable spine in front of the eye, they do have at least three pairs of barbels around the mouth. The gill openings are small, often placed fairly high on the sides of the body. The anal and dorsal fins are small and short and, like the other fins, are not equipped with spines. A single series of eight or more pharyngeal teeth is present. The scales are very small and of the cycloid type.

Many of the homalopterids are noted for their intermittent respiration; they breathe steadily for a period of time, then stop for an interval of variable length. Dissection reveals that many of these intermittent breathers have water-storage compartments formed by enlargement of the pharynx and gill cavities. As a result of this enlargement to form a water reservoir, the usable portion of the external gill openings is reduced to the upper section only.

On the basis of the branching of the rays of the pectoral and ventral fins, the hillstream fishes are divided into two subfamilies (or according to some specialists, two families): (1) the Gastromyzoninae, with only the first ray of the pectorals and ventrals undivided, and (2) the Homaloptinae, with two to five of the anterior rays of the ventral and pectoral fins undivided. The entire group probably includes fewer than fifty species.

Catfishes *(Suborder Siluroidea)*

Catfishes are usually easy to identify because the majority have barbels or feelers extending from each side of the upper jaw, and some also have them on the lower jaw. Although catfishes do not have scales, a number do have bony, platelike armor covering the outside of the body. Spines are often present at the front of the dorsal and pectoral fins; these spines may be saw-toothed and may carry venom glands. Certain species have an adipose fin, which may or may not be preceded by a spine, on the back between the dorsal and tail fins. Because catfishes are very popular with the tropical-fish hobbyists, a wealth of detailed descriptions and life histories of them have been written; many of these will be found in the various aquarium texts listed in the bibliography.

The specialists have many contradictory viewpoints on the classification of the catfishes, so that the number of families in the entire group may range from twenty-five to thirty-one for the more than two thousand species of these fishes known to science. Although not a strictly scientific classification scheme, a division of the catfishes into armored and naked species seems advisable for our purposes. Hence, the three principal families of armored catfishes will be discussed first and the naked catfishes second.

ARMORED CATFISHES

DORADID CATFISHES—Family Doradidae

The four- to six-whiskered, fat-bodied doradids are a South American group noted for their heavy armor, which is composed of a single series of overlapping plates along the sides of the body; the individual plates are usually festooned with hooks and other ornate bucklers. These appurtenances as well as the arrangement of the scales serve to differentiate the doradids from the smooth-armored callichthyids and loricariids, some of which are similar in appearance. Aquarists are familiar with doradids through the activities of the 8-inch talking catfish, *Acanthodoras spinosissimus,* noted for the grunting sounds it produces both in and out of the water. The sounds are apparently the result of activity of the air bladder in conjunction with the motion of the pectoral spines. *Doras costatus* is one of the brilliantly lined species occasionally imported; it has a bright white band along the sides of the body.

CALLICHTHYID CATFISHES
—Family Callichthyidae

Catfishes belonging to the South American family Callichthyidae have smooth armor and may usually be identified by the arrangement of the armor plates in two longitudinal rows along the sides, the upper and lower rows meeting at approximately the center of the side of the body. Two short but fairly conspicuous barbels are located at each corner of the mouth, and in some species there are two more on the lower part of the mouth; spines are present at the front of the dorsal, adipose, and pectoral fins.

The large genus of arch-backed catfishes known as *Corydoras* is a popular one with the tropical-fish enthusiasts, since most of this group are under 3 inches in length and are fairly peaceful in captivity. Although not brilliantly colored, they do have interesting patterns which are useful in identification. For example, the skunk cat, *C. arcuatus,* has a black band running from the nose through the eye and over the back to the tail fin; the black-spotted corydoras, *C. melanistius,* has a blackish area on the front of the head and extending through the eye, and also a black base on the dorsal fin; the leopard corydoras, *C. julii,* has a reticulated pattern formed of many small lines. All the above catfishes spend most of their time on the bottom where catfishes usually stay; however, there is a renegade in the genus—the pigmy corydoras, *C. hastatus,* a magnificent dwarf of 1½ inches. It has a black line through the eye straight down the side to the center part of the tail fin. This species spends a large portion of its time in schooling formation at the center level of the tank, well off the bottom. Among European aquarists this is one of the most popular of the tropical catfishes; it has not achieved this degree of favor in America.

Members of the genus *Callichthys* lack the rounded-head profile of *Corydoras,* and they grow to be somewhat larger. The hassar, *Callichthys callichthys,* reaches a length of 8 inches and is of interest because it refuses to spawn in captivity until a simulated tropical shower is poured on the surface of the tank.

The long-whiskered catfish, *Dianema longibarbis,* looks much like a cross between a *Corydoras* and a *Callichthys.* One of its distinguishing marks is its very flat head.

LORICARIID CATFISHES—Family Loricariidae

The South American loricariid catfishes are usually completely covered with smooth armor formed by overlapping plates, and some of them have peculiar body shapes. An example of this is the very rare striped sailback, *Panaque nigrolineatus* (Plate 22), from Venezuela and Ecuador. Equally strange are the long, slender-bodied twig catfishes of the genus *Farlowella.* Like most of the loricariid catfishes,

Armored Catfish (*Corydoras caquetae*); fresh water; upper Amazon (Frans Gabler).

Farlowella has a high dorsal fin and a V-shaped tail fin with the outer ray of the upper lobe sometimes much longer than the corresponding ray of the lower lobe. The platelike suctorial lips surround the mouth, which is located on the underside of the head. This type of mouth structure is well adapted for vegetarian feeding; the jaw teeth have bilobed or spoon-shaped tips which effectively scrape algae and other minute plant life from rocks and bottom rubble. However, this restricted diet presents problems for the aquarist attempting to keep these fishes alive in captivity; in some cases the feeding problem has been solved by using chopped spinach and other leafy vegetables.

At first glance the loricariid sucking catfishes of the genus *Otocinclus* look very much like some of the

North American minnows. Their habits, however, are entirely different from those of the minnows; they spend most of their time hanging on plants, usually in a vertical position. The pelvic fins and the suctorial disk around the mouth act as aids in holding the fish to the plants.

Heavy-bodied loricariids of the genus *Plecostomus* are often a favorite of the tropical-fish fancier; although some of these fishes grow as large as 15 or 20 inches, the average maximum size in a small tank is around 4 or 5 inches. It is of interest to note that

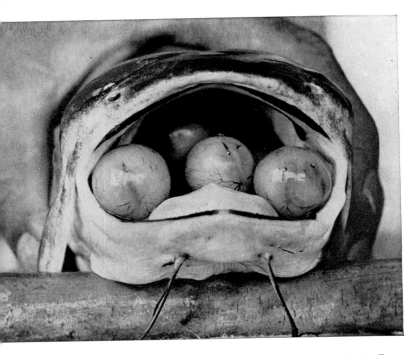

Incubation of eggs in the mouth of the male Gafftopsail Catfish (*Bagre marinus*); marine; Cape Cod to Gulf of Mexico (E. W. Gudger).

baked *Plecostomus* is a favorite food among some of the South American Indian tribes.

Dense barbels are commonplace among some of the members of this family. Certain species of the genus *Ancistrus* have veritable brush piles on top of the snout and around the mouth; another species, *Pareiorhaphis regani,* has slender, bony spines extending straight out, laterally, from the sides of the head; and finally, *Pseudacanthicus histrix* has long, brushlike spines extending outward from the forward edges of the heavy pectoral spines.

NAKED CATFISHES

BANJO CATFISHES—*Family Aspredinidae*

The South American banjo cats are so called because when viewed from the top they look exactly like banjos. Their bony heads sometimes give them the appearance of being partially armored. These are small nocturnal fishes that show little movement during the daytime, when they normally hide in aquatic vegetation and under dead leaves. However, at night and in total darkness they swim actively over the bottom searching for food. *Aspredinichthys tibicen,* from the Guianas, has a very interesting method of brooding the eggs, which is not used by all members of the family. The female incubates the eggs by carrying them about attached to the underside of her body; the eggs are actually anchored to spongy tentacles which develop on the female's abdomen during the breeding season. The head and abdomen of *Aspredinichthys* are both very short, followed by a tail more than three times the length of the forward part of the body; at the end of the tail is a small forked tail fin. The long anal fin runs the complete length of this posterior portion of the body. The adipose fin is lacking, as in all members of the family. All of the typical banjo cats are fresh-water species; however, as pointed out recently for the first time by Stanford's Professor George Myers, there are several species of *Aspredinichthys*-type cats that are brackish- and salt-water species.

The 5-inch two-colored banjo cat, *Bunocephalus coracoideus,* is one of the few aspredinids that have spawned in captivity. The spawning site in one case was a hollow spot in the sand; two spawnings at this same site yielded between four and five thousand fry, which grew rapidly on a diet of rotifers.

ARIID MARINE CATFISHES—*Family Ariidae*

My introduction to the incubation method of the ariid catfishes occurred one day when I visited a fish trap on the shore of the large lake known as Laguna de Bay on the Philippine island of Luzon. I picked up a big Kanduli catfish, *Arius dispar,* by the tail and was astounded to see a number of eggs the size of marbles roll out of its mouth. The size of the eggs was amazing, for—dependent upon the species—they may be as large as $5/8$ or even $7/8$ of an inch in diameter. In all, some forty species of ariid marine catfishes have been recorded as incubating their eggs in the mouth. This is strictly a male function, although in at least one species an occasional female will also incubate eggs in this same manner. Normally, brooding of the eggs takes place in salt water, but it can also occur in fresh water, again dependent upon the species.

Dr. James Atz has described observations made at the New York Aquarium on oral incubation in the sea catfish, *Galeichthys felis,* a small species known on the American Atlantic coast from Cape Cod to Panama. The onset of breeding season, usually in

June or July, is shown by the development of a thickened, triangular, hooklike flap on the inside margin of each of the ventral fins of the female. These are thought to have some function in either temporarily holding or carrying the eggs. Some time later, egg-laying takes place at night, but neither this nor the fertilization of the eggs has ever been observed; nor has the male been observed picking up the eggs. All that is known is that the male carries up to fifty-five eggs in his mouth for the next month before hatching takes place; then for two additional

PLOTOSID MARINE CATFISHES
—Family Plotosidae

The colorful marine catfish *Plotosus anguillaris* is one of the most dangerous fishes found on the tropical reefs of the entire Indo-Pacific region, death often resulting from contact with its fin spines. There are perhaps two dozen species in the family, but whether the others share the poisonous qualities of *P. anguillaris* is not known. The single dorsal and paired pectoral spines are each equipped along the

Eel Catfish (*Channallabes apus*); fresh water; Congo (Gene Wolfsheimer).

weeks he holds the youngsters in his mouth—all this time forsaking food.

The ariid marine catfishes are a tropical and subtropical group, world-wide in distribution, and they are often used as food fishes. Unlike many of the fresh-water cats, they do not spend their time resting on the bottom, but are always on the move, often in schooling formation. They have four to six barbels around the mouth, and the usual complement of predorsal and pectoral spines; they also have an adipose fin. However, they differ from other catfishes in that the anterior and posterior nostrils are close together, the latter covered by a valve.

The cleaned skull of an ariid catfish viewed from the underside often has the appearance of a cross, sometimes with the figure of a man superimposed. In the West Indies and along the coasts of South America these skulls are often sold to gullible tourists as native religious objects of sacred value.

sides with venom glands and are capable of causing extremely painful wounds, even with slight contact. Since these fishes often form schools in shallow coastal waters as well as in estuaries and rivers, they are a constant menace to the unwary fisherman or swimmer.

Plotosus anguillaris has eight barbels around the mouth and a pointed tail formed by the confluence of the long second dorsal and the anal fins; the first dorsal has only a few rays, usually four or five, but the second dorsal and anal fins each have eighty to one hundred rays. Average size of the adult is about 10 to 12 inches, although in Ceylon and South Africa they are recorded as reaching a length of 30 inches. The young of *P. anguillaris* has two bright yellow bands extending from head to tail, one above and one below the eye.

Members of the genus *Plotosus* have, behind the vent, a small, treelike structure which is connected

[125

by a ligament to one of the vertebrae. The function of this structure is still a mystery.

Study of this poison-spined catfish in Japan has revealed that the spawning season occurs during July and August, with the eggs being deposited in cracks and crevices of rocks in very shallow water. There are conflicting reports of the edibility of *Plotosus:* in Japan the taste of the flesh is considered very poor, but in South Africa it is reported excellent.

CLARIID CATFISHES—*Family Clariidae*

Clariids differ from other catfishes in having an auxiliary breathing apparatus contained in a pocket that extends back and upward from the gill cavity;

the treelike breathing organs in this special pocket are attached to the second and fourth gill arches, and are undoubtedly responsible for the ability of the clarids to live out of water much longer than other catfishes. Most of the fishes in this family with some exceptions, do not have an adipose fin nor do they have a spine in front of the usually long dorsal fin, which in some species may actually be attached to the tail fin. The anal fin is also extremely long. The only spines are those of the pectoral fins. Around the mouth are four pairs of barbels rather than the two or three pairs usully found in other catfishes. These fishes are widely distributed from Africa to the East Indian archipelago, and in recent

Wels (*Silurus glanis*); fresh water; central and eastern Europe and western Asia (Otto Croy).

Glass Catfish (*Ompok bimaculatus*); fresh water; India to Indonesia (Gene Wolfsheimer).

years at least one species, *Clarias batrachus,* has been introduced into Guam and the Hawaiian Islands and has become established there. This is a rather hardy fish; it reaches a length of some 16 inches and in captivity lives for a number of years.

The strangest members of the family are the West African eelcats, *Gymnallabes typus* and *Channallabes apus,* which are specialized fishes with the very long dorsal (98 to 150 rays) and anal fins (82 to 130 rays) continuous with the tail fin. At maximum size they are about 1 foot in length, with a very slender body no thicker than a lead pencil. *Channallabes* is the more slender of the two; it may be distinguished from *Gymnallabes* by the fact that it lacks the ventral fins.

SILURID CATFISHES—Family Siluridae

The silurid catfishes are similar to the clariids in that they lack the spine in front of the dorsal fin, but they differ in having a very short dorsal fin, usually with five or fewer rays; in some genera the dorsal fin is entirely lacking. The adipose fin is also missing. The very long anal fin is usually the silurid's most important means of locomotion; normally it is separate from the tail fin, but in the Malayan and Sumatran *Silurichthys* it is continuous with the tail fin. The ventral fins are small and inconspicuous, and in the Bornean *Apodoglanis* are entirely lacking. There are two pairs of barbels, but the lower pair may be poorly developed. These catfishes are fresh-water inhabitants, and they are limited to the Old World from Europe and Africa to Indonesia.

One of the largest known catfishes, the European wels, *Silurus glanis,* belongs to the family Siluridae; it is a giant species, said to reach a length of almost 13 feet and a weight of about 650 pounds. Aquarists are familiar with the silurids through the popular

glass catfishes, a transparent group belonging principally to the genus *Kryptopterus,* found in the Malay-Indonesian region. The 3-inch *Kryptopterus bicirrhus,* a species with some seventy rays in the anal fin and only one ray in the dorsal fin, is the favored species of the tropical-fish hobbyists. *Ompok bimaculatus* is another type of glass catfish sometimes encountered by the aquarist. It is found in the same areas as *Kryptopterus* but grows to a length of 18 inches and is more belligerent. One of the most picturesque species is the Sumatran *Hemisilurus moolenburghi;* in the male the maxillary barbels are short and stiff like a waxed mustache, but in the female the same barbels are much longer and have three to five threadlike filaments branching from the end of their expanded tips.

PIMELODID CATFISHES
—Family Pimelodidae

This group of catfishes ranges all the way from Mexico southward through most of South America; it is the largest family of catfishes in South America. Typically, the pimelodids have very long feelers or barbels, usually in three pairs; the adipose fin is present, and there are spines in front of the dorsal and pectoral fins; the teeth are numerous and comblike. Included in this family are some spectacular flat-headed cats of such genera as *Sorubim* and *Pseudoplatystoma;* in these fishes, the long whiskers, often as long as the body itself, extend forward from the thin, flattened head. *Goslinia platynema* appears to be a form intermediate between the flat-headed catfishes and the typical heavier-bodied pimelodelids. Of considerable interest is the inclusion within the family of a blind cave catfish, *Typhlobagrus kronei,* from the Caverna das Areias, São Paulo, Brazil. In this same region there is a closely related eyed spe-

Tiger Catfish (*Pseudoplatystoma fasciatum*); fresh water; Venezuela to Uruguay (New York Zoological Society).

cies, *Pimelodella transitoria,* living at the surface; this is suspected of being the parent species of the blind *Typhlobagrus.*

Although pimelodids are sometimes imported for the tropical-fish hobbyists, they usually require much space and in a community tank they tear up the plants and attack all the other fishes. One of these is *Pimelodus clarias,* which ranges from Panama to the La Plata River; it has a distinctive spotted and reticulated pattern on the sides and reaches a length of 1 foot. The 3-inch bumblebee catfishes of the genus *Microglanis,* sometimes called harlequin or many-colored cats, have found favor with some aquarists because of their attractive color pattern, which consists of a light yellow background crossed by five or more broad, wavy, fairly irregular bands.

BAGRID CATFISHES—*Family Bagridae*

The bagrids are in some respects the Old World equivalents of the South American pimelodids; there are internal anatomical differences between the two families, but in many respects they are externally similar. The family Bagridae includes some interesting species. *Leiocassis siamensis* from Thailand is a beautiful dark brown color with four or five irregular light yellow or white bands crossing the body; there are two distinct spots, one in the center of each lobe of the tail fin. In or out of the water it is noted for its ability to make noises, which consists of emitting a series of croaking sounds. Its maximum length is about 7 inches. The striped *Mystus vittatus* is a striking 7-inch fish found throughout India, Burma, and Thailand. The stripes begin just behind

the head and extend horizontally to the tail fin; there are usually four light stripes alternating with four dark ones. This family also contains the most incredible catfish in the entire world: *Bagrichthys hypselopterus,* which lives in the rivers of Borneo and Sumatra. When full grown it measures about 16 inches, and it has a remarkable anatomical peculiarity—the spine of the dorsal fin extends obliquely upward for a distance almost equal to the length of the fish, that is, more than twelve inches on an adult fish. The function of this strange development is as much a mystery today as it was over one hundred years ago when it was first discovered.

PARASITIC CATFISHES
—*Family Trichomycteridae*

This is a South American family of small, slender, and naked catfishes that were formerly known as the pygidiids; they lack the adipose fin and have a soft-rayed, spineless dorsal fin. The opercle and pre-opercle are armed with retrorse spines, enabling them to hook themselves to any object with which they come in contact. Many of these fishes are free-living in streams. Some, however, are parasitic on other fishes, obtaining their food by eating the gill filaments and drinking the blood of the host. The infamous candiru, principally *Vandellia cirrhosa* although other species may be involved—sometimes called the only vertebrate parasite of man—is also a member of this group. This 2½-inch fish enters the urogenital openings of men and women bathers, especially if they should happen to micturate while in the water. The reason for this strange attraction is as yet unknown. There are many cases on record describing the excruciating pain resulting from the candiru's swimming up the urethra of a man or the vagina of a woman and erecting its spines. When this occurs, surgical procedures are sometimes the only solution. To guard against this insidious parasite native tribes in the areas where candirus abound wear protective devices over the genitalia when swimming or bathing.

NORTH AMERICAN CATFISHES
—Family Ictaluridae

The ictalurids are "typical" catfishes with four pairs of short barbels around the mouth, an adipose fin, and spines in front of the short dorsal and pectoral fins. The family contains fewer than fifty species, all living in North American fresh waters from Canada to Guatemala. One of the largest ictalurids is the flathead, *Pylodictis olivaris,* a square-tailed species reported to weigh as much as one hundred pounds at a length of about 5½ feet. The flathead is

found throughout the central United States, and it may be identified by the much flattened head and the lower jaw which projects beyond the upper jaw.

The smallest ictalurids are the madtoms, which are also the most dangerous because of the wounds they can inflict with their pectoral spines and associated venom glands. Most of the madtoms reach a maximum size no greater than 5 inches or even less. For example, the normal size range of the adult tadpole madtom, *Noturus gyrinus,* a common form throughout the eastern United States, is from less than 2 inches to 3½ inches. The madtoms can usually be identified by their small size as well as by their very long adipose fin and rounded tail fin; in some madtoms, including the tadpole mentioned above, these two fins are continuous.

The bullheads are square-tailed catfishes that provide the fisherman with a low-cost source of protein. The original distribution of the brown bullhead, *Ictalurus nebulosus,* was limited to the eastern half of the United States, but like other species of icta-

Yellow Bullhead (*Ictalurus natalis*); fresh water; eastern United States (John Gerard: National Audubon Society).

Spotted Upside-down Catfish (*Synodontis acanthomias*); fresh water; Congo (New York Zoological Society).

lurid catfishes, it has been widely introduced through the western part of North America as well as the Hawaiian Islands and Europe. Brown bullheads are mature at a length of about 6 inches and reach an average maximum length of perhaps 16 inches. These fishes are noted for their care of the young. After the embryos hatch and leave the nest as free-swimming juveniles, they form a dense school which is guarded by one or both of the parents. Other common bullheads include the yellow bullhead, *Ictalurus natalis,* and the black bullhead, *Ictalurus melas,* both of which can often be distinguished by their colors.

The white catfish, *Ictalurus catus,* was limited in its original distribution to the Atlantic seaboard of the United States. It is slightly larger than the brown bullhead and differs from it in several features, including a pronounced V in its tail. The channel catfish, *Ictalurus punctatus,* is a very common V-tailed ictalurid catfish, originally found through most of the central United States but subsequently introduced into many other areas. It attains a maximum length of 4 feet and a weight of fifty-seven pounds. The young have spots on the sides, but with growth the channel cat turns dark and the spots are no longer visible. As a food fish for human consumption, it is one of the most valuable North American catfishes.

SCHILBEID CATFISHES—Family Schilbeidae

Schilbeids are fresh-water Afro-Asian catfishes which have an interrupted distribution, being absent through the Near East. The family includes one of the world's largest catfishes—a giant, heavy-bodied, toothless herbivore, *Pangasianodon gigas,* which has been measured at more than 7½ feet with a weight probably around 250 pounds. Although little study has been devoted to these economically valuable fish, they are known to make spawning migrations up the Mekong River as far as the Chinese province of Yunan, where spawning is reported to take place in Lake Tali; after spawning they make the return trip down the river, some of them, fortunately, avoiding the many fishing devices set to catch them. The "trey reach" or royal fish, as the Cambodians call this giant fish, has the usual characteristics of the schilbeid catfishes: (1) a short but quite high dorsal fin of some five to seven rays, preceded by a pungent spine; (2) a very small adipose fin; (3) a forked tail; (4) a long anal fin of twenty-eight to forty rays, distinct from the tail fin; and (5) usually two or three pairs of short barbels around the mouth, occasionally four pairs in certain genera.

There are also small species in the family—for example, the 3-inch *Etropiella debauwi* from the Congo. This is a schooling form which has a flag-like dorsal fin just behind the head. There is a silvery stripe down the side of the body.

UPSIDE-DOWN CATFISHES
—Family Mochocidae

A fascinating experience is that of watching an apparently normal catfish repeatedly reversing its swimming position from right side up to upside down and back again. This is the custom of many of the catfishes belonging to the family Mochocidae, a group entirely limited to tropical African fresh waters. "Squeaker" is one of the appropriate African names sometimes applied to these fishes because of the grunting sounds they produce, which are thought to be the result of the dorsal and pectoral spines rotating in their sockets. Incidentally, the upside-down cats have a locking mechanism on these spines —an anatomical feature possessed by some but not all other catfishes. The spotted upside-down cat, *Synodontis angelicus* (Plate 24), is one of the most attractive members of the family. Courting activity in this species, as observed at San Francisco's Steinhart Aquarium, consists of a pair swimming swiftly toward each other until they collide head on; this is repeated for several minutes at intervals of about thirty seconds. In recent years *Synodontis nigriventris,* a speckled brownish species, has been imported into Europe and the United States in increasing numbers for tropical-fish fanciers. Like the other members of the family, it has a bony head and around the mouth there are six barbels, four of which are branched; there is the usual complement of fins and spines, including an adipose fin between the dorsal and tail fins.

ELECTRIC CATFISH—Family Malapteruridae

A fish more irascible than the electric catfish, *Malapterurus electricus* (Plate 23), would be difficult to find. Its pungnacity is vividly demonstrated when it is put into a tank with other fishes, of either its own kind or other species. As small fish, less than 2 inches in length, electric cats sometimes live together peacefully; but sooner or later, as they grow older, fighting begins, and thereafter they must be kept apart. The ancient Egyptians considered the electric cat a very special fish, for they inscribed its likeness in pictographs on tombs. They also used it for food, as do some present-day Africans, although others avoid the fish for fear it will affect their virility. Actually, there is only one species of this remarkable fish, and it is the only catfish known to have electrogenic powers. It ranges through tropical central Africa and the Nile valley. Its maximum length is about 4 feet, with a weight of fifty pounds. Large electric cats are capable of discharging as much as one hundred volts, which may be delivered in one major jolt followed by a series of lesser shocks. Whereas the electrical polarity of the South American electric eel is positive on the head and negative on the tail, that of the electric cat is the reverse. *Malapterurus* uses its voltage for the capture of food and the avoidance of enemies. Apparently it has no means of using the electric organs as a detection unit, as do the African mormyrids and some of the South American knifefishes. Throughout the animal kingdom, most electrogenic tissue is formed by modification of musculature. In the electric cat the electric cells are located in a layer of fatty tissue just beneath the skin, and are derived from the trapezius muscle.

Malapterurus does well in captivity, feeding readily on almost any protein food offered; however, the aquarist must guard against overfeeding, for it is a glutton and may grow obese and die of fatty degeneration.

Eels *(Order Apodes)*

With the exception of one family of fresh-water eels, all of the members of this order—at least 22 families and perhaps 350 species—are marine in habitat, the majority living in shallow water. The eels have several features which they all share in common. They lack the pelvic or ventral fins, and the dorsal and anal fins are usually continuous with the tail fin. As in the isospondylous fishes, the air bladder has an open duct to the throat. All of the eels lack scales, except for about 3 of the 22 families. Most of them have a strange, transparent, ribbon-like larval form known as a leptocephalus. Because this larva is so radically different from the adult, many leptocephali have been described but not identified with the corresponding adults. At the time of metamorphosis, the leptocephalus, which usually measures from 2 to 8 inches in length, shrinks in size and gradually changes to a smaller juvenile eel. Although most of the eel-like species of fishes are placed in this single order, it is possible that when our knowledge is more complete, several orders will be recognized. As a group, eels are usually more active at night than in the daytime.

FRESH-WATER EELS—Family Anguillidae

The anguillid eels, and especially the common European eel, *Anguilla anguilla* (Plate 30), are widely known because of their food value. Anguillids live in a variety of fresh-water habitats such as

Electric Catfish (*Malapterurus electricus*) yawning; fresh water; central western Africa (Georg Mandahl-Barth, Danmarks Akvarium).

streams, rivers, ponds, and lakes; but at spawning season they return to salt water. In the European eel this occurs when the females are about twelve years old and 5 feet long; the males, however, start their migration from fresh to salt water when they are some four to eight years old and 20 inches long. At this time the eels change from yellow to silver in color; and since they are quite fat, their value as food is then at its peak. Fisheries along the European coasts are consequently designed to catch this eel during its downstream migration. Instinctively, the adult eels head for the Sargasso Sea, a tropical-water area of pelagic marine plants extending for many miles in the region of Bermuda. When the eels finally reach their destination a year later, having traveled three thousand miles without food, they spawn at a depth of fifteen hundred feet, where the water is warm and saltier than it is in any other part of the Atlantic. The adults die after spawning, and the eggs float to the surface, where they soon hatch into leptocephalus larvae. These larvae then start on the return trip, which requires three years. During this time they metamorphose, becoming young elvers of about 3 inches by the time they reach the European streams and rivers. They usually arrive at these fresh waters in the spring of the year, although in some areas they do so from October to December.

At the time the Zuider Zee embankment was constructed no allowance was made for upstream migration of the elvers. The following spring millions of small elvers tried desperately but in vain to get over the obstruction. As a result of this and other experiences, Europeans are now taking great care to preserve the elver runs. For example, in the 1959 construction of the Hellevoetsluis Dam in the Netherlands special tunnels to allow the upstream migration of the elvers were built into the structure.

For many years the life history of the fresh-water eels was a confusing puzzle to scientists because of the fact that the American eel, *Anguilla rostrata,* spawns in almost the same area of the ocean as that used by the European eel. The problem was finally solved by the famous Danish biologist Professor Johannes Schmidt (1906), who found that the larva or leptocephalus of the American eel spent one year in making its journey to the American coast, as contrasted with the three years required by the European eel for its return trip. The American eel is often eaten by man but is not considered so much of a delicacy as the European eel. It ranges from Greenland to Labrador, southward to the Gulf of Mexico and perhaps even to Brazil, and moves as far inland as most of the mid-central states.

About sixteen species of fresh-water eels are recognized, but none is found in the eastern Pacific or South Atlantic. Their absence from these regions has been explained as due to an absence of the essential high salinity and high temperature at the proper spawning depth, as well as of suitable currents for subsequent distribution of the larvae.

The anguillids differ from most of the other eel families in the possession of scales, in this case the embedded cycloid type that are visible only on careful inspection. *Anguilla* blood, surprisingly enough, contains a powerful neurotoxin that causes a serious infection if it gets into a cut or wound when the eel is being prepared for market. The poison has not been studied.

PARASITIC SNUBNOSED EEL
—Family Simenchelidae

The only member of this deep-water family is the small blunt-head *Simenchelys parasiticus,* which is usually found at depths ranging from 2275 to 4550 feet. Like the hagfishes, *Simenchelys* obtains its food by drilling into the bodies of larger fishes and feeding upon the musculature. Characteristically, the square-nosed head has a transverse mouth and the gill openings are almost under the neck. The maximum length reached by this eel is about 2 feet. It has been taken off the American Atlantic coasts, the Azores, and Japan.

MORAY EELS—Family Muraenidae

For anyone living along a temperate or tropical coastline, the word "eel" invariably brings to mind the vicious moray. This is not surprising, for the morays are the commonest of the rock- and reef-dwelling tropical eels, not only in abundance but also in the number of different species. Most morays reach a maximum length of 4 or 5 feet, but there are occasional records of giants measuring as much as 10 feet. Morays are regularly eaten by man in many parts of the world, although at least five species have been reported to be violently poisonous, with death resulting in about 10 per cent of the recorded cases. The muraenids are identified by a combination of characteristics, important ones being the absence of pectoral fins, the dentition, the color pattern, and the profile of the nostrils. One important aspect of the morays is that they are suspected of lacking the leptocephalus stage. About twelve genera and at least eighty species are recognized.

The difference in nostril development within the muraenid family is interesting. The greatest extreme is found in *Rhinomureana,* a small genus of only two species (from the Central Pacific and Indonesia) in which the end of each nostril tube is expanded into a large leaflike structure. A more simplified but still distinctive type is that of the Hawaiian dragon eel, *Mureana pardalis* (Plate 25), in which the nostrils are elongate, simple tubes, but with the posterior nostrils being the longer and set far back on the head, just over the eye.

Although many of the morays are unicolored, like the beautiful Atlantic *Gymnothorax funebris* (Plate 29), there are others that have picturesque patterns like that of the Atlantic blackedge moray, *Gymnothorax nigromarginatus* (Plate 26). Brilliant banded patterns are commonplace among the genus *Echidna,* the members of which also have a modified type of dentition, with flattened, grinding teeth; they often feed on mollusks, sand dollars, sea urchins, and other such invertebrates. About a dozen species of *Echidna* are known; one of the most distinctive is the Indo-Pacific *Echidna zebra,* which has a ground color of rich ochre on which there are some fifty to eighty white rings.

Fishes and invertebrates that remove parasites from other larger fish are called cleaners. This cleaning service is also used by the eels. We are fortunate in being able to present two exceptional photos of eels with such cleaners. The first is of a Hawaiian eel, *Gymnothorax eurostus,* being cleaned by a bluestriped wrasse (Plate 27). The second, which was shot at a depth of ninety feet in a clay cave off La Jolla, California, shows a southern California eel, *Gymnothorax mordax,* visiting a group of shrimp cleaners (Plate 28). Many fishes are known to make periodic trips to the areas where the cleaners reside in order to have these helpful invertebrates and fish provide sanitation services for them. Despite the fact that most of these cleaners could be eaten at one gulp, the larger fishes seem to recognize their value and do not harm them.

Morays are very secretive, usually hiding in the daytime and coming out at night to forage. Even though a heavy population of eels may be present in a given coral area, a swimmer with a face mask would see very few and perhaps none unless he made a population study, using a fish poison. When this method is used, many dozens of eels come boiling out of the reef, some of them reacting in a fantastic manner. Occasionally the head and at least half the body are extended above the water and the eels propel themselves about by tail sculling, looking exactly like the sea monsters in medieval woodcuts.

SNAKE EELS—Family Ophichthidae

While the moringuid worm eels often have broad tails and burrow into the sand headfirst, the snake eels are tail burrowers and accordingly have very sharp, strong, spikelike tails. Handling a living snake eel in a net is like trying to hold onto a greased pig; if there is a small hole in the net, the snake eel will invariably find it and thread its way through tail first. Although the majority of snake eels lack pectoral fins, there are a few that do have very small pectorals. Typically, the dorsal fin starts just behind the head and extends for the full length of the body; the anal fin is much shorter. Most snake eels are small and very slender, measuring less than 3 feet in length. Brilliant banded and spotted patterns are commonplace in this family of more than two hundred species. Distribution is world-wide, mostly in inshore tropical shallow seas; the group is less abundant in more temperate water.

SNIPE EELS—Family Nemichthyidae

The snipe eels are peculiar, elongate, deep-sea fishes with extremely long, needle-like upper and lower jaws; the upper jaw is bent upward and the lower jaw downward so that they cannot be closed. The tail usually tapers out to a long filament. About nine species are recognized from the tropical marine depths of the world. *Avocettina exophthalma* is known from the West Indies, and *Avocettina infans* from the mid-Atlantic. *Nematoprora polygonifera* has been taken in the Hawaiian Islands and *Cercomitus flagellifer* from the Indo-Australian Archipelago.

Green Moray (*Gymnothorax funebris*); marine; New Jersey to Rio de Janeiro (Marine Studios).

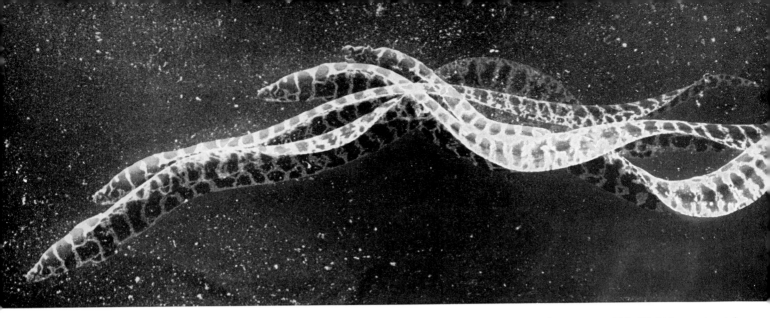

Quadruple exposure showing swimming motion of Chain Moray Eel (*Echidna catenata*); marine, inshore; Florida to Brazil (Fritz Goro: *Life* Magazine, at Lerner Marine Laboratory).

DEEP-SEA EELS
—Families Synaphobranchidae and Serrivomeridae

Superficially, the synaphobranchids look like a cross between the moray and the conger eels. Pectorals fins are present, and the gill openings are under the throat between them. About a dozen species are recognized, mostly from deep water, although the larval forms commonly appear near the surface. *Synaphobranchus infernalis* is a representative Atlantic Ocean form, while *Synaphobranchus bathybius* is widely distributed through the depths of the Pacific Ocean.

The serrivomerids, on the other hand, look as if they were intermediate between the moray eels and the very bizarre snipe eels. The jaws are much elongated but can be closed, and the tail usually tapers to a filamentous tip. Some eleven species and four genera have been recognized from the ocean depths of the world. *Spinivomer goodei* is found in the Gulf Stream and *Stemonidium hypomelas* in the Hawaiian Islands; *Serrivomer sector* occurs in the Pacific and Indian oceans.

CONGER EELS—Family Congridae

The congers usually have pectoral fins and are light colored with a black band around the edge of the dorsal and anal fins. When the conger moves it presents a symphony of motion, enhanced by this black band, as undulating ripples pass down the fins. Although congers are often found in shallow water, it is suspected that some of them require the pressure of deeper water to spawn. For example, the Hawaiian *Ariosoma bowersi* invariably becomes egg-bound when kept in captivity during spawning season. The female swells up like a balloon to about three times her normal diameter and eventually explodes. Examination of the dead female usually shows the presence in the oviduct of a calcareous plug which has prevented the eggs from being expelled. It is believed that the pressure of deeper water would prevent the formation of this plug.

There are many genera and species of congers, some of them ranging in length to about 6 feet. The majority are marine shallow-water forms; however, one species, *Promyllantor purpureus*, has been taken in very deep water, at a depth of more than a mile in the Arabian Sea. The knife-tooth eels, placed by some investigators in the family Muraenesocidae, are included by others in the congrid family. About seventeen species of knife-tooths are recognized, all characterized by a sharp row of large median teeth along the vomer of the upper jaw.

WORM EELS—Family Moringuidae

The worm eels form a small tropical family of about twenty species in two genera. All of them have small pectoral fins and are thought to be head burrowers rather than tail burrowers like some of the eels in other families. The typical moringuid is easily identified by its singular appearance: it looks like a greatly elongated worm, sometimes with one lip, usually the upper one, greatly overlapping the other. Recent studies of the Hawaiian *Moringua macrochir* by Dr. W. A. Gosline at the University of Hawaii have shown that the males and females differ radically in head and lip profile, the difference being further augmented at sexual maturity. The male does not change radically as it matures, but the female develops from a small-eyed, yellow, rudimentary-finned immature worm eel to a larger-eyed, silvery, long-finned adult. It is thought that with maturity there is also a change from the habit of burrowing in the sand in shallow areas to a pelagic mode of life. The Bahaman *Stilbiscus edwardsi* is most often collected around lights at night; this may also indicate a pelagic existence for this species.

Deep-sea Spiny Eels and Their Relatives

(Order Heteromi)

These are greatly elongated fishes that are seldom seen even by ichthyologists, since they live in the depths. Fewer than two dozen species are known. Although superficially they resemble eels, they are not closely related to them. Most of the fishes of the order Heteromi are less than 2 feet in length. They occur in all oceans except in areas where the water is very cold; their depth range is usually between 1200 and 8500 feet. Characteristically they have a very long anal fin with as many as two hundred rays running along the underside of the body to the tip of the tail, which tapers to a point. Some species have luminous organs along the sides of the body and on the head. In one family, the Notocanthidae, the dorsal fin is composed of a series of six to thirty-six separate spines not connected by membranes. In the second family, the Halosauridae, this spiny dorsal is replaced by a small fin of nine to twelve soft rays, usually located opposite the ventral fins. The last family, the Lipogenyidae, has only a single species, *Lipogenys gilli,* which was originally taken offshore southeast of New York at a depth of about one mile. It is a toothless fish which differs from the others in having a few spines in front of the soft dorsal rays.

Needlefishes, Halfbeaks, and Flying Fishes

(Order Synentognathi)

The synentognathous fishes show an interesting gradation in the length of the snout and jaws from (1) the very long, forceps-like jaws of the rapacious needlefishes to (2) the normal upper jaw but extended lower jaw of the halfbeaks, and finally to (3) the more normal jaws of the sauries and flying fishes. Some of the latter still show the extended lower jaw as juveniles, but this is lost as they become adult. A gradation also is shown in the size of the pectoral fins; as the snout decreases in length, these increase in size. The needlefishes are great jumpers, but since their pectoral fins are small, they are incapable of flight. The halfbeaks, with their slightly enlarged pectoral fins, show the beginning of skittering flight in one or two species. And of course the flying fishes, with greatly enlarged pectorals, are well known for their ability to leave the water and "fly" for many yards.

The needlefishes and their relatives show several anatomical similarities: (1) all of the fins are soft-rayed, without spines; (2) the dorsal, anal, and ventrals are usually set far back on the body; (3) the lateral line is usually very low on the side of the body; (4) the lower pharyngeals in the mouth are united to form a single bone; and (5) most of the fishes of this group lay spherical eggs, usually with tendrils which facilitate their being caught by pelagic seaweed. The order Synentognathi, with its four families, is of moderate size, the total number of species being about 117.

NEEDLEFISHES—Family Belonidae

Examination of the mouth of a needlefish leads to the conclusion that it is well named, for these long-jawed, ferocious fishes are armed with many fine teeth that are capable of wreaking havoc among schools of smaller fishes as well as on unwary fishermen. In appearance, the needlefishes are similar to the fresh-water gars of North America or the marine barracudas, but they are probably faster than either. Since they generally remain just below the surface, if the water is reasonably clear they are usually visible when they are in an area. They are tremendous jumpers, and at times it seems almost as though they are trying to become flying fishes. Most of the approximately sixty species are found in all tropical and temperate marine waters and are confined to salt water; however, some species do move into fresh water, and a few, such as the Amazonian *Potomorrhaphis guianensis* (Plate 31), live permanently in fresh water. The dorsal and anal fins are fairly large and are placed opposite each other, just in front of the V-shaped, symmetrical tail; the pectoral and pelvic fins are quite small. Although the bones, and sometimes the flesh, are green, the flesh is quite tasty. Several species, including the Indo-Pacific *Strongylura crocodilus* and the Atlantic *Strongylura marina,* reach lengths of 40 to 48 inches; however, the majority of species are mature at less than 2 feet.

HALFBEAKS—Family Hemiramphidae

If the long upper jaw were removed from a needlefish but the lower jaw were left intact and the size decreased to no more than 12 or at most 18 inches, the result would look like a halfbeak. This peculiar family includes about seventy species, many of which are marine whereas others are restricted to fresh water. The halfbeaks have short pectoral fins, which does not prevent their trying to act like flying fishes, some of them making short, skittering flights. A further indication of their close relationship to the flying fishes is shown by the lopsided flying-fish type of tail possessed by some species, the lower lobe being longer than the upper.

Most halfbeaks fertilize their eggs externally, as do the majority of other fishes, but a few have internal fertilization and young that are born alive. The photograph opposite, showing the birth of a fresh-water halfbeak, is one of the most remarkable fish photos ever taken. The species shown is the 3-inch wrestling halfbeak, *Dermogenys pusillus,* which next to the *Betta* is the most popular fighting fish in Thailand. The males are bred for their fighting ability, which consists chiefly of grasping the adversary by the jaws until he is no longer interested in giving combat. Although blood is sometimes drawn, neither opponent is permanently injured.

Internal fertilization requires the development of some type of copulatory organ, usually a modification of the anal fin. The males of the Indo-Australian halfbeak genus *Zenarchopterus* have a unique variation of this gonopodium: a single ray of the anal fin, usually the third, is greatly elongated, and from it extend a number of smaller, very fine rays, making it look like a feather.

One of the largest halfbeaks, the Pacific *Euleptorhamphus viridis,* reaches a "giant" 18 inches, and is also noted for having the longest pectoral fins of all the halfbeaks, which make it capable of better flight than the others. Another extreme in the half-

Population sample from a tropical reef, Bikini Atoll, Marshall Islands. Large Needlefish (*Strongylura* sp.), upper left, is one of as many as 100 species found in such a collection (Fritz Goro: *Life* Magazine).

Fresh-water Halfbeak (*Dermogenys pusillus*), showing emerging head of young at the moment of birth; Thailand to Indonesia (Gene Wolfsheimer).

beak family is the genus *Nomorhampus,* represented by two species in the fresh waters of Celebes; they look more like topminnows than like halfbeaks since the lower jaw extension is lacking.

Hyporhamphus unifasciatus is one of the most widely distributed of the halfbeaks. It is found in the eastern Pacific and on both sides of the Atlantic; on American shores it occurs from Maine to Argentina.

SAURIES—Family Scomberesocidae

From the standpoint of abundance, the sauries are very important members of the offshore fauna of the world's tropical and temperate seas. They resemble the needlefishes but have short jaws, and they may be identified by a series of five to seven finlets both after the dorsal and after the anal fin. Four species are recognized; all of them are small, 12 to 14 inches being the maximum size. In Japan there are important fisheries for *Cololabis saira,* a species that is also common off the American Pacific coast. *Scomberesox saurus* is a common Mediterranean species that ranges up the European coasts and across the Atlantic to the American side.

FLYING FISHES—Family Exocoetidae

Standing on the bow of a ship moving through tropical or temperate seas, one is fascinated by the schools of flying fish as they leave the water ahead of the ship and scatter in many directions. Does a flying fish actually fly? This question has been debated down through the ages, and only in recent years have high-speed photographic studies enabled us to learn that the adult flying fish normally does not vibrate its wings during flight, but holds them relatively steady. Its gliding is similar to that of the flying squirrels of North America and the flying lizards and flying snakes of Malaya. To have true birdlike flight, the wings would need to vibrate sufficiently to support the body in the air; only among the South American fresh-water hatchet fishes and, to a lesser extent, the African fresh-water butterfly fish is such ability found.

In preparing to leave the water, the flying fish drives very rapidly upward, and if the initial spurt out of the water is not sufficient to get under way—which is usually the case—the long lower lobe of the tail adds impetus by acting as an outboard motor, vibrating rapidly sideways at as many as fifty beats a second, until the flying fish is adequately air-borne. On a flight of 150 feet, requiring some three seconds, the fish may lose momentum and drop down near the water; then the tail again takes over. Average flight speed is about thirty-five miles per hour, and flights as long as thirteen seconds have been clocked. Although most flights are close to the water, at night some fishes have been known to fly aboard ships whose decks were twenty feet above the water.

A light hanging over the side of a drifting ship at night always attracts flying fishes if any are in the area. Not only the adults but also the juveniles are attracted. Many of these youngsters are quite different from the adults, not only because of their variegated color pattern but also because of a pair of large flaplike whiskers that extend downward from the tip of the lower jaw. In some species these whiskers may be longer than the fish itself; for example, a 2-inch juvenile of the Caribbean *Cypselurus cyanopterus* has whisker streamers extending beyond the tail. With growth, these appendages are lost, a fact that explains why juvenile flying fishes have in the past been described as species different from their parents.

Identification of a flying fish is not difficult because of the enlarged "flying fins" and, of course, the lopsided tail, with its lower lobe much longer than the upper. As indicated earlier, the fins are without spines. As a rule, flying fishes are found offshore, usually over deep water; however, there are some inshore forms occurring only in coastal waters. In classification of the individual species of flying fishes, use is made of some of the criteria developed by entomologists; for instance, one flying fish will often be distinguished from another by the branching of one of the veins of the pectoral fins. Because of the spectacular nature of the flying fish, one would imagine that this group had been adequately studied, but such is far from the case. Although there are small commercial fisheries for various species, most of the others are difficult to catch, and only partial life histories of a few species are known.

One major problem in classification has been that of species that are intermediate between the halfbeaks and the flying fishes, for example *Oxyporhymphus micropterus,* which occurs on both sides of the Atlantic as well as in the Pacific. As a juvenile it has an extended lower jaw like the halfbeaks, but as an adult this extension is lost—a change that also occurs among some of the flying fishes. The wings of *Oxyporhymphus* are very short, no longer than those of the majority of the halfbeaks, but the tail is lopsided, with an elongated lower lobe like that of the flying fish. The egg is like that of the halfbeaks—that is, without long tendrils. The fish is capable of getting out of the water and making a short skittering flight.

Among the synentognathous fishes there are a number of problems of this kind which only careful future investigations will unravel. At the present time about forty-three kinds of flying fishes are recognized.

Watching flying fishes as they scatter in front of a ship, one is able to divide them into two categories— the two-wing and four-wing types. The two-wing flying fish has two very large pectoral fins and small, inconspicuous ventrals, while the four-wing type has ventral fins nearly as large as the pectorals. The four-wing types are noted for the beautiful color patterns on their wings.

The largest of the flying fishes is a four-wing species, *Cypselurus californicus,* an 18-inch form that has a limited distribution along the coasts of southern and Baja California. It is caught commercially during the late spring and summer months; some of the catch is sold in the fresh-fish market, and the remainder is used as bait for swordfish and tuna. Other important two-wing species include the 10-inch *Exocoetus volitans,* which occurs around the world in tropical waters; it has a smooth, buoyant egg without the long tendrils characteristic of most flying fish eggs.

Ballyhoo Halfbeak (*Hemiramphus brasiliensis*); marine; both sides of the temperate and tropical Atlantic (Fritz Goro: *Life* Magazine, at Lerner Marine Laboratory, Bimini).

High-speed photograph of California Flying Fish (*Cypselurus californicus*); marine; central and Lower California (Harold E. Edgerton).

The Atlantic *Cypselurus heterurus* is the most common four-wing flying fish found on both sides of the Atlantic, on the American side from the Gulf of Maine to Rio de Janeiro. It has an oblique band extending across the forward wings, and at maximum size is about 12 inches in length.

Topminnows and Their Relatives (*Order Microcyprini*)

The microcyprinids all have the characteristic appearance of fishes that spend much of their time capturing food near the surface of the water: that is, the mouth is in a forward position at the upper end of the head, the most effective arrangement for this type of feeding. Most of the fishes of this order live in fresh water, although a few move into brackish and even salt water. Because of the popularity of tropical fish as a hobby, many of these fishes are as well known as the ubiquitous goldfish.

The seven families in this order include the cave, spring, and swamp fishes, Amblyopsidae; the egg-laying topminnows, Cyprinodontidae; the live-bear-ing topminnows, Poeciliidae and Goodeidae; the four-eyed fishes, Anablepidae; and two small families without common names, the Jenynsiidae and Adrianichthyidae. All of the microcyprinids show the following characteristics: (1) the absence of a lateral line, (2) the absence of an adipose fin, and (3) the presence of an air bladder.

CAVE, SPRING, and SWAMP FISHES —*Family Amblyopsidae*

Cave dwellers in the fish world are represented by several families, one of which is the Amblyopsidae, a group of five North American fresh-water species assigned to three genera. They include the southern cavefish, *Typhlichthys subterraneus;* the ricefish, *Chologaster cornuta;* the springfish, *Chologaster agassizi;* the northern cavefish, *Amblyopsis spelaea;* and the Ozark cavefish, *Amblyopsis rosae.* The maximum size reached by the adults of these whitish fishes is about 3½ inches. Their distribution is closely correlated with limestone formations; for, as pointed out by Loren Woods and Robert Inger of the Chicago Natural History Museum in their recent study of the family: "The amblyopsids, except for one species, are distributed in the limestone region of the central United States between the Appalachian Mountains and the Great Plains, south of the limit of glaciation and north of the Cretaceous Mississippi embayment." For all practical purposes, this is an area of the Mississippi basin limited by 39 degrees north latitude on the north and 32 degrees on the south. The ricefish, *Chologaster cornuta,* seems to have no correlation with limestone areas and is entirely segregated from the other four species; it is found on the Atlantic coastal plain from Virginia to central Georgia. It does not occur in caves, but is found in streams and cypress swamps where the temperature may range between 39 and 80 degrees F. The ricefish has small functional eyes. It may be distinguished from the only other member of the genus, the springfish, *Chologaster agassizi,* by the difference in the number of rays in the tail fin (nine to eleven in *C. cornuta* and twelve to sixteen in *C. agassizi*), and by a dark streak which is present on the sides of the former but absent on the latter.

Although *Chologaster* does have functional eyes, laboratory experiments in which the eyes have been removed have shown that the fishes were able to find their food and survive as well without eyes as they did with them.

The other three species of amblyopsids are blind, although they retain a rudimentary eye. Normally these fishes lack pigment; however, it has been noted that the southern cavefish, *Typhlichthys subterranus,* when kept in daylight in an aquarium for three months gradually developed a dusky color, the pigment being compacted into a wide mid-lateral band with a series of oblique marks at the division points of the muscle segments.

The two species of *Amblyopsis* are distinguished from the other members of the family by the presence of two or three rows of sensory papillae on each half of the tail fin. In addition, the northern cavefish, *Amblyopsis spelaea,* has small pelvic fins, which are not present in any of the other members of the family.

One feature that all the amblyopsids have in common is sensory papillae, or tactile organs, in quite prominent rows on the head, body, and tail; the arrangement of these rows of papillae varies with different species. There are also additional tactile organs beneath the epidermis. These sensory organs, of course, help to make up for the lack of vision in the blind fishes and the rudimentary vision in the eyed forms.

There has been much speculation about the method of distribution of these fishes. Some of the species are rather widely distributed in places where migration by surface water would seem highly unlikely for these blind fishes. For example, *Typhlich-*

thys is found on each side of the Ozark plateau, a distance of only seventy-five miles by land but over one thousand miles by surface water. The area in which *Typhlichthys* and *Amblyopsis* are found is known to be underlined with subterranean limestone channels of water that flow beneath the rivers and surface streams, and it is believed that these channels are used as a means of dispersal by these fishes. One species, *Chologaster agassizi,* is known to migrate for short distances by surface waters, but it is thought to utilize the underground passages as well.

The actual breeding of these fishes has not been observed, but it is known that the *Amblyopsis* female carries the eggs in the gill chamber. In laboratory specimens caught in the wild, these eggs, about seventy in number, hatched after about two months into young measuring about ⅜ inch. It is believed that this method of breeding may be characteristic of all of the amblyopsid family. Two facts lend credence to this belief: (1) the gill chamber is unusually large and the gill filaments quite small, thus making an ideal brooding place; (2) the anus of *Amblyopsis* is in the normal position at birth but gradually moves forward with age until at maturity it lies anterior to the pectorals. This position would make it relatively easy for the ovipositor of the female to reach the gill chamber. Early biologists thought at first that these fishes were viviparous, but this has been proved to be false.

EGG-LAYING TOPMINNOWS
—Family Cyprinodontidae

Sometimes called egg-laying tooth carps, the cyprinodont topminnows include a great many species that have been popularized by aquarists. All of them are small, with a maximum length in the range of 4 to 6 inches. Since many of these fishes are common locally near areas where aquarists abound, they are readily available for capture and study. Included in this category are the various species of the genus *Fundulus,* such as the beautiful golden ear, *Fundulus chrysotus,* which ranges from South Carolina to Florida in fresh and brackish water, and the banded (male) and striped (female) starhead topminnow, *Fundulus dispar,* which ranges through the central and southeastern United States. In southern California there is a tidepool fish, *Fundulus parvipinnis,* which is probably the least spectacular of all the *Fundulus* species but does adapt readily to aquarium life. Its counterpart in the eastern United States is a brackish-water form, the zebra or common killifish, *Fundulus heteroclitus.*

Florida has some outstanding members in this family, such as the spectacular but small (2 inches) American flagfish, *Jordanella floridae,* and the swamp killie, *Leptolucania ommata,* which has a large ocellus on the side of the caudal peduncle just in front of the tail fin. Some of the Florida cyprinodonts lose their color in captivity. The mature male blue-fin topminnow, *Chriopeops goodei,* has a fantastically brilliant blue dorsal and anal fin when first captured, but in tank life this color is almost impossible to maintain. Many young natural history students living along the eastern United States seaboard have started their study of fishes with the attractive little sheepshead minnow, *Cyprinodon variegatus,* a species that reaches a length of 3 inches and ranges from Maine to Florida and Texas in brackish and ocean water. In the western United States enthusiastic aquarists have often made extended trips to collect the Death Valley pupfish, *Cyprinodon nevadensis,* as well as other pupfishes which are found only in isolated desert springs. From Spain and Italy through the Near East are found various species of the genus *Aphanius,* some of which are as popular with European aquarists as the fishes previously mentioned are with American aquarists.

ANNUAL FISHES

The topminnows include a small but remarkable group of highly colorful fishes known as the annuals. Altogether, there are some twenty-six species in five genera from the continents of Africa and South America.

Whereas the lungfish survives the dry period by estivating in a mud ball, the annual fish, although it dies, accomplishes the same thing by laying eggs that are impervious to desiccation and thus allow the species to be carried over until the wet season.

The habitat of these fishes on both continents is one of climatic extremes, with an extensive rainy season followed by hot, dry weather. With the coming of the rains, the streams flow and pools and lakes are formed; at the end of the rainy season, the hot tropical sun evaporates the water until nothing is left but sun-baked mud, frequently covered with the bodies of innumerable dead and dying fishes. This provides ready food for scavenging birds and other animals. The annual fish has a short life: it is born with the rains and is dead within the year, its entire life cycle completed.

Similarity of breeding habits has given these fishes as a group the name of "egg-buriers," for this is just what they do. When their watery habitat gives the warning sign that danger approaches and soon evaporation will leave them stranded, the males seek mates and together they burrow into the soft ooze or sandy bottom of their pond or stream to deposit and fertilize their eggs. Here the eggs remain until the rains come again and release the fry. Certain bacteria, which are said to be necessary to liberate the

fry from the tough-coated eggs, are usually present in the dried mud, together with abundant infusoria nurtured in part by the decomposed bodies of parent fishes. These infusoria provide the fry with its first food.

Because of their great beauty, the annual fishes have long been admired and worked with by aquarists. Among those which have been studied are three species of *Cynolebias* from South America; one each of *Pterolebias* and *Rachovia,* also from South America; four *Notobranchius* from Africa; and about fifteen species of African lyretails, genus *Aphyosemion.* The general pattern of reproduction of all of these fishes is similar, most of the divergence being in the length of time required for hatching the eggs. Depending upon the species involved, this period varies from a few weeks to several months.

Obviously, not all of the annuals necessarily go through a dry period each year, in which case the adults continue to survive for a number of weeks or months. Other fishes are suspected of having latent capabilities of becoming annuals. For example, recent investigations have shown that the unhatched eggs of the common Atlantic killifish, *Fundulus confluentus,* may remain alive and hatchable after as much as three months' exposure. When the eggs are immersed in tap water, hatching occurs within fifteen to thirty minutes.

Because of the peculiarities of the life histories of the annuals, many widely varied methods of breeding these fishes have been developed. For *Rachovia brevis,* a little 2-inch fish from Colombia, pairs are put into a tank with a sandy bottom and shallow water. Evaporation is increased by direct sunlight or even an electric fan, and as the water gets shallower and shallower the pair partially bury themselves in the sand, where they deposit and fertilize the eggs. After the water has evaporated completely (the breeding pair having been removed to complete their very brief remaining life in another tank), the aquarium is allowed to stand for at least two weeks with the sand just barely moist. Then the tank is slowly filled with rain water, about two quarts a day, and soon the fairly large young are seen swimming about. This method has also been used for some of the species of *Cynolebias.* Others of this genus, whose eggs are laid in peat moss or fine plants rather than sand, are raised by removing the eggs and storing them in darkness between layers of barely moist peat moss at a constant temperature of 75 to 78 degrees F. for a period of six weeks or more. Some enterprising fanciers have made a lucrative business of breeding these annual fishes and shipping the eggs in peat moss by mail when they are just about ready to hatch. The recipient merely prepares a tank and puts in the peat moss, and in a matter of hours fry are swimming in his aquarium.

In some species of annuals, notably the Argentine pearlfish, *Cynolebias bellotti,* the difference in the sexes is so great that early ichthyologists sometimes made the error of classifying the male and female as different species. This is not hard to understand, for this species and others of its genus exhibit vastly different color markings and also different fin counts for the two sexes, something which is not common in other fishes.

VIVIPAROUS TOPMINNOWS
—Family Poeciliidae

The Reverend Robert John Lechmere Guppy little suspected, when he discovered some small, beautiful fishes with long, streamerlike tails on the island of Trinidad in 1866, that his name would be made known to millions by this little 2½-inch fish, *Lebistes reticulatus,* commonly called the guppy. In fact, if one fish could be chosen to represent an entire family, the guppy would certainly serve as representative of the poeciliids. As in the other members of this family, the young are born alive. They reproduce so rapidly that at one time they were called "million fishes." Internal fertilization is normal for the family, and one batch of sperm fertilizes several successive broods. The copulatory organ of the male is formed from the elongated anterior rays of the anal fin. This gonopodium, as it is called, is an elaborate, complicated structure, having assorted hooks and spines as well as other anatomical peculiarities which are useful in classification of both genera and species. The gonopodial rays are much longer than the other anal fin rays, a feature which instantly identifies the males of any species in the family (Plate 32). The anal fin of the female is usually rounded and lacking the extended rays.

The family Poeciliidae is a large one, with more than forty-five genera and a great number of species. They are entirely New World fishes, ranging from Illinois and New Jersey in the United States to Argentina.

One of the peculiarities found in the poeciliid family is that some species produce only female offspring. Dr. and Mrs. Carl Hubbs made the first discovery of this in 1932 when they found that the Amazon molly, *Mollienesia formosa,* a species normally ranging through the coastal and inland waters of northeastern Mexico and Texas, existed in nature only as a female population. Since the father contributed nothing to the heredity of his offspring, the species was able to maintain itself by using males of other species occurring in the same area, such as *Mollienesia latipinna* and *M. sphenops.* Experimen-

tally in the laboratory, several other species of males have also been shown to be capable of acting as the male parent of the Amazon molly. Twenty-seven years later (1959) Dr. R. R. Miller and Dr. J. Schultz of the University of Michigan announced the discovery of an intermediate type of inheritance in all-female populations of the genus *Poeciliopsis,* a group of several species living in the coastal streams of northwestern Mexico. In this case some of the father's characteristics may be transmitted to the all-female offspring. These fishes, however, have two kinds of females: one that produces only female offspring and another that looks identical but produces a normal ratio of male and female offspring. Needless to say, geneticists are following the studies in this field with great interest.

The live-bearing topminnows have long been popular with tropical-fish hobbyists. Countless breeding experiments, both planned and haphazard, have resulted in many new domestic strains of these remarkable fishes. The lowly guppy serves as a good example: the wild form has a tail of moderate length, although that of the male is usually longer and more flowing than that of the female; so many domestic tail varieties and other variations have been developed that the guppy-breeders' societies have been forced to establish standards. A few of the recognized tail varieties include the double sword, upper sword, lower sword, pin-tail, and spear-tail; along with this are specific body and tail color patterns. Full-grown female guppies measure about 2 inches in length, whereas the males are usually about half as long. Their normal habitat extends from the islands of the southern Caribbean to the southern part of Brazil.

From the southeastern United States comes the world-famous mosquito fish, *Gambusia affinis.* It is slightly larger than the guppy, with the adult females ranging between 2 and 3 inches and the males slightly smaller. Melanistic forms with erratic spotting are often found in this species. A mark of identification appears on the gravid female in the form of a large black patch on the side of the abdomen just above the anal fin. Although it was one of the first viviparous fishes to become known to aquarists, it does not share the popularity of the guppy; it is somewhat belligerent and not nearly so attractive as many of the other topminnows. The ability of *Gambusia* to consume quantities of mosquito larvae and pupae makes it an item in demand in tropical and temperate areas where those pests abound. In marshes and swamps as well as other standing bodies of water where the vegetation is not too dense, *Gambusia* can substantially cut down the population of larval mosquitoes. For this reason it has been

Egg-laying Topminnows (*Tomeurus gracilis*); female above, male with extended gonopodium below; fresh water; northeastern South America (New York Zoological Society).

imported into many areas of the world where it does not normally occur. In California, for example, many mosquito-control districts maintain supplies of *Gambusia* for free distribution to persons requesting them for the intended purpose.

One of the smallest of the active mosquito fishes is the dwarf topminnow, *Heterandria formosa:* as an adult it is scarcely 1 inch in length. It is easily identified by the black band along the side of the body and the black spot at the base of the dorsal fin. *Heterandria* is found from North Carolina to Florida, and is more a mid-water fish than *Gambusia* and the other topminnows. This was well demonstrated during the early days of field testing of DDT and other insecticides. The topminnows that constantly fed on material near the surface of the water, such as *Gambusia,* were often killed by the insecticidal film at the surface, whereas the fishes such as *Heterandria* that frequented the mid-water between surface and bottom were usually not affected.

Mollies have long been favorites of the aquarists because of the males' beautiful sail-like dorsal fins. The most common species in the southeastern United States is *Mollienesia latipinna* (Plate 32); it reaches a length of about 4 inches and is found from South Carolina to Mexico in both fresh and salt water. Mottled blackish sailfin mollies sometimes occur in nature, and in Florida are most often found in sulphur springs. Aquarists have duplicated many of these melanistic forms and have also produced entirely black mollies (Plate 32). It may be noted that these black mollies have been produced not only from *M. latipinna* but also from other species such as *M. velifera* and *M. sphenops.*

The live-bearing topminnows have made great contributions to medical science, largely through knowledge gained from research on the genetics of the popular "platys" and "swordtails," both types belonging to the genus *Xiphophorus.* For example, when a spotted platy, *X. maculatus,* is crossed with a green swordtail, *X. helleri,* the offspring often develop lethal cancerous growths along the sides of the body just in front of the tail fin. The late Dr. Myron Gordon of the New York Zoological Society discovered that, although inheritable cancers could be developed in the laboratory as the result of special crosses of the type just described, these same fishes would not hybridize in the wild even though they inhabited the same streams of Mexico and Central America. Since some of these inheritable fish cancers are remarkably similar to human cancer, studies of the genetics of platys and swordtails have received the support of medical research foundations. Many color varieties of platys and swordtails are known, and in addition to these, new types have been developed in the course of genetic studies.

Tomeurus gracilis from British Guiana, Venezuela, and Brazil is a strange little 1-inch fish that has presented ichthyologists and aquarists with some puzzling problems. The male has a spectacularly well-developed gonopodium which is in a forward position, almost on the throat. *Tomeurus* has the same mating pattern as a poeciliid topminnow, but the young are not born alive; instead, the female lays a single large, hard-shelled egg which soon hatches into a free-swimming youngster. Because of these differences, some authorities suggest that *Tomeurus* be placed in a distinct family, the Tomeuridae, whereas others consider it a poeciliid although a very aberrant one.

GOODEIDS—Family Goodeidae

In the highlands of Mexico and adjacent areas there is a group of about two dozen species of small

Male Four-eyed Fish (*Anableps anableps*); fresh water; northeastern South America (New York Zoological Society).

fishes known as the goodeids. They have a reproductive pattern intermediate between that of the egg-laying cyprinodont topminnows and the live-bearing poeciliid topminnows. Although the goodeids resemble the poeciliids in that they bear their young alive, they lack the highly developed gonopodium of the latter. Instead, the male goodeids have an anal fin that shows only a small amount of modification, with the first six rays set apart by a notch from the rest of the structure. The poeciliids and goodeids are further differentiated by the fact that the male goodeids are capable of fertilizing only a single batch of eggs at a time. The poeciliids, on the other hand, have spermatophores, or masses of sperms, which are transferred during copulation to the oviduct and remain there to fertilize several successive batches of eggs.

The two-lined neotoca, *Neotoca bilineata*, from central Mexico, is one of the few members of the Goodeidae that have been studied by aquarists. It is mature at a length of only 2 inches. The greenish female is slightly larger than the male and has a different color pattern, with a brilliant green band along the side, whereas the male has a series of longitudinal striations.

FOUR-EYED FISHES—Family Anablepidae

"Cuatro ojos" or "four eyes" is a well-known fish in many areas of southern Mexico, Central America, and northern South America. Two species are recognized, both in the same genus, *Anableps;* they reach a normal maximum length of 6 to 8 inches, although some giants of 12 inches have been recorded.

The four-eyed fish spends much of its time cruising just below the surface of the water with the upper half of its eyes protruding. The water line is at the center of each eye, and at this point the eye is neatly divided by a longitudinal epithelial band so that the upper and lower portions are separate; hence the name "four eyes." Not only is the cornea

divided, but *Anableps* carries this division a step further and has separate retinas in the backs of the eyes. An object out of water is seen through the upper eye and is brought to focus on the lower retina, whereas an object under water is seen through the under cornea and is brought to focus on the upper retina. Air vision requires a different lens system than does underwater vision. *Anableps* solves this problem by having the lens of the eye oval shaped so that an object viewed under water is seen through a portion of the lens that is much thicker than the portion through which an object out of the water is viewed.

Only one other fish is known to have a divided eye. This is a small 3-inch blenny from the Galapagos Islands, *Dialommus fuscus*. Since this blenny apparently spends a great deal of time standing on its tail with a portion of the head and eyes out of the water, the division of the eye into two sections is in the opposite direction from that found in *Anableps* —that is, the eye is divided by a band running vertically from the upper to the lower surface of the fish rather than horizontally from the head to the tail. It has not been recorded whether the four-eyed blenny also has a divided retina with an oval lens.

Land-dwelling vertebrates keep the eyes moist by means of lachrymal glands and ducts. Since *Anableps* lacks these structures, it must keep the eyes moist by popping the head below the surface at frequent intervals.

One of the methods for capturing these fishes takes advantage of their surface habitat. By shining a flashlight upon the water at night, one can easily detect their presence by the beam of light reflected from their eyes, and can approach them without too much difficulty. However, in the daytime the approach of an intruder is quite another matter, for *Anableps* will often leap from the water with the speed of a rocket leaving its launching pad. This jumping ability presents the aquarist with a problem, for unless the tank in which the captive *Anableps* is living is kept securely covered, the fish will soon depart.

It might logically be assumed that *Anableps'* dual vision would enable it to catch insects above the water surface, but this phenomenon has not been recorded. At present, the only known function of the intricate visual system is that of enabling *Anableps* to watch for predators both above and below the surface at the same time. *Anableps* can and does feed below the surface, despite the fact that swimming downward seems to require considerable effort. After going down for food, the fish returns to its customary surface position, floating upward with little movement of the fins.

As is true of other poeciliid-like fishes, *Anableps* is viviparous, the eggs being fertilized internally and hatching within the female before birth. As in other fishes of this group, the anterior rays of the anal fin are modified to serve as a phallic organ. Through the tubelike structure so formed, the *Anableps* male passes the spermatozoa to the female. Compared with other related fishes, there is nothing exceptional about their reproduction up to this point. However, we now come upon one of the most amazing reproductive patterns in the fish world. For coitus to take place, a "left-handed" male must always mate with a "right-handed" female, and a "right-handed" male with a "left-handed" female. To explain this, it should be noted that in some males the modified anal fin or intromittent organ is able to move only to the left and in others only to the right. The female also has a peculiarity; her genital aperture is covered by a special scale which is free on one side and not on the other. In some females the opening beneath the scale is on the right side, in others on the left. Hence it is possible for a sinistral male to mate only with a dextral female, and vice versa. Fortunately, both sexes seem to be about evenly divided in their sinistral or dextral traits. (It should be mentioned that poeciliid males of the subfamily Poeciliopsinae, all of which have asymmetrical gonopodia, are also limited to copulation from one side only.) Personal observation of *Anableps* has shown two males each simultaneously trying to mate with one female, one of which, it is assumed, was unsuccessful.

The female has from one to five offspring. One 6-inch female at Steinhart Aquarium gave birth to a single young measuring 2½ inches; another female of similar size produced four young, each measuring about 1½ inches.

JENYNSIIDS—Family Jenynsiidae

Insofar as breeding habits are concerned, the jenynsiids are very similar to the four-eyed fishes. The male has a tubular copulatory organ or gono-podium, formed from some of the rays of the anal fin, that will work only on one side of the fish. Consequently, as with the four-eyed fishes, a right-handed male must mate with a left-handed female. The young are born alive.

The jenynsiids are usually bluish in color with a series of black stripes, usually four to six, along the side. Adult females reach a maximum length of about 4½ inches and males about 1½ inches. Several species of these fishes have been described from the southern portions of South America. *Jenynsia lineata* is occasionally imported for sale in tropical-fish stores.

ADRIANICHTHYIDS—Family Adrianichthyidae

These peculiar fishes from the fresh-water lakes of Celebes are given family recognition principally because of their scoop-shovel type of mouth, which looks like the result of a cross between a duckbill platypus and a topminnow. Only three species are known: they range from 3 to 8 inches in length and are usually silvery below and yellowish to brown above.

One species, *Xenopoecilus poptae* from Lake Posso, Celebes, is fished by hook and line from November to January in thirty-five to fifty feet of water. The fishing season apparently coincides with the reproductive season, since the fishes when caught expel their eggs at once. The young fish hatch as soon as the eggs are discharged. During these winter months large patches of the lake surface are covered with the broken egg membranes of the hatching fry.

Troutperch and Pirateperch (*Order Salmopercae*)

Three small species placed in two families are the only living representatives of a formerly widespread transitional group of North American fishes with characteristics intermediate between the more primitive troutlike forms and the more advanced spiny-rayed fishes. Two of the species have a fleshy adipose fin on the caudal peduncle between the dorsal and tail fins—a characteristic of trout and salmon. In addition to the normal complement of soft fin rays, all three species have one or more spines preceding the dorsal, anal, and ventral fins.

TROUTPERCH—Family Percopsidae

The blunt-nosed troutperch, *Percopsis omiscomaycus,* sometimes called sandroller, is a 6-inch spotted fish which can be identified by its adipose fin, spiny fins, and rough ctenoid scales. It is found in most of Canada, ranging from Quebec to the eastern border of British Columbia, and southward to Kansas, Missouri, Kentucky, and Virginia. In the Great Lakes it is a forage fish of some importance, and is found abundantly in shallow areas; however, it also occurs as deep as two hundred feet. Spawning takes place in the spring in shallow areas.

The second species of troutperch, *Columbia transmontana,* occurs in the Columbia River basin of western North America. Like *Percopsis,* it also has the identifying adipose fin, and has two spines preceding both dorsal and anal fins; but it is smaller than *Percopsis,* being full grown at 3 to 4 inches.

PIRATEPERCH—*Family Aphredoderidae*

The 5-inch adult pirateperch, *Apredoderus sayanus,* has a surprising anatomical peculiarity that segregates it from other fishes. As the fish grows, the vent, which in the juvenile is in normal position just ahead of the anal fin, migrates forward until in the adult it is located underneath the throat, just behind the gill openings. The pirateperch usually has one ventral, two anal, and three dorsal fin spines, but it lacks the adipose fin. It occurs along the Atlantic coast from New York to Texas, then northward through the Mississippi basin as far as Michigan. Its preferred habitat is ponds and lakes where there is much debris on the bottom along with organic decomposition.

Tube-mouthed Fishes

(*Order Solenichthys*)

The seven families in this group make up two well-defined suborders. The first includes the ever popular pipefishes and seahorses as well as the ghost pipefishes (Lophobranchi); the second includes the other five families: the trumpet, cornet, snipe, and shrimpfishes, as well as the rare freshwater indostomid from Burma (Aulostomi).

The members of this group are noted not only for their bizarre appearance but also for their strange anatomical and biological characteristics, which clearly set them apart from all other living fishes. One feature that they all have in common is a long, tubelike snout. Because of this elongated snout they have become quite adept at siphoning or pipetting their food. This is accomplished by a rapid intake of water that sucks the prey into the mouth. Characteristics exhibited by various families within the order include complete or partial external armor in the form of bony plates, incubation of the eggs within a special external pouch, a primitive aglomerular kidney, and tufted lobelike gills.

PIPEFISHES and SEAHORSES
—*Family Syngnathidae*

Pliny the elder (A.D. 23–79) described the seahorse under the name "hippus," and even today this is retained in the technical generic name of the seahorse, *Hippocampus,* meaning horse-caterpillar. Historically, the seahorse has long been known for its alleged medicinal properties. These range from a supposed aphrodisiac effect when used in a love potion to more prosaic uses as a cure for baldness and pains in the side; or, when a living seahorse has been dipped into oil of roses, for chills and fever.

There are approximately two dozen species of seahorses, 2 of which are found on the American Pacific coast, 6 on the Atlantic, 3 on the European and African Atlantic coasts, and 10 in the Indo-Australian area. On the other hand, there are more than 150 species of pipefishes, with 28 species on the American Atlantic coast and about 14 on the American Pacific coast (Plate 36). Whereas the seahorses are strictly marine in habitat, some of the pipefishes move readily from salt to fresh water and a few are entirely restricted to fresh water. Five hundred feet is as deep as any syngnathid has been collected; the majority of species live inshore in shallow water. One exception is the sargassum pipefish, *Syngnathus pelagicus,* which is found in the North Atlantic throughout the sargassum beds.

Adult pipefishes range in size from approximately 1 inch in the smallest species to slightly more than 18 inches in the largest. The maximum length of the largest species of seahorse, measured from the crest of the head to the tip of the tail, is about 8 inches, with the minimum adult size of the smallest species about 1½ inches.

One ichthyologist has described a pipefish as looking like a pipestem cleaner suddenly come to life. This is not really accurate unless we add an external armor made of bony plates arranged in concentric rings. In addition, we would need to add a marsupium-like brood pouch, but instead of giving it to the female, we would attach it to the underside of the male pipefish. Special tufted gills with blobs on the ends and a primitive kidney without glomeruli would help to complete the picture. To change our synthetic pipefish to a seahorse we would only need to bend the head at right angles to the body, drop the caudal fin, and add a tail even more prehensile than the elephant's trunk.

But the major difference between pipefish and seahorse is to be found in the brood pouch. Depending upon the species of pipefish, the eggs may be attached to the underside of either the abdomen or the tail. They may be fully exposed to the water or may be covered by pouch flaps that extend from the sides of the body toward the center of the egg area. In contrast, the seahorse always has the brood pouch under the tail, and it is sealed for most of its length. Only a small opening directly beneath the dorsal fin permits the entrance of the eggs and the subsequent emergence of the newly hatched seahorses. Regardless of the species of pipefish or seahorse, the female actually deposits the eggs in the brood pouch of the male, who, in turn, incubates them for a minimum of eight to ten days. The total

the opened mouth so rapidly that the observer cannot follow the movement of the hapless creature. Young seahorses may feed for as long as ten hours of each day and consume up to 3600 baby brine shrimp during that time. Although the pipefish has a straight, tubular digestive tract, and the seahorse a convoluted one, digestion is apparently equally rapid in both.

Like a human acrobatic diver on a springboard, the seahorse and to a certain extent the pipefish use the head to control the direction in which they are

Banded Pipefishes (*Dunckerocampus caulleryi chapmani*), showing male (on right) with eggs attached to abdomen; marine; New Caledonia (René Catala at Nouméa Aquarium).

length of the incubation time is dependent not only on the temperature of the water but also on the species involved.

In certain primitive pipefishes the term "brood patch" rather than brood pouch would be more accurate. In these species a naked vascular area without pouch folds or other protection develops either under the abdomen or under the tail. The eggs may be loosely attached or embedded in a spongy matrix. Examples of these types are the European worm pipefish, *Nerophis lumbriciformis,* and the bizarre Australian leafy seadragon, *Phyllopteryx foliatus.*

In watching pipefishes or seahorses, one is soon impressed by the independent movement of the eyes. Much as in the African chameleon, one eye may be looking in one direction and the other roving elsewhere. All of the syngnathids require living food. Since they are unable to move rapidly enough to chase their prey, they have had to develop their own method of capture. This secret weapon consists of a jetlike suction of pinpoint accuracy. A brine shrimp or other planktonic organism swimming within the 1½-inch range of the elongated snout is sucked into

moving. Changing the head position alters the center of gravity and the relationship of the dorsal to the pectoral fins. When the seahorse is swimming at full speed, the fins may oscillate as fast as thirty-five times per second, but at other times the undulations are much slower. Dorsal and pectoral fin movements are usually synchronized at the same oscillation rate.

One of the questions commonly asked at any public aquarium is, "How can I keep seahorses alive at home?" The answer is not to try unless you happen to be an accomplished fresh-water aquarist, and even then there are many problems. Some seahorses are hardier than others. Of the larger species, the Atlantic *Hippocampus hudsonius* (Plate 33) and the Pacific *H. kuda* (Plate 34) do well in captivity. These large species rarely mate in captivity, whereas the pigmy seahorse, *Hippocampus zosterae* from the Gulf of Mexico, may be raised through several generations without undue trouble. It is not unusual to collect large male seahorses of *Hippocampus hudsonius* in a gravid condition. These can be held until hatching time, and if the aquarist is lucky he may be able to bring the youngsters through to adulthood. In the United States this has been achieved on only a few occasions, since young seahorses of the larger species seem to be prone to every known disease. At the Steinhart Aquarium a brood was raised in 1950, but in the many other attempts made there, few have survived beyond the second month.

One of the complications of seahorse birth is that some of the unhatched progeny may die within the pouch before birth, and this soon results in the formation of gas. The male then virtually becomes a balloon and is quickly buoyed to the surface. In its regular habitat the male would immediately be picked off by some hungry fish (pipefishes and seahorses are sometimes found in stomachs of tuna and other carnivorous fishes). However, in the aquarium it is possible to open the pouch carefully and expel the gas by pressing against the sides of the pouch. The seahorse will then return to the bottom and to its normal swimming position.

In raising the first brood of the Miami seahorse at Steinhart Aquarium we were surprised to find that *Hippocampus hudsonius* grew rapidly. Emerging from the pouch about ⅝ inch in size, the youngsters feed continually on any small animal food offered to them. On a diet of newborn brine shrimp (*Artemia*) they reached a length of 2½ inches in two months and 3 inches in four months. At three and one-half months the first appearance of the male's future brood pouch was shown by a heavily pigmented area under the tail. By ten months the maximum size of 5 to 5½ inches had been reached. Cirri, or filamentous appendages, were often present on the youngsters but disappeared as they became mature. Regeneration was rapid. A fin entirely removed could be completely regenerated within two weeks. Nineteen months is as long as any American seahorses have been kept alive in captivity, and it is probable that normal longevity is less than two to three years.

Some of the European aquaria have been able to keep the Indo-Pacific *Hippocampus kuda* (Plate 34) alive for more than two years. Their experiences with the Mediterranean species, *Hippocampus brevirostris* and *H. guttulatus,* indicate that these are also reasonably hardy aquarium fishes.

The jackknife contortions of the male seahorse and the less active movements of the male pipefish during the birth of the young, not to mention the female's depositing eggs in the male's brood pouch, are rarely observed. In some American species these activities apparently occur only at night. In the Chesapeake Bay dusky pipefish, *Syngnathus floridae,* the courting pair perform a preliminary *liebespiel* during which both are in a nearly vertical position. This is soon followed by the actual transfer of the eggs, which takes place as the pair entwine about

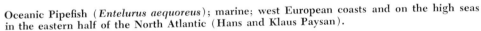

Oceanic Pipefish (*Entelurus aequoreus*); marine; west European coasts and on the high seas in the eastern half of the North Atlantic (Hans and Klaus Paysan).

each other in a figure S. Fertilization is thought to occur as the eggs pass from the female's phallus-like oviduct into the top end of the male's pouch. Each embrace lasts not longer than five minutes, and at least three encounters are usually necessary to fill the pouch. The time between successive coitions is used by the male to make room for the next batch of eggs by working the previous batch farther down into the pouch. To do this properly he apparently requires intelligence as well as experience. When one examines large series of specimens, it is obvious that some males never learn and that others are lackadaisical and do not receive a second clutch of eggs until one to several days after the first. Since the different groups of eggs will hatch at different times, this leads to much confusion in the pipefish world.

In 1954 some very important studies on the reproductive behavior of the Mediterranean pipefishes and seahorses were conducted at the Naples Biological Station by Dr. Kurt Fiedler. In the broad-nosed pipefish, *Syngnathus typhle,* it was discovered that the male entices the female by a shaking action consisting of moving his body from left to right through a 90-degree arc at a high rate of speed. The female, however, is the more active during courtship, often courting the male for several hours. Perhaps it would be more accurate to say "males," since the female seems to show no preference and changes partners often. This species does not entwine the tails during copulation. The transfer of eggs is of very short duration, lasting for less than thirty seconds. At each transfer one to twenty eggs are moved into the pouch. Spawning activity takes place at all times of the day, but at night only under illumination. After seventeen to twenty-one days of incubation, the pouch folds relax and the youngsters move out into the marine world.

Shaking during courting activities is known in both males and females of *Syngnathus abaster,* another pipefish common in the Mediterranean. However, only the males of *Syngnathus acus* show the shaking movement.

The female of the primitive and wormlike European *Nerophis ophidion* does all of the courting; the male simply follows her around. For some reason as yet unknown, the turning of the female's head to the side is stimulating to the male. During copulation the tail of the female is entwined around that of the male. The female then lays two rows of eggs on the bright yellow undersurface of the male's abdomen. The eggs are entirely exposed, since there are no brood-pouch folds or pouch-protecting plates.

The Mediterranean short-nosed seahorse, *Hippocampus brevirostris,* usually starts its breeding activ-

Mediterranean Seahorse (*Hippocampus guttulatus guttulatus*); marine; Mediterranean coasts of Europe (Otto Croy).

ities with the males courting each other. The *H. brevirostris* males may even court males of an entirely different species, such as *Hippocampus guttulatus.* Courtship goes on for several days until the pouch of the male is in proper condition to receive the eggs. During the transfer of the eggs, the male and female are usually near the surface, but the tails are not intertwined. As many as two hundred eggs can be released into the pouch within ten seconds.

By contrast, the courtship of *Hippocampus guttulatus* is more complicated. The pairs actually hold tails, which is an important factor in preventing crossbreeding with *Hippocampus brevirostris.* The males are somewhat belligerent and actually snap at rivals. Courtship pumping of the male is a characteristic of this species, and is thought to have been derived from pumping the young out of the brood pouch. During this courtship pumping the male bends forward as though he were bowing. In so doing he usually pumps his empty brood pouch full of water, which of course must be expelled before he can receive a clutch of eggs. The ejection of the young from the brood pouch is usually preceded for two days by intention movements.

Strangely enough, the toughest of all the seahorses is also the smallest. This pigmy, *Hippocampus zosterae,* is full grown when only 1½ inches long. It is usually considered a shallow-water species, ranging from eastern Florida through the Gulf of Mexico to Campeche. Dr. Kirk Strawn's detailed studies of this species at Cedar Keys, Florida, have shown not only that it is able to survive in water temperatures from 43 degrees to 98 degrees F., but also that its salinity tolerance allows it to live easily in water that is 40 per cent fresh. Breeding takes place during nine months of the year, with no activity from November through January; about ten days are required for the eggs to mature in the male's brood pouch. Two days after delivery he is ready to receive another clutch of eggs; in water of 85 degrees two broods per month is considered normal. The brood pouch can carry a maximum of fifty-five eggs, but the average is usually about twenty-five. The young grow quite rapidly, reach maturity in two to three months, and have a life span of less than a year.

Unguarded carborundum air stones which release air in small bubbles can be disastrous to the courting activities of the male pigmy seahorse. During the courting procedure the male pumps his pouch full of water, but if his tail should happen to be wrapped around an air line or air stone, he is quite likely to suck in one or more air bubbles. This causes him to lose his equilibrium and rise to the surface, more or less permanently disrupting the courtship. The larger species of seahorses do not seem to be disturbed by air bubbles.

Just what is the normal vertical position for the seahorse? Artists often show the tail of the horse curled backward toward the head, but this position is impossible for the adult. Aquarium observations have revealed that the seahorse is remarkably agile for the first two weeks or month of life. In swimming, a youngster may bend the tail backward in a reverse crescent, but the tail is prehensile only in a forward direction. Adult seahorses seldom carry the tail in a straight position, usually having it coiled forward.

Some years ago I became interested in the problem of how the primitive pipefish developed into a seahorse. The answer was to be found in the brood pouch, for I discovered that there were four basic ways by which different kinds of pipefishes could hold the eggs in the pouch. The pouch folds (1) could be very short, hardly covering even the outermost eggs; or (2) they could be long and cover the eggs completely by overlapping at the center; or (3) they might turn inward and divide the eggs within the pouch into two sections; or (4) one flap might turn back upon itself and the other overlap it.

Strangely enough, it was a pipefish with a brood pouch of this last type that gave rise to the true seahorse. We know this because there is one pipefish,

Amphelikturus dendriticus, that is really a missing link. Fewer than two dozen specimens have been found—all in the Bahamas. The missing link has a partially sealed brood pouch intermediate between that of the pipefish and that of the seahorse; it has developed the prehensile tail of the seahorse but still retains the tail fin of the pipefish; and finally, the head is only partially bent, making a 45-degree angle or less with the axis of the body.

Pipefishes as well as many reef fishes show a marked vertical distribution. For example, during the ichthyological studies preceding and following the 1946 atom bomb tests at Bikini and adjacent atolls, it was found that there were ten species of pipefishes in the region. Five of these were common in the intertidal area and had been known for many years. However, from a depth of ten to fifty feet and perhaps deeper, there were five additional species which were entirely new to science and were subsequently described in the first volume of the Bikini fish report (1953).

It is interesting to note that the discovery of the vertical distributional gradients at Bikini was made possible through the development of diving techniques that have since been widely used. Wearing diving gear and carrying a canvas type of desert water bag filled with derris fish poison (derris is a tropical plant), the ichthyological diver can safely poison any reef down to depths of about fifty feet. Most of the early studies were carried out with airline gear, but recent work has been done with self-contained diving equipment using compressed air.

Many of the small and very rare pipefishes are suspected of leading a burrowing and eel-like existence. Dr. Robert Rofen discovered a finless pipefish of this type in 1951 at Christmas Island, where the British subsequently conducted atom bomb tests. It was found at low tide under five feet of water, beneath a foot of coral rubble at the base of a coral head. It turned out to be *Penetopteryx taenocephalus,* which previously had been found only in areas some three thousand miles away. Another member of the same genus, *Penetopteryx nanus,* was found more than fifty years ago in coral rubble on a beach in the Bahamas. Despite intensive collecting in that area in recent years, no additional specimens have been discovered.

GHOST PIPEFISHES—Family Solenostomidae

The ghost pipefishes are the closest living relatives of the true syngnathid pipefishes and seahorses. They are small, and at a maximum length measure no more than 3 to 6 inches. In appearance they look like pipefish getting ready to fly. The head of the ghost pipefish is similar to that of the syngnathid

Shrimpfish (*Aeoliscus strigatus*) in typical head-down position among the spines of a sea urchin; marine; Indo-Australian region (René Catala at Nouméa Aquarium).

pipefish, but there the resemblance ends, for the body immediately behind the head is greatly expanded, forming a base for the long and slender first dorsal and ventral fins. Behind this, the body is again constricted to about the diameter of the head, only to widen again a short distance farther on to form the base of the second dorsal and anal fins. The tail fin is very long and looks like a big broom attached to the body. One genus, *Solenostomus*, with perhaps five species restricted to the tropical Indo-Pacific, makes up this family, which has reversed the procedure so firmly established by the syngnathids. It is the female ghost pipefish and not the male who cares for the young in the brood pouch. In this case the brood pouch is formed by the elongated ventral fins, whose inner margins are attached to the abdomen, thus forming a semi-open pouch area. On the inside surface of these pouch fins are short filaments that serve to hold the eggs within the pouch. As might be expected, the inner margins of the male's ventral fins are not attached to the abdomen. Although some of these fishes occur in shallow water, they are quite rare and almost nothing is known of their biology.

Like the true pipefishes and seahorses, the ghost pipefish retains the peculiar lobed or tufted gills. Because of the similarities between these two families they are sometimes placed in a separate suborder, Lophobranchi. The remaining five families in the order Solenichthys have a normal gill structure and do not provide incubators for the young; they are often grouped together under the suborder Aulostomi.

INDOSTOMIDS—Family Indostomidae

In 1929 a small, strange fish was discovered in Lake Indawgyi of the Myitkyina District of Upper Burma. It looked much like a cross between a pipefish and a stickleback, and it was given the scientific name *Indostomus paradoxus*. This name is most appropriate, for it well describes the various viewpoints that have been expressed about its relationships. *Indostomus* has the isolated dorsal fin spines of the stickleback, but the head and the bony exoskeleton remind one of the pipefish; and the large tail fin looks like one characteristic of the abdominal-pouched syngnathid pipefishes. When the detailed biology and anatomy of *Indostomus* are fully unraveled, they will undoubtedly reveal much needed information about the relationships between the tube-mouthed fishes.

SHRIMPFISHES—Family Centriscidae

Members of the shrimpfish family have a compressed knifelike body covered with a transparent tortoise-shell-like armor arranged in the form of plates. As in the seahorse, the slight movements of the fins give the shrimpfish its mobility. The entire undersurface of the body is extremely sharp; hence the Australian common name, razorfish. The two genera, each made up of two species, are easily distinguished by the difference in the spine at the posterior end of the body. In *Centriscus* the dorsal spine is long and solid, whereas in *Aeoliscus* it is jointed and movable. Shrimpfishes are found in shallow waters from East Africa to Hawaii but are strangely absent in the Atlantic.

Some years ago while visiting the Turtle Islands off the north coast of Borneo, I slipped over the side of the boat and began the usual underwater check of the inshore fish fauna. Visibility was poor through the face mask, but suddenly I came face to face with a living shrimpfish. It was particularly startling because it was swimming with the head pointed downward rather than upward as illustrated in a number of books. Present-day ichthyologists are not entirely in agreement as to the orientation of the swimming shrimpfish. Dr. Robert Rofen has told me of his observations of shrimpfish (*Aeoliscus strigatus*) swimming head down along the bottom of a small underwater cave. As they came to the cave wall, they continued up the wall but in a horizontal position until they reached the ceiling, where they continued to forage even though the body was now reversed in its vertical orientation. He further observed that when disturbed they would turn the sharp underedge of the body toward the intruder. However, if really frightened they would streak off in normal (for other fishes) horizontal position.

Unfortunately, the reproductive pattern and general biology of these very interesting shrimpfishes is still largely unknown.

SNIPEFISHES—Family Macrorhamphosidae

The snipefishes, sometimes called bellows fishes, are a small group of about eleven species divided among four genera. They are deep-bodied fishes with a long snout and a single very long dorsal fin spine that extends backward toward the tail. Characteristically, there are two series of bony plates on each side of the back, forming an imperfect exoskeleton. All species are small, with none reaching a maximum length of more than 10 inches. They are found in tropical and temperate marine zones, ranging from moderate depths to deep water. In appearance the snipefishes suggest that they are in the first stage of progressive evolution approaching their cousins, the shrimpfishes. Some species are silvery, while others are bright red to pink. An outstandingly colorful species is the banded snipefish, *Centriscops obliquus,* from New South Wales and New Zealand, which has a beautiful orange-pink coloration with five oblique dark bands across the body. Aquarium observations by David Graham (New Zealand) show that the banded snipefish usually swims backward as easily as it does forward and that its normal position in the water is with the head pointed downward. This position of the body again suggests a relationship with the "head-down" shrimpfishes. Apparently the snipefish is easily excited; merely turning on the lights is likely to result in its jumping up and out of the water, occasionally onto the floor. They feed with great gusto upon the eggs of starfish or other animals that lay eggs in their tank.

CORNETFISH—Family Fistulariidae

The cornetfishes, sometimes called flutemouths, are fairly common in tropical seas, especially around reefs, where they swim about in loosely formed schools. There are about four species, at least one of which—the red cornetfish, *Fistularia villosa*—reaches a length of 6 feet. Because of its slender body, it weighs only around seven and one-half pounds at this length. The principal identifying mark of the cornetfish is the long filament extending from the center of the tail fin. Almost equally as long as the filament is the tubular snout, which is one of the most efficient food pipettes known in the fish world. Alternately broadening, then narrowing, the snout enables the cornetfish to siphon rapidly into the mouth any small morsels of food in the vicinity. An ichthyologist making a population study of fishes by poisoning the water in a limited reef area sometimes finds that he has taken a great many cornetfish although he may have seen only a few before the poisoning.

TRUMPETFISHES—Family Aulostomidae

The trumpetfish looks much like the cornetfish but lacks the long filament on the end of the tail and is further distinguished by a series of isolated spines in front of the dorsal fin. Maximum length for any of the four species is around 2 feet. These fishes are often found in the same reef areas as cornetfishes, but they are not nearly so common and are often difficult to locate because of their ability to camouflage themselves (Plate 35). They have been observed attempting, usually successfully, to bring

Trumpetfish (*Aulostomus maculatus*); marine; both sides of the tropical Atlantic (Fritz Goro: *Life* Magazine, at Lerner Marine Laboratory, Bimini).

their bodies into alignment with other larger fishes in the same manner as the shark suckers. It has been suggested that this may be a combination transportation and camouflage device.

Codfishes, Hakes, and Rattails (*Order Anacanthini*)

The codfishes and their relatives have soft-rayed fins, usually without spines; they may often be identified by the "cod look," which is partially due to the location of the ventral fins ahead of the pectorals, sometimes under the throat. Another typical feature is the presence of a ductless air bladder. Certain of the deep-sea grenadiers or rattails have a single spine in front of the dorsal fin. A few of the cods and a larger number of grenadiers have luminous glands or ducts that produce light because of luminescent bacteria. As many as six families of anacanthine fishes are sometimes recognized, with a total of several hundred species.

CODFISHES—*Family Gadidae*

The gadids are predominantly a cold- and temperate-water group, and with one exception are all marine fishes; they occur chiefly in the northern hemisphere and to a lesser extent in the southern hemisphere. The family includes some of the world's most valuable food fishes. Since many of these forms live near the bottom, they are often referred to as ground or bottom fishes. Commercial methods of capture include the use of large trawling nets which are dragged over the fishing beds (probably the most frequently used method), set lines, seines, and gill nets. Because of the keeping qualities of dried and salted codfish, fisheries for the Atlantic cod,

Gadus callarias, are among the world's oldest; it has long been one of the most profitable food fishes on both sides of the North Atlantic. The Atlantic cod has a characteristic speckled pattern on the sides of the body, three dorsal fins, and two anal fins; there is a small whiskery barbel under the chin. It is the largest of some 150 species in the family, reaching a maximum of 211 pounds at a length of 6 feet; however, those caught commercially are usually much smaller, ranging from only 2½ to 25 pounds. Spawning generally takes place between January and March, with the female laying a fantastic number of eggs, the record being somewhere around 9,000,000 for a 75-pound fish. The eggs float for some ten to twenty days, and as soon as they hatch, the larval cods become a part of the floating plankton where they remain for the next two and one-half months. By this time they have reached a length of about 1 inch; they then sink to the bottom where they continue to grow fairly rapidly. In two years the cods reach a length of about 15 inches; by the time they are five years old, they are usually capable of spawning.

The smoked fish product called "finnan haddie" is widely known to many who may not be familiar with the actual fish, *Melanogrammus aeglefinus,* the haddock. This species resembles the cod in having three dorsal and two anal fins, but it lacks the cod's reticulated markings along the sides of the body. A large blotch just above and back of the pectoral fin provides ready identification. It is a much smaller fish than the cod, the maximum recorded size being 44 inches and thirty-six pounds. It is widely distributed on both sides of the North Atlantic, and in recent years has been the basis for highly productive bottom fisheries in both regions. However, there has been considerable evidence of overfishing, with the result that in some areas larger sized mesh on the trawl nets is now required in an

Atlantic Cod (*Gadus callarias* or *morhua*); marine; both sides of the North Atlantic (Douglas P. Wilson).

attempt to rehabilitate the fishery by allowing the smaller fishes to escape. The haddock occurs in many of the same areas as the codfish, but has different feeding habits, preferring invertebrates rather than fish, which is predominant in the diet of the codfish. For example, a study of the food in the stomachs of more than twelve hundred haddock from New England's Georges Banks revealed that the 173 kinds of animals found there were mostly crustaceans, followed in order by molluskans, echinoderms, worms, and finally, fish. Vertebral counts correlated with water temperatures show that the haddock stocks of the northwestern Atlantic may be divided into five distinct populations.

Other commercially important North Atlantic species include the pollack, *Gadus pollachius,* a fish with greenish coloration above and a jutting lower jaw without a barbel under the chin. The coalfish, *Gadus virens,* is similar to the pollack in appearance, but it is blackish above and retains the chin barbel. The whiting, *Gadus merlangus,* is a silvery fish lacking the chin barbel; it has an identifying black mark on the upper part of the base of the pectoral fin.

The Pacific cod, *Gadus macrocephalus,* has a mottled pattern along the sides of the body somewhat like the Atlantic cod; however, it is a smaller species, its maximum length being only about 30 inches. It ranges from Oregon to the Bering Sea and south to Japan and Korea. On the American side it is of negligible commercial importance, but in Japan it is one of the most valuable fishes. The Japanese recognize two kinds of "tara," as the Pacific cod is called. One race is sedentary and spends its time on the fishing grounds, whereas the other is migratory and always on the move. The principal fishing season in Japan is from December through April; set lines and gill nets are the gear most often used.

The Pacific tomcod, *Microgadus proximus,* is a 12-inch silvery white species ranging from Alaska to central California; although it is highly esteemed by some as a food item, the total sports and commercial catch is small. The Atlantic tomcod, *Microgadus tomcod,* is slightly larger than the Pacific species and is a greenish color on the upper part of the body. It occasionally moves into fresh water throughout its range from the Gulf of St. Lawrence to Virginia.

The previous species all have three dorsal and two anal fins; other members of the family have different fin combinations. For example, the European five-bearded rockling, *Motella mustela,* an 18-inch inshore fish, has two dorsals, with the anterior one sunk in a groove in the back. The second dorsal is very long, as is the single anal. The most striking feature of this fish is the five barbels: there is the usual barbel beneath the chin, and in addition there are two on the upper lip and a pair on the anterior nostrils. The four-bearded rockling, *Motella cimbra,* has the same fin characteristics as its five-bearded cousin; however, it occurs on both sides of the North Atlantic.

The only fresh-water member of the cod family—and also of the entire order Anacanthini—is the burbot, *Lota lota,* a holarctic species which ranges from the polar regions southward in Eurasia and North America; although it extends as far south as the Black Sea and the high Italian lakes, in England it is found south of Durham only, and it does not occur in Scotland or Ireland. Since it is the only fresh-water fish that has codfish characteristics, it is fairly easy to identify: the ventral fins are ahead of the pectorals; there are two soft dorsal fins and a single anal fin; and a single barbel is present under the tip of the lower jaw. The burbot is a very slender fish, the largest on record measuring 32 inches and weighing only twelve pounds. It is a winter spawner, with the young appearing during the early spring. The eggs, instead of floating as those of the marine species do, lie on the bottom. Not only is it a cold-water species, it is also a deep-water species, having been taken at depths of seven hundred feet in the Great Lakes of North America.

Because of the fact that the hakes have the frontal bones of the head separate (those of the cod are joined) and ribs attached to the anterior vertebrae (in the cod the ribs begin with the fifth or sixth vertebra), some investigators consider the hakes members of a separate family, the Merlucciidae. Externally, the elongated, streamlined hakes look like many of the other codfishes. In the hake the second and third dorsals are combined to form a single very long second dorsal fin, which has a slight notch in the center indicating where the third dorsal would have started had this second portion of the fin been entirely separate. A center notch also is present on the very long single anal fin. The pelvic or ventral fins are placed ahead of the pectoral fins, the lower jaw is longer than the upper jaw, and the barbels under the chin are lacking. The flesh of the hakes is fairly soft and usually does not keep as well as that of other fishes; this may explain why there is so little exploitation of the large hake populations in various parts of the world. There are, however, active fisheries for hake in South Africa and Europe, and the population of the European hake, *Merluccius merluccius,* has actually shown signs of depletion. The European hake is an interesting species with a wide temperature and geographic range, occurring all the way from Norway to Cape Blanco on the northwestern coast of Africa, and also in the Mediterranean. It reaches maturity at a length of 8 inches, and its maximum weight is around twenty pounds. The European hake lives in deeper water than many of the other codlike fishes, having been taken at depths of 2400 feet. It is an active and predaceous species, with other fishes forming a major part of its diet. Spawning of the European hake and the American Atlantic silver hake, *Merluccius bilinearis,* occurs during the summer, whereas that of the Pacific hake, *M. productus,* takes place during the early spring. Hake eggs are buoyant, and they may be identified by the presence of a conspicuous oil globule, which is absent from the eggs of most of the codfishes. During plankton surveys off California the eggs of the Pacific hake were discovered as far as three hundred miles offshore.

The South African hake or stockfish, *Merluccius capensis,* a species reaching a length of 4 feet, is considered the most valuable single commercial species in the region; many of the catches are made by trawlers, some of which operate their nets as deep as eighteen hundred feet.

Bregmaceros macclellandi is an interesting 5-inch codlike fish found throughout the Indo-Pacific region. The first dorsal fin is merely a single long ray on the top of the head; the second dorsal has two distinct lobes, as does the anal. The ventral fins are attached to the throat, and the three outer rays of the ventrals are long, separate filaments which trail backward for about one-half the length of the fish. This species and one or two others are sometimes assigned to a separate family, the Bregmacerotidae. One genus, *Muraenolepis,* a codlike fish from the Antarctic, has a first dorsal composed of a single ray like *Bregmaceros;* in addition, this strange cold-water fish has the dorsal and anal fins continuous with the tail fin. It is also recognized under a separate family, the Muraenolepidae.

DEEP-SEA RATTAILS or GRENADIERS
—Family Coryphaenoididae

Rattails are so named because of their long, tapering tails. The tail fin is missing, and the long anal and second dorsal fins extend almost to the pointed tip of the body. As in the codfishes, the ventral fins are anterior to the pectorals in position. Some species have a single spine in front of the flaglike first dorsal fin; many have a barbel under the chin; and some, such as the Indo-Pacific *Coelorhynchus parallelus,* have long noses that extend forward for a considerable distance ahead of the mouth, which is recessed on the underside of the head. This nose extension undoubtedly aids the fish in grubbing and digging up the bottom. Although there are many genera and species of these grenadiers living in the depths of all the oceans, some in tremendous abundance, they are seldom seen, since only occasionally do they stray into water even as shallow as five hundred feet. They are rather flabby fishes, so that when brought to the surface they have usually lost most of their scales and are in poor condition. The majority of the species are less than 2 feet in length, although there are some that grow larger. The smooth-spined grenadier, *Macrourus berglax,* is a 3-foot cold-water rattail widely distributed in deep water on both sides of the Atlantic.

Opah and Ribbonfishes

(Order Allotriognathi)

The name "Allotriognathi" means "strange jaws," and it is a most appropriate way to describe this rare deep-water group of marine fishes, all of which have soft-rayed fins. In appearance, there is such variation within the group that one would not suspect many of the species of being even slightly related. However, all of them are united by the fact that they have protrusible jaws of a type not found among other fishes.

OPAH—Family Lampridae

When one of these large, oval-shaped, and laterally compressed fishes is caught, it usually is reported in the newspapers, with a vivid description of its spectacular color pattern. The upper surface is blue to gray, changing to rose red on the under surface, and the entire body is covered with a series of white spots. The jaws and the sickle-shaped fins are vermilion, and there is a golden area around the eye. The opah, *Lampris regius,* sometimes called moonfish, is the only member of its family; it reaches a length of 6 feet and a weight of almost six hundred

Tropical Reef Fishes at Bermuda: Longspine Squirrelfish (*Holocentrus rufus*) in foreground, Blue Angelfish (*Holacanthus bermudensis*) in center, spotted Bermuda Chub (*Kyphosus sectatrix*) above, and banded Sergeant Majors (*Abudefduf saxatilus*) on the sides; marine; tropical American Atlantic (George G. Lower).

pounds, and it has flesh of excellent flavor. It is thought that squids and octopuses form a large part of the opah diet. One investigator found the beaks of fifty-four cuttlefish in the stomach of a single fish. In the vicinity of Madeira the food is often composed of crustaceans, especially sea woodlice (isopods). Although the opah occurs in all seas, it is never abundant. For example, on the American Pacific coast its range is from southern California to northwestern Alaska; yet not more than four dozen specimens have ever been recorded from this extended coast line. It is occasionally taken on long lines off Madeira and Japan. Fishery biologists have long looked upon this fish as a future food resource, provided that someone can discover the depths at which it is most abundant, and that commercial fishing gear that will work effectively at such depths can be developed.

RIBBONFISHES: DEALFISHES, OARFISHES, and LOPHOTIDS

These are fragile, offshore, usually deep-water species that are quite spectacular anatomically. The body is very thin—for example, a ribbonfish 8 feet long might have a body 12 inches deep and only 2 inches or even less in width. The dorsal fin usually starts on top of the head as a plumelike topknot and extends down the long body to the tail fin, which is quite long and at a right angle to the body. Actually, this is the upper lobe of the tail fin, the lower lobe being undeveloped. As the juvenile fish grows

older, the topknot usually decreases in size, and the right-angled tail is often broken off, with the remaining portion coming to lie more in line with the body. The ventral fins, originally quite large, decrease in size and may even be lost during this growth process. These radical growth changes explain why so many different species of these fishes have been described. As many as three families of ribbonfishes have been recognized: (1) the dealfishes, family Trachipteridae, which have scales and lack the anal fin; (2) the giant oarfishes, which measure up to 30 feet and are sometimes included with the trachipterids, but are also recognized separately as the family Regalecidae, chiefly on the basis of the very elongated, slender ventral fins from which the oarfish takes its name; and (3) the Lophotidae, a scaleless group of ribbon-like fishes that retain the anal fin but lack the ventral fins.

The origin of many stories of sea serpents may be traced to the occasional appearance of one of the ribbonfishes. The giant oarfish, or king of the herrings, *Regalecus glesne,* which occurs in all seas, has undoubtedly contributed more than its share to these legends. A description of one 11-foot *Regalecus* observed swimming at the surface in Indonesia stated that its undulating motion was most serpent-like, and that whenever the body was touched, the flaglike crest on the top of the head was instantly erected.

Many taboos have developed around the king of the herrings; for example, the ancient Norwegians believed that if one of these fishes were injured, it would keep away the herring. A similar belief was held by the American coastal Indians of the Pacific northwest about another member of the ribbonfish family, the Pacific king of the salmon, *Trachipterus rex-salmonorum.*

Squirrelfishes and Their Relatives *(Order Berycomorphi)*

In some respects this is a transitional group of fishes, intermediate between the primitive forms with fins having few or no spines and the more advanced typical perchlike, spiny-rayed species to be described in the order Percomorphi. The geological record shows that the berycomorphs of earlier times were extremely abundant, both in number of species and in total population. The group is characterized internally by several obscure anatomical similarities and externally by the fact that the dorsal fin is preceded by a series of spiny rays and the many-rayed ventral fins are thoracic in position—that is, just behind the pectoral fins. Most of the sixteen families are deep-sea groups, and many of them are bright red in color. Two suborders are recognized: (1) the primitive Berycoidea, containing ten families including the squirrelfishes and the lantern-eye fishes, the only shallow-water families in the group; and (2) the highly specialized, deep-sea fishes of the suborder Xenoberyces, with six families.

SQUIRRELFISHES or SOLDIERFISHES
—Family Holocentridae

Bright colors—usually some shade of red—and shallow-water tropical reefs are invariably associated with the nocturnal squirrelfishes. In the daytime it is often difficult for a swimmer with a face mask to see many of the squirrelfishes that may be in an area, for they tend to hide in crevices and cracks. At night they are usually much more active, moving out over the reefs to forage. An examination of Plates 37 through 40 will clearly show the general characteristics of these fishes, which are noted for their sharp spines and sharp scales as well as their large "squirrel-like" eyes.

Although the squirrelfishes have a world-wide distribution in tropical marine waters, they still form a small family, the total number of species being only around seventy. As adults, squirrelfishes are not migratory and tend to remain near the bottom in one general area. The larval fishes, with their noses long and pointed like supersonic jet aircraft, look quite different from the adults. Instead of remaining near the bottom, they become a part of the floating plankton and are apt to be swept for many miles by surface currents. Stomachs of offshore tuna are sometimes crammed with these larval squirrelfishes.

The genus *Holocentrus* is the largest genus in the family; these fishes can be recognized by their strong preopercular spine and very long dagger-like anal spine, one of four spines preceding the soft rays of the fin. *Holocentrus spinifer,* which occurs in the eastern Pacific and reaches a length of around 2 feet, is probably the largest species. *Holocentrus xantherythrus* (Plate 37), is a common species around the Hawaiian Islands; the longspine squirrelfish, *Holocentrus rufus* (Plate 38), is an equally common tropical Atlantic form. The wistful squirrelfish, *Holotrachys lima* (Plate 39), has a great number of prickles over the entire body, a feature which helps to distinguish it from the other squirrelfishes. The deep-water squirrelfish, *Ostichthys japonicus* (Plate 40), lives in much deeper water than any of the other members of the family. *Myripristis* is the second-largest genus in the family, and it contains the most important species economically. In body form these fishes resemble the wistful squirrel but have a larger eye and lack the prickles over the body. In

the Hawaiian fish markets, fishes of this genus are known as "menpachi" and command a premium price. *Myripristis*-type squirrelfishes are generally schooling species which move about over the reef more than do members of the genus *Holocentrus,* which are often solitary, exhibiting a strong territorial pattern.

Squirrelfishes have occasionally been described as producing sounds that can be heard even out of water without amplification. One day during a rehearsal for a *Science in Action* telecast on which we were discussing squirrelfishes, we were surprised to hear a series of faint intermittent sounds coming from the studio display tank. Even more startling was the obvious courting activity while the sounds were being produced by a pair of Hawaiian striped squirrelfish, *Holocentrus xantherythrus.* The pair held their tails close together with the forward parts of the body apart, so that a V or Y was formed between the two of them. The studio photographer happened to be there and snapped a picture of this activity, the re-

Courting activity between Striped Squirrelfishes (*Holocentrus xantherythrus*); marine; Hawaiian Islands (**Moss Photography, California Academy of Sciences**).

sult of which appears nearby. This was the first time that prenuptial activity in squirrelfishes had been observed or recorded.

ALFONSINOS—Family Berycidae

The deep-water alfonsinos are often brightly colored and are among the most primitive of the berycomorph fishes. Paleontologists tell us that they were the first of the spiny-rayed fishes to appear in the fossil record, specifically in the Cretaceous deposits. The 24-inch red *Beryx splendens,* one of the most common species, is of world-wide distribution. Its usual depth range is between 1800 and 2400 feet. In both Japan and Madeira, where it was originally discovered, it is considered an excellent food fish. The alfonsinos resemble the squirrelfishes but have a shorter, stumpy body with a very elongated caudal peduncle. The ventral or pelvic fins of the alfonsinos characteristically have seven to thirteen soft rays.

LANTERN-EYE FISHES—Family Anomalopidae

Although there are a number of kinds of fishes that have the capability of producing light, only those in the lantern-eye family have a shutter arrangement that enables them to turn the light on or off at will. All three genera in the family have beneath each eye a broad bar that is actually composed of a series of tubes containing luminous bacteria. Since the bacteria cannot, of course, be turned off and on, the lantern-eyes regulate the visibility of the luminous eye patch in one of two ways: (1) by means of a dark windowshade-type eyelid which can be pulled up over the luminous gland—represented by *Photoblepharon palpebratus* of the East Indies; or (2) by a muscular attachment which allows the gland to be rotated so that the light is no longer visible to another fish—represented by *Anomalops kaptoptron,* also from the East Indies. In swimming, *Anomalops* makes use of the light organ intermittently, turning the light on for about ten seconds and then off for about five seconds. *Photoblepharon* seems to have a steadier light which is kept on for as long as thirty minutes, whereafter it usually becomes erratically intermittent. The latter has a single dorsal fin and is a small fish of about 3½ inches, whereas *Anomalops* has two dorsals and reaches a length of 12 inches. The only other species in the family is *Kryptophanaron alfredi,* from Jamaica in the Caribbean.

BARBUDOS—Family Polymixiidae

The barbudo, a foot-long nonedible type of fish usually living in depths between six hundred and twelve hundred feet, resembles the squirrelfish but has two long whiskers under the chin and small scales. This family is distinguished by a black spot at the forward tip of the dorsal fin and a black margin on the V-shaped tail fin, as well as by the sixty or more scales along the lateral line. At least four species of this widely distributed fish have been described, but it is probable that only one or perhaps two will be recognized: *Polymixia nobilis* from the Atlantic and *P. japonica* from the Indo-Pacific.

PINECONE FISHES—Family Monocentridae

Pinecone fishes are aptly named, for the heavy platelike scales on the outside of the body give them a pine-cone appearance. The two known species resemble some of the squirrelfishes but have peculiarities all their own. The spines of the dorsal fin are not in alignment, but alternate, the first spine being inclined to one side and the next spine to the other side. They also have a tremendous spine on the outer edge of the pelvic fin. Under the lower jaw there are two light organs which produce phosphorescence by means of the activity of symbiotic phosphorescent bacteria. The 5-inch *Monocentris japonicus* is a schooling species found on the bottom in deep water. It has a wide range through the Indo-Pacific region; in southern Japan it is eaten with vinegar, fried, roasted, or in soya bean soup. It is also a very popular aquarium fish. The Australian pinecone fish, *Monocentris gloriae-maris,* is the only other species.

Gibber, Prickle, Bigscale and Whalefishes

(Suborder Xenoberyces)

These small, obscure, deep-sea fishes, comprising six families and about thirty-five species, make up the entire suborder Xenoberyces. The first three families are similar in appearance, having large, cavernous heads with many mucous areas, and large, platelike, deciduous scales on their bodies. The gibberfishes (family Gibberichthyidae) are known from only four specimens taken in the North Atlantic and off Madagascar; they have vertical rows of papillae on the sides of the body—a feature shared only by certain whalefishes. The very spiny pricklefishes (family Stephanoberycidae) are known from two small species, one from the Atlantic Gulf Stream and the other from off the Tuamotus. The bigscale fishes (family Melamphaidae) contain the largest number of species—about twenty in all, and, like the other members of this suborder, are only a few inches in length.

The rare deep-water whalefishes are undoubtedly the most interesting of the Xenoberyces; at one time they were placed in a separate order, the Cetunculi. As of 1959 fewer than two dozen specimens of these luminous, often brilliantly colored fishes had ever been collected. Orange and red are usually conspicuously present on the blackish body, especially around the mouth and on the fins; yet these fishes are blind or have very degenerate eyes and live at depths where they never see light. The whalefishes are very delicate, ranging in size from only 2 to 6 inches; they have very large mouths and are able to swallow other deep-sea fishes as large as themselves. As might be expected, the whalefish's stomach is highly distensible, a feature that is essential in order to hold the very large prey. The soft-rayed dorsal fin is fairly large and is set far back on the body, opposite the equally large spineless anal fin. Both of these fins have luminous areas, usually at the forward end of the fin. This luminosity is thought to be due to an exudate from a special glandular tissue located at the fin base. It is of interest to note that this type of glandular light-producing tissue is found in only one other group of fishes—the deep-sea gulper eels of the order Lyomeri. This similarity is part of the evidence indicating a close relationship between the whalefishes and the gulper eels.

Since the whalefish does not have an air bladder, it has been confronted with the problem of maintaining its position in the water without sinking. Recent investigations by Dr. Robert R. Rofen of Stanford's George Vanderbilt Foundation have shown that this is accomplished in the Cetomimidae by a unique method. The lateral line is made up of an enormous hollow tube which has a series of large holes along its length; between these holes are attached flotation appendages which vary from species to species, but typically are shaped like a dunce cap with the broad base attached to the lateral-line tube.

Most of the whalefishes do not have ventral fins, and so they are placed in a single family, the Cetomimidae, containing ten species and five genera. However, there are two kinds that do have ventral fins: (1) the spiny-skinned *Barbourisia rufa,* which occurs in the Atlantic and off Madagascar, and has been placed in a separate family, the Barbourisiidae; and (2) *Rondeletia bicolor,* a smooth-skinned species assigned to another separate family, the Rondeletiidae. The latter species has a different kind of lateral line, the hollow lateral-line tube being replaced by about twenty vertical rows of papillae, which are the external indications of mucous tubes extending down the sides of the body. In the fish world, such an arrangement is found only in *Rondeletia* and in the gibberfishes discussed earlier.

John Dories and Their Relatives *(Order Zeomorphi)*

The enigmatic deep-sea zeomorphs are a small group of spiny-rayed fishes, usually thin and deep-bodied, that have long presented ichthyologists with classification problems that even today are not entirely solved. They usually have enormously distensible jaws, set at an oblique angle, and ventral fins with six to nine rays.

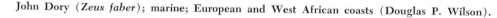

John Dory (*Zeus faber*); marine; European and West African coasts (Douglas P. Wilson).

JOHN DORIES—Family Zeidae

Unlike most of the other zeomorph fishes, which are deep-sea forms, the pouting John Dories are midwater species, found at depths that can easily be fished by commercial gear. These fishes are readily identified by the large, round, black spot surrounded by a yellow ring that is located in the center of the body. As growth proceeds, the spinous dorsal of some ten rays develops long, trailing filaments that may extend almost to the end of the tail fin. Identification is further aided by the presence of a number of small spines or bucklers along the bases of both the dorsal and anal fins. There is also a series of eight or nine spinose plates along the abdomen; the absence of these plates is the chief distinguishing feature of one of the two boarfish families, Caproidae, the members of which otherwise look much like John Dories. The European *Capros aper* is fairly common in offshore waters of moderate depth.

The John Dory, *Zeus faber,* is found from the British Isles southward into the Mediterranean and to the African coasts. Another species, *Zeus japonicus,* replaces it in the Indo-Pacific region. The maximum length of these fishes is about 3 feet. In the regions where they occur they are common market fishes. Food experts do not seem to be in agreement as to the value of these fishes, some declaring that they are gourmet items, others that they are suitable only for reduction to fish meal.

At the Plymouth Aquarium in England experiences with the John Dory have shown it to be a difficult fish to keep alive in captivity unless small living fishes or shrimp are available as food. However, aquarists there found it was possible to train this species over a period of several weeks to accept long pieces of cut squid, which looked like fish as they were dropped into the water and slowly floated to the bottom.

BOARFISHES—Family Antigoniidae

These are bright red fishes that can often be recognized by the extreme depth of the slim body. The horizontal distance from the snout to the end of the caudal peduncle is usually equal to the vertical distance from the base of the dorsal fin to the bottom of the abdomen; thus, in profile, the boarfish usually forms a rhomboid or diamond. Another distinguishing feature is the presence of three anal spines entirely separate from the soft rays of the anal fin and not attached to them. *Antigonia capros* is a widely distributed species known from many parts of the Atlantic and the western Pacific. *Antigonia eos* is occasionally taken by dredge in the vicinity of the Hawaiian Islands from depths ranging between three hundred and seven hundred feet.

GRAMMICOLEPIDS—Family Grammicolepidae

These rare deep-water fishes are sometimes washed ashore after heavy storms or, as in Hawaii, as the result of a volcanic eruption's pouring hot lava into the sea. The grammicolepids have peculiar parchment-like linear scales arranged vertically, much like those of the juvenile surgeon fishes. The latter, however, do not have a separate spiny dorsal fin, a fact that readily differentiates them. Two genera and species are known: *Grammicolepis brachiusculus* from the West Indies and Hawaii, and *Xenolepidichthys dagleishi* which ranges from the West Indies and South Africa to the Philippines and Japan.

Perchlike Fishes

(Order Percomorphi)

This is the largest order of fishes, containing an estimated 8000 species divided among more than 125 families. As might be expected of so large a group of fishes, the range of anatomical variation is great; therefore, it will be easier to discuss each of the fifteen subordinal groups as a separate unit.

Sea Basses and Their Relatives (Suborder Percoidea)

These fishes are rather generalized species, usually with the pelvic fins, each composed of a spine and five soft rays, placed rather far forward on the underside of the body, either in thoracic or in jugular position. About eighty-three families divided into twelve groups are included in this, the largest suborder of percomorph fishes.

GROUPERS and SEA BASSES—Family Serranidae

Among the approximately four hundred species in this family we find many of the world's most important food fishes, as well as a few that have been known to cause poisoning. The serranids have a typical sea bass or grouper appearance which is not difficult to recognize; Plates 41 through 43 and 45 as well as the nearby black-and-white photos show clearly these characteristics. The size range of these fishes is extraordinary, some species being mature at slightly more than 1 inch in length, others matur-

[continued on page 177]

160]

61. Blue-faced Angelfish (*Pomacanthus xanthometopon*); marine; tropical
Indo-Australian region (Mike Wilson: Pix)

62. Rock Beauty (*Holacanthus tricolor*); marine, inshore; Florida to Rio de Janeiro;
lower left: Queen Angelfish (*Holacanthus ciliaris*); northeastern and southwestern
Gulf of Mexico to Brazil (Jutta Dunkel)

63. Blue Chromis (*Chromis cyanea*); marine; offshore; Bermuda and West Indies
(Edmond L. Fisher)

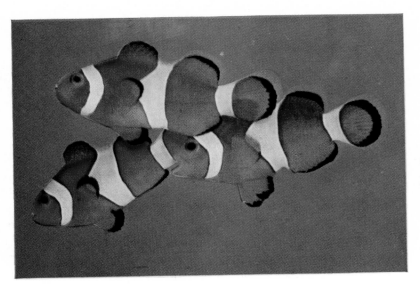

64. Clown Anemone Fish (*Amphiprion percula*); marine; tropical, India to Central Pacific (Gene Wolfsheimer)

65. Garibaldi (*Hypsypops rubicunda*) young; marine; southern and Baja California (Gene Wolfsheimer)

66. Garibaldi (*Hypsypops rubicunda*) adult; marine; southern and Baja California (Ron Church)

67. Cuckoo Wrasse (*Labrus ossifagus*); marine; Norway to the Mediterranean (Douglas P. Wilson)

68. Bluehead (*Thalassoma bifasciatum*) male; compare with young in Plate 69; Bermuda and Florida to Colombia and southwestern Gulf of Mexico (Edmond L. Fisher)

69. Blueheads young male and female; Bermuda and Florida to Colombia and southwestern Gulf of Mexico (Edmond L. Fisher)

70. Twinspot Wrasse (*Coris angulata*); marine; tropical Indo-Pacific (René Catala at Nouméa Aquarium)

71. Saddle Wrasse (*Thalassoma duperreyi*); marine; Hawaiian Islands (Cy La Tour at Marineland of the Pacific)

72. Yellow Jack (*Gnathanodon speciosus*); marine; Africa to America (Ron Church)

73. Great Amberjack (*Seriola dumerili*) young; marine; both sides of Atlantic, Massachusetts to Puerto Rico and Gulf of Mexico (Ernest Libby at Marine Studios)

74. Sweetlips (*Plectorhynchus chaetodonoides*) young; marine; tropical, Singapore to Fiji (Gene Wolfsheimer)

75. Sweetlips (*Gaterin lineatus*) young; marine; tropical Indo-Pacific (Hans and Klaus Paysan at Wilhelma Aquarium, Stuttgart)

76. Sweetlips (*Plectorhynchus goldmani*); marine; tropical, Philippines to New Guinea (René Catala at Nouméa Aquarium)

77. Porkfish (*Anisotremus virginicus*); marine; Bermuda, Florida, and Gulf of Mexico to Brazil (photographed at Seaquarium by Stan Wayman: Rapho Guillumette)

78. Emperor Snapper (*Lutjanus sebae*) with Spotted Grouper riding on side; marine; tropical Indo-Australian region (René Catala at Nouméa Aquarium)

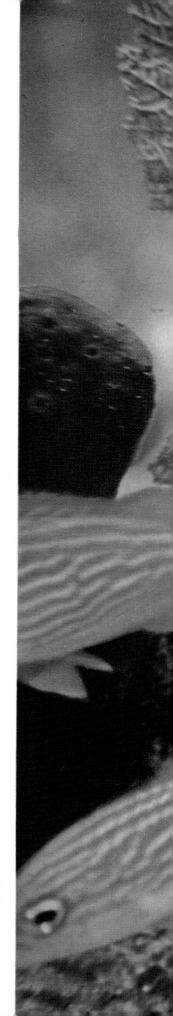

79. French Grunt (*Haemulon flavolineatum*) and White Grunt (*Haemulon plumieri*); marine; Virginia to Rio de Janeiro (Conrad Limbaugh)

80. **Gray Snappers** (*Lutjanus griseus*); marine; both sides of Atlantic, Massachusetts to Rio de Janeiro (Ernest Libby at Marine Studios)

Striped Parrotfish (*Scarus tae-*
terus); marine; West Indies
otographed at Seaquarium by
Wayman: Rapho Guillumette)

82. **Rainbow Parrotfish** (*Scarus guacamaia*); marine; both sides of Atlantic, Florida to Argentina (George G. Lower)

83. Striped Parrotfish (*Scarus croicensis*); marine; Massachusetts to Gulf of Mexico and Brazil (Edmond L. Fisher)

84. Tahitian Parrotfish (*Scarus* sp.); marine; tropical western Pacific (John Tashjian at Steinhart Aquarium)

85. Batfish (*Platax orbicularis*); marine; Indo-Pacific (Hans and Klaus Paysan at Wilhelma Aquarium, Stuttgart)

86. Moonfish (*Monodactylus argenteus*); marine and fresh water; tropical Indo-Pacific (Cy La Tour at Marineland of the Pacific)

87. Jewelfish (*Hemichromis bimaculatus*); fresh water; tropical Africa (Hans and Klaus Paysan at Zoo Aquarium, Duisburg)

88. False Mouthbreeders (*Tilapia melanopleura*); fresh water; tropical central Africa (Herbert R. Axlerod)

89. Antarctic Cod (*Trematomus bernacchi*); marine; antarctic (Richard G. Miller)

[continued from page 160]

ing at about 4 feet at weights of about fifty pounds and eventually reaching weights of a thousand pounds. Large mouths and sharp teeth are important to many of these fishes since the majority are carnivorous. A number of species spend their time sitting on the bottom, waiting for prey; some are active roamers. Serranids are most abundant in tropical seas, somewhat less abundant in temperate waters, and do not occur at all in the Arctic or the Antarctic. Most species are marine, but a few go into brackish and fresh water; and there are a few, like the American white and yellow basses, that are restricted to fresh water.

Aquarists have long been familiar with the tropical sea basses through the importation of young golden-striped groupers, *Grammistes sexlineatus* (Plate 41). This is a widely distributed Indo-Pacific species that sometimes reaches a length of 10 inches. In juveniles the lines along the sides of the body are in the form of a series of short dashes; as the fish grows older, the dashes coalesce to form a continuous line. This species does well in captivity, living for at least a dozen years.

The beautiful blue-spotted argus, *Cephalopholis argus* (Plate 42), is another Indo-Pacific grouper of wide distribution. Like a number of other Pacific species, it is not a native part of the Hawaiian fauna; however, in October, 1956, a number of individuals from the Marquesas Islands were introduced into Hawaii, and it is expected that they will become established there. This species occasionally reaches a length of 18 inches, but most specimens are much smaller. Although considered an excellent food fish, it is one of the species that in certain localities has been known to cause tropical fish poisoning. Because of its quick color changes, the blue-spotted argus proves to be a fascinating fish in the aquarium. There are usually four to six circular whitish bands around the body, beginning at about the second dorsal fin, and there is a conspicuous whitish area under the pectoral fin base. These white patterns are more prevalent in younger fish, but they come and go depending upon the mood of the argus. It is quite startling to see the pattern appear or disappear as one watches a fish swim from one resting spot to another.

The picturesque Nassau grouper, *Epinephelus striatus,* of the Atlantic, is also known for its color-changing ability; it has eight recognized color phases ranging from dark brown to cream. Within a single minute it can go through several of these phases. The Nassau grouper grows to a length of 3 to 4 feet and is fairly common throughout most of its range from North Carolina to Brazil.

The large genus *Epinephelus* includes a great many spotted and mottled groupers ranging throughout the tropical and temperate seas of the world. *Epinephelus elongatus* (Plate 43), from Tahiti, is a good example of one of the small, common Pacific coral-reef species; it is a rather slender fish, whereas the mottled grouper, *Epinephelus fuscoguttatus* (Plate 45), from Ceylon, is one of the heavy-bodied species and reaches a length of about 40 inches.

The weight records for the giant sea basses, sometimes called jewfishes, are of interest since these are the largest American serranids. The California species, *Stereolepis gigas,* has been recorded at 800 pounds and the Atlantic *Epinephelus itajara* at 750 pounds; however, the sports fishermen's tackle records are much less, being 513 pounds (7 feet 2 inches) and 551 pounds (8 feet 4 inches) respectively. A related Australian species, *Epinephelus lanceolatus,* called the Queensland grouper, is a common Barrier Reef fish. It has been known to stalk a shell diver the way a cat does a mouse and has actually rushed a diver in an apparent attack. Since in this area it attains a weight of 800 pounds, divers are often more wary of this fish than they are of sharks. This species is found through many parts of the Indo-Pacific; it is the largest known grouper and is said to grow as long as 12 feet and to weigh around 1000 pounds. This is probably the species involved in the many unauthenticated stories of skin divers being swallowed alive by giant groupers.

The soapfishes are a peculiar group of serranid fishes. As a result of any activity—being handled or threshing about in the water—their body mucus creates a soapsuds-like effect, either in the water or on the hands as the case may be. The three-spined soap-

Mouth of Spotted Grouper (*Epinephelus* sp.); marine; tropical Pacific (Fritz Goro: *Life* Magazine).

fish, *Rypticus saponaceus,* is a 12-inch inshore species found on both sides of the Atlantic.

The wreckfish or stone bass, *Polyprion americanum,* lives in deeper water than some of the other serranids; the normal range of this eighty-pound, 6-foot fish is the Mediterranean and tropical Atlantic as far north on the European coast as England. In the aquarium it is a very attractive but belligerent species, attacking and often killing other fishes even larger than itself. The name "wreckfish" comes from the fact that it is often found near wrecks; for instance, one trawler took five tons of this species from the immediate area of a wreck in 360 feet of water.

Although many of the groupers and other serranids spend much of their time sitting on the bottom, the striped bass, *Roccus saxatilus,* is usually on the move. This trait undoubtedly contributes to its popularity as a sports fish in the regions where it occurs. Its original distribution was along the American Atlantic coast from the Gulf of St. Lawrence to northern Florida. In 1879 and 1882 two shipments totaling 432 fish were transported to California and planted in the San Francisco area; in less than ten years the striped bass population in this region had mushroomed to such an extent that a commercial fishery for them was established. Today the fish is found on the American west coast from the state of Washington to southern California. Stripers move into fresh water for spawning, usually in the spring of the year. Females are generally not mature before reaching an age of five years and a length of 2 feet; males mature at two years when they are about a foot long. The largest striper on record was a 125-pound giant caught at Edenton, North Carolina; a fish weighing 78 pounds has been caught on the west coast; but the angler's record is only 73 pounds.

In addition to the striped bass, the genus *Roccus* includes two other striped species found in fresh water, mostly in the eastern United States: the 18-inch yellow bass, *Roccus mississippiensis,* looks much like the striper, but has an identifying yellowish tinge to the body; the white bass, *Roccus chrysops,* reaches about the same length as the yellow bass. One other species, the 12-inch white perch, *Roccus americanus,* lacks the stripes along the sides of the body; it originally occurred along the United States Atlantic seaboard in both salt and fresh water, but it has moved inland over a period of years.

Jewfish (*Epinephelus* [formerly *Promicrops*] *itajara*); marine; both coasts of tropical America (Fritz Goro: *Life* Magazine, at Marine Studios).

Striped Therapon or Tigerfish (*Therapon jarbua*); marine; tropical Indo-Pacific (Gunter Senfft).

Functional hermaphroditism, originally thought to be a rarity among fishes, has recently been discovered in several families including the porgies and the sea basses. Studies of the small 6-inch belted sandfish, *Serranellus subligarius,* made by Dr. Eugenie Clark of Florida's Cape Haze Marine Laboratory showed that this species is sexually mature at 1¼ inches and that each individual contains both ovum and sperm. Although it is possible to cause the release of both kinds of cells at the same time by pressing against the fish's sides and to fertilize the ovum experimentally with sperm from the same fish, it is not known whether the individual fish under normal circumstances acts as a female at one time and a male at another or as both simultaneously. They have a spawning pattern in which a number of fishes participate at the same time; this may fortuitously result in cross fertilization. These fishes are fairly common on rocky bottom between depths of eight and sixty-five feet.

Another serranid sexual peculiarity occurs in the black sea bass, *Centropristis striatus,* a fish common along the Atlantic coast of the United States. Young fish of this species are predominantly females, producing normal eggs, but by the time they have reached five years a number of them change their sex, becoming functional males.

The anthiids are sometimes classified as serranids or as a separate family, the Anthiidae. These are reef-dwelling sea-bass-like fishes found in deep water throughout many parts of the tropical Indo-Pacific. They are moderate-sized fishes noted for their beauty and brilliant colors, usually shades of red. The small 4-inch *Anthias squamipinnis* is one of the most widely distributed species.

TIGERFISHES or THERAPONS
—Family Theraponidae

This is an Indo-Pacific family of small to moderate-sized fishes found in marine and brackish water, with a few kinds limited to fresh water. The few species are usually conspicuously striped, with the stripes extending onto the tail. In one species, *Therapon theraps,* the very young have five bands around the body; with growth these bands gradually change to dots and then to four longitudinal lines. The three-striped tigerfish, *Therapon jarbua,* is one of the most common species and is sometimes imported as an aquarium fish. The 12-inch adults have on the opercle and preopercle sharp spines which can cause a nasty puncture wound if one is not careful in handling them. Juveniles of about 2 inches display a marked territorial pattern, each fish pushing out a small crater of sand about the size of its own body and fiercely guarding this against other fishes of its own size and kind. It may be that this crater-digging is a special adaptation for maintaining the fish's position in the tidal flow of river mouths, where young tigerfish are often found. By the time the fishes are 3½ inches long, this territorial pattern is lost. The youngsters are often quite susceptible to shock, death sometimes resulting merely from food being put into the tank. Another species, the 8-inch tigerfish croaker, *Pelates quadrilineatus,* is noted for the croaking noise it invariably makes when removed from the water.

AHOLEHOLES—Family Kuhliidae

The aholeholes are silvery, tropical Indo-Pacific fishes that look much like the North American fresh-water sunfishes (family Centrarchidae). Less than a dozen species are known; they may range in size up to 18 inches. The majority are marine species, but they move readily into brackish water; and a few are entirely fresh water in habitat. The 8-inch *Kuhlia taeniurus*, with its five black longitudinal stripes across the tail, is one of the most distinctive. The 12-inch Hawaiian aholehole, *Kuhlia sandvicensis*, is a common fish around the islands. Spawning takes place all during the year, and the young move into shallow areas where they can easily be collected. Ten years ago several thousand of these 1-inch juveniles were transported to San Francisco's Steinhart Aquarium, where they are still alive as adults. Many of this lot have subsequently been shipped to other aquaria all over the United States, a fact attesting to the hardiness of these common Indo-Pacific food fishes.

SUNFISHES—Family Centrarchidae

Bluegill, crappie, and largemouth black bass—these are names that are very familiar to the American fresh-water angler. About twenty-five kinds of these sunfishes are recognized. They were all originally North American fishes; but several species, including the bluegill and largemouth, have been introduced into Europe and elsewhere. Typically, the spiny-rayed and soft-rayed portions of the dorsal fin are continuous, and in some species, such as the black basses, there is a notch between the two sections; in the related perch family, Percidae, the two are entirely separate fins. Some of the species of sunfishes are so similar that it is difficult to distinguish between them; this is especially true of the juveniles. The small species of centrarchids are well known to aquarists. The beautiful 3½-inch pigmy or bluespotted sunfish, *Enneacanthus gloriosus* (Plate 44), is a common species through the eastern and southern areas of the United States. Two other dwarf sunfishes—the banded *Elassoma zonatum*, found in the central United States, and the mottled *Elassoma evergladei*, found in Florida—are both sexually mature at the magnificent length of 1 inch and never grow larger than 1½ inches. The 3-inch black-banded sunfish, *Mesogonistius chaetodon*, which is common from New Jersey to northern Florida, is another attractive species. It is a strange fact that this fish is bred extensively in Germany and shipped to countries all over the world, including the United States. Apparently it is easier to do this than to collect it in its normal habitat.

The centrarchid sunfishes are noted for their nest-building. The male, using his tail as a fan, hollows out a small depression in the sand; then he entices a receptive female to the nest, where she lays her eggs and he fertilizes them at the same time. After the eggs are laid, he jealously guards the nest, chasing off the female and aggressively attacking any intruder.

The largemouth bass, *Micropterus salmoides*, is the largest species in the family, with specimens reported at 25 pounds; the official angler's record, however, is somewhat less, being 22½ pounds for a largemouth measuring 32½ inches. The largest recorded weight for the smallmouth, *Micropterus dolomieui*, is almost 12 pounds for a 27-inch fish. These larger centrarchids often feed upon smaller sunfishes; consequently, normal stocking practice is to introduce with them smaller forage fishes, often the common bluegill, *Lepomis macrochirus*.

The bluegill is usually found in the still water of lakes and ponds where vegetation is present. The dark blotch on the posterior base of the soft dorsal fin and the five to seven vertical bars across the body are good identifying marks. The bluegill usually becomes mature at 3½ inches but has been known to reach a length of 15 inches and a weight of 4¾ pounds.

Sunfishes can sometimes be identified by the nature of the ear lobe, the small extension of the opercle just above the pectoral fin. On the long-eared sunfish, *Lepomis megalotis*, the edge of the very long ear flap is rimmed with white, and the ear flap may often be covered with orange dots or flushed with a reddish color. The pumpkinseed, *Lepomis gibbosus*, has a large blood-red blotch on the end of the ear flap.

The two species of crappies originally occurred only in the eastern part of the United States, but because of their popularity with sports fishermen, they have been widely planted in many waters across North America. The white crappie, *Pomoxis annularis*, is usually found in turbid rivers, lakes, and sloughs, whereas the black crappie, *Pomoxis nigromaculatus*, prefers clear water. Although 12 inches is a respectable length for either of the two species of crappies, specimens ranging between 19 and 21 inches in length and weighing about five pounds have been caught.

The only centrarchid sunfish originally occurring in the western part of the United States—although others have been introduced—was the Sacramento perch, *Archoplites interruptus*, found in California's Sacramento and San Joaquin basins; most of the fish of this species are under 1 foot in length.

CATALUFAS or BIGEYES—Family Priacanthidae

Very large eyes, small rough scales, and bright red color, rarely with a pattern, are the marks of the carnivorous, nocturnal catalufas. Fewer than two

Largemouth Black Bass (*Micropterus* [*Huro*] *salmoides*); fresh water; eastern United States from Great Lakes region south into Mexico; also widely introduced elsewhere (Wisconsin Conservation Department).

dozen species are recognized, but some of these are very widely distributed. They are bottom-dwelling marine fishes, usually found in deeper water than the squirrelfishes, which they resemble. Their maximum size is around 2 feet. The presence of a membrane connecting the inner ray of the ventral or pelvic fins with the abdomen is a great help in identification. The catalufa or common bigeye, *Priacanthus arenatus* (Plate 46), is a representative species; it attains a length of 14 inches and is found on both sides of the temperate and tropical Atlantic. The Hawaiian aweoweo, *Priacanthus cruentatus,* is one of the shallow-water forms, sometimes occurring in water less than six feet in depth. In most regions the priacanthids are considered food fishes of only modest value. In the Gulf of Thailand, however, they are caught on long lines over rocky bottom, salted and dried, and highly prized as food.

CARDINAL FISHES—Family Apogonidae

Many of the cardinals are attractively patterned and often brightly colored; shades of brown or red are commonplace, as in the barred cardinal fish, *Apogon binotatus* (Plate 47), a tropical Atlantic species. Most of them are small, tropical marine fishes, the majority of which are less than 4 inches in length. The largest cardinal fishes are 6 to 8 inches long and are brackish-water species, living in mangrove swamps. There are also a few species that live in fresh-water streams of high tropical Pacific islands on which cyprinid or other native fresh-water fishes are lacking. Cardinal fishes usually occur in shallow water, but there are a few species that are found only in deep water. Two separate dorsal fins and two instead of three anal spines are the identifying features of the family. Many of the species are mouth-

breeders; in some it is only the male that takes the eggs into the mouth for incubation; in others, only the female; and in still others, it is suspected that both the male and female incubate the eggs in this manner. Some cardinal males are described as picking up the eggs and holding them in the mouth only while danger threatens.

Since the cardinals are sometimes fantastically abundant, they play an important part in the food cycles of larger carnivorous forms. Gosline and Brock in their *Handbook of Hawaiian Fishes* (University of Hawaii Press, 1960) describe the collection of more than one thousand specimens of *Apogon brachygrammus*, a 3-inch species that frequents dead coral; these were all taken in a very small area.

The brownspot cardinal, *Apogonichthyoides uninotatus,* is a 3-inch Indo-Pacific species that has a large eye spot just above the pectoral fin; it is noted for the fact that it will often flop over on its side and play dead when an attempt is made to catch it.

One peculiar cardinal fish from the Gulf of Tongking, *Apogon ellioti,* has on the digestive tract three luminous organs, all facing inward toward the lumen of the intestine; each organ is glandular, with structures that look like a reflector and a lens. The function and value to the fish of this strange feature have not been determined. Other luminous cardinal fishes include the members of the genus *Siphamia*, which are common Indo-Pacific fishes living on the bottom of lagoons or deeper coral reefs.

PERCHES, WALLEYES, and DARTERS
—Family Percidae

The familiar yellow perch, *Perca flavescens,* is a small, shallow-water fish found in lakes, ponds, and slow-moving streams; originally, like all American

Walleye (*Stizostedion vitreum*); fresh water; eastern United States and Canada from Tennessee River drainage northward (Wisconsin Conservation Department).

members of the family, it occured in North America east of the Rockies only, but subsequently was widely introduced elsewhere. Although always popular with youngsters and with the casual fisherman, it has had an erratic history as a food dish. Before the turn of the century it was often considered useful only as a fertilizer, and sometimes fishermen could not give it away. Yet today the yellow perch forms an important part of the commercial fisheries of the Great Lakes. Like other members of the family, it has two instead of three anal spines and the spiny and soft portions of the dorsal fin are separated. These features help to differentiate the perches from the centrarchid sunfishes, which often occur in the same waters. The yellow perch is easily recognized by the six to nine blackish bars on the sides of the body; the young are silvery in background color, but as they become mature—usually at 4½ to 12 inches —they develop a brassy or golden body color with orange ventral and anal fins. A 15-inch perch weighing slightly more than one pound is considered a large fish, but the record is held by a fish that was caught many years ago (1865) and weighed 4¼ pounds. Spawning takes place in the spring, the eggs being laid at night in long strings which are usually found stuck to shallow-water vegetation. A single female perch has been known to deposit a string of eggs eighty-one inches in length. Although these eggs were not counted, it is known that the ovaries will produce 10,000 to 48,000 eggs, depending on the size of the fish.

The highly popular European perch, *Perca fluviatilis*, is very similar to the yellow perch; it also has bars on the sides of the body, but is a slightly larger fish, with maximum recorded weights in the five-to-six-pound range. This species is found throughout most of Europe with the exception of Spain, southern Italy, and northern Scandinavia, and ranges all the way to Siberia. It also occurs in brackish waters along the coast of the Baltic Sea; in this area spawning occurs during the summer although in warmer regions it takes place in the spring.

The perches just described make up one of the three subfamilies into which the family is divided. The second group, of which there are a few representatives in both Europe and North America, contains the walleyes, the sauger, and the pikeperches. The third and largest group contains the smallest species, the darters, more than one hundred of which have been described, all from North America.

The walleye, *Stizostedion vitreum*, sometimes also called pikeperch, has a mottled pattern, usually with a large black blotch at the posterior end of the spinous dorsal fin; it also has many small canine teeth. This fish is quite popular with sports fishermen throughout its range in eastern North America and is a valuable commercial species in Lake Erie. Although reported to reach a weight of twenty-five pounds, most of those caught by anglers are in the one-to-four-pound range, fishes of this size usually being three to five years old. When spawning, females generally drop their eggs over the bottom in the shallow areas of a lake; sometimes they migrate into tributary streams and lay their eggs in the shallow rocky sections. The walleye prefers living food, but in a tank it can be trained to take dead food. In the aquarium it shows a strange feeding pattern. All of the fishes invariably huddle together in one area of the tank on or near the bottom; as chopped fish floats slowly down through the water, one fish quickly swims upward, swallows it, then swims back to the bottom again. This procedure is soon followed by another fish and then perhaps by several more until they are all feeding in the same manner. It looks almost as though the more timid fish wait to follow the lead of the bolder ones. The blue walleye and the yellow walleye are recognized geographic varieties of the common walleye.

The sauger, *Stizostedion canadense*, resembles the walleye but has a spotted spiny dorsal fin without the black blotch at the base. It is a smaller fish than the walleye, as shown by the anglers' world record of an 8¼-pound fish with a length of 30 inches.

Other members of the subfamily include the 9-inch pope or ruffe, *Acerina cernua*, and the 16-to-20-inch pikeperch, *Lucioperca lucioperca*, both widely distributed from Europe through Siberia.

Darters are small, quick, bottom-dwelling fishes found in a variety of habitats but limited to temperate North America east of the Rocky Mountains. About one hundred species are known, most of them less than 4 inches in length, the largest reaching only 9 inches. Although some have distinctive markings, a specialist is often needed to be certain of identification. Among the darters are found some of the most brilliantly colored fishes in North America; this is especially true during breeding season, when their colors are greatly enhanced. Some darters distribute their eggs indiscriminately, but others, such as the 2½-inch Johnny darter, *Etheostoma nigrum*, lay their eggs under a rock or in a small cave while in upside-down position; the male then aerates, cleans, and guards the eggs for about three weeks until they hatch.

BLANQUILLOS—*Family Malacanthidae*

Most of the fifteen or so species of blanquillos are very elongated, small fishes less than 2 feet in length, with many-rayed dorsal and anal fins. They are primarily tropical marine species, but a few move into temperate waters. There is one well-known member of the family—the strange tilefish, *Lopholatilus chamaeleonticeps*, a large, beautiful blue, deep-water fish that in the past has occurred in erratic abundance off the American Atlantic coast. It was first discovered in 1879, and almost immediately considerable interest was engendered in the development of a commercial fishery. Unfortunately, though, in 1882, when the fishery was just getting started, millions of tilefish ranging up to fifty pounds in weight were found dead and floating at the surface over thousands of square miles of the western offshore Atlantic. This tremendous mortality was apparently due to a temperature change, but afterward the tilefish could no longer be caught in their old haunts. For a time scientists speculated that the species might be extinct, but it gradually returned to its former abundance until by 1916 some eleven and one half million pounds were marketed. Since then, however, the commercial demand for the tilefish has declined.

The Polynesian name for the 12-inch, square-tailed *Malacanthus hoedtii* is "makaa," which means "bright eyes," a very descriptive name for this western Pacific representative of the blanquillos. The tail fin is white in the center with distinctive black lobes on each side, and there is a sharp spine on the opercle. It swims with sinuous grace. The American Atlantic sandfish, *Malacanthus plumeri*, is a similar although slightly larger species, and has a lunate tail without the black areas.

BLUEFISH—*Family Pomatomidae*

The bloodthirsty feeding habits of the bluefish, *Pomatomus salatrix*, remind one of the South American piranha. Even when these fish have eaten their fill, they continue to slaughter others, seemingly for the pure love of killing. The bluefish is a fast-moving, schooling species, found in tropical and temperate waters around the world with the exception of the central and eastern Pacific. Its movements up and down the American Atlantic coast are to a certain extent correlated with those of the schools of menhanden and other fishes upon which it feeds. The young bluefish, often called tailors or snappers, are common inshore; their feeding habits are the same as those of the adults. Little is known of the spawning areas. The species reaches a maximum weight of twenty-seven pounds, but even in the five-to-ten-pound range the battling bluefish is a favorite of the salt-water angler, not only because of its fighting qualities but also because of its excellent taste. The demand for bluefish is invariably greater than the supply. The fish has a bluish or greenish color and separate dorsal fins with the spiny portion much smaller than the soft-rayed portion. There is an identifying black blotch at the base of the pectoral fin. Only the single species is known.

COBIA—*Family Rachycentridae*

The fast-moving, voracious cobia, *Rachycentron canadum*, is easily identified by the three dark stripes on the sides of the body: one through the eye and along the midline of the body, another beneath the pectoral fin and along the side of the abdomen, and the third along the top of the body. The soft dorsal fin is preceded by a series of seven to eleven short, free fin spines. This is a large, streamlined fish reaching a weight of 102 pounds and a length of almost 6 feet. In appearance the young cobia is very similar to a shark sucker, and because of this similarity it has been suggested that the two kinds of fishes may be related; thus it is quite appropriate that the nearby photograph shows a cobia with shark sucker attached. The cobia does well in captivity; it is primarily a fish-eater but also eats crabs with great

Cobia (*Rachycentron canadum*) with remora attached to abdomen; marine; world-wide in tropical and temperate waters (Fritz Goro: *Life* Magazine at Lerner Marine Laboratory).

gusto. It is an excellent game fish of average food value. There is only the single species, which is world-wide in tropical and subtropical seas.

JACKS, CAVALLAS, SCADS, and POMPANOS —Family Carangidae

Carangids vary greatly in shapes and sizes, but most of them have one thing in common—they move with great speed. Because of their speed, they provide a real treat for the fisherman who hooks one on his line. As a group, they are excellent market fishes, with some, such as the pompanos, bringing premium prices. They occur around the world in tropical and temperate seas, and a few move readily into fresh water. Many of the two hundred or so species are shaped like the yellow jack, *Gnathanodon speciosus* (Plate 72), a 3-foot Indo-Pacific fish easily identified by its color and by the eight to twelve dark bands around the body. The very young of this species are solid gold in color, and, unlike the adults, act as pilots for other larger fishes. Along each side of the caudal peduncle of the tail the yellow jack has a sharp ridge formed by a series of bony scutes or plates; in some species these may extend along the entire lateral line. The scutes are worn down during growth, so that younger fish have much sharper ones than older individuals. An example of the species with extended lateral scutes is the torpedo-shaped Atlantic horse mackerel or saurel, *Trachurus trachurus*, which is much more common on the European side of the Atlantic than on the American side. A similar species, the jack mackerel, *Trachurus symmetricus,* occurs on the American Pacific coast.

There are some species such as the amberjacks that lack scutes on the lateral line; a typical example is the Atlantic *Seriola dumerili* (Plate 73). Some of the amberjacks have very attractive juvenile forms with brilliant golden bands, which are lost as the fish grows.

The beautiful, deep-bodied pompanos are graceful fishes when swimming. The 18-inch common Atlantic pompano, *Trachinotus carolinus,* is a valuable species on the coasts of the Americas. The lookdown, *Selene vomer,* which ranges across the Atlantic, has a most bizarre appearance in that the eye is placed high on the large head, at an inordinate distance from the mouth, giving the fish a supercilious look. The threadfishes of the genus *Alectis* are always sure to attract attention because of the long streamers extending out from the first rays of both the dorsal and anal fins; as these fishes grow, the body proportions change considerably and the streamers shorten, so that the adult is sometimes quite different from the juvenile. The threadfishes are typically inshore species, whereas the other carangids range offshore.

The 4-foot Indo-Pacific rainbow runner, *Elagatis bipinnulatus,* is a cigar-shaped fish with a fantastic blue color on the back; along the side of the body there is a yellow stripe bordered below by a thin blue stripe; the abdomen is light colored. The presence of two small finlets, one after the second dorsal and one after the anal fin, is helpful in identification.

Other common carangids include the leatherjackets of the genera *Scomberoides* and *Oligoplites,* which are sometimes so abundant in tropical waters that it is impossible for a baited hook to reach the bottom without being taken by one or more of these fishes.

Some years ago San Francisco's Steinhart Aquarium brought in some young yellowtail, *Seriola dorsalis,* a renowned sports fish of southern California and Mexico; as the fish continued to grow, approaching 3 feet, it became necessary to break out a tank wall in order to double the volume of their thousand-gallon tank. When the fish were moved into the larger tank, for three months they refused to use the added space, staying always on the eastern half of the larger tank; by four months they began to move over occasionally, but six months had passed before they actually made use of both ends of the tank. Animal psychologists have been at a loss to explain this behavior.

Old-time mariners tell us that the legendary pilot fish, *Naucrates ductor,* will lead lost swimmers, ships, or even whales to safety. However, the truth of the matter is that they do not do a great deal of leading, although they are often found around sharks and other large fishes, as well as ships—in fact, wherever scraps of food are easily available.

Some of the jacks have been implicated in tropical fish poisoning. For example, the black ulua, *Caranx melampygus,* is one of the most common carangids around the Hawaiian Islands, where the majority of those caught are used for food; however, the same species at Palmyra Island, 960 miles south of Honolulu, is known to be deadly poisonous. As might be expected, it is impossible to sell Palmyra Island fishes of any kind in Honolulu.

Threadfin (*Alectis ciliaris*); marine; tropical Indo-Pacific (*San Francisco Chronicle*).

Long-finned Pompano or Palometo (*Trachinotus glaucus*); marine, pelagic; both sides of the tropical and temperate Atlantic (New York Zoological Society).

The most valuable fishes in the Philippines are the jacks and cavallas that swim from the ocean up the Pancipit River into Lake Taal, which is located in an extinct volcano south of Manila on the island of Luzon. These fishes remain in the lake for an undetermined period of time, then return to the ocean. For these fresh-water jacks and cavallas the epicure will pay several times the price of the same fish from salt water. Some of the large rivers in New Guinea also have fair-sized runs of jacks that go upriver but return downriver to spawn.

DOLPHINS—*Family Coryphaenidae*

The name "dolphin" is often confusing, for it is applied to both a fish, one of the most spectacular of the tropical offshore sports species, and a mammal, an air-breathing porpoise.

The 5-foot adult dolphin, *Coryphaena hippurus*, has a long fin of as many as sixty-five rays extending down the back; it also has a forked tail and a beautiful bluish color that is lost soon after the captured fish is pulled on deck. The adult male has a decidedly squarish head and may weigh as much as sixty-seven pounds, whereas the female has a more rounded head and seldom weighs more than thirty-five pounds. Accurate catch records from the Hawaiian Islands show the average weight of all *Coryphaena* in that area to be seventeen pounds. The dolphin is a very fast-moving oceanic fish, with a speed of as much as thirty-seven miles per hour. Occurring singly and in schools, it feeds on a variety of fishes —including flying fishes—and invertebrates; thirty-two species of fishes belonging to nineteen families have been recorded from the stomachs of Atlantic dolphin.

One night when I was on board a ship drifting in the Sulu Sea of the central Philippines, many very small dolphins came swimming around the night light. Under the microscope, they were found to be the small pompano dolphin, *Coryphaena equiselis,* a species previously unknown from that region although widely distributed elsewhere. Later examination in the laboratory showed that most of the dolphins that came to lights all over the Philippines were this species and that very few were the common dolphin, *C. hippurus,* although the latter was caught in the same areas in the daytime. This strange phenomenon has since that time also been observed in the Atlantic. Actually, these two species —the only members of the family—are very similar and are often confused, but they may usually be differentiated by the number of rays in the dorsal fin, the common dolphin having fifty-five to sixty-five and the pompano dolphin forty-eight to fifty-five. As an adult, the latter is a small fish, being mature at 12 inches and having a maximum size of 30 inches.

One surprising fact about the dolphin concerns its edibility. In the Hawaiian Islands "mahimahi" (*Coryphaena hippurus*) is a premium fish and is in great demand; however, in the Philippines and along the tropical American coasts it is considered "third-class fish" and is little sought as a food item.

Dolphin have been kept in large oceanaria and outside tanks on a few occasions, and they do surprisingly well once they become acclimated. Their growth rate is very rapid, as indicated by observations of F. G. Wood, Jr., at Florida's Marine Studios. A group of fifty-two dolphin measuring 18 inches or less and weighing about one and one-half pounds each was introduced into one of the large tanks in late August. Because of their high metabolic rate, they were fed three times a day. Four and one-half months later one of the dolphin leaped out of the tank, and was found upon measurement to be 45 inches long and to weigh nearly twenty-five pounds. Seven and one-half months after their introduction into the tank, two dolphin became wedged between rocks and succumbed; they measured 50 and 50½ inches and weighed thirty-seven and thirty-two pounds respectively. Although further measurements were unavailable, it was obvious that the growth rate was exceptionally rapid. It was postulated that the entire life span, perhaps like that of the sailfish, was quite short, undoubtedly no longer than two or three years.

ROBALOS: SNOOK and GLASSFISH
—Family Centropomidae

The carnivorous robalos run the gamut from large fishes highly prized by commercial and sports fishermen to small species that are popular with the aquarists. An example of the large species is the common marine snook, *Centropomus undecimalis,* shown in the nearby photo; the small species are well

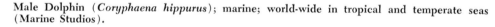
Male Dolphin (*Coryphaena hippurus*); marine; world-wide in tropical and temperate seas (Marine Studios).

Snook (*Centropomus undecimalis*); marine, occasionally entering fresh water; both sides of tropical America (Marine Studios).

represented by the transparent, brackish-water glass-fishes—formerly known as ambassids—such as *Chanda ranga* (Plate 91). These photographs show the general characteristics of the body profile of the family; in addition to the features that can be clearly seen, all centropomids have the lateral line running out to the end of the tail fin. Also included in this small family is the fabulous Nile perch, *Lates niloticus,* which attains a weight of two hundred pounds, as well as several other similar African fresh-water game fishes.

The shovel-headed snooks are a group of about eight species found along both sides of the tropical Atlantic as well as in the tropical eastern Pacific. They readily enter rivers and swim upstream into entirely fresh water. The common snook of Florida, *Centropomus undecimalis,* is found in greatest abundance in mangrove areas. Young fish begin to mature at two years and reach full maturity by three years. Twenty-eight to thirty pounds is the average size of those caught, although they have been known to reach fifty and one-half pounds with a length of 56 inches. Tagging studies have shown that the Florida snook is a relatively sedentary fish. Of fifty-seven individuals caught within a year after marking, 79 per cent were taken within six miles of the original site. The length of time between tagging and recapture apparently had no relationship to the distance traveled.

The small glassfishes, of which there are a number of species, are found from Africa through the Indo-Pacific region along coastlines, in estuaries, and in fresh water. The majority of species belong to the genus *Chanda,* with *C. buruensis, C. nana,* and *C. ranga* being the most commonly imported.

SNAPPERS—*Family Lutianidae or Lutjanidae*

With the exception of the caesios, which in their habits are very similar to sardines, the snappers are shallow-water inshore species. Most species of the genus *Caesio* occur in large schools of billions of fishes throughout the Indo-Pacific region and migrate for long distances foraging for food. With their colors of brilliant, iridescent blues and yellows, a school of them seen underwater is a spectacular sight as they swim with synchronized, quick precision, the entire school resembling a flock of swifts.

In many tropical regions of the world the carnivorous snappers are highly important food fishes, rivaling if not surpassing the groupers and others in this regard. Not only are there a great many kinds, probably more than 250, but the individual species are highly abundant. Many of the species reach lengths between 2 and 3 feet.

It is difficult to describe a snapper so that one can always recognize a fish of this family. Typically, they have sharp jaw teeth and a "snapper" look—which is due to the characteristically flattened top of the snout, giving the fish a shovel-headed appearance. This feature is well shown by the Indo-Pacific emperor snapper, *Lutjanus sebae* (Plate 78), and by the American Atlantic gray snapper, *Lutjanus griseus* (Plate 80). These two examples also demonstrate the extremes in color pattern. Many of the snappers are quite beautiful, with shades of red and yellow predominating. The yellowtail snapper, *Ocyurus chrysurus,* is a 2-foot species widely distributed on both sides of the tropical Atlantic; it has yellow fins and a yellow line along the side of the body, and the upper portion of the fish is blue with yellow spots. Other distinctive American Atlantic species include the red-and-yellow-striped lane or spot snapper, *L. synagris,* and the yellow-and-green-banded muttonfish, *L. analis.*

Plate 78 is a most exceptional photograph, for it demonstrates one of the rare relationships between fishes that is sometimes described but almost never photographed. As Dr. René Catala relates it, this mottled grouper, probably *Epinephelus merra,* acting in the same manner as a shark sucker, customarily rode about in the water on the side of the emperor snapper.

One of the peculiarities of the Hawaiian fauna is that it has very few of the many groupers and snappers that are common throughout the rest of the Indo-Pacific region; in 1956 specimens of *Lutjanus vaigiensis* were introduced from Tahiti in the hope that this species would become established as a valuable market fish.

In spite of the value of snappers as food fishes, they have often been involved in cases of tropical fish poisoning. Some of these widely distributed Indo-Pacific food species are poisonous in certain areas and at certain times of the year. Included in this poisonous category are the twinspot snapper, *Lutjanus bohar,* the onespot snapper, *L. monostigma,* the red snappers, *L. gibbus* and *L. vaigiensis,* and the blue-gray snapper, *Aprion virescens.*

CIGUATERA—TROPICAL FISH POISONING

Including the snappers, at least three hundred species of tropical fishes in the West Indies as well as the Central and South Pacific have at one time or another been proved responsible for a peculiar kind of fish poisoning often called ciguatera. The term is derived from a Cuban name applied to marine snail poisoning. A person who has consumed a toxic fish producing this type of poisoning experiences, among other symptoms, a reversal of sensations of heat and cold—that is, ice cream feels hot to the mouth and hot soup feels cold. The neurotoxic action of the poison shows up within one to thirty hours after the fish is eaten. The first symptom is usually a tingling feeling of the mouth, lips, and throat. The patient may complain of extreme weakness and a variety of muscular pains and aches, nausea, diarrhea, muscular spasms, cramps, and even paralysis. Skin rashes, visual disturbances, and sometimes loss of nails and hair may occur. A mortality figure of 7 per cent has been reported by Dr. Bruce Halstead and his research group. Complete recovery may require many months or even years. Surprisingly, when a person is in the recovery phase, any fish that he eats will aggravate the symptoms.

Medical zoologists have long been puzzled about ciguatera, and especially about the fact that it occurs sporadically in many species of fishes that are normally considered excellent food. There are a number of kinds of fishes, such as puffers and porcupines, that are always poisonous, but we are not concerned with these at the moment. In ciguatera-type tropical fish poisoning we are dealing with some of the most edible fishes in the sea. For example, the common Hawaiian black ulua or jack, *Caranx melampygus,* is an excellent food fish in Honolulu, yet at Palmyra Island, some nine hundred miles away, this same fish is highly toxic. Shorter distances are involved in the Caribbean and the Bahamas, where fishes on the steep windward side of a small island four or five miles long may be highly toxic, while those of the same species on the shallow leeward side are perfectly edible.

The fishes that have been known to cause ciguatera do not include the plankton feeders; all those involved are either piscivores, herbivores, or detritus feeders. Included are such fishes as the barracuda, many species of surgeon fishes, groupers, porgies, snappers, and jacks or cavallas. Moray eels also cause a tropical fish poisoning similar to ciguatera, but there is no reversal of heat and cold sensations; it has been suggested that the absence of this symptom may be due to a more virulent onslaught of the toxin. The ciguatera poison is apparently cumulative within the body of the fish, and seemingly it is not lost if the poisonous fish is removed to an uncontaminated area and fed toxin-free food. This was demonstrated in an experiment in which poisonous snappers and groupers caught at Palmyra Island were transported to Oahu and maintained in an aquarium for fourteen months. At the end of this time they were killed and fed to experimental animals, which then developed severe ciguatera symptoms, thereby indicating that the toxin had not been lost.

One of the most plausible of many hypotheses advanced to explain the cause of ciguatera is that proposed by Dr. John Randall (1958), in which he cites considerable evidence to show that poisonous fishes have often appeared for the first time in areas where a major change in the reef has occurred. Storms resulting in broken reefs and shifted sand, or ships' anchors breaking the coral, as well as overflow from fresh-water streams, provide new growing surfaces for a yet undetermined species of blue-green alga. According to Randall, this unknown blue-green alga must be the primary vehicle for the toxin. This alga is picked up by herbivorous fishes, and then in turn by carnivorous types that feed on the herbivorous forms.

NEMIPTERIDS—Family Nemipteridae

The nemipterids are snapper-like marine fishes found only in the tropical Indo-Pacific. They can often be recognized at a glance by the elongated rays of the upper lobe of the tail fin and by similarly elongated rays of the ventral fins. The very small jaw teeth are cone-shaped and arranged in several rows. There are no teeth on the palate, but some species have canines in the front of the jaws. The two principal genera, *Nemipterus* and *Scolopsis,* each have many species, a large number of which are brightly colored. The majority are less than a foot in length. Although they are often used as food, some species have been involved in cases of tropical fish poisoning.

TRIPLETAILS—Family Lobotidae

The name "tripletail" comes from the fact that the extended dorsal and anal fins together with the tail give the lobotids the appearance of having three tails. The body profile looks somewhat like that of the fresh-water sunfishes. The lobotids inhabit inshore salt water as well as brackish and fresh water; they are found throughout the tropical Indo-Pacific and in the tropical Atlantic. The immature fishes, measuring 2 or 3 inches, camouflage themselves by acting like leaves—they turn sideways and float at the surface. It is rather startling to observe this phenomenon without knowing the habits of the fish. The first time I saw it I thought the fish was actually dead.

The blackish tripletail, *Lobotes surinamensis,* is the most widely distributed species, being found in the Indo-Pacific as well as the Atlantic; it attains a length of about 40 inches. In the fresh and brackish waters of Borneo, New Guinea, and adjacent areas are found two other tripletails; the most picturesque of these is *Datnoides quadrifasciatus,* a four-banded species reaching a length of 12 inches. One other species from off Panama, *Lobotes pacificus,* completes this small family.

SLIPMOUTHS—Family Leiognathidae

These are small Indo-Pacific fishes, chiefly marine in habitat but sometimes living in brackish and fresh water. They have deep, laterally compressed bodies and extremely protrusible mouths which form tubes when extended. Another major characteristic is that the dorsal and anal fins are sheathed along the base with small protective spines. The South African popular name of "slimy" or "soapy" is most appropriate; when these fishes are handled, they secrete a slimy mucus from glands on the body. They are not particularly good to eat, but they are tre-

mendously abundant and form a palatable food when dried. Thus they are very important in the food economy of undeveloped regions, since each fish provides a small amount of low-cost protein.

Members of the three principal genera of slipmouths, *Leiognathus, Gazza,* and *Secutor,* are similar in that they all have luminous tissue around the base of the esophagus, at the point where it joins the stomach. The luminescence can be seen if the fishes are removed from the water and handled. Dr. Y. Haneda, the Japanese authority, has found luminescence in some fifteen species of slipmouths and has been able to culture luminous bacteria from the light organs.

MOJARRAS—Family Gerridae

The small, silvery, shallow-water mojarras are similar in many respects to the slipmouths, and at times the two have been placed together in a single family. The mojarras have the protrusible mouth but have a different sheathing along the base of the dorsal and anal fins, the sheath in this case being formed by a small, scaled extension of the body, so that the fins can be more or less depressed into the resulting groove.

Some of the mojarras have wide ranges—for example the common mojarra, *Eucinostomus argenteus,* which is found from New Jersey to Rio de Janeiro, has an almost equally wide range on the Pacific coast of the Americas, coming as far north as California. In all, there are fewer than three dozen species; they form a tropical marine group extending to some degree into temperate waters. Like the slipmouths, they move readily into brackish water, and some species even go into fresh water.

GRUNTS—Family Pomadasyidae

The grunts receive their name from the sounds they produce by grinding their sharp pharyngeal teeth together; the adjacent air bladder acts as a sounding box, amplifying the sounds. The noise is most audible when a grunt is taken from the water, but it can also be heard under water by means of a hydrophone or other acoustical devices. Some of the grunts rival the croakers (family Sciaenidae) in their noise-producing ability. It is suspected that the majority of species in the family are capable of sound production, although only a relatively few species have been tested.

Externally, the grunts look much like the snappers, but they differ from them primarily in the dentition, having very feeble jaw teeth and very potent pharyngeal teeth. They are mostly tropical marine species. The beautiful French grunts, *Haemulon flavolineatum,* and white grunts, *H. plumieri* (both shown in Plate 79), are typical members of the American Atlantic fauna; an even more striking member is the porkfish, *Anisotremus virginicus* (Plate 77). By contrast, the only grunt in the western United States marine fauna, the sargo, *Anisotremus davidsoni,* is a drab silvery 20-inch species with a single vertical bar on the sides of the body. Some grunts are known for their strange kissing activities, as shown in the nearby photo; whether this is courtship behavior or territorial aggressiveness has not been determined.

The Indo-Australian gruntlike fishes, called sweetlips and a variety of other names, are sometimes included in the Pomadasyidae and sometimes classed as a separate family, the Plectorhynchidae. These attractive tropical marine fishes are exasperating to the classification expert because of the often radical difference in color as well as color pattern of the young as compared with the adult. For example, the young sweetlips of Plate 74, *Plectorhynchus chaetodonoides,* changes to a mottled pattern as it grows. *Gaterin lineatus* (Plate 75) changes its colors with growth and also adds more horizontal lines. *Plectorhynchus goldmani* (Plate 76) probably has the greatest change in the number of horizontal lines, having only nine as a youngster and as many as eighteen as an adult.

The young plectorhynchids are the clowns of the tropical reef. As they seem to flutter through the water, their graceful swimming looks like dancing or the cavorting of clowns. When they grow older they lose this peculiar swimming ability. Some of the young plectorhynchids live in association with the centriscid snipe fishes.

CROAKERS—Family Sciaenidae

Early hydrophone operators on combat submarines, hearing the "boop-boop-boop-boop" from schools of croakers for the first time, often suspected incorrectly that enemy craft were in the immediate area. Later it was found that there were many kinds of noise-makers in the sea, some of which could be heard without listening devices—all producing a veritable cacophony of sound when heard at the same time. In some areas the croakers contribute the major portion of this unearthly din. Submarine commanders quickly learned that they could hide the operational noises of their craft behind this natural sound camouflage.

The sound mechanism of the croakers is under voluntary control; strong muscles attached to the sides of the air bladder work in the same way as the strings on a guitar, with the air bladder acting as a resonance chamber amplifying the snapping of the muscles. The reasons for the sound production are not all understood; however, it is known that the noise increases during spawning season and decreases at other times, and also that it varies during the day and night. In Chesapeake Bay in May and June the sound begins to increase in the evening, reaches a shrill pitch before midnight, and then quickly tapers off until very little is heard. In Japan the croakers of the genus *Nibea* are known to assemble in large schools of up to a million fish and to synchronize their drumming. Most of the croakers produce sound, but there are a few that are practically voiceless because they lack air bladders. Among these are the members of the genus *Menticirrhus,* including the California corbina, *M. undulatus,* and several Atlantic species, such as the king whiting, *M. saxatilis,* and the gulf minkfish,

Kissing Bluestriped Grunt (*Haemulon sciurus*); marine; Florida to Rio de Janeiro (Carleton Ray).

M. focaliger. These fishes nevertheless can still produce a very small amount of sound by grinding their teeth together.

Some years ago at Steinhart Aquarium we installed a hydrophone in the tank containing the yellowfin croaker, *Umbrina roncador,* and the spotfin croaker, *Roncador stearnsi,* both common southern California species. A visitor standing in the viewing corridor could press a button and listen to the sounds made by the "talking fishes." Unfortunately, the croakers became acclimated to their tank and soon stopped "talking" except at feeding time. This problem was solved by using a phonograph which, when the button was pressed, played a recording of the croakers at their noisest.

The croaker family is of moderate size, with perhaps 160 species; they are shallow-water, usually carnivorous, inshore denizens of tropical and temperate seas. Some species move readily into brackish and fresh water, and there is one, the American fresh-water drum, *Aplodinotus grunniens,* ranging from Guatemala to Canada, that does not return to salt water. The croakers have two separate dorsal fins, usually barely connected at the base; a rounded snout is typical of many of them, and some have small barbels under the chin. The majority are considered marketable food fishes.

The Atlantic croaker, *Micropogon undulatus,* which has a normal size range of one to four pounds, is a well-known species throughout most of its range from Massachusetts to Argentina. The spot, *Leiostomus xanthurus,* found from Cape Cod to Texas, is easily recognized by the spot above the base of the pectoral fin as well as by the approximately fifteen oblique bars extending upward from the lateral line to the top of the back. The channel bass, sometimes called redfish, *Sciaenops ocellata,* is also easily recognized by the spot on the upper section of the caudal peduncle, just ahead of the tail fin. Reaching a record weight of eighty-three pounds at a length of 52 inches, this valuable fish ranges from Massachusetts to Florida and the Gulf of Mexico. The genus *Cynoscion* includes a number of croaker-like fishes, among them the California white seabass, *C. nobilis,* and the Atlantic weakfish or common sea trout, *C. regalis,* as well as the various species of Atlantic squeteagues. The largest member of the family, the famed totuava, *C. macdonaldi,* also belongs to this genus; it occurs in the Gulf of California and may weigh as much as 225 pounds.

It is of interest to note that several species of sciaenids have been introduced from the Gulf of California into California's inland Salton Sea, where they are now established and reproducing. The small gulf croaker, *Bairdiella icistius,* forms the basis for the

Striped Drum (*Equetus pulcher*); marine; Florida Keys to the Lesser Antilles (Wilhelm Hoppe).

food cycle of the larger corvinas, which are popular sports and food fishes.

The most spectacular members of the croaker family are the half-dozen species of the genus *Equetus,* a tropical American group. The first dorsal fin of these fishes is greatly elevated, and there are usually irregular bands of black and white over the entire body, as is well shown in the nearby illustration.

GOATFISHES or SURMULLETS —Family Mullidae

Two long, tactile barbels under the chin, constantly working in the same way as a mine detector as they are dragged over the bottom, enable the goatfishes to locate small items of food that might otherwise be missed. These barbels are highly flexible, often moving back and forth even when the goatfish is at rest. When not in use, the barbels can be pulled in under the throat, where they are fairly inconspicuous. The goatfish is rather elongated in shape, and has separate spiny-rayed and soft-rayed dorsal fins and a forked tail. Some have brilliant colors splashed with reds and yellows or with striped patterns. Some are noted for their color changes; one of these changes is strikingly illustrated in Plates 92 and 93, in which photographer Fritz Goro, working at Bimini in the Bahamas, has recorded the change in the American Atlantic spotted goatfish, *Pseudupeneus maculatus,* from a mottled red pattern to one in which the red is entirely lacking. The photographs were taken a few minutes apart, and the position of the goatfish changed only slightly during that time.

About forty-two species of goatfishes are recognized from the tropical and temperate marine waters of the world; the majority are less than 10 inches in length, but a few approach 2 feet. Typically, they are found inshore, often in shallow water. Some species are solitary; others travel in schools. They are carnivorous in diet, feeding principally on invertebrates.

The red surmullet of Europe is primarily a tropical species, common in the Mediterranean but ranging up the European coast to Norway. It has long been a valuable food fish; the archives reveal that in the time of the ancient Romans it was one of the most highly prized fishes. The common goatfish or moano of Hawaiian waters, *Parupeneus multifasciatus,* is distinctly marked with at least three vertical bars, one of which is between the two dorsal fins.

The goatfishes or surmullets should not be confused with the true mullets, which belong to another family, the Mugilidae, and will be discussed later.

LETHRINIDS—Family Lethrinidae

This is a small family—only about twenty species —of snapper-like fishes limited to the tropical Indo-

Pacific. Its members have naked heads, a feature that aids in differentiating them from related fishes. One of the representative types is the 30-inch, blue-striped *Lethrinus nebulosus,* commonly known as the scavenger or Mata Hari; it is a valuable food fish throughout its range from Africa to Polynesia.

PORGIES and SEA BREAMS—*Family Sparidae*

Members of the porgy family look somewhat like a cross between a blunt-headed snapper and a grunt. They are deep-bodied fishes, usually equipped with powerful canine or incisor teeth in the jaws, and they may also have strong molar or grinding teeth. Most of the approximately one hundred species in the family are found in tropical and temperate marine waters, but some have been able to adapt to very cold water and a few occasionally enter fresh water. Perhaps the primary center of distribution is the South African area, for twenty-one of the thirty-four species found there occur in no other area. Included in the South African fauna is the "go-home fish," so called by fishermen because at the times they catch it, no other kinds of fishes are caught, all of them apparently having "gone home." The phenomenal blunt-headed musselcrackers are so named because of their tough molariform teeth. Since these fishes often occur in extremely shallow water, they are very popular as angling fishes with the South Africans. The largest musselcracker, and probably the largest sparid, is *Cymatoceps nasutus,* which may tip the scales at one hundred pounds; a smaller mussel-cracker, *Sparodon durbanensis,* attains a very respectable forty pounds.

There are a number of porgies or sea breams in the Mediterranean, and a few also range northward along the European coast. *Box salpa,* shown in a photograph with barracudas in that section of the text, is a common species off Spain. English fishermen trawl for the common sea bream, *Pagellus centrodontus,* in fairly deep water. Excavations of shell mounds at Oronsay, Scotland, have shown that Neolithic man included this fish in his diet.

There are fourteen porgies in the American Atlantic fauna. Typical of these species are the northern porgy or scup, *Stenotomus chrysops;* the sheepshead, *Archosargus rhomboidalis;* and the pinfish, *Lagodon rhomboides.* The first two are of some value as food and anglers' fishes.

The eastern Pacific is singularly devoid of porgies. There is only a single species, *Calamus brachysomus,* in the California fauna, and only one, *Monotaxis grandoculis,* that reaches the Hawaiian Islands. The latter is a very important food fish in many regions, but it has been involved in tropical fish poisoning. One of the most important Australian fishes is a

Yellow Goatfish (*Mulloidichthys martinicus*); marine; Bermuda and Florida to Panama; and Bluestriped Grunts (*Haemulon sciurus*); marine; Florida to Rio de Janeiro (William H. Longley: U.S. Fish and Wildlife Service).

bump-headed porgy, *Chrysophrys guttulatus;* in Australia, however, it is known as "snapper," because that was the name bestowed upon it by Captain Cook. Another member of the genus, *C. major,* is one of the most valuable food fishes in Japan.

FINGERFISHES or MONODACTYLIDS —*Family Monodactylidae*

The fingerfishes, of which there are about five species, live in both salt and fresh water throughout many parts of the tropical Indo-Pacific. The common fingerfish, *Monodactylus argenteus* (Plate 86), is a favorite of aquarists since it does well in captivity; living for a number of years. Seven inches is its maximum length.

ARCHERFISHES—*Family Toxotidae*

The spitting archerfish was first brought to the attention of the scientific world in 1764, when a communication was read before the Royal Society of London detailing the activities of this strange fish. Unfortunately, the preserved specimen accompanying the letter was an entirely different species, actually a butterfly fish, *Chelmon rostratus* (Plates 50 and 51). This error led to many years of confusion and bitter controversy among the authorities as to whether or not the archerfish could actually spit. It was not until 1926 that two eminent American ichthyologists, Dr. George S. Myers and the late Dr.

[193

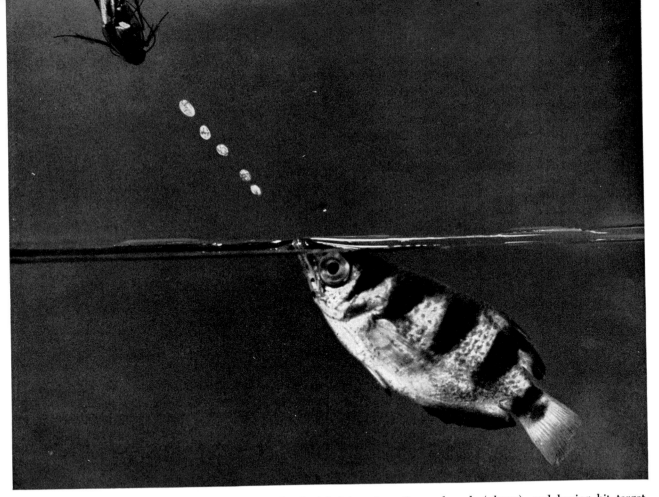

Archerfish (*Toxotes jaculatrix*) firing at captive cockroach (above), and having hit target, receiving food reward (below); fresh, brackish, and salt water; India to Indonesia (Lilo Hess: Three Lions).

Hugh M. Smith, discovered how the archer projects its water pellets. The top of the mouth has a longitudinal groove which acts in the same manner as the upper part of a rifle barrel when the fish's tongue is pressed against it. By compressing the gill covers the archerfish can eject several squirts of water in rapid succession. It is possible to demonstrate this by holding the fish in firing position and pressing the gill covers together with the fingers. This artificial technique will expel a water projectile up to a distance of three feet. The remaining mystery of the archer is that it is able to hit so accurately its out-of-the-water target. Because of the bending of light rays as they enter the water, the target would normally be seen by the fish in a position different from its true one. Yet the archers shoot with reasonable accuracy for distances up to three and four feet and have been credited with hitting a lighted cigarette at ten feet.

The term "pin-point accuracy" has often been used to describe their spitting ability, but this requires modification because differences in individual ability are quite evident. A target only two feet above the water will often be missed by as much as one or even two inches. However, correction of the trajectory usually follows immediately. Also, individuals vary as to the number of shots that can be fired in a period of time. Some can fire with the rapidity of a machine gun; others seem to be capable of only a single shot. If given time, a school of archers can knock down any suitable target within range; but the achievement should be credited to the massed firing power of many rather than the deadly accuracy of a few. It has been suggested that differences in spitting speed and accuracy may be correlated with differences in size, age, and rate of growth; however, this remains to be demonstrated.

One of the most popular exhibits at Steinhart Aquarium was one in which about 150 archers were required to spit at their food daily in order to be fed. This was accomplished by dropping the level of the tank and throwing finely ground hamburger against the exposed portion of the glass. Following this, a period of three minutes usually passed before feeding began. The school of archers ventured toward the glass and appeared to scout the situation; then one or more of the braver ones scurried into the immediate area of the food and jumped out of the water as much as twelve inches, attempting to knock the food off the exposed glass. Following several other jumps, one or more archers cautiously moved in to fire quickly and then moved back away from the glass. Gradually all of the archers came forward, firing a water bombardment, until in fifteen minutes all of the hamburger (one-third of a pound) was washed off the glass.

Archers adapt readily to fresh, brackish, or salt water. The adults, which reach a maximum length of 7½ inches, are considered a good food item in the areas where they normally occur. The four species of archers, all similar in appearance, are found in various parts of the Indo-Australian region. The most common species, and the one often displayed by aquarists, is *Toxotes jaculatrix.*

RUDDERFISHES—*Family Kyphosidae*

Rudderfishes derive their name from the habit some species have of following behind ships, often for long distances. All of the members of the Kyphosidae are oval-shaped, schooling fishes with small mouths and fine teeth. There are not more than a dozen species in the family, most of them widely distributed. Several species are about 30 inches in length when full grown, but the majority are smaller. One of the more common members of this family is the striped rudderfish, *Kyphosus sectatrix,* which is known from both sides of the tropical Atlantic; a similar distribution is shown by the yellow chub, *Kyphosus incisor.*

NIBBLERS—*Family Girellidae*

The nibblers are omnivorous marine fishes that have hinged lips and fine teeth which enable them to nibble very efficiently. Because of their irascible natures and constant pecking and nibbling at other fishes and even at each other, they are disliked intensely by many aquarists. They are nondescript, oval-shaped fishes, greenish, gray, or black in color, and usually less than 18 inches in length. Approximately a dozen species are known, all of them from the Indo-Pacific. In the places where these fishes occur, they are abundantly present in shallow water around rocky areas and in tide pools, the latter being the preferred habitat of the juveniles. The greenish opaleye, *Girella nigricans,* is an inshore California species, common from Monterey Bay to Lower California. Looking down into a tide pool, one can easily identify this fish by the pair of conspicuous white spots on the back on each side of the dorsal fin. Because of its abundance, the opaleye has been used in important temperature tolerance and other experimental studies.

Nibblers are often used as food, especially in Japan, where the "mejina," *Girella punctata,* is a common species.

BATFISHES—*Family Platacidae*

The beautiful batfishes are distinguished by their extremely long dorsal and anal fins. The five dorsal spines are inconspicuously continuous with the soft dorsal rays. When these fishes are young, there are bands across the body (Plate 85), but with growth this pattern is lost and the body shape changes, the height of the fins shortening proportionately. The maximum length of the batfishes is around 26 inches. Like the scats, the batfishes feed upon offal when such "food" is available. *Platax orbicularis,* which ranges through most of the tropical Indo-Pacific, is the most common species.

Once, aboard a research ship in the Sulu Sea, we dipped up some floating sargassum weed to see what kinds of fishes might be lurking in it and found a beautiful 2½-inch batfish. It was carefully placed in the shipboard aquarium, and, because of its likable nature, was soon named the ship's mascot. It was obviously a very intelligent fish, for it quickly learned to come to the surface and feed on small planktonic animals poured into its mouth from a laboratory beaker.

Although several species of batfishes have been described, it is suspected that only a single wide-ranging species exists. This family is closely related to the next family, the spadefishes.

SPADEFISHES—Family Ephippidae

The spadefishes are deep-bodied, laterally compressed fishes with the spinous part of the dorsal fin quite distinct from the soft-rayed portion. In the young there are five or six conspicuous vertical bands extending around the body, but with growth these bands are lost. Also, the young are quite dark, but they tend to become lighter until, at maximum length of about 3 feet, the entire body is silvery. The spadefishes, of which there are several species, are found in the marine waters of the Americas and West Africa, chiefly in the tropical areas and less frequently in the temperate zones.

Most of the spadefishes are schooling fishes, as shown in the title-page photo. One of the best-known species is the American Atlantic *Chaetodipterus faber,* which is found from Cape Cod to Brazil. It has been introduced into Bermudan waters, where it did not originally occur, and now appears to be well established there. This species is noted for its craving for shellfish of all kinds. Sometimes during feeding it produces sound, either by grinding its pharyngeal teeth together or by contracting muscles attached to the very long air bladder, which may be two-thirds the length of the fish.

SCATS—Family Scatophagidae

These popular aquarium fishes have been imported in tremendous numbers because of the attrac-

Bermuda Chub (*Kyphosus sectatrix*); marine; both sides of tropical and temperate Atlantic (Fritz Goro: *Life* Magazine at Lerner Marine Laboratory, Bimini).

tiveness of the juveniles. Found in many parts of the tropical Indo-Pacific, the scats form a small family of perhaps six species, all less than 12 inches in length. The young common scat, *Scatophagus argus,* has a beautiful color pattern of black spots on the body and orange-red color on the dorsal surface, extending downward on the body in the form of bands. With growth the reds are lost but the spots remain, and the scat is much less attractive. Although primarily marine species, they move into shallow brackish water; this is where the young are usually collected for shipment to aquarists. It may be noted that the scats have four anal spines, an exceptional condition which is quite helpful in identification.

The generic name *Scatophagus,* meaning "dung-eater," requires some explanation. It can be traced back to an early ichthyologist in India who studied the food habits of these fishes and discovered that the stomachs of the scats in that area sometimes contained offal.

The banded scats from Australia and New Guinea are silvery fishes of the genus *Selenotoca;* one of these, *S. multifasciatus,* is shown in a nearby photo.

BUTTERFLY FISHES and ANGELFISHES
—Family Chaetodontidae

With few exceptions the small, oval-shaped, laterally compressed chaetodontids are the most beautiful fishes found on the tropical reefs of the world. They are usually solitary, with a few here and a few there. Their range in color and pattern is fantastic; Plates 48 through 62 well demonstrate the beauty of this family. These fishes are usually divided into two groups—or families, according to some—dependent principally upon whether there is a strong spine present on the lower margin of the preoperculum; all of the angelfishes have this spine (note Plates 54 and 58) but the butterflies lack it. There are probably more than 150 species in the family; they are chiefly shallow-water marine forms, although a few do go into brackish water. Some of the angelfishes attain a length of 2 feet, but most of the butterflies are smaller, usually no longer than 6 to 8 inches. The larger species are sometimes used as food.

The chaetodonts have small mouths with many small teeth, and often have extended snouts which are well adapted to picking up small invertebrates from cracks and crevices in rocks and coral. The Indo-Pacific longnose butterfly, *Chelmon rostratus* (Plates 50 and 51), is of interest because for many years it was confused with the spitting archerfish. Although the longnose butterflies, such as *Chelmon,* and the forceps fish, *Forcipiger longirostris,* often come to the surface in an aquarium and spew out small streams of water, they are not capable of

Silver Scats (*Selenotoca multifasciatus*); marine; northern coasts of Australia (Gene Wolfsheimer).

squirting the high-speed water projectiles for which the archerfish, *Toxotes,* is famous.

As a rule, the chaetodonts are peaceful fishes, but there is one, the longnose forceps butterfly mentioned above, that is noted for its fighting nature, especially where its own kind are concerned. The fighting is done with the dorsal fin spines, which are erected as *Forcipiger* turns at an angle to bring the spines into contact with other fish. Because of this aggressiveness, these fish cannot be shipped together in small oxygen-sealed containers, but must be shipped individually or with other species.

Young butterfly fishes usually have a pattern that is similar to that of the adults, so that in many species the juveniles are not too difficult to recognize. Among the angelfishes, however, there are many species in which the juveniles and adults are vastly dissimilar. For example, the angels of Plates 55 and 56 look much alike, but as full-grown adults they are radically different. As an adult, the blue angel (Plate 55) is yellowish on the forward part of the body and grayish or brownish on the posterior portion, with small dark spots over the body. As an adult, the imperial angel (Plate 56) has about twenty-five yellowish bands extending obliquely along the purplish brown body. With growth the young French angel (Plate 57) loses its yellow bands. Changes of this kind are further illustrated by the blue-banded young Atlantic queen angelfish, *Holacanthus ciliaris,* shown in the lower left of Plate 62, which is again greatly different from the adults, shown in Plates 52 and 54. Needless to say, these changes have led to great confusion in classification, the same fish with different patterns having been given as many as four different names.

The butterflies of the Indo-Pacific genus *Heniochus* are an interesting group. They have very deep bodies, most of the depth being due to the highly arched back. The fourth dorsal spine is much longer than the others, sometimes extending for several inches. The white-and-black-banded *Heniochus acuminatus* is one of the most common species.

The angelfishes of the Indo-Pacific genus *Centropyge* are small, usually less than 4 inches in length, and are noted for their beautiful colors, as shown by Potter's angel (Plate 53). One exception is the very drab *C. heraldi,* first discovered at Bikini and other atolls in the atomic testing area of the Marshall Islands.

The largest genus in the family is *Chaetodon,* species of which are found on every tropical reef. Plates 48, 49, 59, and 60 show the characteristic body profile of these fishes.

LEAF FISHES and NANDIDS—Family Nandidae

The Nandidae comprise a fascinating group of small fishes, most of which are well known to the tropical fish hobbyist. Members of this family are found on three continents: Africa, South America, and southeast Asia. This peculiar distribution is in part accounted for by the fact that today's representatives are remnants of an ancient group of fishes once widely distributed.

One of the most interesting fishes in this family is a small 3-inch jumper from India and Burma known as *Badis badis.* Unfortunately, there is no common name for *Badis,* but it probably should be called

Left, French Angelfish (*Pomacanthus arcuatus*); marine; both sides of tropical Atlantic. Right, Gray Angelfish (*Pomacanthus aureus*); marine; tropical American Atlantic (Wilhelm Hoppe).

"chameleon fish" because of its amazing range of pigmentation. Its color changes are often made with great rapidity, and they vary from solid colors to intricate mottled designs. To the uninitiated this fish could easily be mistaken for one of the cichlids, to which it is not even related, although its breeding habits are similar to those of many members of that family.

In the Amazon and Rio Negro basins of South America, we have another member of this family, the fabulous leaf fish, *Monocirrhus polycanthus.* This fish is well named, for its ability to simulate a floating leaf in the water is most remarkable. The body, which measures 3 to 4 inches in an adult, is greatly compressed laterally. The fins are sometimes kept folded and at other times are expanded, showing their serrated edges; both positions enable the leaf fish to resemble leaves of different contours. A fleshy flap or barbel extends from the chin; it looks like a broken leaf stem, thus increasing the camouflage effect. The color is generally a mottled brown but sometimes ranges from light gray or pale tan to black. All of these variations match the fallen leaves that are found floating in the waters of the leaf fish's native habitat. The mode of swimming, generally with the head at a downward angle, again resembles a leaf slowly floating in the water.

Another remarkable feature of this fish is its large mouth, which is equipped with extensible jaws that enable the leaf fish to engulf other fishes at least half its own size. In captivity it has the habit of extending its jaws in what appears to be a prodigious yawn. In capturing its food, the leaf fish drifts slowly and imperceptibly toward the unsuspecting victim or waits patiently until the prey swims within reach. Then in one motion, faster than the eye can follow, the unlucky fish is virtually inhaled and disappears within the cavernous maw.

Although the drifting motion or absence of motion is normal for the leaf fish, it can, if alarmed or excited, take off with great speed, leaping from the water to a height of eight inches or more.

Other members of this interesting family include the mottled *Nandus nandus* of India, Burma, and Siam; the banded *N. nebulosus* from Thailand, Malaya, Sumatra, Borneo, and other East Indian islands; *Polycentrus abbreviata,* the African leaf fish, and *P. schomburgki* of the Guianas and Trinidad.

CICHLIDS—Family Cichlidae

The hardy, aggressive cichlids form a large group of some six hundred spiny-rayed fishes distributed through South America northward to Texas; they are also found in Africa, and there is a single genus of sunfish-like cichlids, *Etroplus,* in India and Ceylon.

Discus (*Symphysodon discus*) with nursing young on the sides of the body; fresh water; Rio Negro and Amazon basins (Gene Wolfsheimer).

The body profile of many of these cichlids is similar to that of the African jewelfish (Plate 87) and the False mouthbreeder (Plate 88). One of their principal identifying marks is a single nostril on each side rather than double nostrils.

In spite of their pugnacity, the cichlids are favorites of the aquarists and the object of many studies. One of the most popular species is the Amazonian scalare or fresh-water angelfish, *Pterophyllum scalare*. In recent years several melanistic varieties of this fish, called black angels, have been developed. The South American discus or pompadour fish, *Symphysodon discus,* which resembles some of the marine butterfly fishes, is considered one of the most beautiful of the cichlids. The spawning and raising of this species has presented a challenge to aquarists, principally because the young normally feed on the secretions of special mucous cells in the skin of the parents. The observations made by the University of California's Dr. W. H. Hildeman (1959) on the normal parent-offspring relationship are interesting:

> Both parents take turns guarding, fanning and mouthing the eggs. The parents pick up the newly hatched fish with their mouths and transfer them together to various surfaces where each remains attached, wriggling violently at the end of a short thread. The fry become free-swimming four days after hatching and promptly move to their parents' sides where they begin to feed from their skin. Although both parents are capable of feeding the young, both take rest periods, and by a flick of the body are proficient at transferring all the fry to the other parent. . . . The young continue to feed on the parental skin for at least five weeks even though an abundance of other live food is available.

Although native Africans have long used cichlids as food, in other parts of the world it is only recently

Spotted Mouthbreeder (*Tropheus moori*); fresh water; Lake Tanganyika and adjacent areas (Wilhelm Hoppe).

that interest has developed in the food value of these fishes, specifically the genus *Tilapia*. Some of the many species of *Tilapia* range up to twenty pounds but the majority weigh less than two pounds. Although many are mouthbreeders, Plate 88 is one of the exceptions. *Tilapia* reproduce rapidly, usually in fresh water, rarely in salt water. Using its mouth the male digs a small crater in the sand or mud, then entices a receptive female to lay her eggs in the depression. The eggs are quickly fertilized, then the female, although in a few species it may be the male, picks up the eggs and holds them in the mouth for as long as three weeks until they hatch; the time required for hatching is dependent upon the species and the temperature. Even after hatching, the young may be held in the mouth for a short time, after which they are carefully guarded for a few more days. With the approach of danger, the youngsters swim back into the parent's mouth.

One of the African mouthbreeders, *Tilapia mossambica*, appeared in Indonesia in 1939, and because of its phenomenal reproductive rate quickly became a popular pondfish. Since then, introduction of this species and other mouthbreeders has been tried in many regions of the world. Where competition with other species is not too great, the mouthbreeders readily become established and provide a practical solution to the problem of low-cost protein, which is acute in some areas.

The Rio Grande perch, *Cichlasoma cyanoguttatum*, is a grayish, blue-spotted, 10-inch fish noteworthy in that it is the only member of its family that has been able to make its way as far northward as the United States. Other cichlids often seen in aquaria include several 4- to 6-inch species of the South American genera *Aequidens* and *Cichlasoma;* included in this latter group are such forms as the greenish black Jack Dempsey, *C. biocellatus;* the flag cichlid, *C. festivum,* which has a distinctive black band extending through the eye to the posterior base of the dorsal fin; and the spectacular firemouth, *C. meeki,* with its brilliant red chest.

The 12-inch oscar or peacock-eyed cichlid, *Astronotus ocellatus,* has often been suggested as a sports fish for the warmer sections of the southern United States, but as yet its introduction there has not been tried. The oscar is easily recognized by the large dark spot surrounded by a bright orange ring on the upper part of the caudal peduncle. The pike cichlids of the genus *Crenicichla* also have a tail spot, but in this case on the tail fin itself; a distinctive bar extending through the eye and sometimes down the length of the body is often present. These are very elongated fishes that grow rapidly up to a maximum of 9 to 12 inches.

The Congo bumphead cichlid, *Steatocranus casuarius,* is an interesting 4-inch species that has developed the same kind of bulbous forehead found among some of the parrotfishes and surgeons.

HAWKFISHES—*Family Cirrhitidae*

The hawkfishes are noted for their ability to perch primly upon bits of coral and rock; they seem to spend most of their lives just sitting, occasionally moving from one resting spot to another. These fishes are limited to the Indo-Pacific; in their habits and to a certain extent in their appearance they resemble the scorpaenid rockfishes, but they lack the rough, spiny heads for which the latter are noted. Cirrhitids have two important identifying characteristics: the simple rays of the pectoral fins are thickened and slightly extended, and there is a fringe at the back of the anterior nostril. The 6-inch *Paracirrhites arcatus,* which is found throughout the tropical Indo-Pacific, is one of the most distinctive forms; it is reddish brown in color and has a definite rectangular mark extending obliquely upward behind the eye. One other very strange-looking hawkfish, the 12-inch *Cheilodactylus vittatus,* has alternating oblique black and white bands and is found most often at depths of a hundred feet. It is sometimes placed in a family by itself, the Cheilodactylidae.

SURFPERCHES—*Family Embiotocidae*

The surfperches, also called seaperches, form a small family of twenty-three species and some fifteen or eighteen genera; they range in size from 3 to 18 inches. With a single exception they are marine in habitat, and all are viviparous, the young being born alive. It should be noted that viviparity occurs among many fresh-water fishes but is extremely uncommon among marine species. The discovery of this reproductive method among the surfperches over a century ago created a tremendous furor in the scientific world. First reports and observations on the viviparous nature of these fishes came from Sausalito, California, and were sent to Harvard to Professor Louis Agassiz, who published a famous paper in 1853, giving the surfperches status as an entirely new family. Immediately thereafter and for the next few years a plethora of papers appeared in scientific journals throughout the world on these "extraordinary" fishes, as Agassiz called them.

There are few records of actual observation of the breeding habits of this family. However, in 1917 Dr. Carl L. Hubbs was fortunate enough to witness the actual impregnation of the female by a male shiner seaperch, *Cymatogaster aggregata,* and published his observations, showing that the anal structure is used during copulation. Subsequent investigations showed that with the exception of the striped seaperch, *Embiotoca lateralis,* the surfperches mature sexually very early, and the first act of copulation takes place soon after birth. The breeding season varies according to temperature; along the California coast breeding usually takes place during the summer, but at the time of copulation the sperm does not come into contact with the eggs, and fertilization does not take place until a later period, ranging from fall to the following spring. The eggs have little yolk, and the young receive their nourishment and respiration through the medium of the ovarian fluid which bathes them.

Two genera with a single species each, *Neoditrema ransonneti* and *Ditrema temmincki,* are found on the coasts of Japan and Korea. All of the other species are from the Pacific coast of North America, ranging from southern Alaska to central Lower California, with the majority being found off central and southern California, where it is generally conceded that the family originated.

As the common name suggests, the majority of these fishes are found in the coastal surf, but many of them enter bays to drop their young. In San Francisco Bay the shiner seaperch, *Cymatogaster aggregata,* is the predominant fish, not only in numbers but often in body volume as well. One species, the pink seaperch, *Zalembius rosaceus,* occurs in fairly deep waters along the continental shelf; two others are generally found in tide pools. Some of the larger species are well known to both sports and commercial fishermen, the white perch, *Phanerodon funcatus,* being the most important commercial species in the family. One species, the tule perch, *Hysterocarpus traski,* is found exclusively in the fresh water of California's Sacramento River Delta. To aquarists this is a mysterious fish because all of the embiotocids except the tule perch are easy to keep alive in captivity; it is difficult to keep this species alive for more than a few weeks. It has been suggested that the presence of a large amount of tule or bog silt may be necessary to provide the proper environment.

Bumphead Cichlid (*Steatocranus casuarius*); fresh water; Congo (Gene Wolfsheimer).

Young Two-striped Damselfish (*Dascyllus reticulatus*); marine; tropical Indo-Pacific (Gene Wolfsheimer).

DAMSELFISHES—Family Pomacentridae

One of the strangest relationships between animals is that exhibited by the damselfishes of the genus *Amphiprion*, known popularly as anemone fishes, and certain tropical sea anemones. About a dozen species of anemone fishes are currently recognized, most of them as beautiful as the clown anemone fish, *Amphiprion percula* (Plate 64). They are usually found living around large colonial anemones and among the tentacles of those animals. The strange aspect of this relationship is that the anemones have explosive stinging cells capable of killing any small fishes that are not immune to their venom. Yet the anemone fishes swim in and out of the tentacles with impunity. Studies carried out at Marineland of the Pacific by Dr. Demorest Davenport and Dr. Kenneth Norris (1958) revealed that the mucus secreted by the anemone fish prevented the anemone from discharging its lethal stinging cells or nematocysts as they are known technically.

Some of the anemone fish are specific in the kinds of anemones they will accept—some will accept only a single species, whereas others will accept several.

Like the fresh-water cichlids, the damselfishes have only a single nostril on each side of the snout. Nearly all of the damsels are small tropical marine fishes, the majority less than 6 inches in length. A few have become adapted to temperate water, as is the case of the 11-inch, brilliant orange garibaldi, *Hypsypops rubicunda* (Plate 66), an attractive inshore inhabitant of the kelp beds and rocky coasts of southern California. The normal depth range of the garibaldi is between four and forty-two feet. Spawning takes place during July and August, and is initiated by the male's cleaning an area surrounding a clump of red algae; it is upon this algae that the female deposits her eggs. The blue-spotted juveniles (Plate 65), which are obviously entirely different in color from the adults, appear between August and November. By the time they are about 2½ inches in length they begin to acquire the color of the adults. In the aquarium, the adults are noted for the highly audible clicking noises produced, especially at feeding time, by their pharyngeal teeth. As is true of many of the damsels, the garibaldis are quarrelsome fishes with strong territorial patterns. In captivity, if they are not given places to hide, they quickly kill the weaker or smaller fish of their kind.

Although many of the damsels are typically inshore species, there are some, such as the American Atlantic blue chromis, *Chromis cyanea* (Plate 63), that are generally found offshore.

Damselfishes of the genus *Dascyllus* are often found around coral heads, several hundred of the same species hovering a foot or so above a large head; if danger threatens—perhaps in the form of a skin diver approaching—they all move, in unison, back into the interstices of the coral. Fishes of this kind include the Indo-Pacific three-stripe damsel, *D. aruanus,* and the two-stripe, *D. reticulatus,* both of which are often imported by aquarists. Another widespread Indo-Pacific species is the spotted *D. trimaculatus,* a dark 6-inch fish with a single spot high on the back on each side of the body and often one above the head. Studies at the Monaco Aquarium by

Dr. J. Garnaud have shown that these fish mature at the age of one year, after which they live as pairs. Spawning takes place early in the morning as often as three times a month; during each spawning some 20,000 to 25,000 adhesive eggs are laid in small distinct clusters. The male then guards the eggs until they hatch four or five days later.

The two largest genera of damselfishes are *Pomacentrus* and *Abudefduf;* the majority of these fishes do not have particularly brilliant markings. One of the most widely distributed fishes in the family is the sergeant major, *A. saxatilis,* a vertically banded 4-inch fish, which occurs not only on both sides of the Atlantic but also in the Pacific.

WRASSES—Family Labridae

There is a tremendous variation in size among the approximately six hundred species of carnivorus wrasses. They range from the tiny 3-inch, pencil-like species of the genus *Labroides* to the giants of the genus *Cheilinus,* measuring 10 feet and weighing several hundred pounds. Many are highly colored and are often the most brilliant fishes on the tropical reefs and in the temperate marine waters where they occur. Startling patterns, such as that of the Indo-Pacific twinspot wrasse, *Coris angulata* (Plate 70), are commonplace. Other distinctive patterns are well shown by Plates 67 through 71. Radical color changes occurring with growth have in the past been the cause of great confusion in the classification of the wrasses. For example, the highly variable young of the Atlantic bluehead, *Thalassoma bifasciatum* (Plate 69), may go through the conspicuous yellow color phase with or without a wide lateral black band along the sides; following this, the males develop the bluehead pattern with the deep crescent tail, shown in Plate 68; the females, however, usually retain the yellow or green color and may also retain the lateral band in the form of blotches, but do not develop the deep crescent in the tail.

The labrids are usually non-schooling fishes noted for their well-developed incisor or canine teeth, which in some cases protrude like a pair of forceps from the protractile mouth. Many of them, with their vile dispositions, use these teeth to remove the fins or even the eyes from other fishes and actually to mutilate members of their own species. For instance, seventy individuals of the beautiful Hawaiian saddle wrasse, *Thalassoma duperreyi* (Plate 71), placed in a thousand-gallon tank will, as a result of their attacks upon each other, be reduced within three months to as few as a dozen fish.

If a single behavior trait were used to identify the wrasses, the one chosen would be their ability to go to sleep, usually buried under the sand. A tank of fifty cigar-shaped 8-inch señoritas, *Oxyjulis californica,* will in the daytime be filled with the fishes swimming about the tank; at night, the tank will be completely barren, all the señoritas having buried themselves in the sand, invariably on their sides. Dr. W. A. Gosline and Mr. V. Brock have pointed out that all except one of the forty-eight species of labrids in the Hawaiian fauna sleep in the sand at night. This one exception, *Labroides phthirophagus,* forms a mucous cocoon around its body as the parrotfishes do.

Around 1950 there began to develop an increased interest in the activity of the cleaner fishes—usually small species of wrasses—which regularly remove ectoparasites from the heads and gills of other larger carnivorous fishes capable of instantly devouring them in a single gulp. Since the cleaners are small fishes, they tend to remain in one place; this place becomes recognized by larger fishes as a cleaner station, and they make periodic trips to it for cleaning services. The genus *Labroides,* which includes several species, is often involved in such activity (Plate 27). Studies made by the University of Miami's Dr. John Randall (1958) in the eastern Pacific showed that many species of large fishes, including jacks, groupers, snappers, parrotfishes, and eels, make use of the services of *Labroides.* Other kinds of fishes that have also been observed to function as cleaners include young blueheads (Plate 98), neon gobies (Plate 100), young porkfish (Plate 77), and many others as well as some invertebrates such as red shrimp (Plate 28).

The cuckoo wrasse, *Labrus ossifagus* (Plate 67), is one of the most attractive labrids; this is especially true during the breeding season. As is characteristic of many vertebrates, the female is less attractive than the male, in this case lacking the bright blue bands which the male has along the sides of his body. Mature fishes measure about 12 inches in length. The normal range of *Labrus* is from Norway to the Mediterranean. Although it has been a well-known aquarium fish for many years, it was only recently that the courtship pattern was recorded, for the first time, by Dr. Douglas P. Wilson of the Plymouth Aquarium. He found that during May the male dug the nest at night by turning on his side and vigorously flapping his tail until a depression about the size of his body was prepared. In one instance, two nests of this type were prepared by a single male. Following this, the courtship of the unwilling female proceeded at a great pace with the male attacking any and all females in the area—biting and swimming at them until one followed him to the nest. The male showed his excitement by a peculiar loss of pigment on the upper part of the head and trunk; this is remarkably well demonstrated in Plate 67. It was thought that this loss in color provided a physiological stimulus for the female to induce egg laying. During normal activity this whitish area did not show.

The Indo-Pacific birdfishes of the genus *Gomphosus* are unusual-looking wrasses with very elongated snouts that curve slightly downward. Two species are known—*G. varius* and *G. tricolor,* both less than 12 inches in length. Another peculiar species is the Indo-Pacific long-jawed wrasse, *Epibulus insidiator,* the lower jaw of which is about twice the usual length and can be extended forward for an even greater distance. This fish is known to have two color phases, which are similar to those of the yellow surgeon (Plate 96).

Among the common Atlantic American labrids are the 3-foot tautog, *Tautoga onitis;* the 2-foot hogfish, *Lachnolaimus maximus;* the 18-inch pudding wife, *Halichoeres radiatus;* and the 15-inch pearly razorfish, *Xyrichthys psittacus.* The first two are food fishes of moderate importance.

PARROTFISHES—Family Scaridae

As one stands above the high-tide line on a tropical shelf reef and watches the incoming tide, the most obvious event seen is the return of the "cattle of the sea"; these are the colorful parrotfishes, which usually appear as many blue-green patches of color moving in over the reefs, much like herds of cattle. Because of their feeding habits, these herbivores with their chisel-sharp, parrot-like beaks are the major sources of erosion on many tropical reefs. Each time the parrotfish removes food from the coral, it also bites out a chunk of the reef, leaving distinct tooth impressions, so that it is usually quite obvious where fishes of this kind have been foraging. Pieces of coral are difficult to pass through the digestive tract, but the parrotfish accomplishes this after first thoroughly crushing the coral and food with its powerful plate-

Blue Parrotfish (*Scarus coeruleus*); marine; Maryland to Rio de Janeiro (Carleton Ray).

like pharyngeal teeth located in the back of the throat. Some parrotfishes have set patterns of travel and certain areas where they defecate regularly, leaving mounds of broken but undigested coral rubble that give mute testimony to the erosive effect of these fishes. Parrots are often creatures of habit and demonstrate a strong homing instinct. For example, at Bermuda the rainbow parrotfish, *Scarus guacamaia* (Plate 82), is a cave dweller, which moves out during the day to forage. When frightened, it swims directly and quickly back to the cave. If a net is stretched across the entrance to the cave, it will repeatedly swim into the net attempting to return to its home.

With growth, some species of parrotfishes go through at least three entirely different color phases; in addition to this, the males and females are sometimes totally different in coloration. This color confusion is to a great extent responsible for the fact that ichthyologists usually consider the parrotfishes among the most difficult of all fishes to identify correctly. This difficulty in classification is partially indicated by the multiplicity of scientific names. Dr. Leonard P. Schultz of the U.S. National Museum, after spending several years studying the some 350 kinds that had been described, finally reduced the number to 80 species for the entire world. This number may be even further diminished by ecological studies such as those carried out underwater at Bermuda by Dr. Howard Winn and Dr. John Bardach (1960). For example, they found that the blue-and-orange-striped parrotfish, *Scarus taeniopterus* (Plate 81), were always males; that the brown-and-white-striped *S. croicensis* (Plate 83) were always females; and that it was possible experimentally to reverse color patterns from female to male by the injection of male sex hormones. Thus the two were found to be the same species, despite the fact that they had been recognized as distinct species for more than 130 years. (The Winn-Bardach report was published after the captions for the plates in this book were printed; hence, we retain the old names.)

Dr. Winn was also responsible for the discovery, in 1955, of the most remarkable biological phenomenon among the parrotfishes. He found that at night certain parrotfishes secreted a loose mucous envelope that surrounded the body as shown in the nearby photograph. Some species required at least thirty minutes or longer to form this envelope, and usually at least the same amount of time to break out of it with the return of either natural or artificial light. Certain species and genera, for example *Sparisoma,* do not show this ability; however, the fishes in Plates 81, 82, and 83 do form mucous envelopes. In some cases formation of the envelope is erratic or occurs only under special conditions. How and why the envelope is formed remains to be determined.

The parrotfishes vary greatly in size, a number of species, such as the Tahitian parrotfish (Plate 84), being adult at lengths of less than 18 inches and others approaching a normal maximum of 6 feet; there have also been a few observations of some gigantic old bulls reaching 12 feet in length and a depth of 6 feet. Most startling among the parrots are the bumphead males, such as the Indo-Pacific *Chlorurus gibbus,* which have smooth foreheads when young but with maturity develop a tremendous hump on the head. The Atlantic *Scarus coeruleus* shown on the facing page is an adult bumphead male.

SANDFISHES—Family Trichodontidae

The sandfishes are scaleless northern Pacific marine species; they have nearly vertical mouths with peculiar fringed lips that provide instant identification. The preopercle has five sharp spines—a further indentifying mark. The sandfish's normal position is that of being buried in the mud or sand on the bottom with only the mouth and eyes showing. Two species are known, both with maximum sizes of about 12 inches: the first, *Trichodon trichodon,* ranges from northern California to Alaska and can be identified by its fourteen or fifteen dorsal fin spines; the second, *Arctoscopus japonicus,* is found from Alaska to Korea and has ten or eleven dorsal fin spines. Since the latter is an important food fish in parts of Japan, its biology is well known. During most of the year it is found at depths of around 450 feet, but during December it moves into water less than 3 feet deep to spawn. The eggs are laid in spherical capsules containing an average of about 750 eggs. Hatching requires up to two months, after which the juveniles remain in shallow water for three months before moving into deeper water.

JAWFISHES—Family Opisthognathidae

The jawfishes are a small tropical group of secretive blenny-like forms, some of which live in burrows of their own construction. All members of the family have large mouths, and a few, such as the Indo-African *Opisthognathus nigromarginatus,* have long, backward extensions of the jawbones, which enable the tremendous mouth to open even wider so that it can scoop up food much larger than the fish's own head. Seven species have been recognized from the Florida keys, the Bahamas, and adjacent tropical areas; one of these, *Opisthognathus aurifrons,* has been studied in some detail. The long-time Tortugas Key diving investigations by Professor William Longley disclosed that this 4-inch fish normally digs a burrow about twelve to fourteen inches

Rainbow Parrotfish (*Pseudoscarus guacamaia*) surrounded by mucous envelope; marine; both sides of the tropical Atlantic (Howard Winn).

in length with an enlarged internal chamber, all of which is eventually lined with bits of rock and coral. Sometimes a small crater is built up around the outside of the opening, perhaps to provide better protection. The jawfish often hovers above the burrow with the body in obliquely vertical position; at the first sign of danger, it darts into its home, usually tail first. In resting position, only a portion of the head and anterior part of the body protrudes from the home. William Braker's observations at Chicago's Shedd Aquarium have shown that the jawfish is a typical "tail stander," using the constantly moving pectoral and tail fins as stabilizing supports for the nearly vertical body. Captive specimens show a strong territorial pattern; another fish entering the surface area of a tunnel excavation is instantly met by the angry owner, who shows his displeasure by erecting his fins, flaring his gill covers, and threatening to bite, although he never does.

Dusky Longjaw (*Opisthognathus whitehursti*); marine; Bahamas and Florida Keys (Charles C. G. Chaplin).

Philadelphia Academy of Science ichthyologists James Boehlke and Charles Chaplin recently discovered that two species of Bahaman jawfishes, *Opisthognathus maxillosus* and *O. whitehursti,* are mouthbreeders, and that the incubating egg masses are so large that the fishes cannot close their mouths. Whether it is the male or female that carries the eggs in the mouth is not as yet known; whether other members of the family are also mouthbreeders remains to be determined.

WEEVERFISHES—Family Trachinidae

The weever family contains only four species of small, elongated marine fishes with long anal and second dorsal fins; the ventral or pelvic fins are under the throat—jugular in position. These are very dangerous fishes, noted for their poisonous spines—specifically, the single long spine of the gill cover and those of the first dorsal fin. Three species of the weevers are found along the European coast and the north and west coasts of Africa, and the fourth one along the coast of Chile. The greater weever, *Trachinus draco,* is a fairly deep-water species, reaching a length of 17 inches, that ranges from the Black Sea to the Baltic; it may be recognized by the oblique bands on the sides of the body. These bands are absent on the shallow-water lesser weever, *Trachinus vipera,* an 8-inch species, which is fairly common from the North Sea to the Mediterranean. Since these fishes bury themselves in the sand, they are a menace to the barefooted skin diver or wader. Weevers are often picked up in trawl nets; although in the past they have had some commercial value, they must be handled with extreme care. The venom contained in grooves on the spines is both a blood and a nerve toxin and causes the victim excruciating pain within thirty minutes after contact. Several months may be required for recovery.

SAND DIVERS—Family Trichonotidae

The trichonotids are small, slender, inconspicuous marine and fresh-water fishes occurring throughout the tropics. They measure only a few inches in length, and are usually found in shallow water, near shore, buried in coral sand. The name "sand divers" is derived from their habit of quickly burrowing head-first into the sand when alarmed. These fishes have many interesting features. Over the tops of the eyes they have intricately shaped silvery "eye shades," which protect them from the bright tropical sun, made even more intense by its reflection from their sandy habitat. The "eye shades" are particularly spectacular in the genus *Trichonotus,* in which they are in the form of radiating silvery bands that shade the eyes like Venetian blinds. Many species in the family have protruding eyes that enable them to lie buried in the sand with only the eyes exposed, waiting for unsuspecting prey. The genus *Chalixodytes* of the central Pacific is remarkable for having "binocular" vision. The eyes can rotate to the front and focus directly forward; this allows the fish to judge more accurately the distance in lunging at its prey. All sand divers are carnivorous, living on small free-swimming animals.

As a rule, the sand divers are slim, elongated, and round in cross section; they have sharply pointed heads, with the upper jaw usually longer than the lower. The dorsal and anal fin bases are long, extending to the base of the caudal fin. There may be one or two dorsal fins. The males of the genus *Trichonotus* have greatly elongated anterior dorsal rays, which are beautifully banded in bright colors. Many of the sand divers are transparent, with a sparse color pattern, so that they blend perfectly with their background.

The family Trichonotidae consists of approximately twenty-two genera and fifty species, most of which are found in the Indo-Pacific region, particularly Australia and New Zealand. They also occur in South Africa and the tropical Atlantic. The sand divers are sometimes divided into several families, some of those recently recognized being the Limnichthyidae, Creediidae, and Bembropsidae. They appear to be related to the dragonets of the family Callionymidae, some of the sand divers having the same vivid coloration of fins and body shown by the dragonets.

SAND LANCES—Family Kraemeriidae

The sand lances of the family Kraemeriidae are little-known, transparent, glasslike fishes 1 to 3 inches long. They live in lagoons and streams along the edge of atolls and high islands in the tropical Indo-Pacific and the coast of Australia, and are extremely difficult to see in the water because they blend completely with their sandy background. So far, the family has been found to be most abundant in such widely separated localities as the Solomon, Palau, and Seychelles Islands, and it has been discovered to inhabit only restricted areas of shore line; it is not known why the habitat is so specific. Most species apparently live in the sand with their upwardly directed eyes protruding, watching for tiny marine animals to pounce upon as prey. They have massive, projecting lower jaws, and the outer edges of their lips are scalloped, presumably to keep sand grains out of their mouths when they snap at food from their hiding places. The female lays eggs that are quite large in relation to her size. There are about ten known species, belonging to two genera,

Southern Stargazer (*Astroscopus y-graecum*); marine; North Carolina to Santos, Brazil (Marine Studios).

Kraemeria and *Gobitrichinotus*. The group is said to be most closely related to the gobies of the family Gobiidae, but sand lances lack the cupped ventral fins of the gobies. They have also been associated with the Trichonotidae. The genus *Gobitrichinotus* seems to be common in streams of the Philippine Islands; the only other record of this genus is at Tahiti. *Kraemeria* is more abundant and widely distributed.

ELECTRIC STARGAZERS
—Family Uranoscopidae

From the standpoint of defense, the marine uranoscopid stargazers are well-equipped fishes; they often have electrogenic organs, formed of modified eye muscles, located in a special pouch just behind the eyes. Discharges of as much as fifty volts have been recorded from this electrical tissue; the stargazers have negative polarity on the upper surface and positive on the lower surface. In addition to their electrogenic equipment, they have two large poison spines just above the pectoral fins and behind the opercle. Each spine has double grooves along the sides and a venom gland at the base; venom from these spines has been known to be responsible for the death of humans. The ventral or pelvic fins are located under the throat, and the mouth, with its fringed lips, is in nearly vertical position. Some stargazers, such as the 13-inch European *Uranoscopus scaber*, have small wormlike fishing lures attached to the mouth; these lures are used to entice passing food fishes as the stargazer lies buried in the sand. When seen in this position, it is obvious why the fish has been named "stargazer," for the eyes are on top of the head and look directly upward. Some stargazers have nostrils that open into the mouth, enabling the buried fish to bring water into the gill cavity with less sediment than if the mouth were used for this purpose, as is normal in other fishes.

About two dozen uranoscopid stargazers are known; they range from shallow to very deep tropical and temperate marine waters around the world. The northern stargazer, *Astroscopus guttatus,* has a limited range from New York to Virginia; it reaches a length of 22 inches and a weight of some twenty pounds. The 15-inch southern stargazer, *A. y-graecum,* ranges from South Carolina southward through the Gulf of Mexico to Brazil.

SAND STARGAZERS—Family Dactyloscopidae

These fishes are almost identical to the uranoscopids except for the fact that they lack the electrical organs and have one spine and three rays in each ventral fin, whereas the uranoscopids have one spine and five rays in each fin. An example of this family is the common sand stargazer, *Dactyloscopus tridigitatus,* which is found from Bermuda and the Gulf of Mexico to Brazil.

ANTARCTIC FISHES

About sixty-six species of fishes are known from around the Antarctic Continent. A few of these are members of families with fairly wide geographical distribution. For example, the fauna includes one hagfish, one ray, two eel cods, five eel pouts, and two snail fishes. These eleven species are not overly abundant, and in population density they account for only 5 per cent of all Antarctic fishes. The remaining 95 per cent of the population (fifty-five species) belong to four families which, with the exception of one genus, are limited to the Antarctic. These are sometimes called the notothenoid group of fishes and include the Antarctic dragon fishes, family Bathydraconidae; the ice fishes, Chaenichthyidae; the plunder fishes, Harpagiferidae; and the Antarctic cods, Nototheniidae (Plate 89). One additional family, the Bovichthyidae, which is sub-Antarctic in distribution, is also included in this notothenoid group.

Although the number of species in Antarctica is limited, it would obviously increase considerably if the sub-Antarctic were included. Depending upon where the boundaries are drawn, 150 to 200 species may be involved. All of these fishes have one thing in common: they face environmental conditions that are hazardous compared with those of more temperate areas. The temperature of the water is usually around 32 degrees F. (0 degrees C.).

ICE FISHES—Family Chaenichthyidae

For over fifty years the Norwegian whalers working in the Antarctic have described to their friends at home a peculiar, transparent, and "bloodless" fish that had white rather than red gills. Recent studies have shown that the blood of these fishes lacks red cells but does have some nucleated cells similar to the white blood cells of other vertebrates. These form about 1 per cent of the total blood volume. This, then, presents a biological puzzle. How can a fish lacking red cells and haemoglobin absorb oxygen into its blood and in turn transport this oxygen to the tissues? Laboratory investigations on *Chaenocephalus aceratus* have shown that the blood plasma is able to absorb only about ¾ of 1 per cent of oxygen by volume, which is about the same capacity as the blood plasma of other vertebrates. By contrast, the blood of other Antarctic fishes has an oxygen-carrying capacity of about 6 per cent by volume. This amount is comparable to that of fishes from temperate regions.

With this added information, the physiological problem of the bloodless fishes becomes a greater enigma than ever. For example, how and why did these fishes lose their red cells and haemoglobin, since obviously they must be descended from fishes that had these characteristics? Only one other fish is known that lacks haemoglobin. That is the larval or leptocephalid eel, but it develops this material as it matures. The lamprey eel, *Petromyzon*, has a blood pigment slightly different from that of other fishes, but all others except the "bloodless" fishes have red cells and the all-important haemoglobin.

Thirteen of the approximately eighteen known species of chaenichthyid ice fishes have been found to lack red blood cells, and it is probable that this condition exists for the entire family. All ice fishes have semitransparent, scaleless bodies and ribs that lack ossification. They are limited to the Antarctic, with the single exception of *Champsocephalus esox*, which ranges northward to Patagonia. *Chaenocephalus aceratus* reaches a length of 2 feet and a weight of two and a half pounds, but the other members of the family are smaller.

Moorish Idol and Surgeonfishes

(Suborder Acanthuroidea)

Fishes of the two families in this suborder are set aside from the sea-bass-like fishes of the previous group principally on the basis of obscure anatomical differences in the relation of the head to the rest of the skeleton. These fishes have vertically compressed bodies and go through a strange "acronurus" larval stage in which the young have vertical ridges on the body.

MOORISH IDOL—Family Zanclidae

Because of its beauty, the spectacular 7-inch moorish idol, *Zanclus canescens* (Plate 90), is usually selected by artists as the typical fish of the tropical Indo-Pacific reefs. Young moorish idols have a sharp spine at each corner of the mouth; as the fishes grow, these spines are lost and protuberances develop in front of the eyes. In the aquarium it is difficult to keep moorish idols in a healthy condition. They fight with other fishes, go into shock easily, and are highly susceptible to a variety of diseases that are not especially troublesome to other tropical marine species.

SURGEONFISHES—Family Acanthuridae

Just in front of the tail, on the sides of the caudal peduncle, the surgeonfishes have sharp "knives," which not only are the source of their name but also are a mark of identification. These knives show particularly well on the yellow surgeon (Plate 96). The members of this species have jackknife-type structures that are hinged so that the blade drops into a hidden groove. The hinge is at the posterior end of the blade and the opened blade faces forward. This arrangement is typical of the genus *Acanthurus* and is the kind of knife possessed by the surgeons shown in Plates 94, 97, 98, and 99. Other surgeons, for instance members of the genus *Naso*, have one to several spines in approximately the same position on the tail as those of *Acanthurus*,

[continued on page 225]

90. Moorish Idol (*Zanclus canescens*); marine; tropical Indo-Pacific
(John Tashjian at Steinhart Aquarium)

91. Glassfish (*Chanda ranga*); fresh, brackish, and
salt water; India and Burma (Gene Wolfsheimer)

92. and 93. **Spotted Goatfish** (*Pseudupeneus maculatus*) showing color change in the same fish; marine; New Jersey to Rio de Janeiro (Fritz Goro: *Life* Magazine)

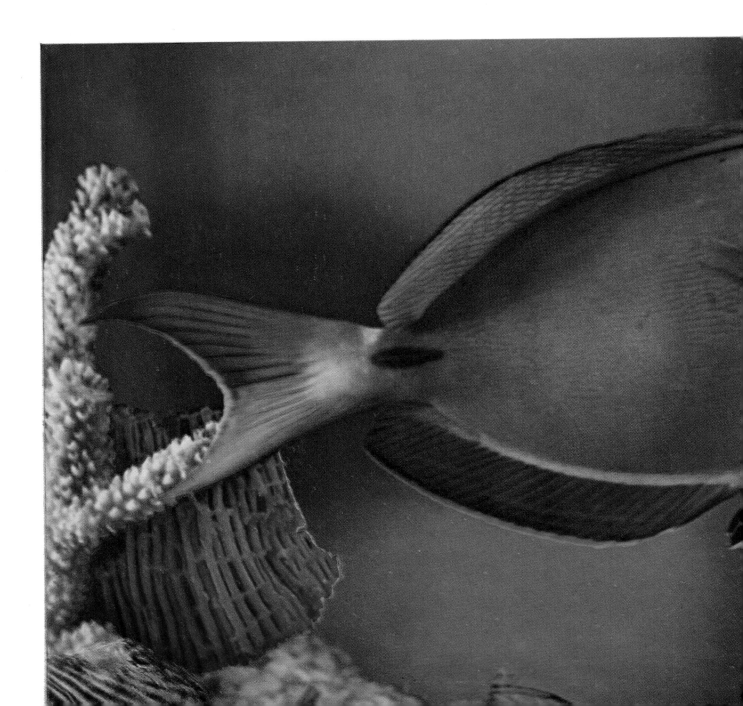

94. Ocean Surgeon (*Acanthurus bahianus*); marine;
Massachusetts to Brazil (photographed at Seaquarium
by Stan Wayman: Rapho Guillumette)

97. Maikoika Surgeon (*Acanthurus leucopareius*); marine; Easter, Marcus, and Hawaiian Islands (Wally Young)

95. Bumphead Surgeon (*Naso tuberosus*); marine; tropical Indo-Australian region (René Catala at Nouméa Aquarium)

96. Yellow Surgeon (*Zebrasoma flavescens*) two color phases; marine; Madagascar to Hawaiian Islands (John Tashjian at Steinhart Aquarium)

98. Ocean Surgeon (*Acanthurus bahianus*) being cleaned by young **Blueheads** (*Thalassoma bifasciatum*); marine; both sides of Atlantic, Massachusetts to Brazil; compare with dark color phase of Plate 94. (Laverne Pederson)

101. Bluebanded Goby (*Lythrypnus dalli*); marine southern California (Gene Wolfsheimer)

99. Blue Tang (*Acanthurus coeruleus*) young; marine; New York to Rio de Janeiro (Edmond L. Fisher)

100. Neon Gobies (*Elecatinus oceanops*); marine; Florida Keys to the southwestern Gulf of Mexico (Edmond L. Fisher)

102. Hairy Blenny (*Labrisomus nuchipinnis*); marine; both sides of the Atlantic, Florida to Rio de Janeiro (William Tavolga)

103. Atlantic Wolf Fish (*Anarhichas lupus*); marine; North Atlantic southward to Cape Cod and France (Hans and Klaus Paysan at Tiergrotten Aquarium, Bremerhaven)

104. Siamese Fighting Fish
(*Betta splendens*) male; fresh
water; Thailand (Gene Wolfsheimer)

105. Great Barracuda (*Sphyraena barracuda*); marine; both sides of the Atlantic,
Massachusetts to Rio de Janeiro (Fritz Goro: *Life* Magazine)

106. Grunt Sculpin (*Rhamphocottus richardsoni*); marine; Alaska to northern California (John Tashjian at Steinhart Aquarium)

107. Flying Gurnard (*Dactylopterus volitans*); marine; both sides of the Atlantic, Massachusetts to Argentina (Douglas P. Wilson)

108. Spotted Irishlord (*Hemilepidotus hemilepidotus*); marine; Alaska to northern California (John Tashjian at Steinhart Aquarium)

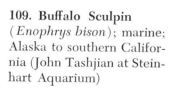

109. Buffalo Sculpin (*Enophrys bison*); marine; Alaska to southern California (John Tashjian at Steinhart Aquarium)

110. California Scorpionfish (*Scorpaena guttata*); compare with red color phase in Plate 112; marine; southern and Baja California (Ron Church)

111. Sailback Scorpionfish (*Tetraroge barbata*); marine, occasionally entering fresh water; Philippines and East Indies (Gene Wolfsheimer)

112. California Scorpionfish (*Scorpaena guttata*); compare with light color phase on opposite page (Plate 110); marine; southern and Baja California (Ron Church)

113. Copper Rockfish (*Sebastodes caurinus*); marine; Alaska to southern California (Ron Church)

114. Kelp Rockfish (*Sebastodes atrovirens*); marine; San Francisco to Baja California (Ron Church)

115. Orange Scorpionfish (*Scorpaena scrofa*); marine; Mediterranean and eastern Atlantic (Douglas P. Wilson)

116. Barbfish (*Scorpaena braziliensis*); marine; New Jersey to Rio de Janeiro (photographed at Seaquarium by Stan Wayman: Rapho Guillumette)

117. Spotfin Turkeyfish (*Pterois antennata*); marine; tropical Indo-Pacific
(Cy La Tour at Marineland of the Pacific)

118. Clearfin Turkeyfish (*Pterois radiata*); marine; Japan to eastern Pacific
(John Tashjian at Steinhart Aquarium)

[continued from page 208]

but the spines are immovable. The bumphead surgeon (Plate 95) and the unicorn fishes are typical of this group. All of these knives are very sharp and capable of inflicting a serious cut on the hand of a careless fisherman.

The herbivorous surgeonfishes comprise a tropical marine group of about one hundred species, most of which are less than 20 inches in length. Some of them are important food fishes. There are a few species, however, such as the Indo-Pacific convict fish, *Acanthurus triostegus,* that have been involved in cases of tropical fish poisoning.

Following the transparent larval or acronurus stage, a few species undergo further radical growth changes, either in anatomy or in color, which sometimes make it difficult to identify the juveniles and adults as members of the same species. For example, the bright yellow color of the juvenile blue tang, *Acanthurus coeruleus* (Plate 99), changes to blue as the fish matures. The bumphead surgeons (Plate 95) usually have smooth foreheads when young, but with growth develop a large bump or, in some species, a blunt spear.

A marked geographical variation in color is shown by the yellow surgeon, *Zebrasoma flavescens* (Plate 96): in the Hawaiian Islands it has the typical yellow color, but throughout the rest of the Indo-Pacific it is dark brown.

The common American Atlantic ocean surgeon, *Acanthurus bahianus* (Plate 94), is one of the species that have been observed to make use of other fishes to remove ectoparasites and other detritus. Mr. M. LaVerne Pederson, who has recorded young bluehead wrasses carrying out this cleaning activity (Plate 98), has written to me of his observations:

> Every five minutes or so one would come over to this little coral head to get cleaned, and would then turn to a dark olive-brown, which seemed to be a signal to the cleaners to start work. The reactions of this doctor fish during the cleaning were rather amusing, and not unlike those of a small boy having slivers removed.

Another interesting observation of Mr. Pederson was that of a fascinating color change that took place when one ocean surgeon became annoyed with another. The angry fish pursued his offender, and in his wrath became white on the front half and very dark on the rear half. This color pattern was retained for almost thirty minutes.

A major portion of the normal surgeon diet is composed of algae, which the fishes obtain by scraping rocks and coral. In most genera all of the teeth are lobate incisors and are firmly anchored in the mouth; however, in the Indo-Pacific genus *Ctenochaetus* there are numerous wirelike teeth, all of which are

Striped Surgeonfish (*Acanthurus bleekeri*); marine; Red Sea to Indonesia (Hans and Klaus Paysan).

movable. The most common species are *Ctenochaetus strigosus* and *C. striatus.* Both of these are difficult to keep alive in captivity since, unlike many other surgeons, they cannot survive on a protein diet.

Rabbitfishes *(Suborder Siganoidea)*

—Family Siganidae

The siganids, popularly known as rabbitfishes because of the rabbit-like appearance of the mouth and rounded nose, can always be identified by the presence of two spines on each ventral or pelvic fin. The two spines are on the margins of the fins and are separated by three soft rays. In addition, the rabbitfishes have an increased number of anal spines— seven of them—preceding the soft rays. These, as well as the thirteen dorsal fin spines, all have along the sides deep grooves containing venom glands. The slightest contact with one of these spine tips produces a very painful puncture wound. Another peculiarity is a very short first dorsal spine that is directed forward rather than upward.

The rabbitfishes are tropical Indo-Pacific species, mostly herbivorous in their feeding habits; they are noted for their ability to make rapid color changes. Most of the species show a marked similarity in appearance, having spots and a mottled or reticulated pattern, but there is one notorious exception: the western Pacific *Lo vulpinus,* which has a moderately long tubular snout and is dark brown on the upper head and chest and bright orange on the rest of the body. Siganids live inshore, usually in salt water but occasionally in brackish water, and there are at least two species that live in fresh water. Most of the approximately thirty species are full grown at a length

Reticulated Rabbitfish (*Siganus vermiculatus*); marine, occasionally entering brackish and fresh water; Indo-Australian region (Georg Mandahl-Barth, Danmarks Akvarium).

of 12 to 16 inches, but a few reach 24 inches. Although they are sometimes eaten, they are not considered very desirable food items; ingestion of certain species may result in food poisoning.

Snake Mackerels and Cutlass Fishes

(Suborder Trichiuroidea)

Unlike the sea basses and their relatives of the previous suborder, the trichiuroid fishes have beaklike, fixed premaxillaries; the tunas also have this feature, but they have a different tail structure. Two families and only forty-two species are recognized, most of them deep-water forms.

CUTLASS FISHES and HAIRTAILS
  —Family Trichiuridae

This is a family of about twenty-two species of oceanic fishes with narrow, laterally compressed bodies and barracuda-like heads armed with fantastic dentition. The body tapers gradually either to a very small V-shaped tail or to a point. The dorsal fin begins just behind the head and extends almost the full length of the body; there is a small anal fin. One of the most widely distributed forms is the 5-foot *Trichiurus lepturus,* which occurs in the Atlantic, Indian, and western Pacific oceans. In the Japanese area it is known to migrate into relatively shallow water in August and September to spawn. In many areas it is a moderately valuable food fish.

DEEP-SEA SNAKE MACKERELS or ESCOLARS
  —Family Gempylidae

The fast-moving, carnivorous gempylids are found in the tropical and temperate marine waters of the world, usually in the depths, although there are some species that commonly occur near the surface. In New Zealand a widely distributed 3½-foot snake mackerel, *Thrysites atun,* known locally as barracouta, is often captured at the surface during summer and fall and at times is taken in very shallow water. Snake mackerels of various species are attracted to lights suspended at night over the side of a ship drifting far from shore.

The gempylids, interchangeably called snake mackerels or escolars, have jutting lower jaws with wicked-looking vomerine teeth. They have two dorsal fins, and some have finlets following the dorsal and anal fins. Double lateral lines on each side of the body are found in two genera. Although they resemble the more slender of the tuna-like fishes, they lack the lateral tail ridge of those forms. About twenty-two species in some ten genera are recognized. Most of these have oily flesh; thus they are not too desirable as food fishes even though some are eaten. One of the most widely distributed species is the 6-foot oilfish, *Ruvettus pretiosus,* which is found around the world, usually at depths of about 2400 feet.

Mackerels, Tunas, Marlins, and Their Relatives (*Suborder Scombroidea*)

Speed in swimming is one of the major characteristics of this group of four families of streamlined fishes. Part of this ability is attributable to the anatomy of the tail, in which the rays of the widely forked tail fin extend over the last vertebra; this arrangement undoubtedly gives the relatively inflexible tail more driving force than would be possible if this structure were hinged as it is in many other fishes.

TUNA and MACKEREL—Family Scombridae

One night some years ago while aboard a fisheries research ship anchored off the island of Celebes in northern Indonesia, I dipped up some of the very small fishes swimming about under the night light. Placing some of these under the microscope, I was amazed to find that they were larval tuna, the first to be found in that part of the world. Although life history data on the Atlantic and Mediterranean bluefin tuna, *Thunnus thynnus,* had been known for many years, similar information on the Pacific forms did not generally become available until after 1940. Since that time several research groups in the Pacific have cooperated in an effort to uncover the life pattern of these valuable food fishes.

A typical mackerel or tuna has a very sleek, cigar-shaped, streamlined body followed by a narrow caudal peduncle and a large, strong tail sharply divided into individual lobes. The second dorsal and the anal fin are followed by a series of small finlets. In some species scalation is limited to a small area under the pectoral fins, called a "corselet." Small keels are conspicuously present on the end of the caudal peduncle just in front of the tail fin. These are usually three in number, the center one being considerably larger than the other two. The mackerels lack the center keel, having only the two small lateral ones.

Scombroid fishes range around the world in tropical, temperate, and even cold seas. Whether they are present at the surface or in the depths is sometimes determined by the water temperature as well as by the composition of the pelagic community.

Although some species of tuna are distinctive and can easily be recognized at a glance, there are others in which identification may depend on counts of the number of gill rakers, fin rays, and finlets as well as internal examination to determine the striations and shape of the liver and the presence or absence of the air bladder. In a newly caught fish the color, which is often lost within an hour, can be a distinct means of identification. The color ranges from the nondescript leaden gray of types such as the frigate mackerel to attractive patterns such as those of the bonitas and skipjacks.

The great bluefin, *Thunnus thynnus,* is the picturesque "titan of tunas," reaching a length of 14 feet and a weight of 1800 pounds. The tremendous battle put up by the hooked bluefin makes it a great favorite of sports anglers and has been the subject of many books and articles by sports writers. Certain details of the movements of the Atlantic bluefin are well known, but there is still much that remains a mystery. They sweep northward up the American Atlantic coast in offshore waters and are present around Long Island and adjacent areas from June through September. Many of these are medium-sized fish (sixty to three hundred pounds) that are believed to winter offshore, north of the Gulf Stream. It is also known that the bluefin found off Norway in the summer form at least part of the same population that is caught off southern Spain in the spring and early summer. It has long been thought that there may be a continuous Atlantic population of bluefin correlated with the circular current system across the ocean. Recent records compiled by Frank J. Mather III of Woods Hole Oceanographic Institution show that two bluefin which were tagged in Martha's Vineyard, Massachusetts, in July of 1954 were recaptured five years later in the Bay of Biscay during July and August of 1959. In spite of the migration shown by these two bluefin, there is evidence indicating that the bluefin populations on opposite sides of the Atlantic have anatomical differences; they also have different spawning seasons.

Several species of bluefin have been described from other parts of the world, including Australia, Japan, and California; some of these are probably separate populations of a single world-wide species, but others may be distinct. Another bluefin tuna, the albacore, *Thunnus alalunga,* is one of the most easily recognized scombrids; its chief identifying feature is its very long pectoral or shoulder fin, which reaches backward beyond the second dorsal and anal fins.

Bluefin Tuna (*Thunnus thynnus*) migrating northward through the Florida-Bahamas channel; marine; tropical and temperate waters of the Atlantic and Pacific (Fritz Goro: *Life* Magazine).

The white meat of the albacore makes it a premium tuna for market and canning purposes; consequently it is fished extensively in the offshore waters of the Pacific and to a lesser extent in the Atlantic. Although eighty-pound albacore have been recorded, most of those caught weigh less than forty pounds. Females are mature when they are six years old; at this time they weigh about thirty-three pounds. Tagging returns on Pacific albacore indicate that these fast swimmers may move across the entire Pacific. For example, an albacore tagged off the American Pacific coast in 1957 was caught off Japan ten months later. On the basis of tagging evidence of this kind as well as other data, the North Pacific population is considered a continuous and homogeneous one, with the mature fishes moving from temperate waters southward for spawning. The South Pacific population is thought to follow the same pattern in reverse. The Atlantic population of albacore has not been studied in such detail.

The yellowfin tuna include several species, some of which are widely distributed around the world, usually in warmer waters than those frequented by the bluefins. The most common species of yellowfin in the Indo-Pacific is *Thunnus albacares,* which at maximum size may be 8 feet in length and weigh 450 pounds. It has been known to gain as much as 60 pounds in a single year. Studies have shown that there are several distinct yellowfin populations in the Pacific and that these populations do not tend to mix. Because of the tremendous abundance of these fishes, they are used to a considerable extent for

canning purposes—especially those weighing less than 90 pounds.

The yellowfin in the Atlantic are not nearly so abundant as those in the Pacific, although they are considered the same species.

Mention should be made of the Allison tuna, which has long been recognized by the sports anglers as a distinct species of yellowfin but is actually only a long-finned growth phase of the common yellowfin.

The widely distributed bigeye tuna, *Thunnus obesus,* looks a great deal like the common yellowfin but apparently spends most of its time in deeper water. The eye is slightly larger than that of the yellowfin, the pectoral fin is longer, and there are striations on the edges of the liver—all features that are not easily recognized and have caused much confusion in the identification of the bigeye.

Kishinouella tonggol is a small yellowfin species, with a maximum weight of only thirty pounds, common in some of the southern areas of the Indo-Pacific region. It can be distinguished from the other yellowfins by its low number of gill rakers and lack of the air bladder.

There are several species of small spotted tuna; these have dark meat and are not considered so desirable as the white-meat types. The spots, varying in number from one to nine or ten, are located under the pectoral fin. The black skipjack, *Euthynnus yaito,* is the common Indo-Pacific species; the little tunny, *Euthynnus alleteratus,* is a similar Atlantic species.

Economically, the most important striped tuna is the skipjack, *Katsuwonus pelamis,* a fish that occurs in all tropical seas; it has a maximum weight of about fifty pounds at a length of 40 inches. Hawaiian investigations have shown that the growth rate is rapid: during the first year the skipjack grows to about 18 inches; during the second year approximately 10 inches are added; and during the third year it grows about 4 more inches, bringing the final length to around 32 inches. Most skipjack apparently do not live longer than four years. This fast-moving tuna supports important local fisheries in many parts of the world. The stripes on the skipjack are on the abdomen. One Australian tuna, *Gymnosarda elegans,* has stripes along the center of the sides.

The bonitas have stripes on the upper part of the body. The Atlantic bonita, *Sarda sarda,* is found on both sides of the Atlantic and has a wide latitudinal range; for example, in the western Atlantic it ranges from Nova Scotia to Argentina. *Sarda chilensis* occurs along the American Pacific coasts from California to Chile, and it is replaced in the central and western Pacific by a similar species, *Sarda orientalis.* Bonita are predominantly white-meat species and consequently are often used for canning.

Heading the list of economically important mackerel is the Atlantic *Scomber scombrus,* which looks like a small tuna. It reaches a maximum length of only 22 inches and a weight of four pounds. The movements of the Atlantic mackerel are well known: it appears each year in American waters off Chesapeake Bay around April and by June and July has moved into the Gulf of Maine; later, usually in September, the reverse migration begins. This fish is sometimes confused with the smaller chub mackerel, *S. colias,* which also occurs in the same areas on both sides of the Atlantic. The latter has nine or ten dorsal spines, as compared with the eleven or twelve of the former, and also has much finer reticulations on the back than the Atlantic mackerel. The Pacific mackerel, *S. diego,* which ranges from Alaska to the Gulf of California, is also an important commercial species, as is the Japanese *S. japonicus.* The pygmy mackerels, genus *Rastrelliger,* are small, deep-bodied fishes usually less than 15 inches in length. Two species are fairly common in the Indo-Australian region: *R. canagurta* and *R. brachysoma,* both of great economic importance.

The Spanish mackerels, genus *Scomberomorus,* are very much elongated tuna-like fishes with a world-wide distribution. The American Atlantic *S. cavalla,* sometimes called kingfish or king mackerel, which attains a weight of one hundred pounds and a length of slightly more than 5 feet, is probably the largest species; however, the widely ranging Indo-Pacific Spanish mackerel, *S. commerson,* grows almost as large. These fishes are excellent food, and important fisheries exist for them in many areas.

Skipjack Tuna (*Katsuwonus pelamis*); marine, pelagic; world-wide in tropical waters (Honolulu Biological Laboratory, U.S. Fish and Wildlife Service).

Live-bait fishing for Australian Yellowfin Tuna (*Thunnus albacares*); marine; world-wide in tropical and subtropical waters (Ern McQuillan: Green's Products Ltd., New South Wales).

For example, in Florida in 1957, the commercial catches of *S. maculatus* were third highest in the state.

Related to the Spanish mackerel is the wahoo, *Acanthocybium solandri,* another fast-moving, very elongated tuna type. It is found around the world in tropical marine waters and at its maximum weight will tip the scale at more than 120 pounds. I have examined many of these fishes, and the end of the stomach of each has invariably contained a single large, pink, leechlike fluke, *Hirundinella ventricosa.* Some species of tuna also have these stomach flukes. As yet no one has solved the mystery of how these parasites get into the stomach.

The frigate mackerels are the least glamorous of all the tuna-like fishes. The meat is dark, and in many regions they are considered "third-class fish."

However, on account of their abundance they do form an important protein resource. *Auxis thazard,* found in tropical marine waters around the world, is the most common species.

The high metabolic rate and nervous disposition of tuna make them difficult to capture alive and transport successfully to an aquarium or open tanks. In 1951 Dr. Albert Tester of the University of Hawaii first worked out, as a part of behavior studies, a technique for the capture and maintenance of yellowfin and little tunny. Skipjack, however, are more flighty and difficult; only recently (1960) the U.S. Honolulu Biological Laboratory staff were able to keep them alive in small outdoor tanks by the simple expedient of not touching the fishes with nets or other standard gear.

From antiquity tuna have been caught by trailing

a flashing lure in the water, the lure of course concealing a barbed hook. These methods are still used today, but modern innovations with outriggers extending from the boat enable the fisherman to troll a series of lines at the same time, thus increasing the catch. Spearing tuna from an open boat is an equally ancient method of capture, and even today it is still practiced to a limited extent in some areas.

The live-bait method of fishing is widely used in catching surface schools of tuna. The fishing vessel moves quietly into the area of the feeding schools; then the tuna are enticed toward the fishing racks of the boat by throwing live bait overboard. If live bait in the form of small sardines, anchovies, or other fishes is readily available, this method is practical as well as effective, for several tons of fish may be caught in less than an hour. In recent years tuna purse seiners carrying tremendous nets have also proved very efficient in offshore fishing along the western coasts of America from Mexico to Peru. Surrounding a single school can result in a catch of as much as one hundred tons!

Tuna are sometimes found in shallow water, especially in places where deep water is immediately adjacent. In some such areas trap fishing for surface schools of tuna has been carried on for generations. This is especially true in the Mediterranean and in the Philippines. In the latter area the large tuna trap or baclad, which is fairly expensive, is usually a community venture; because of the monsoons it must be rebuilt each year. The Moros in the southern Philippines have a special way of handling their traps.

When the net or gate is pulled across the heart of the trap to constrict the area in order to remove the fish, divers are always sent down to the bottom to make sure that the base of the gate works properly. During an operation of this kind I put on my face mask and flippers and swam down to see what was happening; at forty feet I had to struggle back to the surface for another breath of air, but I could still see the men below me, *without diving apparatus,* pulling on the net. Later I sounded the trap and found that the depth at which they were working was eighty feet!

The Japanese were among the first to apply oceanographic methods for determining the most productive fishing area and depth for tuna operations. In their offshore fishing in the western and central Pacific they found that a band of water or temperature isotherm would produce tuna during certain seasons of the year. This band of water might be near the surface or it might be as deep as five hundred feet. To reach the deep-swimming tuna that did not appear at the surface the Japanese developed the long-line technique, using as much

as sixty-five miles of surface line from which baited vertical droplines reached into the proper strata of water. After World War II the United States government established the Pacific Oceanic Fisheries Investigations, later known as the Honolulu Biological Laboratory, to study the waters of the central Pacific. Among their finds were important data on the concentration of subsurface yellowfin tuna, which was greatest near the equator and diminished as one proceded north or south; this abundance of tuna was correlated with an increased abundance of food which resulted from the enrichment of the upper water layers by the interaction of the north and south equatorial currents. One startling discovery was that they could accurately predict the volume of catches of skipjack tuna in the Hawaiian Islands through analysis of the temperature and salinity of the water masses.

At this point a comment on the future food supply for the world's expanding human population may be warranted. Our greatest untapped protein resource is to be found in the upper depths of the ocean, specifically in the schools of tuna and similar fast-moving fishes that are at present caught only accidentally on deep-fishing long-line gear. Development of future fishing techniques, perhaps deep-fishing submarines, will enable the world to make use of this vast protein reservoir.

SAILFISHES, SPEARFISHES, and MARLINS —Family Istiophoridae

This family includes some of the world's most popular marine sports fishes, most of which are also valuable as food. The istiophorids, together with the swordfish—which is set aside in a separate family —are often referred to as billfishes. There are about ten species included in the Istiophoridae; all of them have bills that are rounded in cross section and two ridges on each side of the caudal peduncle, just in front of the tail. By contrast, the swordfish has a flattened bill and a single ridge on the caudal peduncle.

Only in recent years have the life histories and behavior of the billfishes been studied in any detail, and much still remains to be learned. Several species are known to be migratory; in some cases these movements are thought to be feeding migrations. They are fish eaters and often use the bill as a club to maim their victims as they rush through a school of frigate mackerel or other preferred fishes.

Among the istiophorids, the sailfish is undoubtedly the most easily recognized because of the extremely long rays of the dorsal fin as well as the dark spots covering the fin. The ventral or pelvic fins are very slender and longer than the pectorals, and fit into grooves under the body. The Pacific sailfish, *Istiophorus orientalis,* is the largest species, reaching a weight of 221 pounds at a length of almost 11 feet; the Atlantic *I. albicans* is somewhat smaller, with a maximum of 123 pounds at about the same length. The Pacific shortbill spearfish, *Tetrapterus angustirostris,* looks like a sailfish whose dorsal fins have been shortened with a pair of scissors; the longest rays are no longer than the depth of the body. It reaches a length of 6 feet with a weight of 60 pounds and is found throughout the western and central Pacific. The longbill spearfish, *T. belone,* is a similar Atlantic species. The sailfishes, spearfishes, and marlins have ventral fins—a feature that distinguishes them from the broadbill, which lacks these fins.

Because of their great size, which prevents preservation of specimens for study, as well as changes

Pacific Sailfish (*Istiophorus orientalis*); marine; tropical Indo-Pacific (Frank Kuchirchuk).

that occur with growth, the history of marlin identification has been one of such confusion that it is often difficult to know which data and records apply to which fish. The most easily identified of the marlins is probably the Indo-Pacific black marlin, *Istiompax marlina,* which has its pectoral fins permanently extended and incapable of being folded against the body. This is probably the largest species in the family; one specimen caught off Cabo Blanco, Peru, weighed 1560 pounds and measured 14½ feet in length. The Pacific striped marlin, *Makaira audax,* is well marked with ten or more vertical stripes along the sides; the body is laterally compressed in the area of the anal fin, a fact that is helpful in differentiating this species from the Pacific blue marlin, *M. ampla,* which may also show vertical bands on the body. The striped marlin is one of the smaller species, its maximum weight being around 600 pounds, whereas the blue marlin has a maximum weight of about 1400 pounds. The blue marlin of the Atlantic is similar in many respects to the Pacific form; it is found as far north as Long Island. The Atlantic white marlin, *M. albida,* is another well-known sports species; it reaches a maximum weight of 106 pounds at a length of almost 9 feet.

SWORDFISH—Family Xiphiidae

All of the billfishes have respectable nose extensions, but the swordfish, *Xiphias gladias,* carries this development to the extreme, the sword sometimes equaling one-third of the total length of the fish. It is flattened, rather than rounded like the nose extensions of the other billfishes—a feature that is responsible for its being called "broadbill." The sword may be used to impale fishes during feeding, and is even capable of driving through the planking of small boats. Swordfishes are valuable food items in great demand wherever a commercial fishery for them exists. They are found in all tropical and temperate marine waters of the world. The average weight of those caught in the Hawaiian Islands is around 250 pounds; the world's record is held by a specimen that weighs 1182 pounds and measures about 15 feet.

LOUVAR—Family Luvaridae

The louvar is a spectacular, 6-foot, deep-sea fish apparently found in all tropical seas. Only one species, *Luvarus imperialis,* is known; its blunt-headed body profile resembles that of the pilot whale or blackfish, *Globicephala.* It has one anatomical peculiarity: the vent is located directly below the base of the pectoral fins and is covered by the small ventral fins—all a considerable distance ahead of the anal fin, where the vent is normally located. The body is a silvery pink color and the fins are a bright scarlet.

Gobies and Their Relatives (*Suborder Gobioidea*)

Most of the small, colorful gobioid fishes are inhabitants of coral reefs, tropical and temperate shores, and coastal streams; but some species occur in deeper water, living on the continental shelf at a depth of six hundred feet or more, and others are pelagic, living in the open sea. This suborder contains at least six hundred species, ranging from the tiniest known fishes to a few species more than 2 feet in length. The gobioid fishes are usually divided into four families, two of which have under the body a sucking disk formed by the paired pelvic fins.

SLEEPERS—Family Eleotridae

The largest of the gobioid fishes are the eleotrids, which lack the sucking disk. All species have the ventral fins separated either completely to the base or almost to it. They are called sleepers because of the habit most of them have of lying on the bottom, rarely moving except when disturbed. A few of the species, however, do not stay on the bottom but are free-swimming.

Most of the free-swimming species are "hoverers," remaining suspended in midwater and diving into hiding places when danger threatens. Members of the genus *Parioglossus* hover by the thousands in cloudlike swarms over coral heads around tropical islands of the Indo-Pacific. When alarmed, they disappear among the coral branches. The delicately pastel-shaded fishes of the genus *Vireosa* hover over their special hiding places, which are often rock oysters and giant killer clams, and dive inside them when frightened. This action usually startles the oyster or clam and causes it to clamp shut, imprisoning the vireosa until the shells open again. The vireosa emerges without the slightest sign of having been frightened or harmed while inside the bivalve.

Some of the free-swimming gobies, such as the members of the genus *Hypseleotris* of the Indo-Pacific, are pelagic in habitat and swim in schools in the open water.

The largest of the eleotrids is the "guavina" of Central America, *Gobiomorus dormitor,* which may reach a length of more than 2 feet. The next largest are members of the Indo-Australian genus *Bunaka,* which reach almost the same length and are highly prized as food.

Striped Marlin (*Makaira audax*) in Bay of Islands, New Zealand; marine; Indo-Pacific region (Michael Lerner Expedition of the American Museum of Natural History).

GOBIES—Family Gobiidae

All gobies have under the forward part of the body a sucker that is formed by the partial or complete uniting of the two lateral edges of the pelvic fins. They also have two dorsal fins, which distinguishes them from the eel-like Taenioididae. The gobies, with more than four hundred species, form the largest family of fishes that are primarily marine. Most of them are small and colorful and average between 2 and 4 inches in length. The smallest species, *Pandaka pygmaea,* is an inhabitant of freshwater streams and lakes of the Philippine region. It is full grown at less than ½ inch, and on the basis of length (but not weight) is considered the smallest vertebrate animal. Almost equally small are some of the species of *Eviota,* colorful marine gobies that are abundant around coral heads in the Indo-Pacific.

Most gobioid fishes lay elongated eggs attached by stalks to stones, leaves, roots, coral, or the sides of their sand or mud burrows. Many gobies take care of their eggs until they hatch, both parents usually sharing in this duty. The tiny gobies of the tropical genus *Paragobiodon* and their relatives often lay their large eggs in crotches of coral branches; a single small coral head one or two feet in diameter

may have a dozen or more pairs of gobies among its branches, protecting their egg clusters.

The important goby fry or ipon fisheries of the northern Philippines are based on the fact that all fresh-water gobies must return to the sea in order to spawn. After the goby eggs hatch, the transparent fry, measuring a little more than ½ inch in length, move in enormous schools toward the mouths of the same rivers from which their parents came. From September to March, fishermen catch the larval gobies or ipon with a variety of nets and traps across the streams and rivers. The ipon are either fried immediately in oil or made into a fermented fish paste known as bagoong.

Many gobies live in burrows in the mud or sand. The 2-inch arrow goby, *Clevelandia ios,* lives on the coast of California in mud-flat holes shared with a pea crab and a large true burrowing worm, *Urechis.* The arrow goby is a transient "guest" and forages for food over the mud flats. A more elaborate arrangement is found in the Indo-Pacific genus *Smilogobius* and its relatives, which have a symbiotic relationship with snapping shrimps. The shrimps maintain the burrow, constantly digging and hauling sand night and day to keep the hole from collapsing, and the gobies, usually a pair, stand guard, like sentinels, at the entrance. At the slightest sign of danger, the gobies dive into the hole, thereby warning the shrimps. Usually the shrimps will not emerge until the gobies are again posted at the entrance. That the relationship is not completely idyllic is shown by the fact that baby snapping shrimps have been found in the stomachs of the gobies.

Even more dependent upon its host is the 2½-inch blind goby of southern California. This bright pink fish, *Typhlogobius californiensis,* lives its entire life in the gravel in holes that have been dug by the ghost shrimp, *Callianassa.* If the shrimp dies, the blind goby cannot survive unless it finds another host. Other blind gobies are found in Australia and Madagascar.

The spectacular 2-inch neon goby, *Elecatinus oceanops* (Plate 100), is noted not only for its beauty but also for its cleaning of external parasites from other larger fishes. Neons usually spawn twice a year—in the spring and in the fall. The parents select a clean surface, such as the inside of a shell, on which to deposit about one hundred eggs. During the incubation period of usually less than two weeks, the eggs are carefully guarded by the parents. After hatching, the young remain with the parents for several weeks. One year is required for them to reach adult size.

Some of the most interesting gobies are the tropi-

Broadbill Swordfish (*Xiphias gladias*) being pulled aboard fishing launch; marine; world-wide in tropical and temperate waters (Eugenie Marron).

cal mudskippers of the genera *Periophthalmus* and *Boleophthalmus,* which are found from Africa to Oceania, particularly on mud flats and in mangrove swamps. Instead of moving out with the tide as most fishes do, the mudskippers remain on the flats. They skitter away whenever approached; the larger species can jump faster than a man can move, so that it is usually very difficult to collect them alive. Characteristically, the mudskippers have large pectoral fins and protruding eyes that give them a "pop-eyed" appearance. They can stay out of water for long periods if the gills and a part of the body are kept moist. In a small aquarium they may do such odd things as move all of the sand with their mouths from one side of the tank to the other.

The picturesque Catalina or blue-banded goby, *Lythrypnus dalli* (Plate 101), is one of the most beautiful fishes in the entire family. The species was originally described in 1890 from a 1¼-inch specimen dredged at 210 feet in the harbor at Catalina Island and a few other specimens taken nearby. No additional specimens were found for many years. In 1938 Vernon Brock, California's first diving ichthyologist, began investigation of the Catalina fauna and made the amazing discovery that the rare Catalina goby was actually a fairly common fish in cracks

riped Marlin (*Makaira audax*) with remora attached to the abdomen; marine; Indo-Pacific gion (Bingham Oceanographic Laboratory at Yale University).

Mudskipper (*Periophthalmus* sp.); marine; tropical Indo-Pacific (Gene Wolfsheimer).

and crevices of rocky areas at depths from twenty feet downward. Another "rare" fish, the red and blue banded 1¾ inch zebra goby, *Lythrypnus zebra* was also found to be common. Skin divers capture these beautiful fishes for the aquarist by using an ingenious suction device, the "slurp gun," which vacuums the fishes from their hiding places.

EEL GOBIES—Family Taenioididae

Across the tropical Indo-Pacific are about fifteen species of very strange, elongated eel gobies, some living in fresh water and others in salt water. Thirteen inches is the maximum length for these fishes, but most of them are full-grown at half that size. Like the true gobies, they usually have a sucking disk under the body. In life they are pink or blue in color. The extremely long dorsal fin has four to six spiny rays followed by twenty-eight to fifty-nine soft rays, but the spiny-rayed and soft-rayed portions are continuous rather than separate as in the true gobies. The eyes are small or vestigial. The 4-inch *Trypauchen taenia* and five related species all have above the gill cavity a blind pit that opens to the exterior and has no connection with the gill cavity. The function of this pit is unknown. Much remains to be learned about these peculiar fishes.

LOACH GOBY—Family Rhyacichthyidae

One of the strangest of the gobioid fishes is *Rhyacichthys aspro,* the only member of this family. It has two dorsal fins, a flattened head and forebody, widely separated pelvic fins, and a small mouth set under the head. This 9-inch goby is found in torrential streams and large rivers of the East Indies and the Philippines. Its appearance and habits are almost identical to those of the homalopterid loaches of Asia. With its spiny first dorsal fin clipped off, it would be difficult to distinguish the loach goby from the homalopterid loaches.

Dragonets (*Suborder Callionymoidea*)

—Family Callionymidae

A sharp preopercular spine, usually in the form of hooks, and a very small gill opening on the upper part of the head are two of the identifying marks of the dragonets, a group of small, often highly colored fishes with slender, anteriorly flattened bodies. These fishes live on the bottom in tropical and temperate marine waters around the world. The usual size range of the adults is 4 to 8 inches. Internally, the callionymids are distinguished from other perchlike fishes by the absence of certain bones in the skull as well as other features. The ventral fins are located ahead of the pectorals, and the inner rays of the ventrals are longer than the outer rays. The male is usually more brightly colored than the female and generally has a much longer first dorsal and tail fins.

The European dragonet, *Callionymus lyra,* spawns between February and August. The blue-and-yellow male swims enticingly around the female with his fins and gill covers expanded. When the female shows interest, they both swim together slowly up from the bottom with their bodies close together. During this vertical nuptial "flight" the eggs are extruded and fertilized. The eggs float and have a honeycomb appearance; hatching requires about two weeks. The larvae become part of the plankton and remain there until winter, when they drop to the bottom.

The more primitive dragonets are usually recognized under a separate family, the Draconettidae; they have broad gill openings and a spine on the operculum and one on the suboperculum, and are generally found in fairly deep water.

Blennies and Their Relatives (*Suborder Blennioidea*)

Most of the blenny-like fishes are small, rather elongated marine species with the ventral or pelvic fins reduced or entirely absent; if these fins are present, they are located ahead of the pectorals, in jugular position. The very long dorsal fin begins behind the head and extends almost to the tail, in some cases being continuous with it. The majority of the blennies are carnivorous or omnivorous bottom-dwelling fishes, usually found in shallow water although there are a few that do go into deep water. A vast range of variability in anatomy as well as behavior exists among the fifteen or more families in this very successful group of fishes.

Dragonets (*Callionymus lyra*) mating; male on right; marine; European coasts
(Douglas P. Wilson).

Fringehead Blenny (*Blennius tentacularis*); marine; Mediterranean (Hans and Klaus Paysan).

Lumphead Blenny (*Istiblennius lineatus*); marine, tidepools; tropical Indo-Pacific (Gunter Senfft).

SCALELESS BLENNIES—*Family Blenniidae*

The scaleless tropical blennies are divided into two groups according to the way the teeth are anchored. If they are fixed jaw teeth and immovable, the fish belongs in the subfamily Blenniinae; but if they are attached to the gums and can be moved, the fish is a member of the Salariinae. Many of the scaleless blennies, especially those of the subfamily Salariinae, go through a pelagic post-larval stage known as an ophioblennius. This form is so different from the adult that at one time it was recognized as a separate subfamily. Crests, ridges, and fringes on the head are often helpful identification marks of many of the blennies in this family. Members of *Istiblennius, Blennius,* and *Hypsoblennius* are well endowed in this respect. There are a great number of species of scaleless blennies, and they are distributed throughout the world.

Some of the most interesting members of this family are found in the genus *Runnula*. They are brightly colored, striped species with very large fangs in the lower jaw. In the Hawaiian Islands the 3-inch *Runnula goslinei* is noted for mistaking the hirsute legs of swimmers for food and nipping them mercilessly.

SCALED BLENNIES or KLIPFISHES —*Family Clinidae*

The clinids form a large family, mostly of small fishes found in subtropical and temperate seas, predominantly in the southern hemisphere. A number of species are exotically marked and colored and have fascinating life histories. Most of them bear their young alive, and the males have a large intromittent organ.

The 8-inch hairy blenny, *Labrisomus nuchipinnis* (Plate 102), found on both sides of the tropical Atlantic, is a typical representative of the important genus *Labrisomus,* which occurs in both the Atlantic and Pacific. It has the blunt-headed profile characteristic of many of the clinids. On the other hand, the beautiful brown-and-white-mottled 2-foot kelpfish, *Heterostichus rostratus,* the largest member of the family, is a representative of the point-headed group of scaled blennies; it is found from British Columbia to Lower California and is noted for its ability to match the color of its background.

The males of the Florida tube-dwelling pike blenny, *Chaenopsis ocellata,* are known for their aggressiveness in maintaining their territories. If one male invades the territory of another, he is instantly met with the usual combat position—opened mouth and erected dorsal fin. The males may come together and remain in mouth-to-mouth position until one bites the other, usually ending the combat.

The record for the largest mouth in proportion to the size of the fish undoubtedly goes to the sarcastic fringehead, *Neoclinus blanchardi,* a 9-inch Pacific American species with a tremendously elongated jaw that allows the mouth to open like a vast scoop shovel.

The genus *Tripterygion* contains a number of very small tropical fishes with the dorsal fin divided into three separate portions, the first two made up of spiny rays and the last of soft rays. Because of this and other features, these fishes are sometimes placed in a separate family, the Tripterygiidae. The males and females often exhibit different color patterns. The females of *Tripterygion nanus,* found in the Marshall Islands, are mature at less than ¾ inch in length.

PRICKLEBACKS—*Family Stichaeidae*

The fifty-four kinds of pricklebacks usually have moderately elongated bodies covered with overlapping scales. The rays of the dorsal fin are entirely spiny in most species, but in a few there may be some soft rays at the end of the fin. Several species lack the pelvic or ventral fins. The pricklebacks are northern hemisphere, usually cold-water, marine fishes living in shallow water; there is one species, however, the Alaskan longsnout blenny, *Lumpenella longirostris,* that occurs as deep as 1600 feet.

The 16-inch decorated blenny, *Chirolophis polyactocephalus,* ranging from Puget Sound to Alaska, is one of the most spectacular of the stichaeids: it has numerous Christmas-tree-like cirri on the top of the head. Its food habits have not been studied, but two

other members of the same genus in Japan are known to feed on sea anemones. The 20-inch rock blenny, *Xiphister mucosus,* is a common intertidal fish from southern California to Alaska; it can be identified by the presence of two broad bands extending backward in the form of a V from each eye. Anatomically, this species is of interest because of the many mucous canals present over the head and also because of the four lateral lines, two on each side, with many short lateral branches. One of the largest fishes in the family is the California monkey-face blenny, *Cebidichthys violaceus,* which reaches a length of 30 inches.

GUNNELS—*Family Pholidae*

"Eel-like blennies" would be an apt description of the very elongated gunnels, which are shallow-water marine species of the north Pacific and north Atlantic. The dorsal fin is composed entirely of spines, and there is an incomplete lateral line. Gunnels tend to hide under rocks and in crevices so that they are not easily observed. At low tide they are often left exposed, but are able to survive surrounded by moist seaweed. Some of the dozen or so species have bright colors with a pattern of lines across the head and through the eye.

The rock gunnel, *Pholis gunnellus,* sometimes called butterfish, is a common 6- to 12-inch inshore species found on both sides of the North Atlantic. It has about ten spots along the base of the long dorsal fin. During the spawning season, which lasts from December to March, the female deposits a batch of eggs, which she then rolls into a ball ½ inch or more in diameter by curving her body around the egg mass. Both male and female take turns at guarding the eggs for a period of about a month; after hatching, the larvae become free-swimming members of

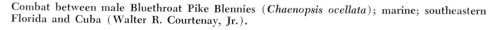
Combat between male Bluethroat Pike Blennies (*Chaenopsis ocellata*); marine; southeastern Florida and Cuba (Walter R. Courtenay, Jr.).

the plankton. When they have grown to slightly more than 1 inch, they sink to the bottom.

WOLF FISHES and WOLF EELS
—Family Anarhichadidae

The giants of the blenny world are found in the wolf-fish family, some of them ranging up to 9 feet in length. The nine species are cold-water marine fishes of the northern hemisphere. They lack pelvic fins, and in addition to the obvious canine teeth in the front of the jaws they have massive grinding teeth in the back of the mouth. There are two types included in the family: (1) the wolf fishes, which have a shorter body with about 85 vertebrae and a small tail fin, and (2) the Pacific American wolf eel, which has a longer body with about 350 vertebrae and a pointed tail.

The 5-foot Atlantic wolf fish, *Anarhichas lupus* (Plate 103), and the 6-foot spotted wolf fish, *A. minor,* are both fished commercially along the European coasts, where they are known as catfishes. Another species in that area, the jelly cat, *A. latifrons,* is also found in the catches, but is not considered a desirable food item and is used only as bait. The first species has a limited commercial importance in the United States along the Maine coast. The Atlantic species seem to do well and feed readily in captivity, but the wolf eel of the Pacific, *Anarrhichthys ocellatus,* has been known to fast as long as nine months before starting to feed. Some of the wolf

Wolfeel (*Anarrhichthys ocellatus*); marine; southern California to Alaska (Arthur Frisch: *San Francisco Chronicle*).

fishes lay spherical egg masses, which are guarded by one of the parents.

EELPOUTS—Family Zoarcidae

The marine zoarcid eelpouts resemble the wolf fishes in many respects. The dorsal and anal fins extend around the tail, which comes to a point; the ventral fins are minute and are located just back of the gills but ahead of the pectorals. The upper jaw projects over the lower jaw, and the lips are quite thick. About sixty species are known, most of them less than 18 inches in length. They range from very shallow cold sea water to depths of more than a mile. Many give birth to living young, for example the European viviparous eelpout, *Zoarces viviparus;* an 8-inch female of this species may give birth to as many as forty young. By contrast, the 3-foot American Atlantic ocean pout, *Macrozoarces americanus,* lays eggs; these are ¼ inch in diameter and are guarded by one or both parents. The zoarcids are common fishes in the waters of both the Arctic and the Antarctic.

Brotulids, Cusk Eels, and Cucumber Fishes

(Suborder Ophidioidea)

The fishes of this small group of three families are usually elongated forms with the pelvic fins reduced in size, sometimes to filaments placed under the throat or chin, or entirely lacking. None of the fins has spines. The dorsal and anal fin rays are more numerous than the vertebrae; this is one of the principal differences between this group and the preceding suborder of blennioid fishes.

BROTULIDS—Family Brotulidae

The brotulids form a medium-sized family of some 155 species; however, the species are so widely differentiated that there are approximately 65 genera recognized within the family. Not only do the brotulids run the full gamut of anatomical variation, but they also cover a great variety of habitats ranging from the greatest depths of the ocean, where some species are blind, to fresh-water caves, also with blind species. For example, the only fish ever taken at a depth of more than four miles belonged to the brotulid genus *Bassogigas;* it was a small (6¼ inches) specimen dredged in the Sunda trench by the Galathea Expedition in 1951. There are three kinds of blind fresh-water cave brotulids known, two from the subterranean waters of Cuba (*Lucifuga subterranea* and *Stygicola dentatus*) and one from Yucatan.

Although the majority of brotulids lay eggs, there are some that bear the young alive. A few of the species reach a length of over 3 feet, but most of them are small, secretive forms, usually less than 18 inches in length. A skin diver working on a tropical reef where brotulids occur would never see one unless he used an ichthyocide to obtain a population sample. A few of the larger, more common species are used as food in areas where there is a high demand for low-cost protein. In this category is *Brotula multibarbata,* a wide-ranging, silvery Indo-Pacific species that reaches a length of 15 inches. The red brotulid, *Brosmophycis marginatus,* is an American Pacific species ranging from Alaska to southern California in water of moderate depths; it reaches a maximum length of 18 inches and has a distinctive color pattern of bright red to brown on the upper surface and white underneath.

CUSK EELS—Family Ophidiidae

The slender cusk eels are similar in appearance to some of the common tide-pool eel-like blennies. Both the dorsal and anal fins have a great many rays beginning just behind the head and extending to the end of the pointed tail. The distinguishing mark of all cusk eels is a pair of very sensitive finger-like whiskers under the chin. Actually, these are the ventral fins that have moved to this forward position. When the cusk eel moves over the botton these slender fins extend downward, and as they are dragged across the bottom they apparently work like a mine detector.

About thirty species of cusk eels are known. They occur around the world in tropical and temperate marine waters. Although most cusk eels are less than 12 inches long when full grown, there are others that grow to a much larger size. In South Africa the famed deep-water kingklip, found in water 180 to 1500 feet deep, reaches a length of 5 feet and is considered a great delicacy. In Peru there is a commercial fishery for two smaller species of cusk eels (maximum length 2½ feet) that live in 120 to 300 feet of water. Although most cusk eels seem to prefer deep water, there are some species that are occasionally taken in the shallow water of tide pools and estuaries.

Some recent specimens of the spotted cusk eel, *Otophidium taylori,* captured in octopus traps while fishing at a depth of 600 feet along the central California coast, demonstrated previously unknown facts about the family. *O. taylori* proved to be a tail stander, for as soon as it was placed in a small tank

Atlantic Wolf fish (*Anarhichas lupus*); marine; North Atlantic south to Cape Cod and France (Georg Mandahl-Barth, Danmarks Akvarium).

Spotted Cusk-Eel (*Otophidium taylori*) resting in tail-standing position; marine; central and southern California (Steinhart Aquarium, California Academy of Sciences).

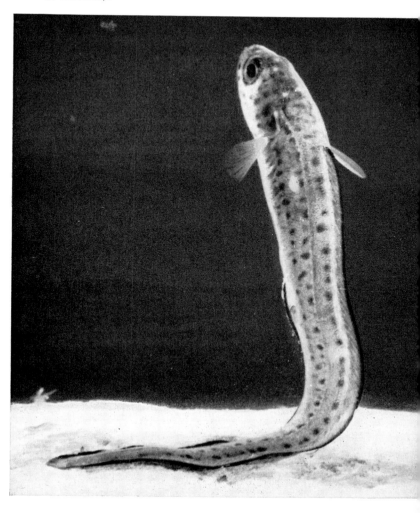

at Steinhart Aquarium it assumed the typical resting posture: standing vertically with the tail pressed against the bottom. External disturbances seemed to have little effect upon this phlegmatic fish. A stick pushed against the side of the body only caused the fish to flutter its pectoral fins rapidly as though attempting to maintain its balance in the vertical position. On one occasion a giant nudibranch slug oozed over the entire trunk and tail of the spotted cusk eel, but again the fish never moved.

In addition to being a tail stander, *O. taylori* is also an active tail borer. It customarily enters cavities and crevices tail first, allowing only a portion of the head to protrude from the hole. When placed in a small tank containing glass tubes, *taylori* will invariably do its tail standing with the tail inserted in one of the tubes. This affinity for backing into unknown apertures has its serious side, for one day *taylori* appropriated an unused submerged aquarium drain pipe for its home. A long pencil inserted into the pipe could barely touch the cusk eel some seven inches down the pipe. Then there began a series of frantic schemes to try to remove it from the pipe without injury. Finally, by means of long forceps, a wriggling salmon fingerling was shoved into the pipe just in front of *taylori*. The cusk eel tried to eat the fingerling, and while it was so occupied, the salmon was pulled out with the eel hungrily attached. Needless to say, this drain was then thoroughly blocked.

CUCUMBER and PEARL FISHES
—Family Carapidae

As adults these slender, knifelike "fierasfers," as they are sometimes called, are usually tail borers, hiding within cracks and crevices by entering tail first. Often these hiding places are living animals such as sea cucumbers (holothurians), clams, starfishes, sea urchins, and even tunicates. The name "pearl fish" is derived from the fact that the host for some species is the pearl shell; on at least one occasion the fish had been permanently trapped by the shell and had become embedded in it like an abnormal pearl.

The life history of a typical cucumber fish is very interesting. Although egg laying has not been recorded, the eggs are known to float at the surface, soon hatching into larvae that pass through two different stages before looking very much like the adult. Either as a second-stage larva or as a subsequent juvenile, the cucumber fish proceeds to find a host of the proper species. For example, *Carapus homei* from the Indo-Pacific will accept any of the animals listed in the above paragraph, whereas the Florida and West Indian *Carapus bermudensis* has been found in only one species of cucumber, *Actinopyga*

agassizi. The prospective host is carefully examined until, in the case of the cucumber, the vent is located. Forcible entry, head first, is then accomplished, and the cucumber fish is now at home within its host. As the fish grows older, it develops a method of tail entry into the holothurian, during which it uses a corkscrew motion, sometimes carrying the body through a full circle of 360 degrees.

To understand this remarkable fish, it is helpful to know something of the peculiar biology of the sea cucumbers. If handled roughly or disturbed, these holothurians have the habit of eviscerating themselves and discarding most of their internal anatomy, which they subsequently regenerate. Thus, it should not bother the sea cucumber if a cucumber fish housed within its body were to feed upon some of its internal organs; the cucumber would merely respond by regenerating replacements. Stomach contents of some cucumber fishes indicate that they actually do feed on the reproductive organs and branchial gills within the holothurian. On the other hand, some observers have suggested that the adult fish does the majority of its feeding elsewhere and merely returns to the sea cucumber for protection. The Mediterranean *Carapus acus*, however, is thought to spend all of its adult life within the sea cucumber, emerging only when thrown out of its host by evisceration.

The cucumber fish can be a difficult species to collect, for one never knows which cucumber has the fish. One way to find out is to place each sea cucumber in a separate bucket of fresh water. Soon the fishes will begin to emerge from the vents of the cucumbers—first the head, then half the body, and then finally the entire fish. If one attempts to pull the fish out, it will usually withdraw into the cucumber and will not emerge until much later.

Laboratory studies using model sea cucumbers have shown that the fish will not react properly to the model unless actual sea cucumber mucus is present along with a current in the water.

The authority on cucumber fishes, D. C. Arnold, indicates that about two dozen species assigned to four genera should be recognized. All share the anatomical peculiarity of having the vent moved far forward under the throat. They lack scales and pelvic and tail fins, and one group of three species of *Encheliophis* has even lost the pectoral fins. The dorsal and anal fins begin a short distance behind the head and are continuous to the tip of the pointed tail.

The largest members of this family reach a length of 12 inches (*Echiodon drummondi* from the British Isles and Scandinavian waters and *Carapus parvipinnis* from the Pacific). Most of the remaining species are less than 6 inches in length. The cucumber and pearl fishes are normally considered shallow-water species; however, some of them have been taken in water as deep as six hundred feet. The family has a world-wide distribution in tropical and subtropical waters, although one or two hardier species are found in temperate seas.

Butterfishes and Their Relatives *(Suborder Stromateoidea)*

The fishes of this marine group share an anatomical peculiarity not found among other fishes: they have an expanded and muscular esophagus armed with ridges, papillae, or even teeth. The three families in the suborder include some valuable food fishes and some small and rare oceanic species.

The oval-shaped, laterally compressed members of the harvest-fish family, Stromateidae, lack the pelvic fins as adults and are usually premium food fishes. Along the American Atlantic shores the best-known species is the 12-inch butterfish, *Poronotus triacanthus;* on the American Pacific coast the only northern representative is the 10-inch California pompano, *Palometa simillima,* which really is not a pompano at all. Young butterfishes are sometimes found under large, floating jellyfish, such as the Portuguese man-of-war, and in this respect they resemble members of the second family in this suborder, the Nomeidae, sometimes called man-of-war fishes.

Most of the nomeids are small and are distinguished from the butterfishes and other members of the Stromateidae by the fact that they have pelvic fins. The 3-inch man-of-war fish, *Nomeus gronovi,* is world-wide in distribution throughout tropical seas; it is invariably found among the long, trailing tentacles of the giant jellyfishes. The black ventral or pelvic fins are very large; when seen from above, the fish in the water resembles one of the short-winged flying fishes. The pattern on the body may be either mottled or banded.

The third family is represented by the squaretail, *Tetragonurus cuvieri,* a fish noted for its tough non-removable scales. It has been aptly described as looking as if it had been carved from wood. It is world-wide in distribution in the depths of tropical and temperate seas.

Labyrinth Fishes
(Suborder Anabantoidea)

—Family Anabantidae

Kissing gourami, fighting fish, and climbing perch are among the more popular members of the family Anabantidae, a group of small, tropical fresh-water fishes found in southeast Asia and in Africa. Because of the special labyrinthine breathing apparatus located in a cavity above each gill chamber and connected to it, the members of this family are called labyrinth fishes. Each cavity is filled with a series of bony plates covered with a rosette-like vascular membrane containing many fine blood vessels, which extract oxygen from the atmospheric air as it passes over them. The fish takes in a bubble of air at the surface and at the same time expels the old air through the gill covers. This accessory breathing apparatus enables the anabantids to live in oxygen-deficient water that would otherwise be lethal.

The walking fish—inaccurately called climbing perch—*Anabas testudineus* is a 10-inch, nondescript, brown fish of India, Malaya, and the Philippines. It is known to walk long distances over land, invariably in quest of another body of water when its own home becomes too dry. To do this, it extends its gill plates, which are equipped with spiny edges, and uses them as "feet." With a rocking motion and great persistence, it is able to proceed as fast as ten feet per minute. In Africa there are other kinds of walking fishes that have mobility on dry and moist land to a greater or lesser extent.

Spotted Climbing Perch (*Ctenopoma acutirostre*); fresh water; Congo (Gene Wolfsheimer).

Kissing Gourami (*Helostoma temmincki*); fresh water; Malaya to Indonesia (Gene Wolfsheimer).

The Siamese fighting fish, *Betta splendens* (plate 104), is another interesting member of this family. In Thailand contests are held in which male bettas are pitted against each other and large sums of money are bet on the outcome. There have been reports of wagerers becoming so enthusiastic as to bet their homes, all their possessions, and even their families. The female bettas are quite docile and do not fight.

In its native waters of Thailand *Betta splendens* is a drab, 2-inch, dull-colored fish with small fins. As a result of centuries of careful breeding and cultivation, there are now bettas of many colors with fantastically long, veil-like dorsal, anal, and caudal fins.

Although many members of this family have had the term "gourami" included in their common names, the true gourami, *Osphronemus goramy*, is the only species to which the name should apply; it is also the only fish in the family that reaches any great length, sometimes growing up to 2 feet. Originally from the East Indies, it has been introduced into India, Thailand, China, and the Philippines, and is now cultivated as food in these areas.

Moonlight Gourami (*Trichogaster microlepis*); fresh water; Thailand (Gene Wolfsheimer).

The famous kissing gourami, *Helostoma temmincki,* always causes comment by its kissing activities. This whitish fish reaches a length of 10 inches and has long been a favorite of tropical fish fanciers. Other gouramis often kept in home aquaria include several species of the genus *Trichogaster,* which range in adult size from 5 to 10 inches. These are imported from southeast Asia and include such species as the pearl, snake-skinned, three-spot or blue, sparkling, and moonlight gouramis. The small gouramis of the genus *Colisia* and the paradise fishes of the genus *Macropodus* are also quite popular with aquarists. The 2½-inch talking or croaking gourami, *Trichopsis vittatus,* is of interest because of the noise the males make at night when they come to the surface for air.

With a few exceptions, breeding takes place in much the same way throughout the family, most of the species being "bubble-nest builders." The male fighting fish produces a nest of bubbles as a place of incubation for the eggs and shelter for the very young fry. He does this by taking into his mouth a bubble of air, coating it with a sticky mucous secretion, and blowing it to the surface; this process is repeated until a nest several inches in diameter and perhaps a half-inch in depth is formed. The male and female then embrace in a U-shaped manner, and as the eggs are squeezed from the female, they are fertilized by the male and drop to the bottom. There they are picked up, usually by the male, and blown into the nest of bubbles. The eggs hatch in a short time, and the young stay in the nest, where they are watched over by the male until the yolk sac is absorbed and they become free-swimming.

All of the anabantids have moderately protrusible mouths; however, there is one member of this suborder that has a greatly protractile mouth—the very slender, cigar-shaped, 7-inch *Luciocephalus pulcher* from the fresh waters of the Malay Peninsula. This species is sometimes placed in a separate family, the Luciocephalidae.

Snakeheads (*Suborder Channoidea*)

—Family Channidae

Snakeheads will live for many hours and sometimes days out of water and are usually sold alive in fish markets. In the Philippines it is well worth a visit to the market just to watch the sale of these fishes. They are placed on a large woven tray, and in order to keep the "dalag"—as they are called—from squirming off the tray, the fishmonger periodically belabors them with a large club she keeps in her hand for that purpose. Her sales talk is delivered in a singsong monotone, reminiscent of the calypso of the Caribbean, punctuated at rhythmical intervals by blows of the club.

Like the anabantids of the previous suborder, the fresh-water snakeheads are air-breathers; but instead of having an intricate labyrinth above the gill cavity, they have a simple vascular chamber. They also have a distribution similar to that of the anabantids, being found in Africa and in Asia. The snakeheads are fairly round in cross section and have long dorsal and anal fins without spiny rays. Six-rayed pelvic fins are present in the genus *Ophicephalus,* which includes all except one of the numerous species in the family. This species is *Channa asiatica,* which is placed in a separate genus because the pelvic fins are lacking. The various species of snakeheads range in size from 6 inches to 3 feet. All of the snakeheads are carnivorous and have the typical bulldog lower jaw which protrudes beyond the upper; the anterior nostril usually has a pronounced tube. The color patterns are usually in shades of gray, brown, and black, often with distinctive markings; for instance, *Ophicephalus africanus* has V-shaped marks along the sides of the body. In a number of species a dark bar extends backward through the eye and may be continuous along the body as a band or a series of blotches.

Snakehead eggs usually float at the surface; they are guarded by the male during hatching and for a short time afterward. Young snakeheads of some species are reddish in color; in muddy ponds as they come to the surface for air, they appear as continual flecks of color breaking the surface of the water. Although the snakeheads have been a boon to the protein economy in some regions, they have also proved a curse in others because of their highly aggressive nature. When newly introduced into ponds, they quickly remove all less competitive species.

Barracudas, Silversides, and Mullet (Suborder Mugiloidea)

Members of this group have the pelvic or ventral fins in abdominal position, each fin composed of five branched rays preceded by a spine. The spiny-rayed portion of the dorsal fin is usually separated from the soft portion by a considerable distance.

BARRACUDAS—Family Sphyraenidae

Divers sometimes fear attack by giant carnivorous barracudas more than attack by sharks. Barracudas are inquisitive, and although they do not exactly stalk a diver, they follow him around. Since they apparently feed by sight rather than by smell, they sample any brightly colored object or anything that makes erratic movements, such as a wounded fish. Unlike a shark, a barracuda makes a single attack and leaves a clean wound with no jagged edges. The jutting lower jaw and fanglike teeth of these elongated, torpedo shaped fishes are so well known that barracudas require little identification. The two dorsal fins are separated by a wide distance. Although they resemble the fresh-water pikes, barracudas are, of course, marine fishes; they are usually found in tropical waters, but some species do range into temperate seas. In spite of the fact that they have occasionally been involved in cases of tropical fish

Snakehead (*Channa asiatica*); fresh water; southeastern Asia (New York Zoological Society).

poisoning, all of the eighteen species are usually considered excellent and tasty food fishes. Six feet is the normal maximum length of the several species of large barracudas, but there are reports of some growing to twice that length. The great barracuda, *Sphyraena barracuda* (Plate 105), occurs on both sides of the Atlantic and in the western Pacific. In the West Indies it is considered a very dangerous species, but in the region of the Hawaiian Islands it has never been known to attack a swimmer. The American Atlantic northern barracuda or sennet, *S. borealis,* is a small, 18-inch species ranging from Bermuda and Massachusetts to Panama and the Gulf of Mexico. The European barracuda, *S. sphyraena,* is the common eastern Atlantic and Mediterranean species; it reaches a length of 5 feet. Another

Schooling Barracuda (*Sphyraena sphyraena*); marine; eastern Atlantic and Mediterranean; and in the background: Striped Porgies (*Sarpa* or *Box Salpa*); marine; Mediterranean and West African coasts (Paul Droz).

fairly large species is the 4-foot Pacific barracuda, *S. argentea,* which is found all the way from Alaska to Lower California; in southern California it is one of the most important market species.

SILVERSIDES—Family Atherinidae

The antherinid silversides are often called "smelt" but are different from the osmerid smelts discussed earlier in that they have two separate dorsal fins, the first one of spines and the second of soft rays. In addition, there is a broad silvery band along the sides and the lateral line is missing. The ventral or pelvic fins are usually in the center of the abdomen. The silversides are chiefly marine species found in tropical and temperate waters around the world; about 150 kinds are known.

One of the best-known silversides is the grunion, *Leuresthes tenuis,* a small, 5-to-7-inch, shallow-water fish found along the shores of southern and Lower California. Its peculiar spawning habits take it high on the beach at night during the period of the highest tides. Here the female wriggles into the sand, burying her eggs at a depth of two inches; at the same time, the male wraps himself around her on top of the sand and fertilizes the eggs. The grunion then flop back to the water and are carried out to deeper water by succeeding waves. The eggs remain in the sand until the next series of high tides, when they

hatch within three minutes after the water first touches them. The spawning runs are correlated with the phases of the moon, usually occurring a day or two after each full or new moon. The grunion has a short life history, being mature at the age of one year and seldom surviving beyond three years. In the upper part of the Gulf of California there is another grunion-like fish, *Hubbsiella sardina,* that has sand-spawning habits like the grunion and shows similar periodicity, but differs in that it often spawns during the daytime.

There are several other silversides that occur along the California coast, the largest being the 22-inch jacksmelt, *Atherinopsis californiensis,* a species that is invariably parasitized by unknown vesicular worms found throughout the flesh. Jacksmelt spawning generally occurs between October and March. The eggs are laid on aquatic weeds; if vegetation is not present—as in an aquarium tank—the eggs may remain in a string attached to the female for as long as a week.

In the eastern part of the United States there are several fresh- and brackish-water silversides, such as the 4-inch brook silverside, *Labidesthes sicculus,* a form which ranges from the Great Lakes to Florida and Texas. Marine species that enter fresh water include the tidewater silverside, *Menidia beryllina,* and the Mississippi silverside, *Menidia audens.*

These species look like typical silversides, but in other parts of the world some of the fresh-water atherinids are entirely different in appearance. For example, in Lake Sentani, New Guinea's largest lake, there are two common 4-to-6-inch species, *Chilatherina sentaniensis* and *Glossolepis incisus,* that are deep-bodied and reddish brown in color. These fishes are important as food to the natives of the region. They are caught in shallow water by traps made of brush into which the fish swim in order to hide. A woven net placed around the outside of the trap allows the brush to be removed and the fish collected without loss.

In the fresh waters of Mexico there are a fair number of species of *Chirostoma,* most of them important market fishes; they reach a length of about 20 inches and are characterized by a jutting lower jaw.

The genus *Iso* contains a few small species scattered across the Indo-Pacific. They are of interest because of the position of the pectoral fins, which are abnormally high on the sides of the body. The abdominal ridge of these fishes is sharp like that of a herring.

In the Mediterranean there are several species of silversides, only two of which come as far north as the British Isles.

MULLETS—Family Mugilidae

The mullets are torpedo-shaped, shallow-water, schooling fishes usually found over sandy or muddy bottom containing detritus, through which they normally grub for food. Most of the one hundred or so species have a muscular, gizzard-like stomach which enables them to grind their food, primarily vegetable, before it starts through the exceptionally long digestive tract. A 13-inch mullet with a digestive tract 7 feet long is not unusual. The structure and curvature of the mouth and the arrangement of the teeth are important factors in determining the various genera. Mullets resemble the silversides in many respects: they have separate spiny-rayed and soft-rayed dorsal fins, the pelvic fins are abdominal in position, and the lateral line is vestigial or absent. But, unlike the silversides, the mullets do not have the silver band along the side of the body, and they usually have fewer vertebrae.

The majority of these world-wide fishes are tropical and temperate marine species, but they move readily into brackish and fresh water. In both the East Indies and the West Indies there are species of mullets that are normally restricted to fresh water.

A mullet measuring 2 feet is considered a reasonably large fish, but the striped mullet, *Mugil cephalus,* reaches a length of about 3 feet and a weight of some fifteen pounds. It is found around the world, usually in warm water, and is the object of commercial fisheries wherever it occurs in abundance. It has a faster growth rate than some of the other species and for this reason is often used in brackish- and salt-water pond culture.

In Europe the mugilids are often known as gray mullets to differentiate them from the red mullets, surmullets, or goatfishes of the family Mullidae. As described earlier, the goatfishes have a pair of distinctive barbels under the chin.

Phallostethids

(Suborder Phallostethoidea)

—Family Phallostethidae

Some of the world's strangest fishes belong to this small family of about eighteen species found in fresh, brackish, and salt water from India to the Philippines; most of them are adult at less than 1½

Spawning Jacksmelt (*Atherinopsis californiensis*); marine; Oregon to Lower California (Steinhart Aquarium, California Academy of Sciences).

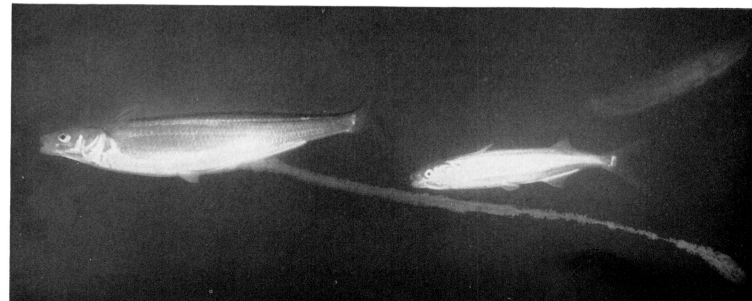

inches. They seem to be related to both the mullet-like fishes and the cryprinodont fishes. There are two dorsal fins, the first having one or two spines. There are no spines on the other fins. Under the throat the male has a muscular and bony copulatory organ accompanied by long curved bones that are used for clasping the female as he fertilizes the eggs; this entire structure is apparently modified from part of the pectoral and pelvic girdles and the first pair of ribs.

One of the authorities on this group, Dr. A. W. Herre of the University of Washington, says in his 1942 review:

> Owing to their small size, lack of color, and translucency in life, most phallostethids are totally unknown to the people of the regions where they occur. Apparently only three species are large enough or abundant enough to be used as food, and then only where good fish are difficult to obtain much of the time.
>
> In general, all phallostethids occur in small schools, swimming at or very near the surface. Their eyes, and a gleam of color in the peritoneum, are the only visible evidence of their presence, and it requires trained and acute vision to see them. When much disturbed, the schools break up, and the individuals escape by hiding on the bottom. Brackish and salt water species advance up tidal creeks in great numbers, with the incoming tide. They keep close to the bank, taking advantage of the vegetation for shelter, and of eddies and backwaters; are borne far up stream by the tide, and even enter fresh water. As the tide goes out they return to quiet sheltered lagoons, bays, and estuaries, or take refuge in mangrove and nipa swamps, or in pools left by the receding tide. These species spawn in mangrove and nipa swamps, and at low tide incredible swarms of young may be seen in favorable areas, well shaded by the jungle. . . . The species of mountain streams stay out of the strong currents, living mainly in eddies and backwaters, where they can obtain a maximum of insect food. Lake dwelling forms live along shore or in quiet bays, where they are protected by vegetation.

Threadfins (Suborder Polynemoidea)

—Family Polynemidae

Typical of the threadfins, sometimes called tassel-fishes, is an anchovy-type head with rounded nose and recessed lower jaw; the mouth, which is on the underside of the head, is not obvious unless it is open. There are two dorsal fins, widely separated, and a deeply forked tail fin. The threadfin takes its name from the peculiar division of the pectoral fin into an upper section with the rays attached to each other, as in a normal fin, and an entirely separate

ventral section composed of four to seven long, filamentous rays not attached to each other. These slender rays are under voluntary control and are thought to have a tactile function; they are often carried close against the body so that they are not visible, but the fish can quickly swing them outward—and often does so—with the result that eight to fourteen slender fingers extend like the tines of a rake beneath the fish. In the young these streamers are very long, sometimes extending beyond the tip of the tail; as the fish grows, the streamers shorten proportionately until in some adults they seldom extend farther than the anal fin.

The threadfins, which are found throughout most of the world's tropics, are usually inshore marine in habitat and are often found in great abundance in estuaries and river mouths. Most of the three dozen or so species are full grown at a length of less than 18 inches, but at least one, the Indian *Eleutheronema tetradactylum,* reaches a length of 6 feet. They are highly prized as food fishes. The barbu, *Polydactylus virginicus,* is a fairly common American Atlantic species known from New Jersey to Uruguay. *P. sexfilis,* known as the Hawaiian moi, occurs throughout the eastern Pacific.

Scorpaenoid or Mailcheeked Fishes

(Order Scleroparei)

The fishes of this group are placed together because all of them have a bony plate, or stay, extending across the cheek from the eye to the gill cover. A number of species belonging to the approximately twenty families assigned to the Scleroparei are very spiny, and some have venom glands. The world's most poisonous fish is included in this order.

SCORPIONFISHES and ROCKFISHES
—Family Scorpaenidae

Many of the scorpaenid fishes have a similarity of appearance, which can readily be seen in Plates 110 through 118. The family includes several hundred species, the majority being found in temperate marine waters and a few in tropical seas. Of the approximately sixty species found on the American Pacific coast, fifty-three occur in the temperate waters of the 850-mile California coast line. Unfortunately, many of these fishes are so difficult to identify accurately that it often requires a specialist to be certain of the species. Most of the scorpaenids spend their time on or near the bottom, often in rocky areas; hence the name "rockfish." The name "scorpionfish" comes from the venomous nature of the dorsal, anal, and ventral fin spines, which, even without a venom gland, can give the careless fisherman a very painful puncture wound. Some species, such as the tropical turkeyfishes or lionfishes of the genus *Pterois* (Plates 117 and 118), have venom glands in grooves along the sides of each spine. Contact with one of these turkeyfish spines has never resulted in death, although there have been several cases that were almost fatal. The majestic *P. volitans* is one of the most widely distributed and well-known species. It will actually attack an object, jabbing at it with its dorsal spines.

The venom carried by the spines of the California scorpionfish or sculpin, *Scorpaena guttata* (Plates 110 and 112), is almost as virulent as that of the turkeyfish. This species, incidentally, is one of a few in the family that do not bear living young. The sculpin lays a peculiar gelatinous egg balloon that may measure 8 inches in diameter; the individual eggs are embedded in the thin wall of the balloon.

The most deadly of all fish venoms is found in the ugly stonefish, *Synanceja verrucosa;* the bulbous venom glands are located near the base of the hypodermic-like dorsal fin spines. This species so closely resembles a small rock on the ocean floor that it is almost invisible as it lies half buried in the sand, its usual resting position. A swimmer accidentally stepping on the fish finds, to his horror, that the pressure of his foot causes the bulbous glands to eject their neurotoxic venom along the grooves in the spines and into his foot. A South African case history of this kind showed that the swimmer survived for about two hours after the accident.

The sailback scorpionfish, *Tetraroge barbata* (Plate 111), is a fascinating 3-inch fish occasionally imported from the Philippines by tropical fish fanciers. The fin does not always remain erect as shown in the plate, but may be raised and lowered depending upon the mood of the fish.

Turkeyfish (*Pterois volitans*); marine; tropical Indo-Pacific (Ernest Palinkas: Pix).

Stonefish (*Synanceja verrucosa*), the world's most poisonous fish; marine, shallow water; tropical Indo-Pacific (Fritz Goro: *Life* Magazine).

Although many of the rockfishes have rather somber colors, there are some that are truly spectacular; included in this category are the barbfish, *Scorpaena brasiliensis* (Plate 116), and the orange scorpionfish, *S. scrofa* (Plate 115).

Commercially, most of the scorpaenids are considered good food fishes. In rocky areas they are caught on hook and line, but in open areas and in deep water, trawl nets are used. The latter is the type employed in catching the rosefish, *Sebastes marinus,* a species common on both sides of the North Atlantic at depths between three hundred and seven hundred feet. Some years ago this fish, which is marketed as ocean perch, was considered a trash fish; however, in 1950 more than two million pounds were marketed in the New England area alone. Although rosefish grow to a length of 3 feet, most of those caught seldom exceed 2 feet and a weight of thirteen pounds. An 8-inch fish may be ten years old. Like other rockfishes, they bear their young alive, as many as twenty thousand being carried at once by a 13-inch female.

SEA ROBINS—Family Triglidae

The highly colorful sea robins have hard, casque-like, bony heads usually armed with spines. There are two separate dorsal fins; the lower rays of the large fanlike pectoral fins are separate and are used as feelers as the sea robin "walks" over the bottom. Some species have spines along the base of each dorsal fin and along the lateral line. All triglids are carnivorous, feeding chiefly on small crustaceans and mollusks. They are found on the bottom from shallow to moderate depths in tropical and temperate waters around the world. The largest members of the family range between two and three feet in length and the people of some areas consider them excellent food.

All of the sea robins are thought to be able to produce sound; in fact, one of the noisiest fishes on the American Atlantic coast is the 16-inch northern sea robin, *Prionotus carolinus,* which occurs from Nova Scotia to Venezuela. It spawns from June through August and is apparently even noisier at this time than usual. Another very noisy species is the striped sea robin, *P. evolans,* which occurs in the same areas as the previous species. The sound that the sea robins make is produced by muscles attached to the large air bladder, which fills about one-half of the entire visceral cavity.

There are a number of sea robins along the European and African coasts. One of the most distinctive species is the tubfish or yellow gurnard, *Trigla hirundo,* which has bright blue on the edges of the pectorals.

ARMORED SEA ROBINS—*Family Peristediidae*

Fishes of this family are quite similar to the preceding group of triglid sea robins, but their entire bodies are covered with armor in the form of heavy plates bearing spines. The snout has two lateral bony projections extending forward as twin fingers. There are barbels attached to the lower jaw, and the pectoral fins have two free rays. Most of the armored sea robins are deep-water tropical and temperate marine fishes and are thought to be more sedentary than their cousins the triglids.

SCULPINS—*Family Cottidae*

Looking down into a tide pool along the shores of the North Pacific, one sees small fishes darting back and forth; many of these are the tide-pool johnnies of the genus *Oligocottus*. The eyes of these fishes are mounted on top of their very large heads, and sharp spines are present on the preopercles. The cottids, a group of some three hundred species, are mostly bottom-dwelling fishes, often scaleless or partially scaled. Many are marine fishes, found in cold northern waters. Some sculpins live easily in brackish water, and there are a number that live only in fresh water. The sculpins have two dorsal fins, either separate or with a notch between the spiny-rayed and soft-rayed portions. The pectoral fins are fan-shaped and quite large, and the ventrals, if present, usually have a spine and two to five soft rays.

Characteristic American Pacific types include the 20-inch spotted irishlord, *Hemilepidotus hemilepidotus* (Plate 108), and the 12-inch buffalo sculpin, *Enophrys bison* (Plate 109); the latter species is noted for the large spine extending from its preopercle. Similar spines are present on several other sculpins, such as the Atlantic longhorn sculpin, *Myoxocephalus octodecemspinosus*.

One of the largest sculpins is the crab-eating cabezon, *Scorpaenichthys marmoratus*, a species that reaches a length of 30 inches and a weight of twenty-five pounds. Its normal range is from British Columbia to Lower California. Despite the peculiar color of its flesh—often green—the cabezon is good to eat, but its roe is poisonous.

Undoubtedly the most common shallow-water, western American marine cottid is the Pacific staghorn sculpin, *Leptocottus armatus*, a species having hooks on the opercle; it is abundant in bays all the way from Alaska to Lower California. Most of those encountered are smaller than 6 inches, but occasional individuals may reach 12 inches. Another cottid with similar hooks on the opercular spines is the Arctic staghorn sculpin, *Gymnocanthus tricuspis*, which is found in the northernmost parts of both the Pacific and the Atlantic.

The American Atlantic sea raven, *Hemitripterus americanus*, has the surprising ability to swallow air and blow up like a balloon when removed from the water. When thrown back into the water, it floats helplessly until it is able to release the air. Although the sea raven grows as large as 2 feet with a weight of five pounds and is said to be edible, it is chiefly used in baiting lobster traps.

The sailorfish, *Nautichthys oculofasciatus*, is a startling-looking cottid from the shores of Pacific northwest America. The first five rays of the dorsal fin are greatly elongated, and the fish often erects them over its head like a tremendous sail.

Most of the fresh-water sculpins are small, as in the case of the 4-inch miller's thumb, *Cottus gobio*, which is found throughout Europe with the exception of Spain and Greece. One of the largest of the many American fresh-water species is the 12-inch prickly sculpin, *Cottus asper*, which ranges from southern California to Alaska. A number of the fresh-water sculpins lay their eggs on the undersides of stones or logs, and the males guard the eggs until they hatch.

GRUNT SCULPIN—*Family Rhamphocottidae*

The big-headed or grunt sculpin, *Rhamphocottus richardsoni* (Plate 106), is the world's most comical fish. As it moves across the bottom, each movement is a series of short jumps aided by the finger-like tips of the pectoral fins. When in a hurry, the grunt swims up from the bottom with all the grace of a captive blimp that has just broken its moorings. The independent motion of the eyes, one moving without reference to the other, adds to its strange appearance. The name "grunt" comes from the noise produced when *Rhamphocottus* is removed from the water. This small 3-inch fish is the only member of its

Leopard Sea Robin (*Prionotus scitulus*); marine; North Carolina to Venezuela (Seaquarium, Miami).

family, and is found along the American Pacific coast from Alaska to northern California. As do many other cold-water fishes, it shows its temperature preference by its vertical distribution in the water; for example, in Washington, British Columbia, and northward the grunt is found in shallow water and even in tide pools, whereas around San Francisco it must go down to a depth of five hundred to six hundred feet to find its preferred temperature of 45 to 50 defrees F.

Despite its bizarre appearance, very little is known about the natural history of *Rhamphocottus*. The only detailed observations are those made by my friend Cecil Brousseau, Director of the Point Defiance Aquarium in Tacoma, Washington. He has described to me how the female chases the male about until she captures him by forcing him into a crevice or other cavern. In the aquarium this nuptial chamber may be any small container such as a broken bottle, a drinking glass, or an old shoe. After the male is forced into this chamber, the female guards the entrance so that he cannot escape, all of this being

Tubfish or Yellow Gurnard (*Trigla hirundo*); marine; Norway to the southwest coast of England (Société Royale de Zoologie d' Anvers).

in the interest of making sure that he will be available to fertilize the eggs which she soon deposits on the sides of the chamber walls. The eggs usually number 150; after fertilization the male is free to leave. This activity takes place at any time during the months of August through October. The incubation period lasts for sixteen weeks when the water temperature is around 50 to 52 degrees or for as long as twenty weeks in colder water of 47 to 49 degrees. Details of hatching and growth have not been studied.

In captivity the grunt sculpin does well, living for several years provided the temperature of the water is kept below 55 degrees, and sufficient food is available in the form of small crustaceans and other natural food.

SEA POACHERS and ALLIGATOR FISHES
—Family Agonidae

The cold-water marine poachers and their relatives look much like some of the South American fresh-water armored catfishes of the family Loricariidae, but the two families are not related. The poachers usually have elongated bodies covered with bony plates; the edges of the individual plates are often saw-toothed. The ventral or pelvic fins are generally located just behind the pectorals in thoracic position; these ventral fins as well as the second dorsal and anal fins are sometimes longer in the males than in the females. The agonids live on the bottom; a few live in tide pools, but the majority are found in deeper water, down as much as two thousand feet. These are northern-hemisphere fishes, most of the species occurring in the North Pacific. The 12-inch sturgeon-like sea poacher, *Agonus acipenserinus* (Plate 124), is one of the largest species; it has the typical appearance of many members of this family. Around the British Isles one of the most common inshore fishes is the pogge or armed bullhead, *Agonus cataphractus,* a small species that ranges from Greenland and Iceland southward in European Atlantic waters.

SNAILFISHES—Family Liparidae

The snailfishes are small, elongated, jelly-like fishes with flabby skin and no scales, although some may have small prickles over the body. The ventral fins are usually modified to form a sucking disk located under the body and directly behind the head. The very long dorsal fin starts a short distance behind the head and has a few spiny rays at its anterior end; because of the fish's flabby body, it is impossible to count the rays without dissection. The snailfishes are carnivorous, cold-water, marine fishes seldom found in water warmer than 60 degrees F. Some 115 species of these bottom fishes are recognized. There are about 6 species in the tropical Pacific, 5 in the Antarctic, 14 in the North Atlantic, and the remainder—about three-fourths of those known—in the North Pacific. They are found at depths ranging from the very shallow water of tide pools to as deep as two miles. Most species are full grown at a length of less than 7 inches, but there are a few that reach 12 inches. When alive, the liparids are usually pink or light tan in color, and some have patterns in the form of spots, blotches, or fine lines. One of the best known of the lined species is the striped sea snail, *Liparis liparis*, a 5-to-10-inch fish found on both sides of the North Atlantic.

LUMPSUCKERS—*Family Cyclopteridae*

Careful examination of a lumpsucker reveals an obvious relationship to the snailfishes; in fact, the two are placed in the same family by some authorities. The lumpsucker has the same kind of sucker under its body that the snailfish has; the small prickles present on some of the snailfishes are greatly enlarged to form tubercles on the lumpsuckers. The body has become globose rather than elongated, and the dorsal fin is usually divided by a notch into two sections.

The lumpsuckers are carnivorous cold-water marine fishes found in the northern hemisphere. On the American Pacific coast they occur as far south as the Puget Sound area, the southernmost species being the 5-inch spiny lumpsucker, *Eumicropterus orbis*. The largest species in the family is probably the Atlantic lumpfish, *Cyclopterus lumpus*, which has been recorded at a maximum of about 2 feet and a weight of thirteen pounds. It has a wide distribution on both sides of the North Atlantic. The males of this species are generally smaller than the females. During breeding season the males develop a reddish color on the undersurface. The eggs are laid in shallow water, one female laying from 79,000 to 136,000. They are then guarded by the male— hence the name "henfish." In Europe male henfish are sometimes smoked and used for food.

OTHER MAIL-CHEEKED FISHES

There are several other small families of the mail-cheeked fishes that space does not permit us to discuss fully. Included among these are commercially important North Pacific forms, such as lingcod (Ophiodontidae), greenlings (Hexagrammidae), and sablefish (Anoplopomatidae). Other interesting Pacific fishes belonging to this group are the caracanthids (Caracanthidae), which look like fifty-cent pieces covered with fur and live in coral heads; and the flatheads (Platycephalidae), which look as if they had been destined to become gurnards or sea

Lumpfish (*Cyclopterus lumpus*); marine; both sides of the North Atlantic (Georg Mandahl-Barth, Danmarks Akvarium).

robins but had failed to do so. The flatheads are important food fishes in some parts of the Indo-Pacific.

Flying Gurnards

(*Suborder Dactylopteroidea*)
—*Family Dactylopteridae*

Although the flying gurnards bear a resemblance to the sea robins, they are placed in a separate suborder because of certain primitive characteristics in the arrangement of the head bones. There are only a few species of these tropical marine fishes. Like the sea robins, they are bottom forms.

Identification of the flying gurnards is relatively easy because of their outstanding characteristics: (1) tremendously enlarged pectoral fins (Plate 107) with the inner rays free, (2) a large bony head, and (3) a single isolated dorsal spine attached to the nape of the neck.

Much remains to be learned about their so-called flying ability. According to some, they are able to propel themselves out of the water and make an ineffectual attempt at flight. However, photographic documentation of this activity, such as that available on the flight of the true flying fishes, remains to be gathered.

Sticklebacks and Tubenose (*Order Thoracostei*)

These fishes have at various times been considered relatives of (1) the pipefishes, (2) the needlefishes, and (3) the mail-cheeked fishes. Only two families totaling about thirteen species are included in this small order: the well-known sticklebacks, which have free ribs; and the tubenose, which has its ribs fused to lateral bony plates. These are northern-hemisphere marine and fresh-water fishes limited to temperate and cold water.

STICKLEBACKS—Family Gasterosteidae

These small, aggressive fishes have long been popular with the aquarist, and in recent years have found new value in their service to mankind as bio-assay test animals used in the study of various aquatic toxins. Of great importance in this regard is the fact that several of the dozen species in the stickleback family live as easily in fresh water as in brackish or salt water. Most sticklebacks are armored with a series of bony plates along the sides of the body; the number of these plates depends upon the species as well as the temperature and salinity of the water, and may vary up to thirty-six. Because of the spines, plates on the sides, and the very narrow caudal peduncle, identification is not difficult.

With the onset of the breeding season, usually in the spring of the year, the male stickleback develops a bright red undersurface and assumes his role as the more active member of the mating pair. His first breeding activity is the construction of a nest, using as a base the stems of aquatic plants. The nest is held together by a threadlike material secreted from a section of the kidney, which becomes specially modified for this purpose during the breeding season. The male usually swims around the nest several times while paying out this binding thread. Then by such actions as nipping at the female's fins, chasing her, and doing a courtship dance, he entices or drives her to lay her eggs in this leafy bower. After she has deposited the eggs, she often leaves by burrowing a hole through the bottom of the nest. The male, noted for his solicitous care of the eggs and the young, then moves into the nest and spews milt over the eggs, thus making sure that they are adequately fertilized. This process may be repeated with several different females, and some males may even have several nests at the same time. Aeration of the eggs during the six-day incubation period is achieved by the male's swimming around the nest and vigorously fanning the eggs with his pectoral fins. The four-spine stickleback, *Apeltes quadracus,* builds a top with two holes in it over the nest and aerates the eggs by putting his mouth against one of the holes and sucking water through the nest. After the eggs have hatched, the male still maintains a watch over the youngsters and attempts to keep them in the area of the nest.

In spite of their spines, sticklebacks are important food items for some birds and other animals. Unfortunately, they are also excellent intermediate host-reservoirs for various tapeworms, which probably have their adult stages in birds. In many areas along the American Pacific coast, the threespine stickleback, *Gasterosteus aculeatus,* is so seriously in-fected with the coenurus stage of tapeworms that large vesicles form on the fish, and it seems almost impossible for the stickleback to move. Strangely enough, these infections seem to be restricted to populations in certain lakes. For example, within ten miles of San Francisco's Steinhart Aquarium there is one lake that is almost 100 per cent infective, others that are intermediate, and at least one that is apparently clear of infection.

Several of the sticklebacks are very widely distributed: the threespine, *Gasterosteus aculeatus,* occurs throughout most of the northern hemisphere in both salt and fresh water; the ninespine stickleback, *Pungitius pungitius,* has a similar distribution but is a more polar species and does not come so far south, New Jersey and central Europe being two of the southernmost limits of its range.

The brook stickleback, *Eucalia inconstans,* is a small (2½ inches) entirely fresh-water species limited to the cold waters of North America from Ohio northward to the latitude of northern British Columbia and Quebec. It may be identified by the four to six—usually five—spines in front of the dorsal fin. The fourspine stickleback, *Apeltes quadracus,* is a common species along the eastern American seaboard from Nova Scotia to Virginia. The fifteen-spine stickleback, *Spinachia spinachia,* can usually be identified by its large number of dorsal spines; it is common in salt water around the British Isles, on the European coasts, and in the North Sea.

TUBENOSE—Family Aulorhynchidae

The slender 6½-inch tubenose, *Aulorhynchus flavidus,* is a marine species ranging from southern California to Alaska and is the only member of its family. In some areas it is so abundant that it serves as a forage fish for others, often being found in the stomachs of larger carnivorous fishes. An indication of the size of some tubenose aggregations is shown by data taken November 16, 1950, by California Fish and Game biologists operating aboard a research ship in eighty feet of water off Santa Rosa Island, southern California. They discovered and accurately measured a dense school of tubenose, one-quarter mile in diameter, that entirely filled the space between the depths of thirty and seventy feet.

The tubenose looks much like a stickleback with two extra inches of length added to the center of the body; there are about twenty-five spines in front of the soft dorsal fin instead of the fifteen or fewer found in the sticklebacks. In aquarium work we have found the tubenose to be extremely susceptible to shock. Of a netful brought into an aquarium tank, perhaps half will go into temporary or permanent shock which eventually causes death.

Nest-building and courtship of the Fifteen-spine Stickleback (*Spinachia spinachia*). Upper left, male Stickleback collecting weed for construction of the nest. Upper right, male passing through and around the nest while secreting a thread with which he "sews" the nest together. Bottom, male driving gravid female into the completed nest by attacking her and biting her tail; marine; western European coasts (Douglas P. Wilson).

The late Conrad Limbaugh, noted diving ichthyologist, in his studies of the life history of the tubenose in the southern California kelp beds, found that their average depth was thirty-six feet but that they did range down to one hundred feet. Normal food consisted of small organisms such as amphipods, mysids, fish larvae, and crab zoae. He observed:

Spawning takes place throughout the year. The male binds seaweed together with a very thin thread which in extruded from the urogenital region. The seaweed chosen is often the new growths in the lower parts of the giant kelp. The eggs are deposited around the seaweed by the females and are closely guarded by the male, who drives off intruders by dashing at them. The translucent orange eggs hatch in about two to three weeks, and the larvae form schools near the bottom, usually in quiet water near rocks or seaweeds. Schooling behavior continues throughout life and is broken up only during spawning, when the male must remain to guard the nest. The young probably take less than one year to mature.

Sea Moths (*Order Hypostomides*)

—Family Pegasidae

A good photograph is certainly worth a thousand words in dealing with the sea moths; thus, Plate 136 is much more adequate than a lengthy description of the strange sea moth, which has been a zoological riddle for many years. The number of years is indicated by the fact that dried sea moths were among the earliest curios brought back to Europe from the Orient and the South Seas in past centuries. Ichthyologists of that time were as lacking in agreement as they are today about the exact affinities of this peculiar fish. The appearance of the body armor, which is composed of bony plates arranged in concentric rings, suggests a relationship with the pipefishes and seahorses or perhaps even the sea poachers (agonids). But the mouth, instead of being at the tip of the elongated snout, is located farther back on the undersurface of the head. The broad, expanded pectoral fins suggest a relationship with the flying gurnards (dactylopterids). There are also small ventral fins, which are lacking on the pipefishes and seahorses. When the life history and embryology of these fishes is well known we may be able to place them more exactly in the over-all classification of fishes. About five species of sea moths are recognized. The range of the group is from Africa to the Hawaiian Islands; it is entirely absent in the Atlantic. The Indo-Australian *Pegasus volitans,* with a length of 5 inches, is the largest and most well-known species.

Flatfishes (*Order Heterosomata*)

When the young flatfish is hatched from its floating egg, it acts like any other larval fish and swims with its body in a normal position. Within a few days, however, something strange begins to happen: one eye starts moving to the opposite side of the head, and soon the larval flatfish has two eyes on the same side. The dorsal fin then begins to grow forward on the head. In many species the mouth becomes twisted and the pectoral fins unequal in size. About this time the young flatfish sinks to the ocean bottom, where it will spend most of the remainder of its life lying on its blind side, with the eyed side up. The blind side of the body does not develop pigment and

so is usually whitish in color. In some flatfishes it is always the right eye that migrates to the opposite side; in others it is always the left eye; and in still others, either eye may make this migration. If both eyes are on the right side of the head, the flatfish is known as a right-eyed or dextral fish; if both eyes are on the left side, it is called a left-eyed or sinistral fish. To further complicate the problem, in certain flatfishes, such as the North Pacific starry flounder, *Platichthys stellatus,* this characteristic may vary with locality. Despite the fact that the starry flounder belongs to the family of right-eyed flatfishes (Pleuronectidae), about 55 to 59 per cent of its population in California have the eyes on the left side of the head; in Alaska this increases to 67 per cent and in Japan to between 98 and 100 per cent.

Included among the flatfishes are many of the world's most valuable food species, such as halibut, flounder, plaice, turbot, and sole. These, however, are only a few of the approximately six hundred species that have been described in this important group. These fishes are chiefly marine and are carnivorous in their food habits. They range in size from very small species only a few inches in length to giants of 10 feet weighing seven hundred pounds. The majority occur in all but the coldest seas, in shallow water or in moderate depths, and a few are found at great depths. In some species the males and females differ in such characteristics as the distance between the eyes or the length of the first rays of the dorsal fins or the pectoral fins.

Some of the flatfishes are noted for their ability to match their body pigment to the color and pattern of the ground on which they happen to be resting. This camouflage feature seems to be dependent upon visual stimuli received by the fish, for blinded experimental fishes lose most of this ability.

The most primitive of the five families of flatfishes is the Psettodidae, which has only two species, both of them found in the Indo-Pacific and on the West African coast. These fishes differ from all other flatfishes in that they have spiny rays in the dorsal and ventral fins and the dorsal fin does not extend forward upon the head.

LEFT-EYED FLOUNDERS—Family Bothidae

Most of the left-eyed or bothid flounders are of moderate size and are found from the shallows to deep ocean water. Some, such as the American Atlantic peacock flounder, *Bothus lunatus* (Plate 138), have very attractive patterns. The females of another member of this genus, the Indo-Australian *B. pantherinus,* have extremely long pectoral fins extending to the tip of the tail, but the males have pectoral fins that are normal in length.

[continued on page 273]

119. Undulate Triggerfish (*Balistipus undulatus*); marine; tropical Indo-Pacific (Hans and Klaus Paysan at Wilhelma Aquarium, Stuttgart)

120. Spotted Triggerfisr (*Balistoides conspicillum*); marine; tropical Indo-Pacific (Hans and Klaus Paysan at Wilhelma Aquarium, Stuttgart)

121. Pinktail Triggerfish (*Xanthichthys ringens*); marine; Atlantic and Indo-Pacific (John Tashjian at Steinhart Aquarium)

122. Queen Triggerfish (*Balistes vetula*); marine; Indian Ocea and both sides of the Atlantic, Massachusetts to Brazil (Fritz Goro *Life* Magazine)

124. **Sturgeon-like Seapoacher** (*Agonu acipenserinus*); marine; Alaska to Puge Sound (Karl W. Kenyon)

123. **Humuhumu-nukunuku-a-puaa Triggerfish** (*Rhinecanthus aculeatus*); marine; tropical Indo-Pacific (John Tashjian at Steinhart Aquarium)

125. **Longtail Filefish** (*Alutera scripta*); marine; world-wide in tropics (photographed at Seaquarium by Stan Wayman: Rapho Guillumette)

126. **Balloonfish** (*Diodon holacanthus*) marine world-wide in tropics, Massachusetts to Brazil (Ernest Libby at Marine Studios)

127. and 128. **Striped Burrfish** (*Chilomycterus schoepfi*); marine; Massachusetts to Rio de Janeiro (Photographed at Seaquarium by Stan Wayman: Rapho Guillumette)

129 and 130. Southern Puffer (*Sphaeroides nephelus*) before and after; marine; southeastern Florida and Gulf of Mexico (Ernest Libby at Marine Studios)

131. Checkered Puffer (*Sphaeroides testudineus*); marine; Rhode Island to Brazil (photographed at Seaquarium by Stan Wayman: Rapho Guillumette)

132. Four-saddle Puffer (*Can-thigaster cinctus*); marine; tropical Indo-Pacific (Gene Wolfs-heimer)

133. Cowfish (*Lactophrys quadricornis*); marine; both sides of the Atlantic, Massachusetts to Rio de Janeiro (photographed at Seaquarium by Stan Wayman: Rapho Guillumette)

134. Blue Trunkfish (*Ostracion lentiginosus*) immature; marine; tropical Indo-Pacific (John Tashjian at Steinhart Aquarium)

135. Blue Trunkfish (*Ostracion lentiginosus*) male; marine; tropical Indo-Pacific (Douglas Faulkner at Waikiki Aquarium)

136. Sea Moth (*Pegasus papilio*); marine; Hawaiian Islands (Douglas Faulkner at Waikiki Aquarium)

137. Spotted Trunkfish (*Ostracion tuberculatus*); marine; Indo-Pacific (Hans and Klaus Paysan at Wilhelma Aquarium, Stuttgart)

138. Peacock Flounder (*Bothus lunatus*); marine; Florida Keys to Brazil (photographed at Seaquarium by Stan Wayman: Rapho Guillumette)

139. Naked Sole (*Gymnachirus williamsoni*); marine; Georgia to Florida, northeastern and southwestern Gulf of Mexico (Ernest Libby at Marine Studios)

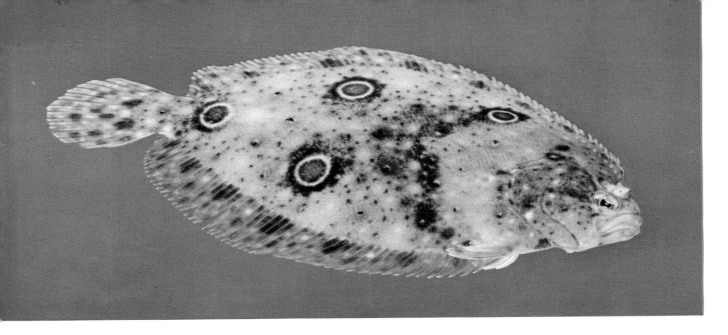

140. Ocellated Flounder (*Ancylopsetta quadrocellata*); marine; South Carolina to Florida and Gulf of Mexico (Ernest Libby at Marine Studios)

141. Torpedo Batfish (*Halieutaea retifera*); marine; deep water, Hawaiian Islands (Douglas Faulkner at Waikiki Aquarium)

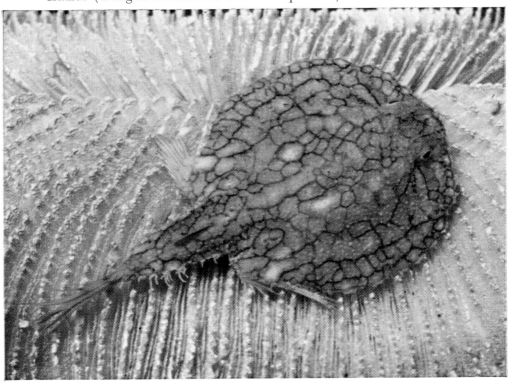

142. **Yellow Angler** (*Antennarius moluccensis*); marine; Hawaiian Islands (Douglas Faulkner at Waikiki Aquarium)

143. **Whiskery Frogfish** (*Antennarius scaber*); marine; New Jersey to Rio de Janeiro (Fritz Goro: *Life* Magazine)

144. Sargassum Angler (*Histrio histrio*); marine; Atlantic and western Pacific, in floating weed (Fritz Goro: *Life* Magazine)

145. Spiny Eel (*Mastacembelus armatus*); fresh water; India to Malaya and Sumatra (John Tashjian at Steinhart Aquarium)

[continued from page 256]

The application of the common name "sole" to some members of this family, such as the American Pacific fantail sole, *Xystreurys liolepis,* is a constant source of confusion because the only true soles are those belonging to another family, the Soleidae. The confusion is further compounded by the use of this name for some of the right-eyed flounders of the family Pleuronectidae.

The small sanddabs of the genus *Citharichthys* are well-known American Pacific left-eyed flounders and are usually listed on the menus of seafood restaurants. The Pacific sanddab, *C. sordidus,* is the most common species. It is a summer spawner and matures at a length of 8 inches, usually during the third year of life. It may live to be ten years old and to reach a length of 16 inches and a weight of two pounds. Also included among the fourteen species of *Citharichthys* is the horned whiff, *C. cornutus,* found from New England to Brazil. In this species the distance between the eyes of the male is twice that of the female.

The California halibut, *Paralichthys californicus,* is one of the larger commercial and sports flatfishes; it reaches a weight of sixty pounds and a length of 5 feet. Although it belongs to the left-eyed flatfish group, there are many individuals that are right-eyed. This species is most abundant in central and Lower California.

The ocellated flounders are a striking group of three American Atlantic species assigned to the genus *Ancylopsetta.* Two of the species have three large ocelli on the eyed side of the body, and the third one, the 10-inch *A. quadrocellata* (Plate 140), has four. The latter is a shallow-water form ranging from North Carolina through the Gulf of Mexico.

Perhaps the most peculiar bothid is the deep-water Hawaiian *Pelecanthichthys crumenalis,* a 10-inch, elongated flatfish with a greatly extended lower jaw, half of which extends beyond the end of the snout.

RIGHT-EYED FLOUNDERS
—Family Pleuronectidae

The story of the giant Pacific halibut, *Hippoglossus stenolepis,* is often cited as an example to show that careful biological study can be used to increase the yield of depleted fisheries. The International Fisheries Commission, composed of Canadians and Americans, through careful study of the Pacific halibut, was able to regulate this depleted fishery so that both the total catch and the yield to the individual fisherman were greatly increased.

Pacific halibut females may reach a weight of 470 pounds at an age of thirty-five years; they grow much faster than the somewhat puny males, which after twenty-five years weigh only 40 pounds. These fish are winter spawners; a 140-pound female lays as many as 2,700,000 eggs, which float in midwater between 900 and 1350 feet. After hatching, the larvae move to the surface and, as the eye migration progresses, drift shoreward, where they later settle to the bottom as young fish. With subsequent growth, they move into deep water. Pacific halibut are found all the way from northern California to northwestern Alaska, but the most productive grounds are from Washington northward.

Even larger than the Pacific halibut is its cousin the Atlantic halibut, *Hippoglossus hippoglossus,* reported to reach a weight of 700 pounds and an age of forty years. It occurs on both sides of the North Atlantic southward to the Bay of Biscay on the European side and to New York on the American side.

The right-eyed flounders are distinguished from the left-eyed flounders not only by the position of the eyes but also by their eggs: the oil globule that is conspicuously present in the egg yolk of the left-eyed flounders is lacking in that of the right-eyed.

Most of the pleuronectids are marine species living on coastal shelves. One exception is the North Pacific starry flounder, *Platichthys stellatus,* which is often found in the brackish water of estuaries and in some areas actually enters fresh water. In Japan, for example, it is found in certain lakes and rivers.

Extensive marking experiments as well as other studies have been carried out in the North Sea on the European plaice, *Pleuronectes platessa,* for this is one of the most important food fishes of that region. One of its principal spawning areas is the Flemish Bight; many of the mature plaice move southward toward this area during the months of January through March. After spawning, they move northward again. Juveniles live in the shallows along the coasts for the first year or two and then gradually move into deeper water. These fishes mature at a length of 7 to 15 inches, depending upon the locality, and may grow to a length of 33 inches. Plaice are marked with orange spots on the body and have bony knobs between the eyes.

The name "turbot" is applied to deep-bodied members of various genera of flatfishes. The 12-inch curlfin turbot, *Pleuronichthys decurrens,* is one of the most desirable of the American Pacific species. A related species in the same area, *P. coenosus,* is equally deep-bodied, and is known as the "C-O sole" because of a C-O mark on the side of the caudal peduncle.

SOLES—Family Soleidae

The term "filet of sole" was originally applied to the common European sole, *Solea solea,* but now is loosely used for any kind of fileted flatfish.

Plaice (*Pleuronectes platessa*); marine; western European coasts (Hans and Klaus Paysan).

In the true soles both eyes are on the right side of the head, and the preopercular margin of the gill cover is never free but is hidden by the skin and scales of the head. These fishes are ribless, and many of them are shaped like the naked sole, *Gymnachirus williamsoni* (Plate 139), one of the more attractive striped species of the American Atlantic coastal areas. Also included in this group is the 6-inch hogchoker, *Trinectes maculatus,* a marine species that is often found in fresh water and occurs from North Carolina to Panama. It has transverse lines across the body and, strangely enough, has a spotted pattern on the blind side.

TONGUE SOLES—Family Cynoglossidae

Eyes on the left side of the head, a pointed tail, and the absence of ribs are characteristics that readily identify the tongue soles. In some respects, these fishes resemble the true soles of the previous family, but true soles have the eyes on the right side of the head and have a small tail fin that is not pointed. The tongue soles are small, teardrop-shaped, inconspicuous species, usually less than 12 inches in length. A few of the larger species in Japan and other areas are used for food, but most members of the family are too small to be of value as market fishes.

Remoras or Suckerfishes

(*Order Discocephali*)

—Family Echeneidae

Shark fishermen sometimes receive an unexpected bonus in the form of small fishes known as remoras or shark suckers that are attached to the sharks by a sucking disk located on the top of the head. As the shark is pulled on board, the shark sucker will either drop off into the water or flop on the deck. Examination of the sucking disk reveals a series of ten to twenty-eight pairs of cross ridges, the number depending upon the species; each ridge is a modification of a spiny ray of the first dorsal fin. If one of these remoras is slapped against the bulkhead of the ship, it remains attached to it. To release the vacuum effect of the sucker, the remora usually slides forward; to increase the adhesive force, it slides backward. Native fishermen have actually used the remora with a line on its tail to catch larger fishes and sea turtles. Although remoras are most often found attached to sharks, they may use other kinds of animals as well as small boats and ships as attachment surfaces. They have even been found inside the gill cavities of large manta rays and ocean sunfish. This wide range of hosts is indicated by the photographs which show remoras attached to a sand shark, cobia, and marlin, respectively. There is one type, *Remilegia australis,* the whalesucker, that is usually found attached to whales of various species. Remoras have long been thought to feed by detaching themselves from their hosts and eating bits of food left by them, then returning to the same hosts or others. Recent investigations have shown that some remoras feed on parasitic crustaceans attached to the host; in this regard, they may function somewhat like the cleaner fishes described earlier.

The approximately eight species in the family have wide distributions through all tropical and temperate seas. The largest species is the striped 36-inch *Echeneis naucrates,* which uses sharks as hosts; the smallest species is the 7-inch *Remoropsis pallidus,* which prefers tuna and swordfish.

Triggerfishes, Puffers, Ocean Sunfishes, and Their Relatives

(*Order Plectognathi*)

Although the plectognaths probably descended from a surgeonfish-like ancestor, there is little in the external appearance of these peculiar fishes to indicate this relationship. All of them have small openings from the gill cavities and small mouths with strong teeth. A few have scales; others have bony plates, spines, or a leathery skin. These carnivorous fishes live in all tropical marine waters, and a few stray into cooler seas. A large number of these fishes have poisonous organs and flesh, but in spite of this, they are eaten regularly in some parts of the world, occasionally with fatal results. The seven best-known families will be discussed here.

TRIGGERFISHES—Family Balistidae

"Humuhumu-nukunuku-a-puaa" is a fish name well known to many who may not associate it with the 8-inch triggerfish, *Rhinecanthus aculeatus* (Plate 123). Actually, the name is also applied to another species very similar to this, *R. rectangularis,* which has a broad triangular black mark on each side of the caudal peduncle. The two humus do not get along well together, and one usually shows its displeasure with the other species by seizing it by the pectoral fin and dragging it all over the tank.

As a group, the bony-scaled triggers have very attractive patterns; this is well demonstrated in Plates 119 through 123. Similarity of body profile among the triggers is an asset in group identification; recognition of one trigger makes it easy to identify others. Triggers have an outer series of eight teeth in each jaw as well as an inner series of six platelike teeth in the upper jaw. The pelvic fins are lacking, but a pelvic or ventral spine is usually present.

Triggers receive their name from the locking mechanism of the first and second dorsal fin spines. When the long first dorsal spine is erected, the second, which is very small, moves forward and locks the first into upright position. A frightened triggerfish reacts by diving into a coral head and erecting the spine, thus insuring its safety from predators or ichthyological collectors, who cannot remove the fish without breaking down the coral. The small second trigger spine must be released before the large first spine can be depressed.

Triggers are shallow-water, tropical marine species, usually solitary and slow-moving in their habits. Some are noise makers; when removed from the water, they make a grunting sound that is produced by the air bladder. None of the thirty species exceeds about 2 feet in length.

Sole (*Solea solea*); marine; western European coasts from latitude of Scotland southward (Hans and Klaus Paysan).

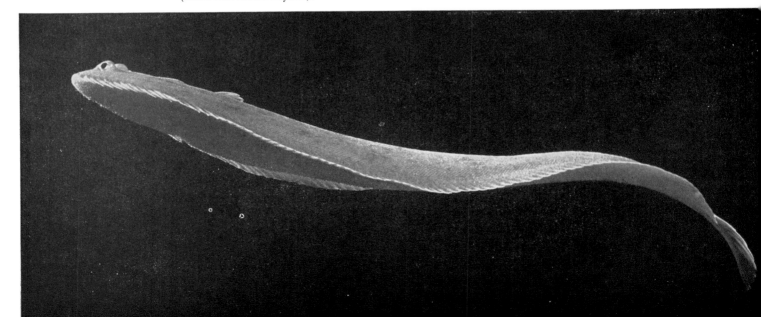

Red-tooth Triggerfish (*Odonus niger*); marine; tropical into Pacific (Wilhelm Hoppe).

FILEFISHES—*Family Monacanthidae*

The tropical marine filefishes resemble the triggers but have much narrower bodies. The first dorsal spine is placed farther forward, usually over the eyes, whereas in the trigger it is posterior to the eyes. The files receive their name from the filelike, sometimes velvety, nature of the scales. The ventral fins are lacking. Between the chin and the anal fin there is a well-developed, usually distensible, pelvic flap that looks like a dewlap.

Many of the filefishes are full grown at a length of 5 to 10 inches, but the longtail filefish, *Alutera scripta* (Plate 125), the largest species in the family, may reach a length of 40 inches. All of these fishes have very small mouths. The longtail, if placed in an

Filefish (*Amanses fronticinctus*); marine; east African coast (Wilhelm Hoppe).

aquarium tank with other tropical reef fishes, will usually starve to death unless given special feeding attention. Its mouth is so small, like that of many other filefishes, that it requires very small food and a long time to feed.

PUFFERS—*Family Tetraodontidae*

When a puffer is pulled from the water, it immediately reacts by swallowing air so that it quickly blows up like a balloon. An expanded puffer thrown back into the water floats upside down for several minutes or sometimes much longer before it is able to expel the air and return to its normal swimming position. The fish's appearance before and after swallowing air is well shown by the southern puffer, *Sphaeroides nephelus,* in Plates 129 and 130. It should be noted that puffers can also swallow water in the same way they swallow air.

The mouth of the checkered puffer, *S. testudineus* (Plate 131), shows the very sharp, incisor-like beak with its division in the center. This division is one of the principal differences between the puffers and the porcupine fishes, which have a solid beak with fused teeth. The puffers form a large group of about ninety species of carnivorous fishes found throughout all warm and most temperate seas. Their maximum size is 36 inches, but the majority of the species are fully grown at less than 18 inches.

In spite of the fact that the organs and sometimes the flesh of many puffers contain a deadly poison, tetrodotoxin (which has important medical uses), these fishes are eaten with great relish in some parts of the world, especially in Japan. In order to cook fugu, which may be prepared from several species of Japanese puffers, a cook is required to have a certificate of graduation from a licensed fugu school. Food poisoning as a result of eating improperly prepared puffers is fatal in 60 per cent of the cases.

SHARP-NOSED PUFFERS
—*Family Canthigasteridae*

Characteristic of the members of this family is a nose that is narrow, somewhat sharp, and quite long, with nostrils that are very inconspicuous. The body is slightly compressed, and the external gill openings are very small—about one-half the length of the pectoral fin base. All of these features distinguish the small sharp-nosed puffers from the previous family of common puffers. In appearance, the four-saddle puffer, *Canthigaster cinctus* (Plate 132), is typical of the dozen species in this family, all of which are found in tropical seas around the world.

Head-on view of Longtail Filefish (*Alutera scripta*) marine; world-wide in tropics (Fritz Goro: *Life* Magazine at Lerner Marine Laboratory, Bimini).

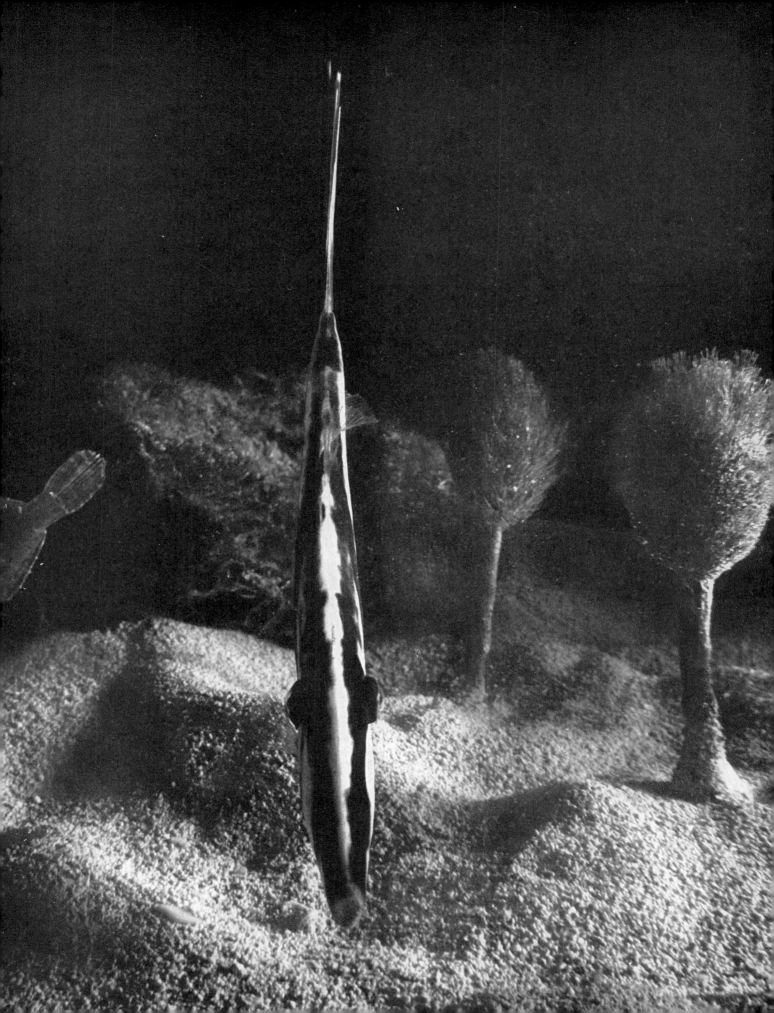

These fishes have a maximum length of about 5 inches; because of their small size, they are popular with tropical fish hobbyists.

PORCUPINE FISHES and BURRFISHES
—Family Diodontidae

A newcomer making his first trip through Chinatown usually stops to admire one of the large, conspicuous balloon lamps covered with spines. Close examination shows that it is the dried outside skin of a porcupine fish with a light bulb placed inside. The porcupine fish is, actually, a puffer with spines added to the outside of the body. The species with large spines hold them in against the body while swimming, and it is only when they begin to swallow air or water that the spines are fully evident (Plate 126). The small burrfishes, sometimes called spiny boxfishes, of the genus *Chilomycterus* (Plates 127 and 128) have short spines that are immovable and always extended. About fifteen kinds of porcupine fishes and burrfishes are known from the tropical marine waters of the world.

Northern Puffers (*Sphaeroides maculatus*); marine; Nova Scotia to Florida and the northern Gulf of Mexico (Roy Pinney).

TRUNKFISHES—Family Ostraciontidae

A trunkfish, sometimes called cowfish or boxfish, may aptly be described as a solid bony box with holes for the mouth, eyes, fins, and vent. Plates 133 through 135 and 137 show the characteristic shapes and beautiful patterns of members of this family. Identification is sometimes complicated by the fact that the males and females of a single species have different color patterns. For example, the females as well as the immature individuals of both sexes of the Indo-Pacific blue trunkfish, *Ostracion lentiginosus,* have the polkadot appearance of the big-eyed, shy fish shown in Plate 134, but the adult males look entirely different, as shown by Plate 135.

In the Hawaiian Islands, Vernon Brock recently showed that these fishes, when handled, discharge a toxin that kills other fishes kept in the same container. The water retains the unknown toxin even after all fishes are removed.

Generic identification of the trunkfishes is based on the contours of the exoskeleton—whether it has three, four, or five angles, and whether there are spines over the eyes. Most species are small, 20 inches being the maximum length attained. Although the adults contain toxins, they are roasted like chestnuts and eaten by some island people of the Pacific.

OCEAN SUNFISHES—Family Molidae

The ocean sunfish looks like a giant puffer that has had the posterior half of its vertically compressed body chopped off just behind the long dorsal and anal fins. There is a tail fin at the end of the truncated body, but one must look carefully to see it. The pelvic bones and pelvic fins are lacking. The larval ocean sunfish has a number of spiny projections and does not even slightly resemble the adult. It swims like a normal fish—that is, vertically—and the fast-moving juveniles also swim this way. As they grow older, they spend a great amount of time on their sides, lazily flapping the elongated dorsal or anal fin out of the water. A full-grown common ocean sunfish, *Mola mola,* may measure 11 feet in length and may weigh as much as two thousand pounds. The 30-inch *Ranzania typus* is similar in appearance to the common ocean sunfish but has a more elongated body. The point-tailed sunfish, *Masturus lanceolatus,* is another giant 11-foot species. These three species, which make up the entire family, are members of the offshore tropical and temperate marine faunas of the world but are never common. They are not considered edible. In captivity they do not survive for long since they have a tendency to swim against a wall and then blindly continue to drive against it. Feeding is not a prob-

Expanded Balloonfish or Porcupine Fish (*Diodon holacanthus*) Fritz Goro: *Life* Magazine.

Spawning pair of Balloonfish or Porcupine Fish (*Diodon holacanthus*); marine; world-wide in tropical and subtropical waters (Gene Wolfsheimer).

lem. They automatically siphon in squid, clams, or other food placed in front of the mouth.

Ragfishes (Order Malacichthys)

—Family Icosteidae

A ragfish when dropped on the floor acts just like a rag—it seems to be entirely boneless. This amazing flexibility is partially accounted for by the large amount of cartilage in the skeleton. Little is known about the biology of these aberrant deep-sea fishes of the North Pacific. Only two species have been discovered. The 18-inch fantail ragfish, *Icosteus aenigmaticus,* has a deep, laterally compressed body that lacks scales, but it does have small spines along the lateral line and covering the fins. The 7-foot brown ragfish, *Acrotus willoughbyi,* lacks the spines, scales, and pelvic fins, and has a more elliptical body than the fantail. The brown ragfish is sometimes found in the stomachs of sperm whales.

Clingfishes (Order Xenopterygii)

—Family Gobiesocidae

A large adhesive sucker under the forward part of the body enables the clingfish to maintain its position of attachment to rocks and seaweed in shallow water, usually in the intertidal zone. The anterior part of the sucker is formed from the ventral or pelvic fins; the posterior part is a fold of skin. Externally, the clingfishes resemble the gobies, but they have only a single dorsal fin without spines, whereas the gobies have a double dorsal fin, the first dorsal composed of spines. All of the gobiesocids are small and have very broad heads that taper off to slender bodies. They are chiefly a tropical and temperate marine group with a few species occurring in the fresh-water streams of Panama and the Galapagos Islands.

Many of the clingfishes, of which there are about one hundred species, are full grown at a length of less than 3 inches. The 6-inch northern clingfish, *Gobiesox maeandricus,* which ranges from California to Alaska, is one of the larger species. Probably the largest is the South African rocksucker, *Chorisochismus dentex.* So firmly can this fish hold onto a rock that when it is hooked, the fishing line will snap before the fish's hold is broken.

Toadfishes and Midshipmen (Order Haplodoci)

—Family Batrachoididae

Toadfishes are slow-moving, bottom-dwelling fishes with large mouths well equipped with many sharp teeth. The heavy, broad head is depressed anteriorly and tapers to a long, slender tail. The small spinous first dorsal with two to four spines is followed by a long soft-rayed dorsal fin. In all members of the family the spines of the first dorsal are solid except in the genera *Thalassophryne* and *Thalassothia.* The pelvic or ventral fins are placed under the throat ahead of the fanlike pectoral fins. Only three pairs of gills are present. The toadfishes are found from shallow to deep water in temperate and tropical seas, and a few occur in brackish and fresh water. About thirty species are known.

The bagre sapo or *Thalassophryne* and *Thalossothia* toadfishes of the tropical American coasts possess an extremely efficient venom-injection apparatus similar to the fangs of rattlesnakes. They have two large dorsal fin spines and a spine at the upper edge of each gill cover; each of these spines is hollow and has at its base a poison gland. Fortunately the toxin produced by these glands is not sufficiently virulent to cause death, but it can produce a painful wound. Since toadfishes hide in shallow areas among debris, a person wading in such an area should be especially careful not to step on one.

A number of these fishes make migrations from deep to very shallow water and later return; these migrations are often correlated with spawning activities. They are able to live out of water, sometimes for several hours, and can live in oxygen-deficient water that would be lethal to most other fishes. Most toadfishes and midshipmen make some sort of sound, usually grunts or raucous growls or a single boat-whistle blast. The sound is usually produced by the air bladder.

The Oyster toadfish, *Opsanus tau,* is a shallow-water 10-inch fish common along many sections of the coast from Maine to Florida; there are similar species in the Gulf of Mexico. Toadfishes are very belligerent and quick to bite, especially during the breeding season of June through July. Their eggs are laid inside old tin cans, shoes, or other debris where the toadfishes naturally seem to congregate. The male guards the eggs for ten to twenty-six days until they hatch.

The midshipmen of the genus *Porichthys* have 600 to 840 small light organs under the body. The light organs are arranged in definite patterns that are useful in species identification. Experimentally, the lights can be made to glow brightly enough for one to read a newspaper ten inches away. Although toadfishes usually do well in captivity, midshipmen often refuse all food and eventually die of starvation. The 15-inch northern midshipman, *P. notatus,* is the common species on the American Pacific coast; its counterpart on the east coast is the 8-inch Atlantic midshipman, *P. porosissimus.*

Oyster Toadfish (*Opsanus tau*); marine, shallow water; Maine to Florida (New York Zoological Society).

Anglerfishes *(Order Pediculati)*

A lure at the end of a movable fishing pole suspended over the mouth is one of the distinctions of many of the anglerfishes, a group of three suborders and sixteen families that are chiefly deep-sea forms. The fishing pole is the modified first spiny ray of the dorsal fin. These fishes move very slowly, but when live food in the form of a smaller fish is in the area, they can gulp or siphon it into the mouth with such speed that the human eye cannot follow its movement. The gills are reduced in number, and the small circular gill opening is behind the broad pectoral fin. "Pediculati" means "small foot" and is a descriptive term for the elbowed pectoral fins as well as the footlike ventrals. The pelvic or ventral fins, when present, are ahead of the pectorals. More than 225 species of anglerfishes are known.

GOOSEFISHES or MONKFISHES
—Family Lophiidae

These repulsive fishes are among the largest of the anglers, some reaching a length of 4 feet and a weight of forty-five pounds, and there is a record of one that weighed seventy pounds. In spite of their ugly appearance, their meat is quite excellent and they are marketed as food in Europe, Japan, and other areas. The goosefish spends its time on the bottom, often camouflaged against its background. It is an odd-shaped fish: the width of the huge, flattened head is equal to about two-thirds the length of the fish. The mouth is almost as wide as the head and is armed with a battery of wicked-looking teeth. A fringe of small flaps extends around the lower jaw and along the sides of the head onto the body.

The fishing pole, modified from the first of six dorsal fin spines, has at its tip a flap of flesh that acts like a flag as the goosefish whips it back and forth in front of the mouth. The goosefish is apparently very successful at stalking its prey, for the food in the crammed stomach may weigh as much as one-third of the total weight of the fish. Anything that moves is fair prey, including sea birds, small sharks, all kinds of fishes, and crabs.

Spawning takes place during the spring and summer. The eggs, which float at the surface, are embedded in a sticky, jelly-like mass that may measure forty feet in length and two feet in width. The strange-looking larval fishes have extremely long ventral fins, which diminish in size as the fish grows.

Goosefishes and monkfishes are found in all tropical and temperate marine waters of the world. About a dozen species are recognized. On the American Atlantic coast *Lophius americanus* occurs from Newfoundland to Brazil, in shallow water in the north and in deep water in equatorial areas. Its counterpart in European and African waters is the monkfish, *L. piscatorius*.

FROGFISHES—Family Antennariidae

On some frogfishes, such as the American Atlantic whiskery or split-lure frogfish, *Antennarius scaber* (Plate 143), and the sargassum angler, *Histrio histrio* (Plate 144), the fishing pole is well developed and is used to great advantage. But, on the Pacific yellow angler, *Antennarius moluccensis* (Plate 142), it is slender, wirelike, without a lure, and seems to be totally ineffective although it is still waved back and forth as is characteristic of most members of the family.

Frogfishes are capable of slow color changes; for example, the 12-inch yellow angler has a brick-red color phase. In the aquarium it has been observed to go from one phase to the other in a period of a month. The sargassum angler can make slight changes in its color pattern to match its background, but seems to be limited to those shades found in the sargassum weed. This species, which grows as large as 7½ inches, is pelagic in habitat. It is found wherever sargassum floats in the tropical oceans of the world. The pectoral fins of this fish are remarkable because of their prehensile ability; they actually clasp the sargassum as *Histrio* moves slowly through the drifting weed. The other fifty-seven species in the family are more sedentary; they usually spend their time sitting on the bottom waiting for food to swim by, then wave their lures to attract it. Many do move, but very slowly, toward food that is also slow-moving.

The carnivorous frogfishes have balloon-shaped bodies covered with loose skin that is usually roughened by many small denticles. The females extrude their eggs in the form of a long, ribbon-like mass that floats at the surface. Frogfishes are found around the world in all tropical and temperate seas.

BATFISHES—Family Ogcocephalidae

The comical batfish waddles across the bottom on its large armlike pectoral and small leglike ventral fins as though it were an armored tank. It occasionally gets up off the bottom and swims awkwardly as if it were entirely unaccustomed to this method of progression. The bat's fishing pole is hidden in a small tube just above the mouth, and whenever the batfish is angling—which is whenever it is hungry—the piston-like fishing pole is pushed out of the tube and is usually rotated so that the small, hinged, lumplike lure at the tip is vibrated to either the right or the left, depending upon the individual fish. In the aquarium some batfishes always vibrate the lure to the right and others vibrate it to the left.

The thirty or so species of batfishes are flat-bodied, scaleless marine forms living in tropical and temperate waters. The largest are about 14 inches in length, but most of them are less than half that size. Although the family is primarily a deep-water one, there are a number of shallow-water species, such as the American Atlantic shortnose batfish, *Ogcocephalus nasutus,* and the longnose batfish, *O. vespertilio.* Typical of the moderate-depth species is the attractive 2-inch torpedo batfish, *Halieutaea retifera* (Plate 141), from the Hawaiian Islands.

Deep-sea Anglers

(Suborder Ceratioidea)

Eleven families of fishes are represented in this deep-sea group of about 120 species, all of which

Mottled Angler (*Antennarius oligospilos*); marine; tropical Indo-Pacific (Wilhelm Hoppe).

differ from the other anglers by the absence of the ventral fins. Whereas the other anglers live on the bottom from shallow to deep water or, in a few cases, at the surface, the deep-sea ceratioid anglers are mostly midwater forms, ranging in depth from perhaps one thousand to several thousand feet. Only the females have fishing poles. Since in the depths it would be difficult to see the lure, the tip is usually equipped with a light-producing organ of some kind. It is not known for certain how this light is produced; one suggestion is that luminescent bacteria are responsible.

Four families of the deep-sea anglers demonstrate a most surprising biological phenomenon: the males are parasitic on the females. These males never grow very large and at an early age attach themselves by their mouths to the much larger females and become permanently anchored, their circulation fusing with that of the female. Thus the male becomes nothing but a sperm-producing appendage.

Spiny Eels (Order Opisthomi)

—Family Mastacembelidae

The spiny eels form a strange group of some fifty species of eel-like fresh-water fishes ranging throughout Africa and Asia. They are not related to the true eels, and because of their anatomical peculiarities they are given a separate order by themselves. The reason for this is apparent upon examination of Plate 145 (*Mastacembelus armatus*), which shows the characteristic elongated shape that is the mark of all masticembelids. The snout is very sensitive and is supported by a special cartilage; at the end of the snout are the tubular anterior nostrils, which together with the snout form a trilobed appendage; the posterior nostrils are located farther back on the head, near the eyes. The name "spiny" comes from a series of seven to forty detached, depressible spines preceding the soft dorsal fin. Some of the spiny eels have the disagreeable habit, when picked up, of wriggling backward, thus spiking the unsuspecting fisherman with the suddenly erected spines. Following the spiny portion of the dorsal is a very long portion with as many as ninety soft rays. The anal fin also has a large number of rays and is preceded by one to three spines. The tail fin is continuous with the dorsal and anal fins in all African species but is separate in a few Oriental species. The ventral fins are absent.

The genus *Mastacembelus* contains all the species in the family with the exception of the elephant trunk fish, *Macrognathus aculeatus*. This species can be identified by its extremely long, mobile, and

Deep-sea Angler (*Melanocetus* sp.), with pencil holding up the "fishing pole"; marine, deep water; Atlantic and Pacific (*San Francisco Chronicle* photo from Galathea Expedition, 1950–1952).

prehensile snout. On its undersurface, as contrasted with *Mastacembelus*, is a series of twenty to twenty-six paired, toothed plates which are an extension of the premaxillary bone. Like many of the spiny eels, the elephant trunk fish is nocturnal and in the daytime hides in the mud with only the tips of the nostrils protruding. Burrowing is accomplished by a rocking and forward-wriggling motion which submerges the entire body at a uniform rate.

Many of the spiny eels are air breathers and can survive in mud and oxygen-deficient water for an indefinite time; although tests have shown that some species will drown if prevented from reaching the surface, authorities are not in agreement on the validity of these experiments.

The largest spiny eel, *Mastacembelus armatus* (Plate 145), reaches a length of 3 feet, but most of the others are less than 15 inches long when full grown. In some regions they are an accepted part of the human diet, but in others, such as in Punjab and Sind, they are considered unfit for human consumption merely because of their snakelike appearance.

Swamp Eels (Order Synbranchii)

—Family Synbranchidae

Although called "eels" because of their appearance, the synbranchids are not true eels; they are air-

hortnose Batfish (*Ogcocephalus nasutus*) with "fishing pole" retracted in tube between eyes; marine, inshore; Gulf of Mexico to Bahia, Brazil (Fritz Goro: *Life* Magazine at Lerner Marine Laboratory, Bimini).

[285

breathing fishes the exact affinities of which are still in dispute. They lack the paired fins—that is, the pelvic and pectoral fins—and the dorsal and anal fins are reduced to a ridge. About eight species of swamp eels are recognized. They are found in tropical fresh and brackish waters of Africa, Asia, the Indo-Australian Archipelago and from Mexico to South America; there is one marine species.

The 2½-foot rice eel, *Monopterus albus,* occurs in fresh water throughout southeast Asia, the Philippines, and Indonesia. In many areas it is used as food. In recent years it has been introduced in the Hawaiian Islands and has become established there. Like the lungfish, the rice eel is able to survive in deep mud pockets during the dry season when the water in the ponds dries up. It has three rudimentary gills, and the two very small gill openings are located under the throat. These gills are inadequate, and most of the respiration is carried on by the membranes in the throat. Rice eels usually spawn during the summer months, and one, or perhaps both, of the parents builds a bubble nest in which the eggs float at the surface.

Other synbranchid eels have different gill ar-

rangements. For instance, *Synbranchus marmoratus,* a 3- to 5-foot species of Middle and South America, has four well-developed gills and a single gill opening under the head.

The only marine synbranchid is the 8-inch *Macrotrema caligans* of the Malay Peninsula. It has four well-developed gills, and the gill openings are of normal size but are continuous with each other under the throat.

The cuchia, *Amphipnous cuchia,* of India and Burma is usually placed in a family by itself because of the two separate lunglike air sacs that connect with the gill cavity.

Lobe-finned Coelacanths

(*Order Actinistia*)

The day was December 22, 1938; the place, the Indian Ocean three miles off the Chalumna River near East London, South Africa; the depth, thirty-seven fathoms. A trawler was routinely dragging its net over the bottom in an area seldom fished by commercial gear. When the net was pulled aboard, there,

Polkadot Batfish (*Ogcocephalus radiata*) with "fishing pole" extended; marine, inshore; North Carolina to Santos, Brazil (Fritz Goro: *Life* Magazine, at Lerner Marine Laboratory, Bimini).

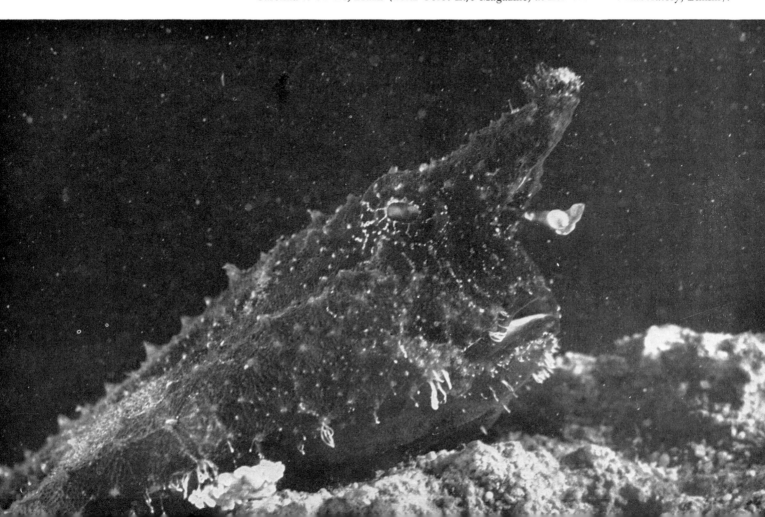

Young male Coelacanth (*Latimeria chalumnae*); marine, moderate depths; east coast of Africa from Madagascar southward (J. Millot).

flopping on the deck in the midst of a three-and-one-half ton catch, was a weird-looking fish that no zoologist had ever seen. It was about 5 feet long and weighed some 127 pounds. Obviously it was a very hardy fish, for it lay on the deck for another three hours before it expired. The skipper was curious as to what it could be and decided to save it for the East London Museum.

That fish was the now-famous coelacanth, later named *Latimeria chalumnae* Smith. Fishes of this kind had supposedly become extinct at least sixty million years ago. Although paleontologists had long known the coelacanths from fossil records, no one had ever expected to see one alive. Even today, zoology has not fully recovered from the impact of this remarkable discovery. Its importance is indicated by the fact that at one time, some 320 million years ago, one of these early forms, named *Eusthenopteron,* was undoubtedly the ancestor not only of all the present-day amphibians, reptiles, birds, and mammals, but was also the direct ancestor of the later coelacanths like *Latimeria*. Here, then, was a marvelous opportunity to unravel some of the past and to learn whether the paleontologist's interpretation of the fossil coelacanths was accurate or needed modification.

The first *Latimeria* had been made into a taxidermist's mount and the internal organs discarded before Professor J. L. B. Smith had an opportunity to study them. The external anatomy provided preliminary answers to many questions, but knowledge of the internal anatomy was still needed to complete the picture.

Obtaining another specimen was not an easy matter. For fourteen years the world waited for the next catch to be made. During all of this time Professor Smith blanketed the coast of South Africa with reward circulars describing the strange fish and giving instructions concerning what should be done if one were caught. On December 20, 1952, the long-awaited telegram arrived. It came from Anjouan, one of the Comorro Island group in the north end of the Mozambique Channel between Madagascar and Mozambique. This was some nineteen hundred miles north of the East London site of the first capture. The Prime Minister of South Africa made his personal plane available for an emergency flight to obtain this all-important second coelacanth. This specimen lacked the first dorsal fin as well as the middle tail fin. Consequently, it was described as a new coelacanth, *Malania anjouanae*. Study of later specimens, however, suggested that these characteristics were undoubtedly aberrations and that *Malania* was in all probability the same species as *Latimeria*. Unfortunately, the internal organs of *Malania* were poorly preserved, and many questions still remained unanswered.

The third coelacanth was caught nine months later, September 24, 1953, also in the Comorro Island area. Since that time a number of others have been taken in the same region. However, until the eighth specimen was taken, all of the coelacanths brought in had been so severely battered and beaten by the fishermen that they could not be kept alive for biological observations. In order to obtain a specimen that could survive long enough for such study, the Institute of Scientific Research of Madagascar, through its Director, Professor J. Millot, offered a double reward to anyone who could bring in a live, uninjured coelacanth. As a result, the eighth specimen, a 56-inch, ninety-pound female, was successfully brought ashore and kept alive for seventeen and a half hours within the sunken hull of a twenty-two-foot whale boat. Observations made on the living fish confirmed the suspected extreme mobility of the leglike fins, for they seemed to be able to move in all directions with ease. The death of the fish was thought to have been caused by a combination of decompression and exposure to warm water. In this area there is a marked difference in temperature between the surface water and the water at a depth of 840 feet, where the eighth coelacanth was caught.

It was rather deflating to scientists to learn that *Latimeria*, the greatest zoological discovery of the century, has long been known to the Comorro Islanders under the native name of "kombessa." As a food fish they do not consider it particularly good unless dried and salted. They even use the rough surface of the kombessa scales as an abrasive in the repair of tubes and bicycle tires.

From our newly acquired knowledge of *Latimeria* we have learned that it is a deep-water, strong, heavy-bodied, carnivorous fish with a maximum weight of about 160 pounds. The pectoral and pelvic fins are modified into stalked flippers which undoubtedly allow the coelacanth to creep or walk over the bottom and pounce upon its food. It has (1) a large, elongate, pseudo-lung filled with fat, and (2) an almost linear heart, (3) a sharklike intestine with a spiral valve, (4) a hypophysis or pituitary still connected to the roof of the mouth (most vertebrates show this only during embryonic life), and (5) an axial skeleton that is nothing more than a hollow tube of cartilage. The fin spines are also hollow cartilage. It is from these hollow fin spines that this group of fishes derives its name: the word "coelacanth" means "hollow spine." The color of the freshly caught fish varies from brown to dark blue. It is an extremely mucilaginous species, for not only do the scales exude mucus but the body also contains a great amount of oil which oozes out continually.

Most of the coelacanths have been caught with oil-fish (*Ruvettus*) bait on very rocky and inclined bottom at depths between seventy-five and two hundred fathoms. The two records for shallow water include the East London specimen, taken at thirty-seven to forty fathoms, and an underwater photograph made in the Comorro Islands by an Italian skin diver working in less than fifty feet of water. The photograph appeared in a popular Italian volume on the expedition. The authenticity of this shallow-water record based upon the photograph has been questioned.

It is interesting to speculate on the fact that the two oldest kinds of living fishes occupy adjacent areas. The coelacanths have always been predominantly marine in habitat, while the lungfishes have lived in fresh water. Today we find *Latimeria* in the coastal region of southeastern Africa and lungfishes in central Africa. Could their ancestors have had the same distributional relationship in the Africa of 350 million years ago? Since the African lungfishes have evolved into four distinct species, is it plausible to expect that several species of coelacanths may eventually be discovered? Zoologists look hopefully to the future for the answers to many questions of this kind.

Lungfishes (*Order Dipneusti*)

Only one species of fish is known to be able to survive out of water for as long as four years: the African lungfish, *Protopterus annectens*. To find out how the lungfish came to have this amazing ability, it is necessary to go back three hundred million years to Devonian time—an era known to the geologist as the golden age of fishes, for they were then the predominant types of animal life. Most of the world was covered by water that teemed with vast schools of fishes. Down through the years the waters gradually subsided and a number of regions that were formerly supplied abundantly came to have water only during the wet seasons of the year. Many kinds of fishes, not able to adapt themselves to the changing environment, became extinct. The lungfishes, however, evolved a most successful way of survival: as the waters receded, they merely went into a dormant state, forming a tough, desiccation-proof cocoon around the body. Remaining in a torpid condition, they estivated until the rains came.

Although most of the early fishes disappeared, there were others that evolved into new forms. Today only two groups remain of that great prehistoric assemblage: the lungfishes and the coelacanth. From the early fossils we know that these two groups of present-day fishes are surprisingly like their ancestors. Whereas evolution has taken place at a normal rate among many kinds of fishes, little change is shown by the surviving members of these two primitive groups.

A number of species of fossil lungfishes have been described from geological formations all over the world. Six living species are known today: one in Australia (family Ceratodontidae), one in South America (family Lepidosirenidae), and four in Africa (family Protopteridae). Although the usual maximum size for all species of lungfishes is between 2 and 3½ feet, there are a few records of much larger fish. The Australian lungfish has been recorded

African Lungfish (*Protopterus annectens*); fresh water; central and western Africa (*San Francisco Chronicle*).

at 6 feet and one hundred pounds; and a specimen of the African lungfish *Protopterus aethiopicus,* caught in Lake Victoria, measured 7 feet.

The Australian lungfish, *Neoceratodus forsteri,* is in many respects the most primitive species. It has large scales, flipper-like paired fins, and a fishlike body. It does not estivate in a mud tube or chamber and has only one lung. In well-oxygenated water it does not need to come to the surface for air. In the aquarium it is a docile, seemingly phlegmatic species until it finds itself caught in a net; then the rugged strength of the brute becomes apparent. In captivity it does well with other fishes, having none of the pugnacious characteristics of its African relatives. In its original distribution it was limited to the Burnett and Mary rivers of northeast Australia, but has since been successfully transplanted to a number of lakes and reservoirs in Queensland.

The South American and African lungfishes have small embedded scales, filamentous paired fins, and tubular eel-like bodies. They have two lungs, and are as much alike in appearance as they are unlike the Australian species. When necessary, they estivate in mud tunnels (South American) or mud balls (African), and must have air to survive. If held under the water, they drown. One of the principal anatomical differences between the African and the

South American species is that the former has six gill arches and five gill clefts, whereas the latter has one less of each—that is, five arches and four clefts. The South American lungfish, *Lepidosiren paradoxa,* is a slender and docile species that lives fairly well in captivity among other fishes. On the other hand, the African species are known for their ferocious dispositions. Not only do they kill their own kind, but they wreak mayhem upon most other fishes. Occasionally young African lungfishes can be kept together in an aquarium, but sooner or later one will neatly remove the fins and many of the scales from the other. Fortunately, they regenerate injured parts with great rapidity.

African lungfishes survive nicely in the foulest mud imaginable. It is therefore interesting to note that the New York Aquarium staff found that *Protopterus* could not live in New York City drinking water even though it had been dechlorinated, but that it could live very satisfactorily in the same water if it were distilled!

Although the Australian, South American, and African lungfishes are easily distinguished from each other by appearance alone, the four African species are so similar that careful study is necessary to segregate them. *Protopterus amphibius,* from East Africa, is much darker than the others. The mem-

Young African Lungfish (*Protopterus annectens*) with larval gill filaments; fresh water; central and western Africa (New York Zoological Society).

branes attached to the pectoral and pelvic fins are wider than those of the other species; it retains the three larval gills longer in the adult stage (up to 15 inches); and it has the smallest number of ribs (twenty-seven to twenty-nine). The common *P. annectens,* which is widely distributed throughout West Africa, is often confused with *P. amphibius.* The former is typically gray in color with black

markings, whereas the latter is very dark. The rib count of thirty-three to thirty-seven provides fairly accurate identification of *P. annectens*. *P. aethiopicus* is found in the Nile, the Congo, and in the large lakes, but does not occur in West Africa. It has an increased number of ribs (thirty-seven to forty-one), and loses the external gills at the smallest size (shorter than 6 inches). *P. dolloi,* which is found in the Congo and Ogooué River areas, has the greatest number of ribs of any African lungfish (forty-seven to fifty-four), and as might be expected, is the most slender species. Of the four African species, it most closely resembles its cousin, the South American lungfish.

Some zoogeographers have used the close relationship between the African and the South American lungfishes as important supporting evidence of the suspected existence of an early land connection between Africa and South America.

It is not difficult to induce an African lungfish to form a cocoon and go into estivation. However, if the mud is not suitable, the lungfish will not perform satisfactorily. A pure mud without organic debris is not acceptable. Addition of aquatic plants, grasses, fibers, and organic detritus usually provides an adequate conglomerate. The sides of the container should have a precoated hard mud covering, since an encystment against glass or nonmud surface invariably results in the death of the lungfish. The African lungfish always encysts with the head upward and the tail bent forward covering the eyes. Without this eye protection, the lungfish usually does not survive the mud-ball stage.

While in the cocoon, the lungfish must carry on all normal body activities: it must breathe, have nourishment, and excrete wastes. The breathing may well be the least difficult part. The lungfish secretes around its body a mucous cocoon that quickly hardens and becomes leathery. The only opening through the cocoon is a small one into the mouth. Since the lungfish is oriented vertically, the mouth is close to the narrow breathing tunnel or tunnels leading to the surface. One of the remarkable facts about the encystment stage is that the lungfish does not use its stored fat for nourishment as do other animals during hibernation or estivation. Instead, it absorbs its muscle tissue. For example, a fish remaining encysted for six months dropped in weight from 13.2 ounces to 10.2 ounces and in length from 16 inches to 14⅜ inches. One month after coming out of the cocoon, it had gained back all of the lost weight and length. In one additional month it grew to 14.6 ounces and 16¾ inches. Thus, in six months the loss was 16½ per cent in weight and 9 per cent in length. Upon coming out of the mud ball, the gain in two months was 32½ per cent in weight and 13 per cent in length. It has been postulated that over a long period of estivation, the lungfish might lose one-half of its entire weight due to this muscle absorption.

During the cocoon stage the lungfish faces a serious problem in the storage of waste products. This problem is solved in a most ingenious manner. The kidney separates the urea from the water and allows the water to be used over and over again in the slow metabolism of the encysted fish. In most vertebrates the presence of 10 parts per million of urea results in a fatal toxemia, but in the remarkable lungfish the concentration may climb as high as 20,000 parts per million without ill effects. In a matter of hours after coming out of the mud ball, the concentration of urea drops back to normal.

The mud-ball cocoon can be useful and convenient as a means of shipping African lungfishes. However, great care must be taken in handling the mud ball since it is quite fragile. Several years ago the Steinhart Aquarium received a shipment of this kind from Nigeria. Eagerly opening the container, we were aghast to find that it had apparently been dropped repeatedly, for there were only broken bits of lungfish and pieces of cocoon in the container. Sadly we discarded $158 worth of Nigerian mud, only to learn too late that it should have been saved for its analgesic effect upon sick lungfishes.

A comparison of the spawning and nesting activities shows a primitive pattern for the Australian lungfish and a more complex one for the South American and African species. The Australian form merely lays its eggs among aquatic plants and then forgets about them. In contrast to this, both the South American and the African species build simple nests by digging a cave or tunnel into a mud bank or mud bottom. When the cavity is completed, the female deposits as many as five thousand eggs in it. The male now takes up one of his principal duties, acting as guard over the eggs. Woe betide the unwary fish that strays into the area, for the male attacks the intruder with great viciousness. By means of his own body movements, he drives intermittent water currents over the eggs. Perhaps as an aid in respiration during this nest-guarding period, the South American male lungfish develops a brushy, gill-like structure on the paired ventral fins.

As soon as the eggs hatch, the larval lungfishes move up on the sides of the nest, hanging vertically with the head upward. Four pairs of external gills are conspicuously present. In about a month the young lungfishes are ready to move out of the nest. By this time one pair of external gills has been lost. The larval South American lungfish loses all four pairs of external gills within the first fifty days, whereas some African species may retain two or three pairs for many months. One African species, *P. amphibius,* usually retains the external gills until it is at least 15 inches in length. In contrast, the Australian lungfish never develops the external gills.

No discussion of lungfishes would be complete without mention of *Ompax spatuloides,* the most fantastic ichthyological hoax of all time. In August of 1872 the director of the Brisbane Museum, visiting in northern Queensland, was told that for breakfast there was being prepared, in his honor, a very rare fish said to have been brought in by aborigines from a distance of eight to ten miles. It had a heavy body with large scales, flipper-like fins, and a paddle-like nose. Because of its curious appearance, he had a sketch made of the fish before consuming it. Following his return to Brisbane, he forwarded his notes and the sketch to Count F. de Castelnau, one of the leading ichthyologists of that region. From these data was described *Ompax spatuloides,* a new genus and species of lungfish. Through the years thereafter, the relationships of this peculiar creature puzzled many zoologists. Some even questioned its existence, but *Ompax* still appeared in all the checklists of Australian fauna. The *Ompax* enigma remained unsolved until one day in 1930 when an unknown author, using the pseudonym Wananbini, published a short note in the Sydney *Bulletin.* It was an account of the great joke played on the Brisbane Museum director, and it described how *Ompax* had been synthesized from the nose of a platypus, the head of a lungfish, the body of a mullet, and the tail of an eel. Exit *Ompax!*

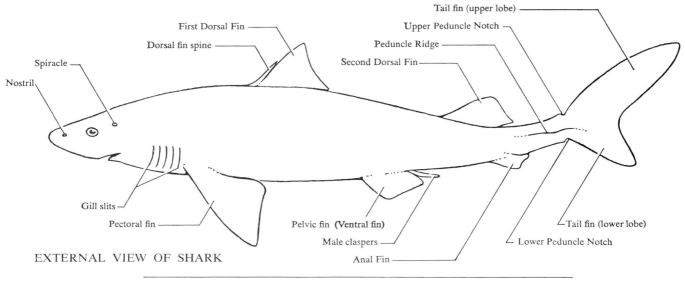

Tail fin (upper lobe)

First Dorsal Fin

Upper Peduncle Notch

Dorsal fin spine

Peduncle Ridge

Spiracle

Second Dorsal Fin

Nostril

Gill slits

Pectoral fin

Pelvic fin (Ventral fin)

Tail fin (lower lobe)

Male claspers

Lower Peduncle Notch

Anal Fin

EXTERNAL VIEW OF SHARK

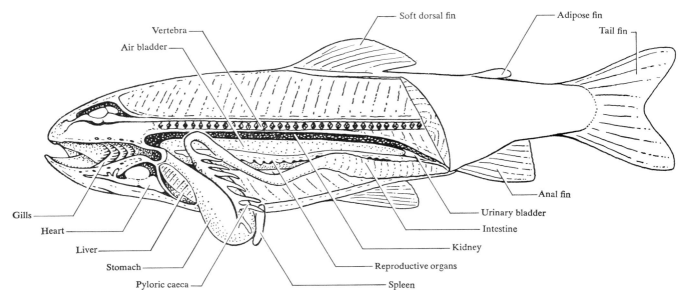

Soft dorsal fin

Adipose fin

Vertebra

Tail fin

Air bladder

Gills

Heart

Anal fin

Liver

Urinary bladder

Stomach

Intestine

Pyloric caeca

Kidney

Reproductive organs

Spleen

INTERNAL ANATOMY OF A SOFT-RAYED FISH (TROUT OR SALMON)

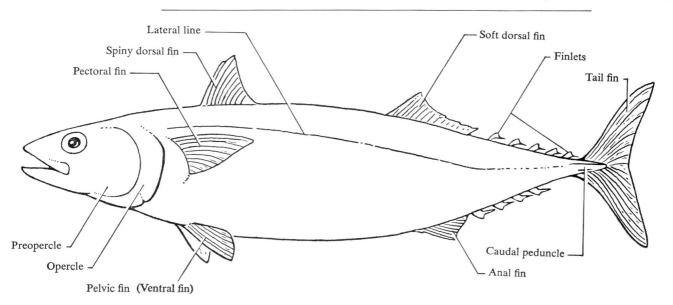

Lateral line

Soft dorsal fin

Spiny dorsal fin

Finlets

Pectoral fin

Tail fin

Preopercle

Caudal peduncle

Opercle

Anal fin

Pelvic fin (Ventral fin)

EXTERNAL VIEW OF A SPINY-RAYED FISH (MACKEREL OR TUNA TYPE)

Glossary

Abdomen—Belly.

Adipose fin—A small, fleshy fin, without rays, located behind the dorsal fin on the back of some fishes.

Air bladder or **swim bladder**—A gas-filled sac located in the body cavity below the vertebrae.

Anal fin—The fin on the median ventral line behind the anus.

Anterior—In front of, or toward the head end.

Anus or **vent**—The posterior external opening of the intestine.

Barbel—A slender, tactile, whisker-like projection extending from the head of some fishes.

Branchial—Pertaining to the gills.

Buckler—A bony shield.

Canine teeth—Elongated conical teeth.

Caudal—Pertaining to the tail.

Caudal fin—The tail fin.

Caudal peduncle—The slender portion of the fish's body just in front of the tail fin.

Cirri—Fringelike tendrils, whiskers, or tufts of skin.

Claspers—A pair of elongated reproductive organs on the pelvic fins of male sharks, skates, and rays.

Dorsal fin—The main fin on the back.

Finlets—A series of small, usually separate fin rays located behind the main dorsal or anal fin.

Fry—The young of fishes.

Gill arches—The bony supports to which the gills are attached.

Gill filaments—The threadlike structures of which the gills are composed.

Gill membranes—Membranes covering the gill openings.

Gill opening—The opening leading from the gills or gill filaments.

Gill rakers—A series of bony projections attached to the inside of the gill arches, used to strain food from the water.

Gills—Filamentous respiratory organs of aquatic animals.

Gill slit—The exterior opening between any two gill arches.

Gonads—Sexual glands: ovaries, testes, or the hermaphrodite glands.

Gonopodium—The modified anal fin functioning as a copulatory organ in certain fishes.

Gular plate—A hard plate covering the under part of the throat; present in some fishes.

Incisors—Front teeth flattened to form a cutting edge.

Jugular—Pertaining to the neck or throat.

Lateral—Pertaining to the side.

Lateral line—Longitudinal line on each side of fish's body, composed of pores opening into sensory organs.

Mandible—The lower jaw.

Maxillary—The second and usually the larger of the two bones forming the upper jaw.

Milt—The sperm of fishes.

Molars—Grinding teeth.

Opercle or **operculum**—The gill cover.

Opercular flap—A fleshy extension of the rear edge of the opercle.

Osseus—Bony.

Otoliths—Two or three small, somewhat spherical bones found in the inner ear of fishes.

Ovary—The female reproductive gland.

Oviparous—Egg-laying.

Ovoviviparous—Producing eggs with definite shells which hatch within the body of the female, so that the young are born alive.

Pectoral fins—The paired fins attached to the shoulder girdle.

Pelvic or **ventral fins**—The paired hind fins.

Pelvic girdle—The bones supporting the pelvic fins.

Pharyngeal teeth—Grinding teeth located in the pharynx.

Pharynx—The section of the alimentary canal joining the mouth cavity to the esophagus.

Photophore—A luminous or light-producing organ or spot.

Premaxillaries—The paired bones forming the front of the upper jaw in fishes.

Preopercle—The anterior cheek bone.

Protractile—Capable of being thrust forward.

Pseudobranchiae—Small gills on the inner side of the gill cover.

Roe—The eggs of fishes.

Scute—An external horny or bony plate or scale.

Spiracle—A small respiratory opening behind the eye in sharks, skates, and rays.

Spiral valve—A corkscrew-like partition in the digestive tract.

Swim bladder—Air bladder.

Testes—The male reproductive glands.

Thoracic—Pertaining to the thorax or chest.

Ventral fins—Pelvic fins.

Vent or **anus**—The posterior external opening of the intestine.

Vertical fins—The unpaired fins along the median line of the body—the dorsal, anal, and caudal fins.

Vestigial—Small and imperfectly developed; rudimentary.

Viviparous—Bringing forth young alive.

Weberian ossicles—A chain of four small bones connecting the air bladder with the ear in the order Ostariophysi.

Bibliography

THE following are some of the more generalized large works used in the preparation of this text. Those most suitable for the general reader have been marked with an asterisk.

*AXELROD, H. R., and SCHULTZ, L. P. (1955). *Handbook of Tropical Aquarium Fishes.* New York: McGraw-Hill.

BAILEY, R. M., *et al.* (1960). *A List of Common and Scientific Names of Fishes from the United States and Canada.* 2nd ed. Ann Arbor, Mich.: American Fisheries Society, Spec. Publ. No. 2.

*BARNHART, P. S. (1936). *Marine Fishes of Southern California.* Berkeley: University of California Press.

*BEEBE, W., and TEE-VAN, J. (1933). *Field Book of the Shore Fishes of Bermuda.* New York: Putnam.

BERG, L. S. (1947). *Classification of Fishes, Both Recent and Fossil.* Ann Arbor, Mich.: J. W. Edwards.

BIGELOW, H. B., and SCHROEDER, W. C. (1948–1953). *Fishes of the Western North Atlantic.* Memoir No. 1, Part 1: *Cyclostomes and Sharks;* Part 2: *Sawfishes, Guitarfishes, Skates, Rays and Chimaeroids.* New Haven: Yale University, Sears Foundation for Marine Research.

BOULENGER, G. A. (1909). *Catalogue of the Fresh-Water Fishes of Africa.* 4 Vols. London: British Museum (Natural History).

*BREDER, C. M., JR. (1929). *Field Book of Marine Fishes of the Atlantic Coast.* New York: Putnam.

BRIGGS, J. C. (1958). A List of Florida Fishes and Their Distribution. *Bull. Florida State Mus., Biological Sciences,* Vol. 2, No. 8. Gainesville: University of Florida.

BROWN, M. E., ed. (1957). *The Physiology of Fishes.* 2 Vols. New York: Academic Press.

*CLEMENS, W. A., and WILBY, G. V. (1946). *Fishes of the Pacific Coast of Canada.* Ottawa: Fisheries Research Board of Canada, Bull. No. 68.

*COATES, C. W., and ATZ, J. (1954). *Fishes of the World (The Animal Kingdom,* Vol. 3, Book 4). New York: Greystone.

*COPLEY, H. (1952). *The Game Fishes of Africa.* London: Witherby.

*COPPLESON, V. M. (1959). *Shark Attack.* Sydney & London: Angus & Robertson.

*EDDY, S. (1957). *How to Know the Freshwater Fishes.* Dubuque, Ia.: W. C. Brown Co.

*———— and SURBER, T. (1943). *Northern Fishes.* Minneapolis: University of Minnesota Press.

FOWLER, H. W. (1948–1955). Os Peixes de Aqua Doce Do Brasil. São Paulo, Brazil: *Arquivos do Zoologia do Estado de São Paulo,* Vols. 6 and 9.

———— (1928–1949). The Fishes of Oceania. *Memoirs of the Bernice P. Bishop Museum,* Vol. X plus 3 supplements. Honolulu: Bishop Museum.

GOSLINE, W. A., and BROCK, V. E. (1960). *Handbook of Hawaiian Fishes.* Honolulu: University of Hawaii Press.

*GRAHAM, D. H. (1932). *A Treasury of New Zealand Fishes.* Wellington: A. H. and A. W. Reed.

GRASSÉ, P. P., ed. (1958). *Traité de Zoologie,* Vol. 13 (three parts of *Agnathes et Poissons*). Paris: Masson.

*HALSTEAD, B. W. (1959). *Dangerous Marine Animals.* Cambridge, Md.: Cornell Maritime Press.

*HARLAN, J. R., and SPEAKER, E. B. (1951). *Iowa Fish and Fishing.* 2nd ed. Des Moines, Ia.: State Conservation Commission.

*HUBBS, C. L., and LAGLER, K. F. (1958). *Fishes of the Great Lakes Region.* 2nd ed. Bloomfield Hills, Mich.: Cranbrook Institute of Science.

*INNES, W. T. (1956). *Exotic Aquarium Fishes.* 19th ed. Philadelphia: Innes Pub. Co.

*IRVINE, F. R. (1947). *The Fishes and Fisheries of the Gold Coast.* London: Crown Agents for the Colonies.

*JENKINS, J. T. (1936). *The Fishes of the British Isles.* 2nd ed. London: Warne.

*JORDAN, D. S. (1925). *Fishes.* New York & London: Appleton.

———— and EVERMANN, B. W. (1896–1900). *The Fishes of North and Middle America.* Washington: U.S. Nat. Mus. Bull. No. 47 (four parts).

*LA GORCE, J. O. (1952). *The Book of Fishes.* Washington: National Geographic Society.

*MCINERNY, D., and GERARD, G. (1958). *All About Tropical Fishes.* New York: Macmillan.

MEEK, S. E., and HILDEBRAND, S. F. (1923–1928). *The Marine Fishes of Panama.* Chicago: Field Mus. Nat. Hist., Zool. Ser., Vol. 15 (three parts).

MUNRO, I. S. R. (1955). *The Marine and Fresh Water Fishes of Ceylon.* Canberra: Australian Dept. of External Affairs.

NORMAN, J. R. (1934). *A Systematic Monograph of the Flatfishes,* Vol. 1. London: British Museum.

*———— (1947). *A History of Fishes.* 3rd ed. London: Benn.

*———— and FRASER, F. C. (1938). *Giant Fishes, Whales and Dolphins.* New York: Norton.

*OKADA, Y. (1955). *Fishes of Japan.* Tokyo: Marusen.

*RAY, C., and CIAMPI, E. (1956). *The Underwater Guide to Marine Life.* New York: Barnes.

*ROUGHLEY, T. C. (1951). *Fish and Fisheries of Australia.* 2nd ed. Sydney & London: Angus & Robertson.

SCHULTZ, L. P., et. al. (1953–1960). *Fishes of the Marshall and Marianas Islands.* Washington: U.S. Nat. Mus. Bull. No. 202, Vols. 1 and 2.

*————, and STERN, E. M. (1948). *The Ways of Fishes.* New York: Van Nostrand.

SMITH, H. M. (1945). *The Fresh-water Fishes of Siam, or Thailand*. Washington: U.S. Nat. Mus. Bull. No. 188.

SMITH, J. L. B. (1953). *The Sea Fishes of Southern Africa*. 3rd ed. Johannesburg, South Africa: Trustees of the Sea Fishes of Southern Africa Book Fund.

STERBA, G. (1959). *Susswasserfische Aus Aller Welt*. Berchtesgaden, Germany: Zimmer & Herzog.

*STOKELL, G. (1955). *Fresh Water Fishes of New Zealand*. Christchurch, N. Z.: Simpson & Williams.

*TRAUTMAN, M. B. (1957). *The Fishes of Ohio*. Columbus: Ohio State University Press.

*WAITE, E. R. (1923). *The Fishes of South Australia*. Adelaide: Government Printer.

WEBER, M., and DEBEAUFORT, L. F. (1911–1953). *The Fishes of the Indo-Australian Archipelago*. 10 Vols. Leiden: E. J. Brill.

*WHITLEY, G. (1940). *Fishes of Australia;* Part 1: *Sharks, Etc*. Sydney: Royal Zool. Soc. of New South Wales.

*——— and ALLAN, J. (1958). *The Sea-horse and Its Relatives*. Melbourne: Georgian House.

INDEX

NOTE: A numeral in parentheses refers to a color plate; a page number followed by an asterisk indicates a black-and-white illustration.

THIS BOOK has been printed and bound by Kingsport Press, Inc. Color engravings by Chanticleer Company. Design and typography by James Hendrickson. Color layout by Nancy H. Dale. Black and white pages arranged by Jean Tennant.

COMMITTEE FOR
TECHNICAL EDUCATION

COMMITTEE FOR
TECHNICAL EDUCATION